THE DRAMATIC CRAFTSMANSHIP OF CALDERÓN
HIS USE OF EARLIER PLAYS

THE

DRAMATIC CRAFTSMANSHIP

OF

CALDERÓN

HIS USE OF EARLIER PLAYS

BY

ALBERT E. SLOMAN

VICE-CHANCELLOR, UNIVERSITY OF ESSEX

Oxford

THE DOLPHIN BOOK CO. LTD.

1969

To Marie

First edition, 1958

Photolithographic reprint, 1969

© Albert E. Sloman

PRINTED IN SPAIN FOR THE DOLPHIN BOOK CO. LTD., OXFORD,
BY ARTES GRÁFICAS SOLER, S. A. - VALENCIA (ESPAÑA)

Depósito Legal: V. 4.556 - 1969

PREFACE

SOME of Calderón's finest and best-known plays —*El alcalde de Zalamea, El médico de su honra, El príncipe constante,* even *La vida es sueño*— derive directly from other plays, sometimes the work of earlier dramatists like Lope de Vega, Tirso de Molina and Vélez de Guevara, sometimes works in which Calderón himself had collaborated with his contemporaries like Pérez de Montalbán and Antonio Coello. In the following chapters I shall examine in turn eight of these plays: reverting to Calderón's starting-point I shall try to reconstruct the process of their creation. Not all the plays offer the same scope for this type of study, but I have deliberately limited myself to a single chapter for each play, concentrating on what seemed to me the principal problems which it posed for Calderón. In a final chapter I have gathered together the points that have emerged from the separate studies and have attempted to draw some conclusions which may serve as a preliminary survey of Calderón's craftsmanship in general. It is hoped that the individual comparative studies will help to elucidate the plays in question, and that taken together they will contribute to a clearer understanding and a deeper appreciation and enjoyment of Calderón's dramatic art.

A serious problem for the student of Calderón's plays is the state of their texts. Few are available in reliable editions, and even these often, like Buchanan's *La vida es sueño,* have long been out of print and are absent from many libraries. I have consulted the earliest extant texts and the important editions of all the plays here studied. For the convenience of the reader, however, I quote whenever possible from the accessible edition of Don Luis Astrana Marín, though well aware of its shortcomings; and I have noted variant readings of, say, the *Parte* or the Vera Tassis texts only to correct obvious misprints or when they seriously affect the interpretation of a passage under discussion.

It is a pleasure to record my gratitude to the many Calderonian scholars whose names appear in the following pages or in the appended bibliography. I am particularly indebted to Professor A. A. Parker who kindly read a first draft of my book; as a result of his generous advice it has been revised and enlarged, and it incorporates many of his suggestions and corrections. I am grateful also to my colleague Mr. H. B. Hall for assisting me with the proofs and for his helpful comments.

Liverpool.   A. E. S.
November 1957.

CONTENTS

I

INTRODUCTION

P O E T S may draw upon what men have written as well as upon what they have done, upon literature as well as upon life. More often than not their debt to earlier writers is fortuitous and unintentional, but sometimes they borrow deliberately, taking over an idea or an image, the general theme or even the very structure of another work. This need not compromise their integrity nor detract from their originality. Provided that the borrowing is imaginative, that by the impact of their minds the appropriated material is transmuted, their work will be new and different and unique. A few of the best plays of Calderón de la Barca were based directly upon plays of his predecessors. Their closeness to their model varies. Some preserve the detailed pattern of scenes and acts of the source-plays, others retain only a bare outline of the earlier stories, or the principal characters, or a striking dramatic situation. Yet in all of them Calderón used what he borrowed to write plays that are new. Neither haste, nor laziness, nor an impoverished mind led him to have recourse to the work of earlier dramatists, but an irrepressible will to perfect, an urge to exploit to the full their dramatic and moral potential. The very failure of another dramatist with material that had the makings of a great play was for him a challenge. Far from being a plagiarist on these occasions, he was an imaginative imitator, inspired by the sources to write some of Spain's greatest plays.

The work of Calderón and his contemporaries marks the culmination of a drama which, though reaching back to the sixteenth-century pieces of Encina, was orientated and established by Lope de Vega. The early plays of Lope, dating from the 1580s and 1590s, were written for a new kind of stage, the apron stages of Madrid's first permanent theatres, and for the new audiences which they attracted. They were novel, experimental. By the first decade of the seventeenth century, when the novelty had worn off, the *comedia* may be regarded as entering upon a second phase, one of consolidation. The lead given by Lope and his fellow dramatists was decisive. The non-classical type of play was confirmed; a drama which imitated life and satisfied the particular demands of a Spanish audience had been preferred to one based on precept and fitted to the requirements of Aristotle. Calderón and the other dramatists who began to write for the stage in the twenties and thirties had the advantage of a tradition of some forty years and more of play-writing, and play-writing within much the same conventions and for almost exactly the same stage conditions.

Their debt to their predecessors, however, was often far greater and more precise. They recast earlier plays. Just as many of the lyrics of Burns are the remaking of old folk-songs, so many of the plays of Calderón, Moreto and others are *refundiciones* of the plays of the older dramatists. The indebtedness of Moreto in this respect is notorious. One recalls the taunt of Don Jerónimo Cáncer in his *Vejamen;* all the poets of Castilla go to the rescue of Apollo except the young Moreto who was too busy looking for material in some old, worthless *comedias.* Professor Ruth Kennedy claims that fifteen of the thirty-two plays which Moreto wrote by himself derive from source-plays, and close parallels have been found for six others; eight of the sixteen written in collaboration have known models. She adds the comment that such facts go far to justify Schaeffer's assertion that if all the plays of the Golden Age were available a dramatic source would be found for every one of Moreto's plays. Calderón's borrowing from the work of his predecessors is far less than Moreto's; yet those of his plays which are known to be based on earlier plays include his best.

The reason for the number of *refundiciones* by the generation of Calderón is not simply that now for the first time large numbers of old *comedias* were available for reworking. With the passing of years the attitude towards the *comedia* changed. Its first exponents set a premium on novelty. Juan de la Cueva in his *Ejemplar poético* requires the poet to be 'new and rare in invention':

> Ha de ser nuevo en la invención y raro,
> en la historia admirable, y prodigioso
> en la fábula, y fácil el reparo.   (I, 232-34)

and Lope, in the famous passage of *Lo fingido verdadero,* wrote:

> Dame una nueva fábula que tenga
> más invención, aunque carezca de arte,
> que tengo gusto de español en esto,
> y como me le dé lo verosímil,
> nunca reparo tanto en los preceptos,
> antes me cansa su rigor, y he visto
> que los que miran en guardar el arte
> nunca del natural alcanzan parte. (Acad. IV, 57b)

As the *comedia* developed the emphasis shifted from novelty to perfection, from invention to artistry. In the passage cited Lope sets invention against 'el arte'; and although for him 'arte' often meant no more than the rules of the ancients, many of which were inapplicable to the new drama, his remarks reflect an approach to playwriting which is different from that, say, of Calderón and Moreto. It must be added that, whereas Lope was a prodigy of inventiveness, some of the later dramatists were deficient in creative imagination; and although, as we shall see, originality and even novelty were not incompatible with the imitation of earlier plays, many *refundiciones* were by common consent no more than plagiarisms.

Precisely because many of the early Spanish plays were artistically so imperfect they invited recasting. Contemporary criticism of the *comedia* was not always as misguided or perhaps as ineffective as it is often made out to have been. Take, for example, that of Suárez de Figueroa, writing at the beginning of *El pasajero* (1617). In his condemnation of the mingling of the comic and tragic and the ignoring of the unities he was, of course, being doctrinaire, setting his face against the very kind of play to which Spain, at that date, was irrevocably committed. Yet some of his comments were valid and apposite:

> Ahora consta la comedia (o sea, como quieren, representación) de cierta miscelánea donde se halla de todo. Graceja el lacayo con el señor, teniendo por donaire la desvergüenza. Piérdese el respeto a la honestidad, y rompen las leyes de buenas costumbres el mal ejemplo, la temeridad, la descortesía. Como cuestan tan poco estudio, hacen muchos muchas, sobrando siempre ánimo para más a los más tímidos. Allí, como gozques, gruñen por envidia, ladran por odio y muerden por venganza. Todo charla, paja todo, sin nervio, sin ciencia ni erudición. Sean los escritos hidalgos, esto es, de más calidad que cantidad; que no consiste la opinión de sabio en lo mucho, sino en lo bueno.

The passage recalls Cervantes's criticism of *comedias* in *Don Quixote*, I, 48:

> ...estas [comedias] que ahora se usan, así las imaginadas como las de historia, todas o las más son conocidos disparates y cosas que no llevan pies ni cabeza...

Lack of unity, carelessness, triviality, irresponsibility, these were indeed defects of many *comedias*, and defects which were remediable.

Lope de Vega did achieve dramatic unity and formal excellence in his best plays, but these serve to throw into relief the shortcomings of so many others, plays of the sort which Calderón and his contemporaries chose to rewrite. Many of Moreto's *refundiciones*, in particular the comedies of character, are vast improvements upon the source-plays; and if they reflect a lack of creative talent they illustrate also their author's search for perfection. The source-plays which will be studied in these pages are mostly mediocre and of little consequence; Calderón's recastings in contrast are all important, and some have long been accepted as outstanding examples of his dramatic art. Their formal superiority—as well as many of the details of technique that have contributed to it, such as the absence of sub-plots that are not pertinent to the main plot, the careful motivation of entrances and exits, the telescoping of the time that elapses in the course of the action, the few scene changes—, and their greater significance, may be taken as indicative of the development of Golden-Age drama in the first half of the seventeenth century. It is perhaps noteworthy that of the three major exponents of Aristotelian precept in Spain at this time—El Pinciano, Cascales and González de Salas—it was Salas, the near-contemporary of Calderón, who was most tolerant towards the new drama. When El Pinciano's *Philosophia antigua poética* was published in 1596 the *comedia* was new and experimental. Even twenty years later, when Cascales was writing, it was still often shapeless and trivial, despite the excellence of a few plays. By the early thirties, however, when Salas published his *Nueva idea de la tragedia antigua*, Calderón had written plays which by their remarkable craftsmanship and universality represented a new and peculiarly Spanish classicism.

At least eight of the major plays of Calderón were based on earlier plays. [1] The relationships are as follows:

SOURCE	CALDERÓN
El médico de su honra Attributed to Lope de Vega.	El médico de su honra
El privilegio de las mujeres Calderón, Pérez de Montalbán, Coello.	Las armas de la hermosura
La venganza de Tamar Tirso de Molina.	Los cabellos de Absalón
Polifemo y Circe Mira de Amescua, Pérez de Montalbán, Calderón.	El mayor encanto amor
La niña de Gómez Arias Vélez de Guevara.	La niña de Gómez Arias
La fortuna adversa del Infante D. Fernando de Portugal Attributed to Lope de Vega.	El príncipe constante
El alcalde de Zalamea Attributed to Lope de Vega.	El alcalde de Zalamea
Yerros de naturaleza y aciertos de la fortuna Coello, Calderón.	La vida es sueño

Though the nature and extent of the borrowing varies from play to play, Calderón's debt to the source is in each case indisputable and, almost certainly, direct. [2]

More than a century ago Schack in the first edition of his *Geschichte der dramatischen Literatur und Kunst in Spanien* (1845) called attention to Calderón's use of the work of other dramatists, and listed a number of plays which derived, in his view, from works'

---

[1] I make no claim to have exhausted the list of plays which can be set against their sources. There is, for example, *El jardin de Falerina*, the joint production of Rojas Zorrilla, Antonio Coello and Calderón, written probably about 1636, a MS copy of which is preserved in the BN (No. 17.320), which was recast by Calderón in the form of a *zarzuela*, dated by Cotarelo y Mori in 1648, and published in Part V (Madrid and Barcelona, 1677). All the important known examples are, however, considered here.

[2] Since the completion of this book I have seen Don Angel Valbuena's new study of the Spanish drama, *Historia del teatro español* (Barcelona, 1956), in which he suggests that Calderón's *El alcalde de Zalamea* and perhaps his *El médico de su honra* might have been written before the plays that have hitherto been regarded as their sources, cf. pp. 321 and 271, although this contradicts what he says elsewhere in his book, e.g. p. 70:
Se refundirán argumentos de Lope y su escuela con otro sentido distinto. Se llegará así a obras como *El alcalde de Zalamea*, *El médico de su honra* o *La niña de Gómez Arias*, bien distintas de las obras de Lope o Vélez. I shall take up the suggestion in notes to the relevant chapters, but it can be stated here that the evidence against it is conclusive.

of Tirso de Molina and Mira de Amescua. In the *Nachträge*, which appeared with the new edition in 1854, he made it known that *Los cabellos de Absalón, El médico de su honra, El alcalde de Zalamea, El príncipe constante* and *La niña de Gómez Arias* were taken directly from earlier plays, three of them with the same title. No one fully availed himself of the opportunity offered by Schack's discoveries, least of all Schack himself who regarded the plays in question as 'tan sólo arreglos de obras de poetas anteriores'. [1] Hartzenbusch made a brief comparative study of the two *Alcaldes*, and Krenkel appended the text of the first *Alcalde* to his critical edition of Calderón's play. *La venganza de Tamar*, the source of *Los cabellos de Absalón*, has always been accessible, but no one to my knowledge has studied in detail the manner of Calderón's borrowing. Menéndez y Pelayo included the text of the first *El médico de su honra* in the Academy edition of the works of Lope de Vega, and briefly compared it with Calderón's. Though *Polifemo y Circe, El privilegio de las mujeres* and *Yerros de naturaleza* appear in modern editions of plays in which Calderón collaborated, the first two have never been compared in detail with the famous works of Calderón which derive from them, and there has been no satisfactory study even of the relationship between *Yerros de naturaleza* and *La vida es sueño*. The source of *El príncipe constante* was until recently available only in a single extant text which for many years was regarded as lost; and Vélez de Guevara's *La niña de Gómez Arias* is still inaccessible, extant only in rare eighteenth-century *sueltas*.

In the absence of comparative studies, which alone could have revealed Calderón's originality in these plays, it has often been assumed that many of them are mere plagiarisms. The following extract from an essay by Fitzmaurice-Kelly is typical:

> Like most Spanish dramatists, Calderón wrote too much and too speedily, and he was too often content to recast the productions of his predecessors. His *Saber del bien y del mal* is an adaptation of Lope de Vega's play *La mudanza de la fortuna y sucesos de Don Beltrán de Aragón;* his *Selva confusa* is also adapted from a play of Lope's which bears the same title; his *Encanto sin encanto* derives from Tirso de Molina's *Amar por señas,* and, to take an extreme instance, the second act of his *Los cabellos de Absalón* is transferred almost bodily from the third act of Tirso's *La venganza de Tamar.* It would be easy to add other examples of

---

[1] Spanish translation by Eduardo de Mier, IV, 206n.

Calderón's lax methods, but it is simple justice to point out that he committed no offence against the prevailing code of literary morality. Many of his contemporaries plagiarized with equal audacity, but with far less success." [1]

Discounting the inaccuracies of this statement, its main point is one which many critics have made. Calderón, it has often been argued, exceeded his own imaginative powers, and to provide new plays was obliged to take over the work of others. Such plays were regarded as exemplifying his 'lax' methods. Here, for example, is the judgement of Sr. Cotareli y Mori in 1924:

> Calderón, como todos los autores de aquel tiempo, escribía a veces con prisa, ya por exigencias de Palacio o ya por compromisos con los autores o empresarios de los teatros, y entonces echaba mano a obras ajenas, ya olvidadas, o acudía a la colaboración de los poetas cómicos más propincuos o más desocupados. [2]

H. C. Heaton went even further to question the integrity and, by implication, the competence of Calderón. He argued, for example, that for *La selva confusa* Calderón simply copied out the text of a work of Lope's, inserting lines of his own and making a few minor alterations to cover up his theft. And as recently as 1952 he called in question the authorship of *La devoción de la cruz* and *El mágico prodigioso,* and expressed his doubts about *Amor, honor y poder.* Calderón, he claimed, not only borrowed from other dramatists but stole whole plays and attempted to disguise them with minor alterations, alterations which at the same time reflect upon his competence as a dramatist. I have dealt elsewhere with the charges of Heaton. [3] *La selva confusa* and the Yepes text of *El mágico* can both be accepted as the authentic work of Calderón. Indeed, there is no evidence that Calderón was ever guilty of the practice suspected by Heaton.

Source-study serves the purpose often of clearing up difficulties or explaining inconsistencies in a text where the author has failed properly to assimilate what he has borrowed. Incidents and characters which are irrelevant, or at least dispensable, have been retained;

---

[1] *Encyclopaedia Britannica,* Eleventh Edition (1910-1911).

[2] *Ensayo sobre la vida y obras de D. Pedro Calderón de la Barca* (Madrid, 1924), 120-21.

[3] '*La selva confusa* restored to Calderón', *HR,* XX (1952), 134-48 and '*El mágico prodigioso:* Calderón defended against the charge of theft', *HR,* XX (1952), 212-22.

others which have been omitted make certain scenes or passages obscure. Such shortcomings are rarely found in Calderón's plays. They testify not to his negligence but to his scrupulous care and remarkable assiduity. But our studies are not conceived merely to give the lie to a view of Calderón which few responsible critics would share to-day. They are intended to show that he was one of the most accomplished dramatic craftsmen of all time. In eight outstanding works we can, as it were, look over his shoulder and watch him at work. We can study in detail his transformation of the source-plays: his omissions and additions to the action and its rearrangement, his provision of new characters and alteration of those he takes over, his new language and imagery. At the same time, it is hoped that these studies will throw some light on Calderón's stagecraft in general. Admittedly he is here building on foundations already laid; the material which he uses has already been fitted, however imperfectly, to the dimensions of the stage and he could draw perhaps on a brilliant dramatic idea, a fine situation or a striking character. But the problem of transforming an undistinguished play into a great work of art is essentially the same as that of writing a play from non-dramatic material. And although our eight plays have not been selected for their representativeness, they are all serious and significant examples of Calderón's work of the thirties and forties.

Calderón's procedure ranged from the rewriting of the source-play within the same pattern of scenes to a complete departure from the original structure. This has dictated the order of these studies. For *El médico de su honra* and *Las armas de la hermosura* Calderón reproduced almost exactly the structural scheme of the sources. For *Los cabellos de Absalón, El mayor encanto amor* and *La niña de Gómez Arias,* by omitting much of the source material and adding new, he followed closely only certain parts of the source-plays. *El príncipe constante* and *El alcalde de Zalamea* are coextensive with their models, but Calderón's new conception of the stories required changes of such consequence that scarcely a scene in common remains. Finally, *La vida es sueño* bears superficially no resemblance at all to its source. All eight are new plays. If *Las armas de la hermosura* and *El médico de su honra* have a structural similarity to their sources which is not found in other plays, they are no less the original and very personal work of Calderón. For some of the plays Calderón's theme could be accommodated to the original structure, in others to only part of that structure. In some, almost all the characters of the source could be utilised, in others only a few. In some, the original theme is developed and elaborated, in others the theme is new. The different fate of the source-plays depended, not upon the stage of Calderón's development as a dramatist, much less upon the whims or mood of the moment, or upon haste or carelessness, but upon considerations which were, above all, dramatic. His concern was, primarily, to write a better play.

II

EL MÉDICO DE SU HONRA

THE plot of *El médico de su honra* [1] may briefly be summarised as follows. Prince Henry of Trastamara falls from his horse whilst accompanying the King, his half-brother Peter, to Seville. He is carried to a nearby house which belongs to the lady he once loved, Doña Mencía, and his love is rekindled. When later Mencía's husband, Don Gutierre, is detained in Seville as a result of a dispute arising out of an earlier love-affair with a certain Leonor, she is revisited by Henry, and though she resolutely rejects his advances, she helps him to escape when Gutierre returns unexpectedly. Gutierre fails to recognize the intruder but he finds a dagger which he is able to identify as Henry's. Thus his suspicions against his wife are first roused; and they are strengthened when she gives him reason for believing that she is expecting another visit from Henry. Meanwhile, Henry comes to blows with the King and is obliged to leave Seville in haste, and Mencía, fearing lest his sudden departure will be associated with her, writes to him to stay. Her husband finds the half-written letter which he takes to be confirmation of her guilt, and since Henry, being of royal blood, is inviolable, his honour requires him to dispose of his wife. This he proceeds to do, after giving her time to make her peace with God, by making a blood-letter open her veins with Henry's dagger. King Peter discovers what Gutierre has done but, though he refers to his

---

[1] Texts used are:

Source:

Parte XXVII (extravagante), Barcelona, 1633.
Ed. M. Menéndez y Pelayo, *Obras de Lope de Vega* (Madrid, 1899), IX, 407-39.

Calderón:

Segunda parte, 1637, QC, Q.
Ed. Vera Tassis, II, 1682.
Ed. J. J. Keil, I, 353-76.
Ed. J. E. Hartzenbusch, BAE, VII, 347-65.
Ed. L. Astrana Marín, 183-214. (Madrid, 1945, 3.ª ed., revisada.)
Ed. A. Valbuena Briones (Madrid, 1956).

Unless otherwise stated, page references are to the Menéndez y Pelayo text of the source and to Astrana Marín's text of Calderón's play.

cruelty, he gives his approval and orders him to accept the hand of Leonor.

It is not difficult to see why *El médico de su honra* has achieved such notoriety. Gutierre murders a wife who is wholly innocent of the guilt which he imputes to her: she is not adulterous. On the other hand, Mencía's suitor, Henry, who is the only wilfully evil character of the play, escapes scot-free. Nor is this all. Calderón ends his play in a manner familiar to readers of the Spanish *comedia;* he brings on the King to give approval to Gutierre's action. So it is that Calderón has been accused of condoning the murder of an innocent wife. Schack dismissed *El médico* as a tragedy which, to him, was horrible, repugnant and offensive; and, to cite a recent judgement, Mr. Gerald Brenan has written: "This secret, premeditated murder of an innocent wife is held up to us as a course to be followed. It is for this reason that the murderer is not tried for his crime, but on the contrary secures the King's approbation." [1] Mr. Brenan, one assumes, deliberately overstated his case, but he was voicing what seemed to be the unanimous opinion of critics.

This view of *El médico de su honra,* and of Calderón's other plays on secret vengeance, has been challenged by Professor E. M. Wilson. [2] Calderón, he argues, did not approve of don Gutierre's rash deductions and savage actions, his jealousy and dissimulation. Don Gutierre is linked in the play with the King. Both are cruel men, if both are just men. It is simply 'in character' for the King to approve of Gutierre's vengeance, and the audience should recognize that the cruelty of both receives punishment, some time after the curtain falls, at Montiel. Doña Mencía, moreover, earned her death because she did not know how to act with such a husband in such an age. Such is the conflict of opinion. On the one hand, a view of the play which makes Calderón, who is remarkable for the consistency with which he commends Christian precept, approve the brutal murder of an innocent wife; on the other, an interpretation which is diametrically opposed to that unanimously held by critics and, it might appear, to the immediate

---

[1] Gerald Brenan, *The Literature of the Spanish People* (Cambridge, 1951), p. 284.

[2] 'La discreción de Don Lope de Almeida', *Cla,* II, No. 19 (1951), 1-10 and 'Gerald Brenan's Calderón', *BC,* IV, i (1952). I take this opportunity of acknowledging my debt to these important studies of Professor Wilson.

impact of the play in the theatre. In the circumstances, it is of particular interest to set the *El médico de su honra* against the play from which it derives.

Calderón's play is known to have been performed at the Royal Palace, by the company of Juan Martínez de los Ríos, on August 26, 1635. [1] Two years earlier a play of the same title, attributed to Lope de Vega. formed part of *Parte XXVII (extravagante)* published in Barcelona: *El médico de su honra, Comedia famosa de Lope de Vega Carpio. Representóla Avendaño.* Professors Morley and Bruerton regard the play as very doubtful Lope. [2] The 1236 lines of *redondilla*, running to 46.6 per cent of the play, point to a date before 1620; the 41.9 per cent of *romance*, on the other hand, suggests that it was written in the twenties, but not after 1630. Whether the play is by Lope or not, it is probable, though not certain, that it was written before Calderón's. Setting the two plays against each other, however, there can be no doubt of the order of precedence. And this is confirmed by other details. For example, the ultimate source of the last scene of Act II in both plays is the ballad *La amiga de Bernal Francés.* There also a husband, believing that his wife is expecting a visit from her lover, returns unexpectedly to his house and speaks to her in the darkness. The wife takes him for her lover and the husband assumes that his suspicions have been confirmed. And the ballad has the same association between the putting out of the light and the extinction of life. The *Médico* attributed to Lope is much closer to the ballad than Calderón's. Its author set the scene in the wife's room as in the ballad and perpetuated the *romance* metre; in Calderón's play the scene is shifted to the garden and the metre is *silva.* For this scene, as for the other scenes of his play, Calderón was following the source-play. For *El médico* Calderón kept closer to the structure of the source than in his other plays; but his general procedure in transforming the source conforms perfectly to that which he adopted with the other source-plays studied in these chapters. [3]

---

[1] Cotarelo y Mori, op. cit., p. 167.

[2] *Chronology of Lope de Vega's Comedias* (New York, 1940), pp. 311-12.

[3] The priority of the text attributed to Lope has recently been questioned by Don Angel Valbuena in *Historia*, p. 321, and by his son, ed. *Dramas de honor*, I, c. Don Angel is misled by his assumption that, if Calderón did follow the other text, he was guilty of plagiarism. But, as I shall show, his play is, on the contrary, remarkably different and original.

What did Calderón remove from the earlier play, and what has he added? What changes has he made which modify or transform the characters of, say, Don Gutierre and Doña Mencía? Why is the total effect of the plays so different? Both the plot and characters of Calderón's *El médico de su honra* derive from the source-play, though all but the two historical characters have been renamed: [1]

SOURCE	CALDERÓN
Don Jacinto Ribera	Don Gutierre Alfonso de Solís
Galindo	Coquín, *lacayo*
Doña Mayor	Doña Mencía de Acuña
Mencía	Jacinta, *esclava herrada*
Elvira	Teodora, *criada*
El infante D. Enrique	El infante D. Enrique
Don Alvaro	Don Arias
Don Pedro	Don Diego
Don Alonso	—
Doña Margarita	Doña Leonor
	Inés, *criada*
El Rey D. Pedro	El Rey D. Pedro
Un barbero	Ludovico, *sangrador*
Sánchez, *viejo*	Un viejo
	Un soldado
	Pretendientes
	Acompañamiento
	Música
	Criados, criadas

Calderón borrowed also the pattern of action of the source-play. In both, the distribution of scenes is:

Act I: 1.   Outside Sevilla: husband's house.
          2.   Sevilla: Royal Palace.

---

[1] Andrés de Claramonte's play, *Desta agua no beberé*, published in 1630 in *Segunda parte de comedias nuevas de Lope de Vega y otros autores*, seems to have provided Calderón with the names Don Gutierre Alfonso and Doña Mencia de Acuña, though Mencia is also the name of the servant of the earlier Mayor. And the plot of Claramonte's play bears some resemblance to that of *El médico de su honra*, centring on a husband whose wife is the object of attention of a royal person (in this case King Pedro himself) and who is charged with infidelity by the lady he formerly loved. But whatever the relationship between *Desta agua no beberé* and the first *El médico*, Calderón at least seems to have drawn on Claramonte only for the names of two characters, attracted to the play, perhaps, by the similarity of plot. A second play which resembles *El médico* is Antonio Enríquez Gómez's *A lo que obliga el honor*, where, as in Claramonte's play, the offender is Pedro, though this time before becoming King. The handling of the action, however, is quite different; so, too, is the *dénouement* in which the husband, Don Enrique de Saldaña, removes his wife, Doña Elvira de Liarte, by pushing her off a rock. Miss Sylvia Winter, in her critical edition of the *A lo que obliga el honor* (London M. A. thesis, 1953) shows that it was probably written in 1640, that is, after Calderón's *El médico*, which, in any case, owes nothing to it.

Act II:	1.	Outside Sevilla: husband's house.
	2.	Sevilla: Royal Palace.
	3.	Outside Sevilla: husband's house.
Act III:	1.	Sevilla: Royal Palace.
	2.	Sevilla: husband's house.
	3.	Sevilla: streets.

So close has Calderón remained to his model that, in the single case of his rearranging the action, he has simply interchanged two events in the source-play: Arias's proposal to Leonor in Act II, xii in Calderón's play corresponds to Alvaro's proposal to Margarita, Act III, i in the source, and Gutierre's appeal to the King, Act III, i in Calderón to Jacinto's appeal to the King, Act II, ii in the source. This interchange is the full extent of Calderón's rearrangement of the action of the source-play. And, even within each scene, his general handling follows closely that of the source dramatist.

For all that, Calderón's play is new. Indeed, it is a conspicuous illustration of his independence and originality that, having borrowed so much, he did not borrow more. The language of his play is his own; nor was he merely expressing in his own words the thoughts of another dramatist. He was writing a new play with all the care of a skilled craftsman, concerned with the fullest, and a very personal, dramatic expression of his theme. Within the borrowed framework, the minor changes in handling and the new language have far-reaching effects. Superior technique and new language, however, only partly explain the total transformation which Calderón has achieved. The story has been conceived anew. If Calderón took over the structure of the source-play, it means simply that he was able to accommodate his own conception of the material to the original framework. A comparative study of parallel scenes reveals changes of emphasis which are of particular significance in a work where Calderón is keeping so close to his source; the sumtotal of these divergencies accounts for the remarkable disparity between the impact of the two plays.

By a series of minor changes, which at the risk of being tedious we shall have to consider in some detail, Calderón transformed the character of the play's protagonist. Jacinto, in the source, is pre-

sented from the outset as a faithless and jealous husband. [1] He is
denounced by Doña Mayor his wife as the victim of lust, neglecting
her to seek pleasure in Seville:

> ...que tiene, aunque más repares
> en la quinta los pesares
> y en Sevilla los placeres...
> Mira, no hay cosa tan vil
> como el humano apetito.   (408b-409a)

Finding Prince Enrique in his house, Jacinto is at once overcome
by suspicion and jealousy; and though he strives to control himself,
Mayor remarks to her servant:

> Mira a mi esposo
> y verás cómo le roban
> los colores de su cara
> algunas pasiones locas. (412a)

Gutierre, on the other hand, in Calderón's first scene is the dutiful
and trusting husband of Mencía. Mencía, it is true, confesses that
the marriage to Gutierre was forced upon her, and she refers to his
earlier affair with Leonor. But whereas the earlier Jacinto regards
Prince Enrique with suspicion on his first appearance in his house,
Gutierre's only lapse is to ask the Prince the reason for his leaving
at once for Sevilla; and he reminds himself:

> Necio en apurar estoy
> vuestro intento; pero creo
> que mi lealtad y deseo...
>
> D. ENRIQUE.   Y si yo la causa os doy,
> ¿qué diréis?

---

[1] Menéndez y Pelayo based his text of the first *El médico de su honra* on a
defective copy of *Parte XXVII (extravagante)*: a torn corner in this copy left his
text incomplete in two places in this first scene. I supply below the missing parts
from the perfect copy of this *Parte* available in Barcelona:

> Doña Mayor.
>   ... le aguardo que venga.
> Infante.
>   ¡Cielos!
> ¿Qué es ésto? No, no, no *informan*
> ya los *sentidos al alma*
> que tal he escuchado. ¡Ola!
>   411a
>
> Don Jacinto.
>   Por aver, señor, sabido
> *que un* bruto con rigurosa
> *obstinación* los preceptos
> *de las riendas* belicosas
> rompiendo y desbaratando...
>   411b

> D. GUTIERRE.   Yo no os la pido;
> que a vos, señor, no es bien hecho
> examinaros el pecho.   (187b)

Dramatically this is important, since it anticipates the later behaviour of Gutierre; and it provokes the Prince to lie, thereby provid-
ing an opportunity for a more serious lapse by Doña Mencía.
Perhaps, too, we are intended to find his excuse for leaving Mencía
excessively flattering and ingenious. But it is only a minor indiscretion compared with the behaviour of Jacinto.

Calderón's second scene of Act I, at Sevilla, reveals Gutierre's
relationship with Leonor. Gutierre was formerly Leonor's lover and
had given his word to marry her; but, having seen one night a
man leave her house, he abandoned her and married Mencía. The
fears of Gutierre were unjustified; the man in question was Don
Arias, who had been visiting a second lady in the same house. This
explanation had evidently already been given to Gutierre and he
had refused to accept it:

> D. GUTIERRE.   Y aunque escuché
> satisfacciones, y nunca
> di a mi agravio entera fe,
> fué bastante esta aprensión
> a no casarme;   (193a)

Gutierre, then, is susceptible in points of honour, and it has led
him to act imprudently. This susceptibility prepares the audience
for his attitude towards Mencía, and the curses of Leonor foreshadow the dishonour which will overtake him. When, however, he
is imprisoned, his first thoughts are for his wife:

> D. GUTIERRE.   (Ap.) No siento en desdicha tal
> ver riguroso y cruel
> al Rey; sólo siento que hoy,
> Mencía, no te he de ver.   (193b)

And love it would seem, rather than suspicion, impels him to absent
himself for a night. It is clear, moreover, from the differences between this and the corresponding scene in the source that, whilst
underlining the excessive punctiliousness of Gutierre, Calderón does
not wish the Leonor affair to reflect unduly upon his character.
Even taking into account Leonor's curse upon Gutierre, Margarita
was far more outspoken in her criticism of Jacinto, whose behav-

iour is presented as infamous. In the scene itself, too, Gutierre, unlike Jacinto, is a model of discretion. To the King's request for an explanation of his conduct towards Leonor he is tactfully brief and vague; he is unwilling to slander a lady in her absence and pleads with the King:

> D. GUTIERRE. Suplícoos no me apretéis;
> que soy hombre que, en ausencia
> de las mujeres, daré
> la vida por no decir
> cosa indigna de su ser.   (192b)

Only under duress does he reveal why he has left Leonor. Jacinto had no such qualms of conscience, and his reply to the King is as insolent as Gutierre's is prudent. If Gutierre was susceptible in the Leonor affair, he is for all that a man whose honour and integrity are to be respected; so much so that even Leonor defends him subsequently against the slanderous charges of Don Arias.

Only in the first scene of Act II does Gutierre's confidence in Mencía begin to waver, when he returns to surprise a stranger in his house, and discovers the dagger. Even here Calderón interpolates further evidence of Gutierre's integrity. In the source-play there is, at this point, a considerable part for the *gracioso*; [1] in Calderón's his only part is to suggest to his master that he should break his word and not return to the Sevillan prison, provoking Gutierre to his heated retort:

> ¡Vive Dios, necio, villano,
> que te mate por mi mano!
> ¿Pues tú me has de aconsejar
> tan vil acción, sin mirar
> la confianza que aquí
> hizo el alcaide de mí?   (196b)

---

[1] Another torn corner left Menéndez y Pelayo's text defective in this scene in two places:

> Mayor: Que no fuesse cortesia
> os hize, ni pude hazer*os*,
> solo por entretenér*os*,
> y llega a ser demasía...   419b
>
> Enrique: Mas ¡ay! que a la puerta ¡cielos!
> *llaman;* ya estoy sin reposo.
>
> Jacinto: Abre Inés.
>
> Mayor: *Este es mi esposo.*
> ¡*Qué* mal lograreys, desvelos!
> *Agora que* hemos de hazer
> morir, por matarme estoy.   420a

The lack of principle of Coquín emphasizes the principles of Gutierre. But the man who deserted Leonor on seeing a stranger leave her house is not slow to recognize the meaning of the dagger which he has found. Suspicion and doubt are at once aroused:

> (Ap.) Mas engañóme, ¡ay de mí!,
> que esta daga que hallé, ¡cielos!,
> con sospechas y recelos
> previene mi muerte en sí.
> Mas no es esto para aquí.   (197b)

And they are intensified by Mencía's unsolicited protests of innocence. Gutierre's conception of honour had prevented him in Act I from slandering Leonor, and earlier in this scene from breaking his word with his Sevillan gaoler. But that same conception of honour had led him to make unwarranted assumptions about Leonor, and leads now to duplicity and dissimulation. Enrique's visit indeed induces both partners to deceit; Mencía succeeds in securing Enrique's escape by lying to her husband, and Gutierre keeps secret his finding of the dagger. Acting with the best intentions, yet misguidedly, both help to set in motion a train of events which results ultimately in tragedy. At this point Calderón appropriately includes the clearest foreshadowing so far of the play's *dénouement*:

> D.ª MENCÍA.   Al verte así, presumía
> que ya en mi sangre bañada,
> hoy moría desangrada.   (198a)

At Sevilla, in scene II, Gutierre has an opportunity of comparing the dagger with Enrique's sword, as in the source-play, and of discovering the identity of the intruder. It is significant that, at this important stage in the progress of the action, Calderón departs from the structural pattern of the source. Jacinto, taking the likeness between dagger and sword as evidence enough of the threat to his honour, goes immediately to the King. Not so Gutierre, whose visit to the King is postponed until Act III. Calderón, moreover, by making Enrique, and not (as in the source-play) the lady, responsible for the release of Gutierre and Arias from prison, allows Gutierre an opportunity of addressing Enrique in terms which he alone can understand; and Enrique's silence leaves no doubt about his intentions in respect of Mencía. In spite of this, Gutierre, with far more patience and restraint than Jacinto, awaits further evidence before appealing to the King. And here Calderón interpolates the famous monologue of Gutierre. In contrast with the impetuosity of Jacinto, Gutierre acts with restraint and self-control, reviewing the facts of the situation and carefully weighing the conflicting arguments. The situation calls for *valor* and *paciencia*, as he reminds himself:

> ¡Ahora, valor, ahora
> es tiempo de que se vea
> que sabéis medir iguales
> el valor y la paciencia! [1]   (200a)

Yet he cannot but doubt the integrity of the woman he loves and has to admit to his own jealousy. It must be conceded that he has some reason to fear that his honour is in danger; and his prescription for curing his malady, like his diagnosis, is cool and controlled:

> Yo os he de curar, honor,
> y pues al principio muestra
> este primero accidente
> tan grave peligro, sea
> la primera medicina
> cerrar al daño las puertas,
> atajar al mal los pasos.
> Y así os receta y ordena
> *el médico de su honra*
> primeramente la dieta
> del silencio... (200b-201a)

Gutierre, compared with Jacinto, is acting with commendable moderation; but his behaviour is motivated by a code of honour which upheld secrecy and dissimulation, and the consequences are tragic. The soliloquy serves also to direct attention to Gutierre and to the problem which confronts him as a man of honour; and his vain attempt to convince himself of his wife's innocence is forceful and dramatic.

After Gutierre's monologue, Calderón has included, in place of the husband's appointment with the King in the source-play, the exchanges between Don Arias and Leonor based upon a scene in the third act of the source. But an interview, which in the first *El médico* contains little more than the advances of Alvaro rejected by Margarita, now takes on a new significance. Arias does propose to Leonor, whose honour he has compromised, and his proposal is

---

[1]   QC, *paciencia*, Astrana Marín, *prudencia*.

refused; but the interview is primarily a discussion about Gutierre and serves to clinch the points which emerged from the previous scene. Leonor has no doubt about the rights and wrongs of Gutierre's deserting her; she refers to it as 'un mal formado delito'. And the words of Arias:

> En mi vida he conocido
> galán necio, escrupuloso
> y con extremo celoso
> que en llegando a ser marido
> no le castiguen los cielos.   (202a)

emphasize the jealousy and susceptibility of Gutierre. But Leonor rejects at once Arias's allegations concerning Gutierre's honour, and defends the integrity of the man who has deserted her:

> Señor don Arias, no quiero
> escuchar lo que decís,
> que os engañáis, o mentís.
> Don Gutierre es caballero,
> que en todas las ocasiones
> con obrar y con decir
> sabrá, vive Dios, cumplir
> muy bien sus obligaciones...   (202a)

Before leaving, Leonor reprimands Arias for slandering his enemy:

> pues si fuérais noble vos,
> no hablárades, vive Dios,
> así de vuestro enemigo.   (202a)

Leonor's defence of Gutierre and the slanderous remarks of Arias (contrast Gutierre who, in Act I, strove to spare the good name of Leonor) are additions to the scene of the source-play which call attention to the integrity of Gutierre, however misguidedly he may act. The attitude of Leonor towards Gutierre anticipates also her acceptance of his hand at the play's end.

Act II ends in both plays with the scene in which the husband deceives his wife by calling to her in the darkness. The earlier Jacinto has no scruples about posing as Enrique; his test is carefully planned and he climbs the walls of his house to carry it through. Gutierre, too, climbs into his house, but only to see for himself if the intruder of the previous night has returned. When he finds everything quiet and Mencía asleep, he is satisfied that all is well; his confidence in Mencía is unshaken. And then, suddenly, he doubts, and on the spur of the moment calls to Mencía in the darkness. Even so, the first words of Mencía seem to remove any fears he may have had:

> *(Ap.)* Ella me ha conocido

But a moment later the fateful words 'Tu Alteza' betray that she has taken him for the Prince. The new effect of Calderón's scene is largely due to the admirable suspense and the striking poetic beauty which are scarcely hinted at in the source-play. Gutierre, however, behaves differently from Jacinto. Though he comes in secret to spy upon Mencía, his calling to her in the darkness without identifying himself is not premeditated as with Jacinto. The lines of Calderón need no commentary:

> Bueno he hallado mi honor, hacer no quiero
> por ahora otra cura,
> pues la salud en él está segura.
> Pero ¿ni una criada
> la acompaña? ¿Si acaso retirada
> aguarda?... ¡Oh pensamiento
> injusto!, ¡oh vil temor!, ¡oh infame aliento!
> Ya con esta sospecha
> no he de volverme...   (203a)

And a moment later:

> Mato la luz, y llego,
> sin luz y sin razón, dos veces ciego.   (203a)

Gutierre's action is morally reprehensible —of that Calderón leaves no doubt— but it is presented as the lapse of one whose reason is momentarily blinded by his suspicions. Where Jacinto is contemptible Gutierre commands our pity.

In both plays the reactions of the wife in answer to a call from the darkness are singularly unfortunate, but Calderón gives greater weight to the point in order to insist on Mencía's imprudence. She is made to refer to the first visit of Enrique and to her deception of Gutierre to secure his escape; and, believing that Enrique has now returned, her only concern seems to be that Gutierre might find out. Mencía must bear some responsibility for the tragedy which follows. If Gutierre has drawn unwarranted and wrong conclusions

from Mencía's words, it must be granted that the words were
remarkably ill-advised and imprudent. Gutierre's exchanges with
Mencía with which the act ends are closely modelled on lines in the
source:

SOURCE

MAYOR.   Sospechas
o celos de mí parece
que tenéis.

D. JACINTO.   Pues ¿hay quién pueda
darme a mí celos, o yo,
si en mi pensamiento apenas
sospechas acreditara,
más pedazos no os hiciera
que átomos el sol deslumbra,
que peces el mar navegan?
¿Más rigores no inventara
que la tiranía cuenta,
si llegara a concebir
rasgo o minuto en mi ofensa?
¿No supiera el homicida,
aunque el rey Enrique fuera
quitar la vida, y subir
mi honor hasta las estrellas?
Mas ¿qué es esto? ¿Yo, Mayor,
os hablo de esta manera?
¿Yo descompuesto con vos?
Alguna cólera fiera
me ha precipitado; esposa,
dadme aquesos brazos, ea,
y perdonadme.   (427b-428a)

CALDERÓN

D.ª MENCÍA.   (Ap.)   El sentido dudo.
Parece que celoso
hablas en dos sentidos.

D. GUTIERRE.   (Ap.)   Riguroso
es el dolor de agravios;
mas con celos ningunos fueron sabios.
¡Celoso! ¿Sabes tú lo que son celos?
Que yo no sé qué son, ¡viven los cielos!
Porque si lo supiera,
y celos...

D.ª MENCÍA.   (Ap.)   ¡Ay de mí!

D. GUTIERRE.   ...llegar pudiera
a tener..., ¿qué son celos?
Átomos, ilusiones y desvelos,
no más que de una esclava, una criada,

<pre>
                     por sombra imaginada,
                     con hechos inhumanos
                     a pedazos sacara con mis manos
                     el corazón, y luego
                     envuelto en sangre, desatado en fuego,
                     el corazón comiera
                     a bocados, la sangre me bebiera,
                     el alma le sacara,
                     y el alma, ¡vive Dios!, despedazara,
                     si capaz de dolor el alma fuera.
                     Pero, ¿cómo hablo yo desta manera?
D.ª MENCÍA.   Temor al alma ofreces.
D. GUTIERRE.   ¡Jesús, Jesús mil veces!
                     Mi bien, mi esposa, cielo, gloria mía,
                     ah mi dueño, ah Mencía,
                     perdona, por tus ojos,
                     esta descompostura, estos enojos;
                     que tanto un fingimiento
                     fuera de mí llevó mi pensamiento:
                     y vete, por tu vida; que prometo
                     que te miro con miedo y con respeto,
                     corrido deste exceso.
                     ¡Jesús! No estuve en mí, no tuve seso.   (204b)
</pre>

Both the violence of Gutierre's words and the admission that he is 'corrido deste exceso' are foreshadowed in the source. But by intensifying the anger of Gutierre Calderón accentuates also the restraint which he exercises in overcoming it, to the extent at least of postponing revenge upon a wife whose guilt seemingly he had just discovered. The struggle within Gutierre is the more impressive since he so nearly succumbs.

At the beginning of Act III Gutierre seeks an audience with the King. Calderón has postponed Gutierre's appeal until he has extracted from his wife what appears to be proof of her complicity. Yet in contrast to that of the source, Calderón's scene between the husband and the King has warmth and feeling. Whereas Jacinto in his appeal is concerned only with his honour, Gutierre comes in tears, his love for Mencía in conflict with his sense of honour:

<pre>
                     No te espantes que los ojos
                     también se quejen, señor;
                     que dicen que amor y honor
                     pueden, sin que a nadie asombre,
                     permitir que llore un hombre;
                     y yo tengo honor y amor.
</pre>

> Honor, que siempre he guardado
> como noble y bien nacido,
> y amor, que siempre he tenido
> como esposo enamorado...   (205a)

Here are lines which, in their humanity and pathos, are without precedent in the source-play. Later, Gutierre will contrive a brutal death for the wife he loves, but this should not blind us to the deeply human conflict which rages in his mind for most of the play, and which reaches its climax in this scene. Gutierre's references to Enrique, the enemy of his honour, unlike those of Jacinto, are restrained; and he assures the King that, being a Prince, Enrique has nothing to fear on his account:

> No os turbéis: con sangre digo
> solamente de mi pecho;
> que Enrique, estad satisfecho,
> está seguro conmigo.   (205a)

He comes to the King to prevent an outrage which has not yet taken place:

> Sólo a Vuestra Majestad
> di parte, para que evite
> el daño que no hay...   (205b)

He is concerned not with revenge but with a remedy. But remarks of Enrique reveal that he is determined to press his suit:

> Es cierto, pero
> el tiempo todo lo rinde,
> el amor todo lo puede.   (206b)
>
> ...en fin, doncella la quise.
> ¿Quién, decir, agravia a quién?
> ¿Yo a un vasallo...

D. GUTIERRE.   *(Ap.)*   ¡Ay, infelice!

D. ENRIQUE.   ...que antes que fuera su esposa, fué...?

REY.   No tenéis que decirme.   (206b)

This from Enrique's own lips! And Gutierre witnesses the dagger incident between the King and Enrique, which leaves him no hope of seeing his honour saved by the King's intervention. Only by disposing of Mencía, the person through whom dishonour may come, can Gutierre remove the threat which hangs over him:

Arranquemos de una vez
de tanto mal las raíces.
Muera Mencía, su sangre
bañe el lecho donde asiste; [1]
y pues aqueste puñal
hoy segunda vez me rinde
el Infante, con él muera.   (207a)

The conception of the dramatic situation of this scene derives from the source, but the effect in Calderón's play is quite different. Coming after the garden scene, it represents a new stage in the action; having confirmed, as he thinks, that the threat to his honour is a real one since Mencía is privy to Enrique's advances, Gutierre discovers now from Enrique himself his designs upon Mencía which the King is powerless to prevent. Gutierre's conception of honour leaves him no alternative but to remove Mencía.

We return to the pattern of the source-play with the second scene of Act III in which the wife is surprised by her husband with a half-finished letter to Enrique, pleading with him not to leave Sevilla. Here Calderón leaves no doubt about the imprudence of Mencía's action. The idea of writing to Enrique comes from her slave-girl Jacinta, and she accepts it unwillingly as the better of two evils. But, as in the garden scene, responsibility for what ensues rests with both Mencía and Gutierre, for, if Mencía's action is ill-advised, Gutierre's interpretation of her action is unwarranted and mistaken. Resolved, in despair, to dispose of Mencía (he asks that a thunderbolt may come to take his own life: "...¿No hay un rayo para un triste?" [207b]) the half-written letter of Mencía is, for him, corroboration of her guilt, and he locks her in her room to await her fate. Again, one notes, Gutierre's is no act of impulse. If his honour requires Mencía's death, his love for her makes him think of her spiritual welfare:

Ya que la cura he de aplicar postrera
no muera el alma, aunque la vida muera.   (209a)

This is the content, too, of the notorious note which he appends to her letter:

El amor te adora, el honor te aborrece; y así el uno te mata y el otro te avisa. Dos horas tienes de vida; cristiana eres, salva el alma, que la vida es imposible. (209b)

---

[1] QC, *lecho*, Astrana Marín, *pecho*.

3

Gutierre, of course, is careful to dispose of Mencía in a way in which she may be thought to have died a natural death, so that his dishonour will not be suspected. But there is nothing in the source-play to suggest his concern for his wife's soul. The effect of Calderón's scene is to present a man who, if he acts with the cruel hand of honour, is in perfect control of himself.

Calderón's portrait of Gutierre has prepared us for the manner in which he will clear his honour. The engaging of a doctor to bleed his wife to death is not the impulsive act of a desperado; it is the carefully-considered stratagem of one whose mind is made up, and whose concern is only the secrecy with which the affair can be carried through. In both plays the surgeon acts under threat of death. But Gutierre delays his orders until he has ensured personally that Mencía has made her peace with God:

> Tiempo es ya
> de que entres aquí...   (210a)

And the surgeon himself is made to describe what he sees in the adjoining room: a veiled figure lying on a bed, with two candles and a crucifix. Gutierre now proceeds with his plan without a sign of weakening, the plan of one who is convinced that his act is just. In the source-play, whilst the doctor is bleeding his wife, Jacinto has some sixty lines in which he reconsiders his action: he cannot take his mind off what is happening next door, his sentiments express a mixture of hesitation, self-justification and pity. He curses the law of honour which requires such cruelty and is so moved by his wife's death that he would seem to doubt the justice of what he is doing. Calderón's procedure is totally different. Gutierre is a person who has no doubts about the justice of his act, and his monologue, if cold and cruel, reflects the attitude which one might expect of a person who has resolved on such a deed. His lines have no mention of Mencía; love and honour having proved incompatible, love has been stifled. Gutierre's final act of love was to give Mencía two hours' grace before her death. His only concern now is the manner in which his honour is being cleared, and above all the need of secrecy; so he plots even to dispose of Ludovico, the only person who knows what has happened.

The differences between the endings of the two plays, though slight, are most important. Jacinto, we have seen, curses the code of honour whilst the doctor is bleeding his wife:

> Mal haya, amén, el primero
> que este género de honor
> impuso con tal rigor,
> tan bruto, bárbaro y fiero.   (434b)

He is made to refer to it again when the King comes to his house:

> ¡Ay honor, lo que me cuestas!
> ¡Que tu ley tan rigurosa
> sea, que sólo con sangre
> ufana viva tu pompa!   (437a)

Calderón does not allow his protagonist to criticize the laws of honour on either occasion; such criticism on the lips of Gutierre would have been out of character. Yet Calderón's attitude to Gutierre's action and to the code which prompted it is plain. Like the source dramatist he makes the King excuse the murder:

> Cuerdamente
> sus agravios satisfizo.   (212b)
>
> Tomó notable venganza.   (213b)

Gutierre has acted strictly in accordance with the rules of behaviour which were upheld by the society in which he lived, and it is right that the law, in the person of the King, should excuse his crime. But the King represents *ley,* not *derecho.* Throughout the play, moreover, Calderón criticizes the King's own moral error and, as we shall see, links him by his severity and cruelty to Gutierre. Yet the King himself is made to say:

> Gutierre sin duda es
> el cruel que anoche hizo
> una acción tan inclemente.   (212b)

and earlier Coquín had commented:

> Gutierre, mal informado
> por aparentes recelos,
> llegó a tener viles celos...   (212a)

The crucifix above Mencía's bed, as Wilson has pointed out, symbolizes divine forgiveness, which contrasts so violently with the law of honour.

But this is not all. The source dramatist seems to predict a rosy future for Jacinto, even though his marriage to Margarita is to be governed by the same code of honour which has brought death to Mayor:

> siendo mi amigo, mi amparo
> siendo mi privanza toda,
> siendo un ejemplo de vida,
> siendo archivo de la honra,
> siendo un sol de mi justicia,
> siendo cláusula que exhorta
> mi vida y mis pensamientos
> siendo en caso que se nota
> desta suerte, amigo firme,
> cuyo amor tenga en memoria
> el tiempo en cuantas edades
> borde el sol por las trionas
> líneas y altos paralelos,
> dejándote escrito en hojas
> de bronce y mármol. (438b)

Calderón's play has no corresponding passage. On the contrary, its emphasis is on the dangers that lie ahead for Gutierre. He is obliged to marry Leonor, whom he no longer loves, in order to repair her injured honour, and Calderón includes a gruesome exchange between the two which has no precedent in the source:

> REY. Dádsela, pues, a Leonor;
> que yo sé que su alabanza
> la merece.
> D. GUTIERRE. Sí la doy. (Dale la mano.)
> Mas mira que va bañada
> en sangre, Leonor.
> D.ª LEONOR. No importa;
> que no me admira ni espanta.
> D. GUTIERRE. Mira que médico he sido
> de mi honra: no está olvidada
> la ciencia.
> D.ª LEONOR. Cura con ella
> mi vida, en estando mala.
> D. GUTIERRE. Pues con esa condición
> te la doy. (214b)

Gutierre is allowed to go on living, but it is grimly clear that his second marriage is based not upon love and mutual trust but upon hatred and suspicion, with the sword of revenge hanging over it. Hence the significance, I suggest, of Gutierre's protest to the King that, with the ashes of one fire still hot, he is allowed no respite, and that, with the storm still raging, he is obliged again to put out to sea:

D. GUTIERRE.	Señor, si de tanto fuego aún las cenizas se hallan calientes, dadme lugar para que llore mis ansias. ¿No queréis que escarmentado quede?
REY.	Esto ha de ser, y basta.
D. GUTIERRE.	Señor, ¿queréis que otra vez, no libre de la borrasca, vuelva al mar? (213b)

Calderón's portrait of Gutierre in outline is the same as that of Jacinto, but minor changes transform the total effect. In Act I, in contrast to the faithless and suspicious Jacinto, Gutierre is constant and trusting; if the Leonor episode shows him to be unduly susceptible, he has acted according to his own conception of honour in good faith, and, unlike Jacinto, declines to slander the lady he once loved. In Act II his love for Mencía impels him to leave the Sevillan prison to which, as a man of honour, he insists on returning. His suspicions are roused by the discovery of the dagger which he identifies as Enrique's but, whereas Jacinto appeals at once to the King, Gutierre awaits confirmation of his suspicions. Leonor, despite her grievance against Gutierre, defends his integrity and sense of honour. In the garden scene, Gutierre's deception of Mencía is not premeditated as in the source-play, and for all his anger at discovering what appears to him proof of his wife's complicity, he avoids committing any act of violence, and goes to the King to remove the threat to his honour peaceably. Only when he discovers that Enrique will continue his dishonourable advances does he resolve on disposing of Mencía. Before doing so, though receiving as he thinks corroboration of her guilt, he grants Mencía two hours' grace to make her peace with God. At every point of the play Calderón has made Gutierre's conduct superior to that of Jacinto. His motives are unexceptionable, and he acts punctiliously in accordance with a code of behaviour which he believes to be right. To this extent Calderón has ennobled his protagonist and given him the stature of a tragic hero.

But if, in the first instance, the outcome of the play is the safeguarding of his honour by a man of undoubted integrity, it is also tragedy, the tragedy of a husband who kills the wife he loves. Throughout his play Calderón has shown, in a manner which is without parallel in the source, that Gutierre's very pursuit of honour has involved him in serious moral error which leads inevitably to confusion and tragedy. Honour for Gutierre meant the code which, for all its positive moral values, permitted suspicion, dissimulation, cruelty and even murder. Though in this respect manifestly evil, it was on such a code that Gutierre's principles and his whole moral behaviour were based. He is a person of integrity and nobility, but as the play advances this nobility becomes progressively more distorted and Gutierre himself more unbalanced. The difficulties with which he is confronted are such that only by trust and love could he overcome them; but trust is turned to suspicion, love to hatred. Gutierre is unequal to the challenge which life presents to him. He accepts the rules of behaviour of his day, and we pity him as a victim of those rules. But a greater man would have recognized that they were leading him into moral error, and rejected them. For all his good intentions Gutierre must be held culpable.

Calderón made changes of importance also in the other characters, though I shall have to deal with them more briefly. There is, first, Doña Mencía. Her virtue, like that of Doña Mayor, is beyond reproach. She consistently opposes the advances of her lover Enrique, and, fully aware of the threat to the family honour, she tries to conceal from Gutierre the visit of Enrique. Later, fearing that Enrique's departure from Sevilla will be associated with her, she risks sending a letter to him to persuade him, for her sake, not to leave. Mencía's good intentions are never for a moment in doubt, but the very steps she takes for the sake of honour lead Gutierre eventually to the conviction that she is guilty. Her dissimulation over Enrique's visit, her words to Gutierre from the garden, her half-written letter, confirm for him her complicity with Enrique, and she pays with her life. In all this Calderón is following closely the source-play.

We note, however, some interesting changes of detail. Before Enrique takes leave of Mencía in the play's first scene, he accuses her indirectly of deceit. Mencía, provoked by this charge, offers to

explain why, in spite of her love for him, she has married Gutierre.
In so doing, unwittingly she is inviting Enrique to see her again, a
point which later Enrique does not fail to make:

> Esto es tomar tu consejo.
> Tú me aconsejas que escuche
> disculpas de aquella dama,
> y vengo a que te disculpes
> conmigo de mis agravios. (194b-195a)

and Mencía herself admits:

> Es verdad, la culpa tuve...   (195a)

There is no parallel in the source-play. Mencía's words in Act I serve
the purpose of anticipating Enrique's visit in Act II; but they also
call atention to Mencía's share of responsibility for the visit. Again,
when Gutierre announces that he is going to Sevilla she tries to
dissuade him in language which leaves no doubt about her jealousy
and disquiet. The point was well made by Viel-Castel:

> On sent que Mencía n'est pas sincère, qu'elle est troublée, agitée et que
> c'est précisément pour cacher son émotion qu'elle a recours à ces artifices
> d'une coquetterie raffinée. Déjà elle n'est plus complètement innocente. [1]

In the first scene of Act II, when her husband returns unexpectedly,
Mencía, like Mayor, tries to get Enrique out of the house without
arousing suspicion; but Calderón, by interpolating first a revealing
aside of Mencía's and then, after Enrique's escape, a short exchange
between Mencía and her servant Jacinta, underlines the rashness of
this deception:

> D.ª MENCÍA.   (Ap.) En salud me he de curar:
>   ved, honor, cómo ha de ser,
>   porque me he de resolver
>   a una temeraria acción.   (196a)
>
> JACINTA.   Grande atrevimiento fué
>   determinarte, [2] señora,
>   a tan grande acción ahora.
>
> D.ª MENCÍA.   En ella mi vida hallé.
>
> JACINTA.   ¿Por qué lo hiciste?

---

[1] Louis de Viel-Castel, *Essai sur le théâtre espagnol*, I (París, 1882), p. 322.
[2] QC, *determinarte*, Astrana Marín, *me*.

D.ª MENCÍA.   Porque
si yo no se lo dijera,
y Gutierre lo sintiera,
la presunción era clara,
pues no se desengañara
de que yo cómplice era;
y no fué dificultad
en ocasión tan cruel,
haciendo del ladrón fiel,
engañar con la verdad.   (197b)

At the end of Act II, Mencía's remarks from the garden to the person she takes to be Enrique are, as we have noted earlier, singularly unfortunate. Calderón emphasizes the point:

D. GUTIERRE.   El venir no ha extrañado
del Infante, ni dél se ha recatado;
sino sólo ha sentido
que en ocasión se ponga (¡estoy perdido!)
de que otra vez se esconda.   (203b)

In the same way, when in Act III Mencía writes the letter to prevent Enrique from leaving Sevilla, the gravity of Mencía's action, far from being glossed over as in the source-play, is given due prominence. Mencía adopts the suggestion of Jacinta, her slave-girl, only in the last resort, cognizant of the danger involved:

D.ª MENCÍA.   Pruebas de honor son peligrosas pruebas;
pero con todo quiero
escribir el papel, pues considero,
y no con necio engaño,
que es de dos daños éste el menor daño,
Si hay menor en los daños que recibo.   (208b)

Coquín later refers to it as an 'error cruel'.

By calling attention to those instances in the play in which Calderón, in contrast to the source dramatist, shows the imprudence of Mencía, I may perhaps appear to have exaggerated her share of responsibility for the final tragedy. She is, in fact, the victim of a brutal code. Virtuous and well-meaning, her slight imprudence has disastrous consequences only because of the abnormal circumstances in which she finds herself and the abnormal persons with whom she is involved. She resorts to dissimulation to safeguard her good name, and her misguided efforts to conceal the threat to her honour aggravate the suspicions of Gutierre and hasten on her death. Mencía dies on account of the unscrupulousness of Enrique and the cruelty of her husband. But Calderón shows how, in the kind of society in which she lives, her own actions, however human and understandable, are imprudent. By her failure to see the consequences of these actions she herself must bear some responsibility for her own death.

Prince Enrique is the only character of the play who is wilfully evil. The lover of Mencía before her marriage to Gutierre, he wishes to re-establish a relationship which can only bring dishonour upon Mencía and her husband. Enrique's advances are in defiance of all the laws of honour; yet, because Gutierre respects the inviolability of his person, he is not involved in the final tragedy. Enrique's rôle is unambiguous, and Calderón has transferred him from the source-play with no changes of importance, except to insist upon his contempt of the honour of a vassal:

> Pues yo, señor, he de hablar:
> en fin, doncella la quise.
> ¿Quién, decid, agravia a quién?
> ¿Yo a un vasallo... (206b)

Even so, Calderón shows that Enrique's guilt leads to tragedy only through the errors of other persons involved, above all Gutierre and Mencía.

In addition to Gutierre, Mencía and Prince Enrique, three other characters are involved in what occurs: the King, Doña Leonor and Don Arias. The source dramatist had set the action against the background of the enmity between King Peter and his bastard brother Henry of Trastamara. He presented King Peter both as 'el justiciero' and 'el cruel', and on more than one occasion foreshadowed his death at the hand of Enrique. Calderón followed this lead. At the same time, however, as Wilson has shown, he drew a parallel between the King and Don Gutierre. In the two plays, of course, Enrique is the enemy of both the King and Gutierre, and the dagger which symbolizes his offence against the honour of Gutierre cuts the hand of the King; and just as he emerges unscathed from his escapade with Gutierre, so he escapes from his quarrel with the King whom he will later murder. Both dramatists comment upon the King's severity and anger. At the very outset of their plays, for example, he abandons his injured brother Enrique; and at Sevilla he is impulsive and quick-tempered. But Calderón insists upon the severity of the King by means of a contract between him and the *gracioso* Coquín. Coquín is to receive a hundred *escudos* each time he makes the King laugh; if he fails he will lose his teeth. The contract brings out the cruelty and the inhumanity of the King; since he is incapable of laughter, the contract is unjust. At Sevilla, the King is high-handed with the *pretendientes;* the second comments in an aside:

<blockquote>Pocas palabras gasta.   (189b)</blockquote>

His promotion of the soldier and his generosity to the beggar are unconsidered and precipitate.

Nor is the King in Calderón's play a mere spectator with whom Gutierre is compared. He is directly involved in the disaster which overtakes Gutierre. At Sevilla, with Leonor in hiding, he obliges Gutierre against his better judgement to tell why he has deserted her. The point is important because it is only when Gutierre has given his reason that Leonor shows herself and provokes a quarrel which leads to the imprisonment of Gutierre, and to the opportunity for Enrique to visit Mencía. Without the King's insistence, this visit, with the train of events which ensues, would not have taken place. A parallel incident occurs in Act III where the King interviews Enrique with Gutierre in hiding. As a direct result of what he overhears, Gutierre takes it upon himself to dispose of Mencía. This time Calderón makes the King admit it in an aside:

<blockquote>(Ap.) ¡Válgame Dios, qué mal hice
en esconder a Gutierre!   (206b)</blockquote>

Of the ultimate fate of the King Calderón leaves no doubt. As in the source-play, the dagger incident between the King and Enrique serves as a premonition of his violent death:

<blockquote>SOURCE
No sé qué agüero he tenido
en ver qué instrumento ha sido
Enrique, de haber así
mi sangre yo derramado;
mas vaya ¿qué puede ser?
¿Agüeros ha de temer
quien tiene valor sobrado?   (429b)</blockquote>

CALDERÓN

¡Válgame el cielo! ¿Qué es esto?
¡Oh, qué aprensión insufrible!
Bañado me vi en mi sangre,
muerto estuve. ¿Qué infelice
imaginación me cerca
que con espantos horribles
y con helados temores
el pecho y el alma oprime?
Ruego a Dios que estos principios
no lleguen a tales fines,
que con diluvios de sangre
el mundo se escandalice.   (207a)

But Calderón insists on the point by including a specific reference to Montiel in a ballad which the King overhears in the streets of Seville:

Para Consuegra camina
donde piensa que han de ser
teatros de mil tragedias
las montañas de Montiel.   (211a)

Leonor's part is similar to that of Margarita in the source, but she is better integrated into the main structure. Much of what was irrelevant to the action in Margarita's part has been removed, in particular a speech to the King of some two hundred lines with unimportant details of her early life. Leonor's imprudence links her with Doña Mencía: at Sevilla, for example, she comes out of hiding to defend her honour, an action which is, on her own admission, rash:

que menos perder importa
la vida, cuando me dé
este atrevimiento muerte,
que vida y honor perder.   (193a)

And she admits to Arias some measure of blame for her dishonour:

Yo tuve la culpa, yo
la pena siento, y así
sólo me quejo de mí
y de mi estrella.   (201b)

By her punctiliousness, however, she is linked with Gutierre. Her honour has been compromised by Gutierre and, despite her love for him, she is ready to kill him:

> Y yo, aunque ofendida estoy,
> y aunque la muerte le diera
> con mis manos si pudiera,
> no le murmurara hoy
> en el honor, desleal.   (202b)

The same sentiment is expressed in the phrase of Gutierre's final
note to Mencía:

> *El amor te adora, el honor te aborrece.*   (209b)

The death of Mencía allows Leonor to recover her lost honour by
marrying Gutierre. But Gutierre no longer loves her, and it is a
marriage based upon suspicion and hatred.

An examination of the source-play suggests that Calderón
intended a parallel between Don Arias and Enrique. Arias derives
from the earlier Alvaro and his relationship with Leonor resembles
that of Alvaro's with Margarita. But Alvaro in the first *El médico*
defends the King against the aspersions cast by Don Pedro:

D. PEDRO.	No ha sido fineza poca para su severidad, apearse.
D. ÁLVARO.	¿Quién ignora su resolución, midiendo las palabras con las obras?
D. PEDRO.	¡Buena visita de hermano!
D. ÁLVARO.	Su entereza en todas cosas el mundo admira. (408a)

And in Act III he accompanies him in his wanderings around
Sevilla. Don Arias, on the contrary, is made the friend and adviser of
Enrique, and in Calderón's first scene he is the critic, not the
defender, of the King:

> Esta ocasión
> de su fiera condición
> ha sido bastante prueba.
> ¿Quién a su hermano dejara,
> tropezando desta suerte,
> en los brazos de la muerte?
> ¡Vive Dios!   (184a)

Privy to Enrique's affair with Mencía, Arias is the first to recognize
her in Act I. In Act II he is released from prison through the

intervention of Enrique, and when rejected by Leonor leaves to join his master. Calderón insists on the link again in Act III:

REY.	Y Enrique, ¿quién lleva que le acompañe?
D. DIEGO.	Don Arias.
REY.	En su privanza. (209b)

Arias, like Enrique, is the enemy of Gutierre; if Enrique is Gutierre's rival for Mencía, Arias is Gutierre's rival for Leonor. And he slanders him in order to win her affections for himself, provoking Leonor to defend him. To this extent Arias mirrors Enrique as the enemy of Gutierre's honour. Arias, too, is made to bear some share of the responsibility for what befalls Mencía, for if Enrique starts off the chain of events which will lead to Mencía's death, Arias is responsible, unintentionally, for Gutierre's desertion of Leonor. Recklessly—'atrevimiento de enamorado'—he has entered Leonor's house, and, in so doing, has brought upon her the suspicion of Gutierre. In the source-play, Arias's presence in Leonor's room goes unexplained; in Calderón's play, Arias himself recognizes his *culpa*.

The only remaining part of standing is that of Don Diego, evidently an elderly attendant of the King, who replaces the earlier Don Pedro and Don Alonso. Don Diego, throughout the play, is the wise counsellor. It is he who in the first scene, for example, warns Don Arias when he is criticizing the King, and who in Act II reminds the King himself that, though he is right to be 'un Argos de su reino' he did wrong to take on incognito a party of toughs in the streets of Sevilla. In Act III he accompanies the King on his nocturnal wanderings and interprets for him the songs they hear.

Of greater importance as a character is the *gracioso* Coquín. In outline Coquín derives from the earlier *lacayo* Galindo and his appearances correspond almost exactly with those of Galindo in the source. But whereas Galindo is exclusively a figure of fun, a simpleton who is constantly harping on food and wine and who is involved in a long exchange with the servant Elvira, Coquín has a rôle which is both serious and important; he provides, it is true, a certain amount of humour and performs some dramatic odd jobs, but at the same time he contributes to the development of the play's theme. Coquín is best remembered for his contract with the King, an idea which may have been suggested to Calderón by the earlier

Galindo's reply to his master's suggestion that he should take a
candle and look for the intruder in Mayor's bedroom:

> Señor, sacarme una muela
> aquí, tanto no sintiera
> como llevar instrumento
> con que afrente el pensamiento
> del desdichado que espera.   (420b)

The contract is the excuse for some humour, but, as I have said
earlier, it is a perpetual reminder of the King's severity and cruelty.
But the key to Coquín's contribution to the play comes in Act III
when his pity for Mencía makes him seek out the King in an
attempt to save her life. He begins by making the point that he
is now in earnest and to be taken seriously:

> que aunque hombre me consideras
> de burlas, con loco humor,
> llegando a veras, señor,
> soy hombre de muchas veras.   (212a)

Then, at the same time as he informs the King that the life of his
mistress is in danger, he is made to comment on both her own
behaviour and that of Gutierre. Mencía, he admits, is guilty of
moral error *(error cruel)* but she is not unfaithful; Gutierre is the
victim of 'viles celos'. Coquín's own pity throws into relief Gutierre's
cruelty. The *gracioso* who failed to make the King laugh brings
him a story of such poignancy that he should weep:

> que quiero hacerte llorar,
> ya que no puedo reír.   (212a)

The King observes:

> No es ahora tiempo de risa.

to which Coquín retorts:

> ¿cuándo lo fué?

Professor Parker has pointed out to me that in the light of these
exchanges Coquín's earlier interventions take on a new significance.
We recall first his comment upon the terms of his wager with
the King:

> Dicen, cuando uno se ríe,
> que enseña los dientes; pues
> enseñarlos yo llorando,
> será reirme al revés.   (191b)

The society in which the innocent Mencía is brutally murdered is topsy-turvy, a society in which love is smothered by honour and moral values are confused. And in this society laughter is transformed into tears. We recall too Coquín's comments upon Gutierre's insistence that he should return to prison:

> ¿Y heme de dejar morir,
> por sólo bien parecer?
> Si el morir, señor, tuviera
> descarte o enmienda alguna,
> cosa que de dos la una
> un hombre hacerla pudiera,
> yo probara la primera
> por servirte; mas ¿no ves
> que rifa la vida es?
> Entro en ella, vengo y tomo
> cartas, y piérdola: ¿cómo
> me desquitaré después?
> Perdida se quedará,
> si la pierdo por tu engaño,
> desde aquí a ciento y un año.   (196b)

Coquín's lack of principle emphasizes the punctiliousness and integrity of his master. But his defence of his attitude calls attention to the danger of a rigid adherence to a principle to the extent of sacrificing life itself for the sake of appearances. And this is precisely what Gutierre will do. These words of the *gracioso* Coquín early in Act II epitomize the play's theme.

The combination of these changes in the borrowed characters accounts to a large extent for the different impact of the two plays. All the characters of Calderón's play are made to share some responsibility for the tragedy which occurs. Don Arias, in the first instance, recklessly enters the house of Leonor. He is discovered by Gutierre, whose susceptibility makes him deaf to explanations so that he deserts Leonor to marry Mencía. Enrique, Mencía's first lover, continues his advances in face of Mencía's and her husband's honour; and Mencía's own imprudent remarks serve to encourage him. The rashness of the King and Leonor's indiscretion at Seville lead to the imprisonment of Gutierre and Arias and the opportunity for Enrique to visit Mencía. In a society whose behaviour is determined by the code of honour, slowly but inexorably the characters bring their tragic fate upon themselves. There is suspense and mounting tension as the imprudence of Mencía, the jealousy, susceptibility and cruelty of Gutierre, and the complete disregard for honour of Enrique lead Gutierre first to suspect and then seemingly to confirm the threat to his honour and Mencía's complicity, and to carry through his cruel murder. Calderón has established the whole train of events leading up to Mencía's death; he does not even exempt her father:

> D.ª MENCÍA. Nací en Sevilla, y en ella
> me vió Enrique, festejó
> mis desdenes, celebró
> mi nombre... ¡felice estrella! ;
> fuése, y mi padre atropella
> la libertad que hubo en mí:
> la mano a Gutierre di... (189a)

The source not only lacks the cohesion and unity of Calderón's play but, through the dramatist's failure to bring out so clearly and forcibly the responsibility of the characters and the distorted values of the society in which they lived, it lacks too its gravity and grim significance.

The major differences between the two *El médico* plays were required by Calderón's conception of the characters. Some, however, are evidence simply of a superior technique. In the recasting of a scene, for example, Calderón had a sure eye for achieving the maximum dramatic effect. Take the first meeting of Prince Enrique and Doña Mencía in Act I. The earlier dramatist anticipated it by lines in which Doña Mayor informed her servant (and, more to the point, the audience) of the advances made to her by the Prince. Calderón brought Mencía and Enrique together without any such preamble, and the relationship between them is made to emerge from snatches of conversation like:

> D. ARIAS. ...Pero ¡qué miro!
> ¡Señora!
> D.ª MENCÍA. ¡Don Arias!

D. ARIAS.   Creo
              que es sueño o fingido cuanto
              estoy escuchando y viendo.
              ¡Que el infante don Enrique,
              más amante que primero,
              vuelva a Sevilla, y te halle
              con tan infeliz encuentro,
              puede ser verdad?   (184b)

Calderón delayed, too, the return to consciousness of Enrique,
allowing Mencía a monologue, whilst she watches over him alone,
in which she gives expression to the conflict between her love for
the Prince and her duty towards her husband. This situation, with
the effective suspense prior to Enrique's recovering consciousness,
was not exploited by the source dramatist.

Another example is provided by the last few lines of the first
scene of Act II where the husband embraces his wife with Enrique's
dagger in his hand:

SOURCE

D. JACINTO.   Volvedme, esposa, a abrazar,
               ea, y sosegaos.
(Vala a abrazar, y la daga que halló lleva desnuda, y ella
        entiende que la quiere matar, y se retira.)
MAYOR.   ¡Ay, cielos!
               ¿Por qué matarme queréis?
D. JACINTO.   ¡Yo! ¿Qué decís? ¿Qué tenéis?
               ¡Ah! Espacio, señores celos.
MAYOR.   ¿Con el acero desnudo
               os venís a mí, señor?
D. JACINTO.   Mayor, aquese es error,
               que sólo sacarle pudo
               mi enojo, para matar
               al que escondido estuviera,
               si acaso se defendiera.
               Pero venid a cenar,
               y ese miedo que os desvela
               dejad. ¡Cielos, no es engaño!
               Sólo quien comete el daño,
               del castigo se recela.
               Triste voy: vamos.   (421b-422a)

CALDERÓN

D.ᵃ MENCÍA.   Los brazos da
               a quien te adora.

4

D. GUTIERRE.   El favor
          estimo.
(Al ir a abrazarle, doña Mencía ve la daga.)
D.ª MENCÍA.   ¡Tente, señor!
          ¿Tú la daga para mí?
          En mi vida te ofendí,
          detén la mano al rigor,
          detén...
D. GUTIERRE.   ¿De qué estás turbada,
          mi bien, mi esposa, Mencía?
D.ª MENCÍA.   Al verte así, presumía
          que ya en mi sangre bañada,
          hoy moría desangrada.
D. GUTIERRE.   Como a ver la casa entré,
          así esta daga saqué.
D.ª MENCÍA.   Toda soy una ilusión.
D. GUTIERRE.   ¡Jesús, qué imaginación!
D.ª MENCÍA.   En mi vida te he ofendido.
D. GUTIERRE.   ¡Qué necia disculpa ha sido!
          Pero suele una aprensión
          tales miedos prevenir.
D.ª MENCÍA.   Mis tristezas, mis enojos,
          vanas quimeras y antojos,
          suelen mi engaño fingir.
D. GUTIERRE.   Si yo pudiera venir,
          vendré a la noche, y adiós.
D.ª MENCÍA.   Él vaya, señor, con vos.
          (Ap.) ¡Oh, qué asombros! ¡Oh, qué extremos!
D. GUTIERRE.   *(Ap.)* ¡Ay honor, mucho tenemos
          que hablar a solas los dos! *(Vanse.)*   (197b-198a)

The source dramatist conceived a fine situation but failed to exploit it to the full, and dissipated much of its effect by prolonging the scene with exchanges between the servants Elvira and Galindo. Calderón heightened the drama of the situation itself and with it rounded off his scene. At the same time he used it to foreshadow more explicitly than hitherto the play's dénouement.

Calderón used a variety of devices, in particular imagery and song, to point to the impending tragedy. The play opens with a bad omen —Enrique's fall from his horse—and its first scene contains in its language numerous hints of the tragedy to come. Act I ends with Leonor's prophetic curse. In Act II suggestion gives way to explicit foreboding, first when Mencía sees her husband with the dagger, and even more unmistakably in the exchanges at the end of the Act. The examples could be multiplied. Nothing goes unmotivated or unexplained in Calderón. Enrique, for example, does not suddenly appear, as in the first *El médico*, in the presence of Mencía in Act II; a bribed slave, Jacinta, arranges for his admission. In the scene in which Gutierre discovers Mencía with the half-written letter to Enrique, Calderón has removed the conventional 'unexpected return' of the source. Mencía is informed of Enrique's departure, not by Gutierre but by a letter of Enrique himself brought by Coquín; Enrique's charge, incidentally, that Mencía is responsible for what has happened makes her subsequent conduct more probable. Gutierre, therefore, needs to make but one appearance. This, too, is handled more subtly. Don Jacinto had simply overheard the servants' conversation which conveniently referred to Mayor's writing a letter; Calderón makes Gutierre sense that something is amiss. Similarly in his play's final scene Calderón clears up the inconsistency of the earlier *barbero's* story; though he claims that he has been led to the uttermost parts of Sevilla, the King comes immediately upon Jacinto's house. Calderón brings on Gutierre's servant Coquín, who explains that his master has locked his wife in a room and that her life is in danger; and it is he who directs the King's party to Gutierre's house.

The language of *El médico* is as authentically Calderonian as that of any of his works, and I have not noted a single line which has been appropriated from the source. Even when he follows the source dramatist so closely that he describes precisely the same object as, for example, the horse offered by the husband to Prince Enrique, the descriptions themselves have nothing in common:

SOURCE

Si Vuestra Alteza me honra
en aceptar un caballo
de piel negra y frente corta
de brazos y pies ligeros,
cola crespa, crin redonda,
podrá, por ser sosegado,
si (como dice) le importa
llegar a Sevilla presto,
ser la jornada tan corta;
que aunque en el distrito ponen
cuatro leguas, en una hora
logre Tu Alteza su gusto.   (412a-b)

CALDERÓN

Si es del que hoy habéis caído,
no subáis en él, y aquí
recibid, señor, de mí
una pía hermosa y bella,
a quien una palma sella,
signo que vuestra la hace:
que también un bruto nace
con mala o con buena estrella.
En este prodigio, pues,
proporcionado y bien hecho,
dilatado de anca y pecho,
de cabeza y cuello es
corto, de brazos y pies
fuerte, a uno y otro elemento
les da en sí lugar y asiento,
siendo el bruto de la palma
tierra el cuerpo, fuego el alma,
mar la espuma, y todo viento.   (188a)

The symbolism of the physician who finds the remedy for his injured honour through the drawing of blood derives, of course, from the source, but Calderón extended it and enriched it far beyond the bounds reached by the earlier dramatist, so that a large part of the vocabulary is medical: words like, *médico, salud, curar, remedio, enfermo, sanar, prevención, sangría, antídoto, lesión, herida, accidente,* recur throughout the play.

The imagery of *El médico* closely resembles that of the other serious plays of Calderón, particularly those concerned with honour, and there is little precedent in the source either for its richness or its complexity. Consider, for example, the striking contrast in the play between light and darkness. It will have been observed that a large part of the action of both plays, and certainly the major incidents, occur at night: the first and last scenes of Act II and almost the whole of Act III. But whereas the source dramatist took little advantage of the opportunities which were offered for symbolism, Calderón exploited them to the full. Honour was conventionally compared with brightness and splendour, and in both plays the wife is compared to the sun and light; one recalls, for example, the extended comparison of Gutierre, in which he explains that the sun of Mencía has eclipsed the star of Leonor. Calderón often

returns to the image: when Gutierre discovers the advances of
Enrique, he refers to the cloud which threatens to obscure the sun:

> Pero sí puede, mal digo:
> que al sol una nube negra,
> si no le mancha, le turba;
> si no le eclipsa, le hiela.   (200b)
>
> hasta que tirana fué
> la nube que turbar osa
> tanto esplendor en mi esposa
> y tanto lustre en su fe. [1]   (205a)

The equating of life with light is also found in the source, but it is
only in Calderón's play that it becomes significant. Here, for example,
is the extended comparison at the end of Act II:

> No me espanto, bien mío;
> que el aire que mató la luz, tan frío
> corre, que es un aliento
> respirado del céfiro violento,
> y que no sólo advierte
> muerte a las luces, a las vidas muerte,
> y pudieras dormida
> a sus soplos perder también la vida.   (204a)

Ludovico tells the King of Mencía's death in these words:

> No la vi el rostro, mas sólo
> entre repetidos ayes
> escuché: "Inocente muero;
> el cielo no te demande
> mi muerte." Esto dijo, y luego
> expiró; y en este instante
> el hombre mató la luz...   (211b)

The complementary association of death with darkness is no less
important:

> D. GUTIERRE.   que el día
> ya en la tumba helada y fría
> huésped del undoso dios,
> hace noche.   (188b)
>
> D. GUTIERRE.   En el mudo silencio
> de la noche, que adoro y reverencio
> por sombra aborrecida,
> como sepulcro de la humana vida...   (202b)

---

[1] QC, *su*, Astrana Marín, *mi*.

Gutierre is the 'soplo', 'aire', 'aliento respirado del céfiro violento' which extinguishes the 'luz' Mencía.

Calderón's imagery is by itself a pointer to the elucidation of his play. Gutierre's jealousy is compared to a viper's poison:

> ¿Celos dije?
> ¡Qué mal hice! Vuelva, vuelva
> al pecho la voz. Mas no,
> que si es ponzoña que engendra
> mi pecho, si no me dió
> la muerte (¡ay de mí!) al verterla,
> al volverla a mí podrá;
> que de la víbora cuentan
> que la mata su ponzoña
> si fuera de sí la encuentra.   (201a)

Like a thief it works in the dark:

> tienen los celos pasos de ladrones.   (203a)

Gutierre acts blindly in Act III, not only because he puts out the light, but because his reason is clouded by jealousy:

> Mato la luz, y llego,
> sin luz y sin razón, dos veces ciego.   (203a)

If, like an eagle, he dares look at the sun, his royal rival, like a moth he will perish in the flame; he is lynx-eyed but he is also blind:

> ...mi aliento, lince y ciego,
> entre asombros y desmayos,
> es águila a tantos rayos,
> mariposa a tanto fuego.   (187a)

Darkness, blindness, madness, these are the dominant associations which Calderón uses for Gutierre. The virtue of Mencía shines like the sun, and she is as chaste as Lucretia, Porcia and Tomyris. Enrique surprises her as Actaeon surprised Diana:

> Acteón
> con Diana me disculpe.   (194a)

He attacks her as a hawk attacks the heron. The King is:

> un Atlante, en quien descansa
> todo el peso de la ley.   (190b)

He is an Argos, an Apollo. But the stone with which he is twice associated is the diamond, harder than any other known substance. These are some of the important images which owe little or nothing to the source.

As if to remove any doubt about the originality of his language, Calderón avoided, in every scene except one, the stanza form of his model:

		SOURCE	CALDERÓN
Act I:	i.	romance O-A	redondilla
		redondilla	romance E-O
		romance O-A	décima
	ii.	redondilla	silva
		romance O-E	octava
		redondilla	romance E
Act II:	i.	redondilla	romance U-E
		romance E-A	redondilla
			décima
	ii.	redondilla	romance A-E
		décima	décima
			romance E-A
			redondilla
	iii.	romance E-A	silva
		silva	
Act III:	i.	redondilla	décima
			romance I-E
	ii.	silva	
		redondilla	silva
	iii.	redondilla	romance A-E
		décima	redondilla
		romance O-A	romance A-A

The percentages, as provided by Morley/Bruerton and Hilborn, are:

	Source	Calderón
Redondilla	46.6	12
Romance	41.9	50
Décima	7.6	20
Octava	—	2
Silva	3.8	15
Sestina	—	(12 lines)

If comment is required, it is that the versification of the source-play is remarkable for its limitation to four metres, and in particular for the absence of *quintilla* and *octava*. The relatively high percentage of *décima* and *silva* in Calderón's play would seem to owe nothing to the source.

Neither play presents any difficulty in staging. All the important dramatic situations are, as we have seen, perpetuated in Calderón's play, and often the details of staging are the same: in both plays, for example, the second lady hides behind a screen to listen to the King's interview with her former lover, and later the husband hides behind the same screen to listen to the King's interview with Prince Enrique. But Calderón varies the settings of the play by shifting two of the husband's interviews with his wife from the house to the garden. At the beginning of Act II, in the earlier play, the Prince enters Mencía's house by an open door; when the husband appears, he hides behind a bed set in the inner stage. After he has escaped, a curtain is drawn to reveal the dagger which has been left behind:

> Saca [D. Jacinto] luz y corre un tafetán; aparece una cama
> cerrada con sus colgaduras, y en un alamar una daga do-
> rada y desnuda, pendiente.   (421a)

Calderón transfers this scene to the garden. The Prince, admitted by a servant, first hides behind some shrubs, represented perhaps by the screen used in the Palace scene, covered with branches:

> Estas verdes hojas
> me escondan y disimulen.   (194a)

At the appearance of the husband Mencía tells him:

> Detrás de este pabellón,
> que en mi misma cuadra está,
> os esconded.   (195b)

and he too, it would seem, hides in the inner stage. But when he escapes, there is no reference to a 'discovery'. Calderón similarly sets the scene at the end of Act II in the garden, so that Mencía is presented with the same situation. Both plays contain two 'discoveries' in Act III, first when the husband surprises his wife writing to the Prince, and second when she lies dead upon her bed. For the latter scene the source dramatist introduced a note of stark realism:

> Corre la cortina, aparece la cama colgada y en ella acos-
> tada y muerta MAYOR, los cabellos sueltos.   (437b)

Calderón anticipates the scene by making Ludovico describe what he sees before he murders Mencía, through presumably an opening representing a window:

D. GUTIERRE.   Asómate a ese aposento.
               ¿Qué ves en él?
LUDOVICO.   Una imagen
          de la muerte, un bulto veo
          que sobre una cama yace:
          dos velas tiene a los lados,
          y un crucifijo delante.
          Quién es, no puedo decir;
          que con unos tafetanes
          el rostro tiene cubierto.   (210b)

This is what is disclosed in the inner stage when, later, Gutierre breaks off his account of what has happened and bids the King see for himself. The *Parte* text reads simply:

     Descúbrese a Doña Mencía en una cama desangrada.

The disturbing 'discovery' of a dishevelled heroine of the source is replaced by one of calm and serenity appropriate to a person who has made her peace with God, and the crucifix is a timely reminder of God's forgiveness. If by this date the mouth of the inner stage was covered by a 'flat' rather than a curtain, it could have contained the opening required for Ludovico.

The twelve lines of song of Calderón's play have a serious dramatic purpose. In the first scene of Act II Teodora sings for her mistress, Doña Mencía, whose husband is in Sevilla:

         Ruiseñor que con tu canto
         alegras este recinto,
         no te ausentes tan aprisa,
         que me das pena y martirio.   (194b)

The theme of the song is, significantly, absence; Gutierre himself is symbolized by the nightingale, and the words *pena* and *martirio* foreshadow the tragic consequences of his absence. The remaining eight lines come in Act III in a song overheard by the King as he wanders incognito through the streets; in this case the idea at least derives from the source-play in which music is heard off-stage. The song tells of Prince Enrique's departure for Sevilla:

         El infante don Enrique
         hoy se despidió del Rey;
         su pesadumbre y su ausencia
         quiera Dios que pare en bien.   (210a)

Para Consuegra camina,
donde piensa que han de ser
teatros de mil tragedias
las montañas de Montiel.   (211a)

Here, as Wilson has shown, are clear forebodings of the King's own death to confirm his own grim vision; his cruelty, like Gutierre's, will end in tragedy.

The foregoing pages will have shown, first, that *El médico de su honra*, despite its closeness to the source, has at every stage considered and significant changes which, taken together, make it a new and original play; it differs from those which we shall examine later only in so far as the transformation which Calderón has effected is the result, not of radical structural alterations, but of the accumulation of minor changes. I hope, too, that some light has been thrown upon Calderón's conception of a play which has given‧ rise to conflicting interpretations. Gutierre is a man of principle who acts scrupulously in accordance with the laws of honour of his day. His murder of Mencía, however cruel, is the act of a person who has exhausted all other means of clearing what he believes to be an offence against his honour. But the code which Gutierre followed, despite its positive values, countenanced dissimu-lation and insisted upon revenge, and in this ran counter to Christian teaching. Gutierre is a man of integrity but he is also inhuman. 'Calderón' as Wilson has said 'took the laws of honour and shewed their virtues and their cruelty.'[1] He was no more recommending the distorted sense of honour of Gutierre than, say, the author of *La estrella de Sevilla* was recommending the exaggerated sense of loyalty of Busto Tabera and Sancho Ortiz. It is clear too that he disapproves of the villainy of Enrique, the severity of the King, the imprudence of Mencía and Leonor and the slander of Arias. The whole society presented here is one whose moral values are confused, and the consequences are necessarily tragic. Calderón's play is a vigorous criticism of the code of honour.

---

[1]   *BC*, IV, i.

III

LAS ARMAS DE LA HERMOSURA

Las armas de la hermosura [1] is a play about Coriolanus. Its chief claim to fame would appear to be its extraordinary anachronisms and falsification of history, for it has served critics of Calderón for centuries as a convenient target for attack. The play opens with Coriolanus repulsing a Sabine onslaught on Rome. He returns to the city in triumph only to discover that, in his absence, the Senate has issued an edict depriving the women of Rome of their traditional rights and privileges. Coriolanus is in love with Veturia, and incited by her he protests against the edict and defies the Senate. In Act II he is publicly tried and exiled, and he gains asylum with his former enemies the Sabines. In due course, as Commander-in-chief of the Sabine army, he besieges Rome and starves her into submission; but he refuses all peace terms and threatens to destroy the city. Veturia alone is able to persuade him that it is nobler to pardon than to avenge, and prevails over him to spare Rome. Disaster is thus averted. Coriolanus clears the Sabine grievance without bloodshed and restores the rights of Rome's women. In Act I a longish speech by the *gracioso* announcing the details of the Senate's ban on beauty-aids incorporates the provisions of a sumptuary decree promulgated in Calderón's own day.

Las armas de la hermosura contains some strange variations upon the familiar legend of Coriolanus, and it is not perhaps surprising that it was cited by Alberto Lista, when he censured Calderón for the liberties which he was accustomed to take with legend and history:

---

[1] Texts used:
 El privilegio de las mujeres:
  Comedias famosas de varios autores, XXX, 1636.
  Ed. J. E. Hartzenbusch, BAE, XIV, 397–412.
  Ed. Astrana Marín, pp. 1353-81.
 Calderón:
  Comedias escogidas de los mejores ingenios, 46, 1679.
  Ed. Vera Tassis, IX, 1691.
  Ed. J. J. Keil, IV, pp. 444-73.
  Ed. J. E. Hartzenbusch, BAE, XII, 187-209.
  Ed. Astrana Marín, pp. 579-618. (Madrid, 1945, 3.ª ed., revisada.)
 All quotations are from the edition of Astrana Marín.

> Nadie ignora que Calderón tomó al pie de la letra el *quidlibet auden-di* de Horacio, en materia de historia, de cronología y de geografía, y las desfiguró a su placer muchas veces, sin que se conozca ningún motivo plausible de su infidelidad. Pero en la comedia de *Las armas de la hermosura,* en la cual abusó quizás más que en otras, y en todos los sentidos posibles, de aquella libertad... [1]

Schack labelled it "una de las obras más desgraciadas de Calderón", and went on:

> La dicción es enfática y alambicada, y los personajes desaparecen por su falta exagerada de consistencia... Dios sólo sabe cuáles fueron las fuentes históricas... [2]

Later, Menéndez y Pelayo, dealing with Calderón's plays on ancient history, wrote:

> Algunas de estas obras son indudablemente las más endebles del autor. Empiezan por carecer de todo colorido de época; la historia está falseada arbitraria y caprichosamente, no sólo en el espíritu íntimo que distingue unas épocas de otras, sino hasta en los lances y en los hechos más triviales y familiares, hasta suponer, v. gr., en *Las armas de la hermosura,* que Coriolano se une con los Volcos contra Roma con el fin de hacer anular una ley suntuaria sobre los trajes de las mujeres, convirtiendo así a aquel rudo guerrero romano de los primeros tiempos de la república, en un galante caballero de la corte de los Felipes..., por eso sus dramas tomados de asuntos de la historia romana, no deben ser citados cuando se habla de él en concepto de gran poeta; por más que siempre se encuentran trozos notables de versificación ahogados en un mar de palabrería culterana. [3]

Needless to say, Menéndez y Pelayo's conception of poetry was one obstacle in the way of his understanding *Las armas de la hermosura,* but it was not the only one. Few would deny that the freedom with which Calderón dealt with history and legend and the numerous anachronisms of his plays are, for the uninitiated at least, strange and disturbing; but it does not follow that his departures from historical fact were arbitrary and capricious. Unfortunately this freedom with history has, apparently, blinded critics to the many merits of *Las armas de la hermosura,* to Calderón's skilful accommodation of the story of Coriolanus and the persons involved in his fate to a single significant theme, to its moving and intensely dramatic

---

[1] Alberto Lista, 'De Calderón, considerado como poeta lírico', *Revista de Madrid,* III (1839), in BAE, XIV (Madrid, 1850), p. 694b.

[2] Op. cit., IV, p. 398.

[3] Marcelino Menéndez y Pelayo, *Calderón y su teatro* (Madrid, 1910), 4th ed., pp. 376-77.

incidents, and—a point observed by Don Angel Valbuena [1]—to the incomparable lyrical beauty of so many of its lines. *Las armas de la hermosura* is unquestionably a play of first importance.

For *Las armas de la hermosura* Calderón recast an earlier play, *El privilegio de las mujeres*, one which he himself had written in collaboration with Coello and Pérez de Montalbán. *El privilegio de las mujeres* was first published in *Parte XXX de comedias* (Zaragoza 1636). Cotarelo y Mori takes the lines of the *gracioso* in Act I, v, to refer to the *pragmática* of 12 October 1636, but this seems to leave too narrow a margin for publication in that year. Professor Ruth Lee Kennedy tells me, however, that the references to the *guardainfante* and *jaulilla* make it certain that the passage was written in the 30's, probably not much before 1636. [2] *Las armas de la hermosura* was first published in 1679 in volume 46 of the series *Comedias nuevas escogidas*. Hartzenbusch believed that Calderón wrote the play in 1652 with the end of the war in Cataluña in mind, and that the last lines, celebrating the sparing of Rome by Coriolanus, are an allusion to Philip IV's mercy towards the Catalans. [3] The argument is by no means conclusive. If 1652 is correct, some fifteen years would have elapsed between the writing of the two plays. It is not perhaps surprising, even so, that *Las armas de la hermosura* remains close to its model, for Calderón was here rewriting a work of which he was part-author and probably architect. More experienced as a dramatist than either Montalbán or Coello, Calderón wrote the first act of *El privilegio de las mujeres*; and it seems probable that the conception of the play was his. He may even have prepared a detailed plan from which his collaborators could work. As writer of the first act, in any case, his was the initiative: he presented the scene, set the action in motion and defined the main characters. His share of responsibility was certainly greatest. When he chose to rewrite the story of Coriolanus, he worked on the general structural plan of *El privilegio de las mujeres*.

The act-divisions of the two plays come at the same point, and within each act most of Calderón's scenes have their exact parallel in the source:

---

[1] *Calderón* (Barcelona, 1941), p. 128.
[2] Cf. Cotarelo y Mori, p. 177, Hilborn, p. 20 and J. H. Parker, 'The Chronology of the plays of Montalbán', *PMLA*, LXVII (1952), 209.
    BAE, XIV, 677.

El privilegio de las mujeres.			*Las armas de la hermosura.*	
Act I:	1.	Sabine camp	1.	Rome
		—	2.	Battlefront
	2.	Rome	3.	Rome
Act II:		—	1.	Rome
	1.	Rome—trial	2.	Rome—trial
	2.	Walls of Rome	3.	Walls of Rome
Act III:	1.	Sabine Camp		
	2.	Rome	1.	Rome
	3.	Sabine camp	2.	Sabine camp

The characters too are the same:

El privilegio de las mujeres.	*Las armas de la hermosura.*
Coriolano	Coriolano, *joven galán*
Morfodio, *gracioso*	Pasquín, *gracioso*
Veturia, *dama*	Veturia, *dama*
Tisbe	Livia, *criada*
Aurelio, *viejo*	Aurelio, *viejo*
Enio	Enio
Flavio	Lelio
	Flavio, *viejo*
El rey Sabino	Sabinio, *rey*
Astrea, *reina*	Astrea, *reina*
Romanos y romanas	Romanos, romanas
Soldados romanos	Soldados romanos
Soldados sabinos	Soldados sabinos
	Emilio, *soldado*
	Un relator
	Damas
	Criados
	Música
	Acompañamiento
	Gente

Calderón has kept the same names for the main characters, except for the substitution of Lelio for Flavio.

The same theme underlies both plays, and Calderón's principal departures from the traditional story of Coriolanus derive from his source. The kernel of the legend remains: Coriolanus, a Roman patrician, displays great valour in relieving a siege, is then accused and condemned to exile, takes refuge with the enemy King, advances against Rome in command of the enemy army, refuses reasonable peace terms and is won over by a lady. But there are significant changes. According to tradition, the siege was of the town of Corioli by the Volscians; in both *El privilegio de las mu-*

jeres and *Las armas de la hermosura,* on the other hand, Rome is besieged by the Sabines in revenge for the rape of the Sabine women. Traditionally, Coriolanus was impeached for attempting to deny the tribunes their rights; the source dramatists and Calderón have him banished for championing the rights of women. In both plays Veturia is Coriolanus's lover, and no mention is made of his mother. Both incorporate the details of a seventeenth-century sumptuary decree banning beauty-aids. Coriolanus is presented as a feminist who defies the law and risks death to champion the cause of women; but when he returns at the head of the Sabine army to destroy Rome in revenge for its injustice to women, he is prevailed upon—by a woman—to pardon rather than punish. In both plays the theme is pardon. In *Las armas de la hermosura,* then, Calderón is returning to a theme which he had treated, in collaboration with Montalbán and Coello, in an earlier play. As with *El médico de su honra,* he keeps close to his model, though he rewrote all but a few passages. A collation of the two plays reveals, however, that within the same framework there are numerous changes of detail which give the play its remarkable complexity and unity.

El privilegio de las mujeres opens in the Sabine camp outside Rome where King Sabino recalls for his young wife Astrea the rape of the Sabines, and swears revenge; he is interrupted by the news that the Roman army is marching against them, headed by Coriolano. The rest of the act takes place in Rome. Calderón opens his play in Rome, and transfers to Enio much of the content of the speech of the Sabine King. Whereas the first scene of the source directed attention to the Sabines, Calderón appropriately begins a play about Rome in Rome, and gives prominence at once to his two main characters. The opening scene shows a crowded banqueting table in the garden of Veturia. Coriolano and Veturia, at the head of the table, declare their love for each other, and their sentiments are echoed by two choruses:

> Coro 1.º de música: *No puede amor*
> *hacer mi dicha mayor.*
> Coro 2.º *Ni mi deseo*
> *pasar del bien que poseo.*

Cor.

Sin duda, Veturia bella,
esta canción se escribió
por mí, pues sólo fuí yo
feliz influjo de aquella
de Venus brillante estrella,
pues benigna en mi favor...

Él y Coro 1.º:

No puede amor
hacer mi dicha mayor.

Veturia:

Mejor debo yo entender
su benévolo influir,
pues dándome qué sentir,
me deja qué agradecer;
y más el día que a ser
llegue la ventura mía
tu esposa, pues ese día
no podrán mi fe, mi empleo...

Ella y Coro 2.º:

Ni mi deseo
pasar del bien que poseo.

579a-b

Poetry, music and spectacle are combined in these idyllic, brilliantly lyrical lines.

A few moments later drums and trumpets are heard offstage, and Aurelio, the father of Coriolano, comes on with news of war. Enio gives the details of the Sabine attack but he prefaces his account with some background history. Romulus was responsible for the rape of the Sabine women and in revenge the Sabines had twice besieged Rome, though in vain. Now that Romulus is dead, however, they are renewing their attacks, inspired by their Queen Astrea who has Spanish blood. In this scene Calderón underlines the conflict of opinion between Coriolano and Aurelio, his father. Aurelio disapproves of love which, he argues, makes men effeminate, and he violently upbraids Coriolano and his friends for their junketing and revelry. He speaks of their 'torpe olvido' and of their lying in 'el infame / sepulcro de la pereza', and he brands them 'bastardos hijos del ocio / cultos al amor'. Coriolano vigorously defends Rome's women and in particular Veturia. It is Rome herself, he says, who is responsible for their being there; having abducted them, they owe them affection and courtesy:

La culpa fué del primero
que robadas las violenta,
no de los que, ya robadas,
procuran que estén contentas,
que para tenerlas tristes,
mejor fuera no tenerlas.   (582b)

Nor is love irreconcilable with true honour. Mars was Venus's lover, and Coriolano himself will prove that his love for Veturia detracts in no way from his valour:

> Y para que mejor veas
> que ser galán en la paz
> no es ser cobarde en la guerra,
> el primero seré yo
> que de la patria en defensa
> al opósito le salga.   (582b)

The opening lines of the play with their picture of love, and Calderón's insistence in the exchanges which follow upon the conflict between the attitude towards women of Coriolano and of his father Aurelio, are a significant pointer to what is to follow. The play is a vindication of woman's place in society. The two great dramatic moments of the play, first at the end of Act I when Coriolano defies the unjust edict of the Senate and second at the end of Act III when he overcomes his desire for revenge and shows mercy to Rome, represent the triumph of a woman. In both instances Veturia prevails upon Coriolano to act rightly. She inspires in him the spirit of self-sacrifice which makes him defy the Senate regardless of danger, and she teaches him mercy. Love and valour are not incompatible. In Plato's *Symposium* Phaedrus claims that love inspires men to noble deeds; and this is its achievement in *Las armas de la hermosura*. Veturia's lover, Coriolano, is the first to answer the call to arms in defence of his country and, acclaimed the leader of the Roman forces, it is he who leads them to victory. And Veturia herself pledges the support of the Sabine women of Rome in the war against their own people; they belong now to Rome and will take arms themselves to defend it.

For scene two the action shifts to the battle-field, and we see in action the Roman victory over the Sabines which is only described in the source. In this scene Calderón introduced an important episode which is not found in *El privilegio de las mujeres*. The Sabine Queen Astrea is taken prisoner by the Romans. When, however, Coriolano realises that his captive is a lady he releases her and orders Enio to accompany her back to the Sabine camp. The new incident has its germ in a detail of the second act of the source, where the Sabine King refers to his having been defeated and freed by Coriolano:

5

SABINO. Dime: ¿tú no me venciste?
CORIOLANO. Confieso que te he vencido.
SABINO. ¿No me diste libertad?
CORIOLANO. Es verdad.   (1371b)

It serves a double purpose. Astrea's deliverance by Coriolano provides a motive for her protecting him when he is banished from Rome. At the same time it calls attention again to Coriolano's attitude to women. He tells Astrea:

> ...has llegado a puerto
> donde las mujeres tienen,
> con franca escala el respeto,
> cortesanos pasaportes
> de inviolables privilegios.   (587b)

Coriolano's courtesy and generosity to women are such that it is enough to know that his prisoner is a woman for him to release her and see her escorted safely back to her own camp.

This second scene is notable for the violence and confusion it portrays. Coriolano describes the battle in the following words:

> Disputada la batalla,
> crece, con que al sol cubriendo,
> nubes de pluma las flechas,
> tempestad parece, siendo
> del eclipse de sus rayos
> cajas y trompetas truenos,
> de quien relámpagos son
> las chispas de los aceros.
> Todo es horror, todo es grima,
> todo asombro, todo incendio.   (586a)

Earlier Astrea calls for a war 'a sangre y fuego'. There are, too, violent changes of fortune. First the Romans, then the Sabines, prosper. Astrea, mistaking the Roman lines for her own, assumes that there is a Sabine victory, only to discover that it is Rome's; then, expecting death from the hands of her foes who have captured her, she finds both life and freedom. She herself refers to the fickleness of fortune:

> ¡Oh tú, de la fortuna
> transmutado teatro...   (584b)

> ...(¡oh tú, otra vez, varia fortuna,
> condicional imagen de la luna!)...   (585a)

And there is confusion; both armies, for example, use mottoes with the letters S. P. Q. R., and Astrea is misled by this into assuming that the Sabines have been victorious. Calderón contrasts the violence and chaos of war with the harmony and order of peace in scene one.

The final scene of Act I has a counterpart in the source-play. Coriolano returns at the head of the victorious Roman army; but he is met by Veturia who inveighs vigorously and eloquently against an edict, promulgated by the Senate, which bans beauty-aids. In both plays Veturia protests not so much against the terms of the edict as against the affront to women which it implies:

> No lo sentimos por ellos,
> que es por lo que lo sentimos
> por la desestimación,
> el desdén, el descariño,
> el ultraje, el ajamiento. (591b)

Women are to be deprived of their freedom and reduced to the status of slaves. Coriolano, persuaded by Veturia, defies the Senate. There is, however, a significant difference of emphasis in the two plays. In El privilegio de las mujeres the Romans are shown to have been degraded and made effeminate by women. A bare thousand volunteered to fight against the Sabine aggressors and even they have taken their wives with them:

> porque los romanos, ciegos,
> tan rendidos yacen todos
> a ese universal veneno
> de las mujeres y al ocio,
> muerte segunda del cuerpo,
> que nadie las armas toma
> por no apartarse un momento
> de las mujeres, y todos
> el animoso instrumento
> de trompas y cajas yacen
> sordos, desnudos y muertos... (1356b)

This is the reason for the Senate's edict. Coriolano, moreover, though recognising the injustice of the edict, wavers between love and patriotism before recognising finally the superiority of love:

> Más pesa aquesta balanza.
> Amor, amor ha vencido. (1362a)

> Pues, piérdase el honor mío
> a trueco de que me quieras;
> que poderoso y antiguo
> de la mujer el imperio
> siempre con el hombre ha sido.   (1362b)

In *Las armas de la hermosura* there is no evidence that women have demoralized the men. This, it is true, is the fear of both Aurelio and Flavio, the spokesmen of the Senate, but their fears are shown to be without foundation. The edict is inspired, not by any adverse effects which the women have had, but by the Sabine attack. Moreover, if the circumstances of Coriolano's rebellion are the same in both plays, love and patriotism are no longer represented as mutually exclusive. The point is important because it is precisely this view of love and true honour which Calderón is commending throughout his play. Opposed to Coriolano are Aurelio and Flavio. Aurelio's view of women is manifest in the play's first scene; he regards them as irreconcilable with honour. The last line of Act I recalls his earlier speech against women, since it completes an incomplete section of that speech:

> ¡Nunca acá hubierais venido!   (592b)

Would that the Sabine women had never come! Aurelio's attitude could hardly be more unrealistic, for without women there would be no succession. Flavio's view is similar; he assumes that women will bring discredit upon Rome. Coriolano, on the other hand, recognises woman's place in society. Not only does he deny that love is incompatible with valour, but he accepts Veturia's claim that if women are dishonoured so also are men:

> ...siendo las mujeres
> el espejo cristalino
> del honor del hombre, ¿cómo
> puede, estando a un tiempo mismo
> en nosotros empañado,
> estar en vosotros limpio?   (591a)

Coriolano's decision to defy the Senate is not the weakness of a man whose love for Veturia is stronger than his patriotism, but the strength of one whose love has shown him the true path of honour and whose act of defiance is in the best interest of his country.

Calderón's principal structural change comes at the beginning of Act II. In the source-play Montalbán's second act starts in at once with the trial scene; in a second scene Coriolano is formally exiled. Coriolano's trial and exile are, of course, the direct outcome of his espousing the cause of Rome's women. But Montalbán allows no place for Veturia and only a passive role for Coriolano; Veturia has only a few lines of farewell to her lover and Coriolano's speech of defence merely repeats what is already known. Calderón interpolated a long scene, which is entirely new, in which Veturia, feeling personally responsible for Coriolano's imprisonment, contrives a plan to rescue him. She takes Enio into her confidence and asks him to deliver a note to Coriolano and a file by which he might free himself from his chains. The action then follows Enio to the prison where he delivers the file and arranges for Coriolano's escape that same evening. Just as he is leaving Aurelio enters and, guessing at the reason for Enio's visit, makes him personally responsible for Coriolano's safe-keeping. Coriolano thereupon refuses the chance of freedom which would endanger the life and compromise the honour of his friend. It is interesting to note that both this addition and the new incident in Act I involving the capture and release of Astrea have exact counterparts in *El príncipe constante*: Coriolano, like Fernando, generously spares the life of his adversary, and refuses freedom at the expense of his friend's honour. Calderón's scene provides rôles of importance for Coriolano and Veturia as well as Enio, and gives emphasis to their sense of honour and obligation.

This new scene takes up a considerable part of Act II, enabling Calderón to treat Coriolano's trial and exile with far more economy than Montalbán. He can dispense, for example, with the strange manoeuvres of Aurelio in the source-play to interfere with the course of justice by influencing the votes of the other two judges, and with Coriolano's long speech which tells the audience what it already knows. The outcome of the trial is the same in both plays: Coriolano is exiled. But Calderón has altered the verdict of each of the three judges: Aurelio votes for his son's death, not his acquittal; Lelio for his acquittal, not (as the earlier Flavio) for his exile, and Enio for his exile, not for imprisonment. Aurelio cannot hide his love and concern for a son, but he condemns one who has defied a Senate's edict. Both dramatists emphasize his divided loyalties, and both make what he regards as his duty as a judge take precedence over his affection as a father. But Montalbán's

procedure is curious; though Aurelio feels obliged to condemn his
son, he has no scruples about interfering with the course of justice
by giving advice to his two colleagues. Then, in giving judgement,
confused by his conflicting feelings, he writes not what he intended
to write but what in his heart he has ardently desired.

Calderón did not preserve this psychological point of Montalbán's. Though he repeats almost exactly the lines of Aurelio's speech
before recording his vote, Aurelio is made to vote as he has argued,
that his son should die. But Calderón's change is more fundamental
than this: Aurelio's decision, though appearing to be noble and
disinterested, is shown by Calderón to be selfish and inhuman. He
is concerned with appearances and, though clearly desiring his
son's pardon, he publicly votes for his death for the sake of his
own honour:

> Y es tan grande del Senado
> la autoridad y el honor,
> que el que eligió senador
> no puede ser recusado:
> dando a entender que ha de ser
> tan recto en la ejecución,
> que interés, sangre o pasión
> no ha de poderle vencer.   (597b)

He counts, moreover, upon a similarly 'honourable' decision from
his fellow-patrician Lelio, whose father was killed in the rioting
which followed Coriolano's defiance of the Senate:

> ...que si un padre le condena
> un contrario, ¿qué ha de hacer?   (599a)

Lelio does not fail him; though resolved upon revenge and
determined that Coriolano shall die, for the sake of his honour—he
must act, he says, as a *caballero*—he votes for Coriolano's exile,
imposing thereby a measure of punishment and at the same time
safeguarding the life of his friend. The openness of Enio is contrasted
with the lack of frankness of Aurelio and Lelio when, at the end
of the scene, the latter are made to reveal their secret motives in
asides:

> AURELIO. Mi esperanza en eso estriba;
> que al ver tan sin ejemplar
> mi voto, es fuerza ganar
> afectos para que viva.

LELIO. No mal de su juicio espera
        mi voto lograrse, pues
        sabrá la nobleza que es
        que viva para que muera.   (599b)

It is significant too that in Calderón's play it is Enio's judgement
which is decisive, since the votes of Lelio and Aurelio cancel each
other out.

The scene in *El privilegio de las mujeres* in which Coriolano is
taken beyond the walls of Rome and stripped of his insignia is
replaced by a similar scene in Rome with the public announcement
of the sentence upon him and the official ceremony of banishment.
In both plays Coriolano is abandoned in the mountains, but Calderón uses the occasion to foreshadow Coriolano's later attack on
Rome and to show how Rome brings her fate upon herself:

        ¿En fin, hijo aborrecido,
        patria, me arroja tu centro,
        como bruto a las montañas,
        como fiera a los desiertos?
        Pues teme que, como fiera
        rabiosa, que como fiero
        bruto irritado, algún día
        me vuelva contra mi dueño.   (603a)

Once again Calderón establishes a causal sequence which is not
brought out in the source. By challenging the Senate's edict, Coriolano has offended against the law of the state; but the edict was
unjust, so that, though illegal, his act is morally right. The Senate,
therefore, is morally wrong in banishing him; by abandoning him
amongst the beasts of the mountains they must bear some responsibility for his behaving like a 'fiera rabiosa' when later he has it
within his power to be avenged.

In a brief final scene in both plays Coriolano is granted asylum
by the Sabines. In Montalbán's act the Sabine King recognises Coriolano, who had defeated him in battle and had spared his life, and
offers him command of his own army. Calderón, as we have seen,
inspired probably by this detail of Montalbán's, shows in Act I how
Astrea was captured and released by Coriolano. It is Astrea, therefore, who in *Las armas de la hermosura* wishes to repay Coriolano's
generosity by ensuring his safety. But, at the same time, Calderón
makes the Sabine King suspect treachery and attempt to kill Corio-

lano, and he is prevented from doing so only by the intervention of Astrea. The King wishes to be avenged of Coriolano:

> Válgome deste pretexto
> para acabar con él, pues
> no tiene otro eficaz medio
> vencer una opuesta estrella
> que destruirla el objeto.   (605b)

And Coriolano, having been spared, at once swears revenge against Rome. But Astrea's prevailing upon the King to show mercy foreshadows the achievement of Veturia in Act III.

In Act III of both plays Coriolano returns to Rome as commander-in-chief of the Sabine forces to be avenged both for himself and for the people whose army he leads. Calderón interchanged the two first scenes of the source; by opening his act with Coello's second in Rome, and by combining Coello's first and third scenes for his second, he has tightened the action. In his third act Calderón leans quite heavily upon the language of the source-play. In the first scene, corresponding to Coello's second, in which Veturia prevails upon Aurelio to seek peace terms, he uses the stanza form of the source, *romance* in U-E, and appropriates a number of passages. Indeed, except for a considerable passage in which Enio describes the Sabine strategy, he keeps very close to Coello's scene. Aurelio urges the Romans to continue their resistance and, when Enio shows the futility of hoping for any change of fortune, he despairs and prays that a thunderbolt may end his life. At this point in both plays Veturia is given a speech in which she urges the Romans to ask for a truce, confident that the Sabines will be merciful. But Calderón here includes some lines which have no exact counterpart in the source. Veturia argues that it is right for a noble to show mercy and that to ask for a truce is no dishonour:

> No, Aurelio; ni es bien que dudes
> cuán hija de la nobleza
> es la piedad...   (608a)

> No es desaire del valor
> ni es bien que por tal se juzgue
> ceder a mayor violencia
> fortunas que el hado influye.   (608b)

These lines are a rebuke to Aurelio who, recognizing his error, agrees to go himself to sue for peace.

For his second scene Calderón turns to the *silva* passage with which Coello had begun his act, and again he copies many of Coello's lines verbatim. So close, in fact, is Calderón to his model at this point that Hartzenbusch has felt justified in completing a defective passage in *El privilegio de las mujeres* by reference to Calderón's text.[1] The setting is the Sabine camp where Coriolano in a monologue swears revenge upon the Romans and warns them not to expect mercy. Assuming the text of the two plays to be good, Calderón alters and expands Coriolano's speech to compare Rome with the hydra, and to emphasize her responsibility for Coriolano's insistence upon revenge, as for example:

> *El privilegio de las mujeres.*
>   Un hijo despechado,
>   de su paterno amor desheredado,
>   hoy severo te aflige,
>   siendo su agravio quien su espada rige.   (1372a)

> *Las armas de la hermosura.*
>   Un hijo aborrecido,
>   de su paterno amor destituído;
>   un hijo desdichado,
>   de su paterno amor desheredado,
>   es hoy el que te aflige,
>   siendo su agravio quien su espada rige.   (609a)

He goes on to explain to the Sabine King and Queen that his victory over the Romans will be bloodless; having laid siege to the town he declines to be drawn into a fight and will oblige his enemy to capitulate by sheer inaction. At this point a white flag is hoisted upon the Roman wall and envoys come to ask for a truce. In both plays the first envoy is Aurelio, who pleads in vain for Rome's pardon. Coriolano is adamant and, in the following exchange borrowed from Coello, lays the blame for his cruelty upon Aurelio himself:

> AURELIO.   ¿Quién te dió tanto rigor?
> CORIOLANO.   El padre que me ha engendrado,
>   padre y juez en un estrado,
>   tal vez fué juez, padre no;
>   ¿qué mucho, pues, si él faltó
>   a ser padre por ser juez,
>   siendo juez e hijo esta vez,
>   que falte a ser hijo yo?

----

[1]   BAE, XIV, 408b.

AURELIO.   Él procedió cuerdo y sabio,
pues ejerció la justicia,
castigando una malicia.

CORIOLANO. Yo castigando un agravio.

AURELIO.   Él con la pluma y el labio,
que lavó una afrenta, piensa.

CORIOLANO. Yo lavo una infamia inmensa.

AURELIO.   Él con el extremo que hizo,
una culpa satisfizo.

CORIOLANO. Yo satisfago una ofensa.   (611b)

Aurelio is made to taste his own medicine. If for the sake of his honour he has publicly voted for his son's death, Coriolano in turn insists upon retribution for this grievance; he has learnt both cruelty and inhumanity from his father. And, Calderón makes Coriolano add, one does not expect pity in war:

No te admire, oh Palas nueva.
No te admire, oh nuevo Marte,
que estando yo de tu parte,
a lástima no me mueva,
sin que a perdonar me atreva
de Roma la tiranía,
más por vuestra que por mía.   (612a)

Whereas in Coello's act the only other envoy is Enio, Calderón brings on Lelio as a second patrician representative. Lelio, it will be recalled, is the nobleman whose father was killed in the rebellion caused by Coriolano, and who was the patrician representative at the trial. Lelio's mission is as unsuccessful as Aurelio's, and Calderón admits another passage imputing responsibility for Coriolano's intransigence to the treatment he received in Rome:

LELIO.   Arrogante
estás.

CORIOLANO.   Harto estuve humilde,
aherrojado en una cárcel,
y arrojado en un desierto.   (614a)

Coello gave the tribune Enio a part similar to that of the patrician Aurelio; deputed to plead with Coriolano on behalf of the people, he fails in his mission. Only at this point, when the Romans have abandoned all hope of an armistice, does Veturia go alone to Coriolano and, in a brief exchange of words, browbeat him into retracting his threats. Coello's handling of Coriolano's submission to Veturia is perhaps the weakest part of the source-play. Calderón, it is true, draws freely upon Coello's scene, transferring many of the lines of the earlier Enio to his Veturia, but he made radical changes which transform the total effect. In the first place he combined the visits of Enio and Veturia; in this way Veturia's prevailing upon Coriolano to pardon Rome is associated with the people, and the success of the deputation of the *plebs* is contrasted with the failure of that of the Senate. This is a point to which I shall return but it will have been noted that, as Veturia reminds Coriolano, the *plebs* have associated themselves with his grievance:

> el pueblo, que a tu lado
> siguió tus parcialidades,
> lloró tus desdichas preso,
> y desterrado tus males,
> hasta que le enmudecieron
> las mordazas de lo infame... (616a)

In *Las armas de la hermosura*, too, Coriolano tries to persuade Veturia and Enio to stay with him; but they reject his suggestion and insist on sharing the fate of their fellow-citizens. Another important change by Calderón was to replace the few abusive lines of Veturia in the source by a long speech in which she reproves Coriolano for his obstinacy, leading up to lines which state simply and directly the theme of the play:

> El desagravio del noble
> más escrupuloso y grave
> no estriba en que se vengó,
> sino en que pudo vengarse.
> Tú puedes, y también puedes
> dar tan precioso realce
> al acrisolado oro
> del perdón; que en el semblante
> del rendido luce más,
> con el primor de su esmalte,
> lo rojo de la vergüenza
> que lo rojo de la sangre. (616a-b)

But Coriolano is unmoved by Veturia's arguments and only when, taking her leave of him, she weeps does he submit:

> Viva, pues, triunfante Roma,
> ya que han podido postrarme
> a sus siempre victoriosas
> municiones de cristales. (617b)

The two plays end with Coriolano's conditions for Rome's pardon; in both he insists that women shall be free and that in future they shall be the arbiters of honour:

El privilegio de las mujeres.

> y por mayor privilegio,
> más grave y más eminente,
> pues yo por una mujer
> sin honra me vi, se entregue
> todo el honor de los hombres
> al poder de las mujeres,
> porque han de ser absolutos
> dueños de la honra siempre.   (1381a)

Las armas de la hermosura.

> Y por mayor privilegio,
> más grave y más eminente,
> pues por las mujeres yo
> sin honra me vi, se entregue
> todo el honor de los hombres
> a arbitrio de las mujeres.   (618b)

It is remarkable, however, that Calderón, following so closely the text of Coello, omits the stipulation that women should kill their husbands if they are unfaithful:

> y que podáis, si ofendidas
> de vuestros maridos fuereis,
> castigar, como los hombres,
> su adulterio con la muerte.   (1381a)

At the same time, he insists upon the theme of mercy by means of a chorus which chants, at intervals during the final exchange, the words:

> ¡Viva quien vence!
> Que es vencer perdonando
> vencer dos veces.   (618a)

In *Las armas de la hermosura* Coriolano is subject to violent reversals of fortune. He is first reprimanded by his father and then chosen to lead Rome's army; the battle with the Sabines goes against him before he finally triumphs; the Senate which welcomes him is soon demanding his imprisonment; Enio brings him hope of escape which, a moment later, is dashed; he is decorated by the

Senate and then impeached; despairing in exile, he is given refuge by the Sabines. Calderón not only added to the changes of fortune of the source-play, but missed no opportunity of drawing attention to them and making his characters comment on fortune's fickleness. I can quote only a few of the many passages in question:

> (¡oh tú, otra vez, varia fortuna,
> condicional imagen de la luna!)   (585a)
> ¡Oh, quién aquí hacer pudiera
> exclamación de cuán varia
> la fortuna, en un instante
> tan de extremo a extremo pasa...   (594a)
> ...es fácil deidad, y es fuerza
> que por instantes se mude.   (607a)

Coriolano believes himself to symbolize man's subjection to the vagaries of fortune:

> ¡Ay de quien nace a ser trágico ejemplo,
> que a la fortuna representa el tiempo!   (604b)

Two passages in Coriolano's speech early in Act III are, however, significant. He is explaining to the Sabine King that Rome might be taken by attack or simply by doing nothing. The King would have attacked and in the ensuing battle would have been at the mercy of fate:

> en cuya ardiente lid hubiera sido
> árbitro la fortuna,
> llena y menguante, imagen de la luna;
> y cuando los vencieras (que no hicieras),
> a gran costa de sangre los vencieras.   (609b)

Coriolano chooses to do nothing and thereby leaves nothing to chance:

> que esta victoria
> sin sangre ha de escribirla la memoria:
> y sin dar parte alguna
> a la neutralidad de la fortuna.   (609b)

Fortune, he states, is neutral; and man exposes himself to chance only in the confusion of war. Rome's survival, in any case, depends not upon chance but upon the conscious decision of Coriolano. Persuaded by Veturia, he chooses to champion the rights of women and at the play's end to save Rome. Far from being a pawn of fortune, he plays his part in shaping his own destiny and Rome's. And the very circumstances in which Coriolano finds himself are shown to be less the result of the fickleness of fortune than of the moral error of man. Rome, we are reminded on more than one occasion, is a theatre; the actors are not puppets but persons with freedom of will whose fate is largely of their own making.

Coriolano's two momentous decisions are inspired by Veturia. And here we see the reason for Calderón's major departures from the legend of Coriolanus. A woman prevails upon Coriolanus to pardon Rome; with this as the starting point *El privilegio de las mujeres* and *Las armas de la hermosura* are conceived as plays in which women reveal to men true honour. It is appropriate, therefore, that the motive for Coriolano's impeachment should be his championship of women and that the outcome of the plays should be the restoration of their rights. The other startling departure from tradition, the association of the Coriolanus legend with the rape of the Sabines, is no more surprising in a dramatist so insistent upon thematic links. In a play about the rights of Rome's women it is inevitable that reference should be made to the occasion when those rights were first and most flagrantly abused, and, by making the Sabines rather than the Volscians the attackers, Calderón could trace the events in Rome back to the their first cause. The Romans carry off the Sabine women; the Sabines seek revenge and attack Rome. This causal sequence which Calderón establishes makes it clear that it is man himself rather than fortune which has shaped the conditions of war and violence of the play's first act. In the rest of the play the same pattern of injury and revenge is repeated. The Senate, because of the Sabine attack, deprives women of their rights; and Coriolano, imprisoned and banished for defiance, returns against Rome to be avenged. At every stage Calderón clearly shows the moral responsibility of all the characters involved for the disaster which is averted at the last moment by Veturia's intervention.

The rights of Rome's women are removed by an edict of the Senate, so that the major responsibility for what happens rests upon the Senators, above all upon Aurelio. At the beginning of the play Aurelio argues that women make men effeminate and assumes that love is incompatible with valour. At the end of Act I he opposes his son because he has challenged an edict of the Senate, without recognizing the injustice of the edict. In the trial scene he votes that the son he loves should be killed. In Act III, when Rome's defeat is inevitable, it is with difficulty that he is persuaded to sue for peace terms. Aurelio has much in common with Gutierre in *El médico de su honra*. He is a man of principle and of iron will; in the dilemmas with which he is faced he acts in good faith in accordance with his own conception of honour and duty. Yet Calderón leaves us in no doubt that he is wrong. Coriolano gives the lie to his argument that love cannot be reconciled with valour; and the Senate's edict is manifestly iniquitous. In the trial scene Aurelio is shown to be both cruel and hypocritical for the sake of appearances. And he was wrong to despair in Act III; like Coriolano, he learns the lesson that mercy is nobler than revenge.

Flavio, the Senator who loses his life, has no part in *El privilegio de las mujeres*, though reference was made to his death. In Calderón's play it is Flavio who incites the citizens of Rome against Coriolano at the end of Act I:

> Ciudadanos, a impedir
> su arrojo venid conmigo.   (592b)

Earlier he is the most outspoken critic of Rome's women:

> No; que otra habrá en que se vea
> que las -mujeres no son
> tan dueños nuestros que puedan
> en descrédito poner
> de Roma el valor.   (583b)

Flavio is the one person who dies in the course of the play and it is characteristic of Calderón that he makes him in some way responsible for his fate.

Lelio is Flavio's son who replaces his father as Senator and is one of Coriolano's judges. In *El privilegio de las mujeres* Lelio (under the name of Flavio) makes his only appearance in the trial scene. Calderón greatly extended his part, in the first instance probably in the interest of symmetry. Aurelio is Coriolano's father, Enio his friend, and Lelio (because Coriolano was responsible for his father's death) his enemy. Calderón gives Lelio a part commensurate with the parts of Aurelio and Enio. In Act I he leads the patrician contingent against the Sabines; in Act II he is the patrician representative at the trial; and in Act III he sues for peace terms. At the same time, Lelio's part is closely linked to the play's theme. He is shown to be jealous of Coriolano. When, for example, Coriolano is acclaimed leader of the Roman forces, Lelio remarks in an aside:

> ¡Que también sea
> hijo yo de senador,
> y de mí...! ¡Oh envidia, deja
> de afligirme!   (583a)

But he controls his envy and at the battlefront serves willingly under Coriolano:

> Que una cosa es
> callar yo mis sentimientos,
> y otra que mi honor no diga
> que es mío.   (586a)

Later he accompanies Coriolano on his triumphal return to Rome:

> Pues
> aunque otra lid desigual
> lucha en mí, no es tiempo ya
> della, pues contrapesó
> el socorro que me dió
> a la envidia que me da;
> con que en uno y otro muestro
> que ni uno ni otro permito.   (590b)

Lelio is envious of Coriolano but, as a man of honour, must not show it; he does not overcome his envy, but conceals it. He is happy, therefore, when Coriolano defies the Senate, so that he can openly take sides against him:

> No es mala ocasión, envidia,
> de acriminar su delito.   (592b)

This same self-control is evident in the trial scene. Coriolano now is not only the object of Lelio's envy, but he is a rebel against his country and the alleged murderer of Flavio. Lelio is resolved upon revenge, but he must act, he says, as a *caballero* and he votes for Coriolano's acquittal. In Act III Lelio goes to Coriolano to ask for peace terms. Coriolano assumes that he is interested only in revenge and makes ready for a duel; but Lelio subordinates his personal grievance to his mission for Rome:

LELIO.	Hay precisas ocasiones en que conviene que atrase por los ajenos, un noble sus propios particulares.
CORIOLANO.	¡En Roma hay nobles! ¡En Roma hay nobleza!
LELIO.	Y grande.
CORIOLANO.	Sí será, si es que entre todos, la que yo dejé, reparten.
LELIO.	Por la nobleza de Roma... (613b-614a)

and he is not provoked by Coriolano's remarks. Lelio is a man of exemplary self-control; but he behaves in accordance with a conception of honour which, in its concern for appearances, its coldness and its insistence upon revenge, is censured.

In contrast to these Senators is the tribune Enio, whose role corresponds to that of the earlier Enio in *El privilegio de las mujeres*. But Calderón extended his part and, more important, closely associates him with Veturia. It is Enio to whom Veturia entrusts the file which will allow Coriolano to escape from prison and who is willing to sacrifice both life and honour for the sake of his friend; later, in the trial scene, Enio's vote for Coriolano's exile is decisive and he is able to achieve as a judge what he failed to achieve as a friend. At the beginning of Act III Enio shows Aurelio the futility of continued resistance to the Sabine attack. Subsequently he goes with Veturia to Coriolano and, like her, insists on returning to Rome to share its fate. Throughout the play Enio, as the representative of the *plebs* is set against Lelio as the representative of the patricians. At the battlefront he defends the left flank whilst Lelio defends the right, and it is significant that Lelio's flag is red and Enio's white:

| LELIO. | Tremole el viento
la siempre roja bandera
del Senado con el nuevo
jeroglífico, a quien sigan
todos mis parciales.   (586a) |
| ENIO. | Despliegue también el aire
su blanca bandera el pueblo;
que no es el que menos sabe
dar victorias a sus reinos.   (586a) |

The *pundonor* of the noble, with its insistence upon revenge and the shedding of blood, is symbolized by the red flag. The white flag, in

6

contrast, is the flag of truce. It is fitting, therefore, that Enio should accompany Veturia on her successful mission to Coriolano, and that her success should be associated with the people.

Of the remaining characters the most important are the Sabine King and Queen. Calderón extended considerably the part of the latter. Hers is the initiative in the battle against Rome and her prevailing over her husband links her with Veturia:

> hizo extremos
> tales, que hasta persuadirle
> a que volviese de nuevo
> a sitiarla, no dejó
> de instarle, valida a tiempos
> de la maña del cariño
> y de la fuerza del ceño.   (588a)

Despite her wish to avenge the Sabine grievance Astrea recalls with gratitude her treatment by the Romans when she was taken prisoner. At the end of Act II, when the King wishes to take the life of Coriolano, Astrea persuades him to offer Coriolano asylum. In Act III she reminds Coriolano that Enio has escorted her to safety. At the end of the play both she and the King accept their victory over Rome and the restoration of the rights of Rome's women as sufficient redress for their people's injury, and they give their approval to the mercy shown by Coriolano.

The economy of El privilegio de las mujeres was such that Calderón needed to dispense with none of its characters. His contribution was to extend the parts of the principal characters, notably those of Coriolano and Veturia, and by a number of additions and minor changes to establish the train of events running from the rape of the Sabine women down to the deliverance of Rome. The theme of Las armas de la hermosura, like that of El privilegio de las mujeres, is mercy: it is nobler to pardon than to punish; and since punishment and revenge are associated with so-called men of honour, and forgiveness with women, the plays embody a criticism of the formal honour of men and a championship of women. Calderón's play is at once a clearer and more cogent dramatic statement of the theme of mercy than the source. It shows how the conventional concept of honour of the patricians like Aurelio has led to war and bloodshed so that Rome herself is brought within an ace of destruction. Their confused moral values have led to the confusion of war. Rome is saved only by the intervention of a woman who shows the futility of both war and revenge.

Though he is a patrician, Coriolano is, from the outset of Calderón's play, contrasted with the other patricians, and particularly with his father, by his attitude to women. Whilst Aurelio despises women, Coriolano defends them and is himself in love with Veturia. It is this which accounts for his dramatic decision to defy the Senate at the end of Act I. But, by his imprisonment and exile, Coriolano is forcibly divorced from Veturia's influence; treated like an animal he behaves like one, and in Act III with Rome at his mercy he insists on revenge. Coriolano's attitude coincides now with that of his father; if Aurelio was prepared publicly to sentence his own son to death, Coriolano will destroy his native city and with it the woman he loves. Such were the demands of conventional honour. Yet, although Coriolano resists even the arguments of Veturia, he is won over by her tears. Veturia is the representative of womanhood. She is herself a victim of the crimes against the Sabine women committed by Rome and at the play's end, by going to Coriolano, she can see that crime revenged and be assured of her personal safety. Yet it is Veturia who pleads that Rome should be pardoned. Women, the play asserts, are an essential part of human society; their tenderness, symbolized by their ability to weep, is the necessary antidote to the sternness of men. At the play's end their freedom is restored and their rights assured. But Calderón, like Coello, goes further, and one of the stipulations of Coriolano is that women shall in future be the arbiters of honour. Unlike Coello, however, Calderón does not go on to suggest that women should be allowed to punish with death their unfaithful husbands, as previously husbands had disposed of their wives. For this, although ensuring the equality of women with men, means perpetuating the barbarity of the code of honour and perverting the natural attributes of women, which are tenderness, gentleness and forgiveness. True honour is consistent with such qualities. And since the patricians of Rome have shown themselves to be pitiless and vindictive, women are made the guardians of honour. What clearer indictment could there be of the *pundonor* of Calderón's own day?

El médico de su honra and *Las armas de la hermosura* are new plays, but in both instances Calderón's conception of the story could be fitted to the basic framework of the source-play. More changes were required by *Las armas de la hermosura*, but, as with *El médico de su honra*, most of its scenes have their exact parallel in the source, offering ample opportunity for the study of details of Calderón's technique. Again, space permits only a summary of the more important points. One notes, at once, the scrupulous care with which Calderón has proceeded. No incident in the play is allowed to go unmotivated, and time and again a situation is better exploited. A single example must suffice: at the end of Act II, Coriolano in both .plays is banished from Rome and granted asylum by the Sabines. Yet Calderón, having to do precisely what the source dramatist has done, is content neither to copy the original nor simply rewrite it in his own language. In *El privilegio de las mujeres* Coriolano bids farewell to Veturia and in despair goes to throw himself in the Tiber. He is prevented from doing so by the Sabine King who at once recognizes him and is acquainted with the treatment he has received from his countrymen. In acknowledgment of his prowess and generosity in the recent battle, the Sabine King offers him protection and gives him command of the Sabine army. Contrast the technique of Calderón. Coriolano enters blindfold, lamenting his fate, and the Sabine King and Queen listen to him without knowing who he is. The Queen then removes the bandage and recognizes the person who earlier had saved her life; Coriolano in turn recognizes her. Neither, however, knows the identity of the other. At this point Calderón brings on the *gracioso* Pasquín who has just been captured, and it is he who reveals that the exile is Coriolano. And when Coriolano explains that he has been banished on account of a lady, Astrea erroneously assumes that she is the person in question and feels obliged to protect him. By careful motivation and the skilful use of surprise and suspense, Calderón has transformed an unexciting scene of the source-play into one taut with drama.

Calderón's careful motivation allows him to dispense with the many monologues and expository speeches of the source-play which are required as a running commentary on the action. At the beginning of Act II, for example, Pérez de Montalbán first introduces

Aurelio, who explains to the audience his attitude towards Coriolano; then, after a brief interview with Enio, the *gracioso* Morfodio
comes on to describe the outcome of Coriolano's protest. Calderón's
method is at once more subtle and convincing. Veturia, having
conceived a plan for Coriolano's escape, naturally turns for help
to Coriolano's friend Enio. But Enio has been delegated to escort
Astrea to her camp and, being absent from Rome, does not know
the circumstances of Coriolano's arrest. Hence the need for
Veturia's explanations which, at the same time, allow the audience
to keep pace with what is happening. Calderón achieved too a
remarkable tightening of the action. In Act III we have seen how,
by interchanging the first and second scenes of Coello's act in *El
privilegio de las mujeres*, he removed a change of scene. Elsewhere
there are the familiar Calderonian devices to make scene changes of
the source-play less abrupt. In Act I he has bridged the gap between
his first scene in Rome and his second at the Sabine camp by inter-
linking with the last lines of scene i the war cries of the Sabines
off stage which anticipate scene ii. Roman soldiers march off and the
Sabines march on, and the scene has shifted from Rome to a hill
outside Rome. Act II opens in the house of Veturia, but the action
is not fixed; the scene moves with Enio, first into the street and
then to the prison tower of Coriolano. Calderón strove to achieve,
as far as possible, continuity of scene, and he dispensed with as
many breaks in the action as he could. By beginning his play,
moreover, with a scene in which Coriolano and Veturia look
forward to the time when they will be united in love, and ending
it after so many vicissitudes with the announcement of their
marriage, Calderón suggests the wholeness and completeness of the
action.

In *El médico de su honra* Calderón kept strictly even to the
scenes of the source-play, but rewrote them down to the last line.
In *Las armas de la hermosura*, too, most of the borrowed scenes
are rewritten, except in the third act where, particularly in the
first half, Calderón borrowed a considerable number of Coello's
lines. In Act I Calderón is rewriting an earlier act written by himself, and often with more or less the same purpose in mind. Yet he
has borrowed actual lines in only two places: in the long passage
of *romance* in which the *gracioso* lists the items of the Senate's ban,

and in Veturia's declamation. In these two speeches he sometimes repeats earlier lines, but more often he revises. The following passage, taken from the peroration of Veturia, shows him following closely his own writing in *El privilegio de las mujeres:*

El privilegio de las mujeres.

<blockquote>
que yo en nombre de las otras,
a ti, cielo donde vivo;
a ti, gloria donde anhelo;
a ti, centro donde aspiro,
quejosa, ofendida y ciega,
despreciado el artificio,
la lengua anegada en quejas,
la voz ardiente en suspiros,
ajado y triste el semblante,
muerto el color o perdido,
brotado el aliento en rayos,
destilado el llanto en hilos,
sin parcialidad la gala,
sin preceptos el aliño,
sin ley vagando el cabello,
sin orden puesto el vestido,
te empeño, te pido y ruego,
te propongo y te suplico
que por galán, por osado,
por cortés, por entendido,
o por hombre solamente
(y harto al empeño te obligo),
que aquesta infamia derogues,
haciendo que aqueste arbitrio
se borre de las memorias
y se escriba en el olvido.   (1361a)
</blockquote>

Las armas de la hermosura.

<blockquote>
Y así, yo, en nombre de todas
en ira envuelto el sentido,
la lengua anegada en quejas,
la voz ardiendo en suspiros,
brotado el aliento en rayos,
destilado el llanto en hilos,
sin puntualidad la gala,
sin preceptos el aliño,
sin ley vagando el cabello,
sin orden puesto el vestido,
vuelvo a que en nombre de todas
digo a todos lo que a él digo.
Por noble, pues, Coriolano,
por galán, por entendido,
por cortesano en la paz,
en la guerra por invicto,
</blockquote>

> o por hombre solamente
> (que harto con esto te obligo),
> si como dama, te ruego,
> si como esclava, te pido
> que aquesta infamia derogues,
> haciendo que su designio
> se borre de la memoria
> y se escriba en el olvido.   (592a)

Parallelisms which play so important a part in Calderón's language are an outstanding feature of the passage from *El privilegio de las mujeres,* and it is not perhaps surprising that Calderón should wish to reproduce it in his new play. In the absence of autograph copies of the two plays one must be cautious in comparing these texts, but it would appear that Calderón has added to an already complicated structure of parallel phrases. One notes, for example, the two series of five parallel lines, and within the series more subtle variations of the nature and order of the constituent elements. On the other hand, Calderón would seem to have omitted the simple enumerations of the original:

> quejosa, ofendida y ciega...
> te empeño, te pido y ruego,
> te propongo y te suplico

By minor omissions and additions he enhances the poise and equilibrium of the pasage.

Only in the two instances mentioned has Calderón taken over lines of Act I of *El privilegio de las mujeres*; elsewhere, he has at times been inspired by its language. In *El privilegio de las mujeres,* for example, the Sabine King gives a long narrative account of Rome's foundation and the rape of the Sabines; this digression is transformed in *Las armas de la hermosura* into the very beautiful lines of Astrea, carefully woven into the fabric of the play:

>   Ya desde aquí diviso,
> aunque no bien, aquella
> que ayer vil choza, y hoy fábrica bella,
> tan elevada sube,
> que empieza en muro, y se remata en nube.
> ¡Oh tú, de la fortuna
> transmutado teatro, cuya escena,
> no sé si diga de piedades llena
> o llena de crueldades
> (que tal vez son crueles las piedades),

en yerto albergue dió primera cuna
a aquellos que arrojados
de ignoradas entrañas
hambrienta loba halló, que en sus montañas
recién nacidos, ya que no abortados,
eran espurios hijos de los hados!
¡Oh tú, que en lo voraz de su fiereza
mudando especie la naturaleza,
viste, en vez de ser ellos de su hambriento
furor destrozo, en cándido alimento
trocar la saña, haciendo que ellos fuesen
los que della, al revés, se mantuviesen!
Si a sus pechos criados,
si a su calor dormidos,
si de roncos anhélitos gorjeados,
crecieron, arrullados a gemidos,
¿qué mucho que bandidos,
sañudamente fieros,
se juntaran con otros bandoleros
para vivir sin Dios, sin fe, sin culto,
del homicidio, el robo y el insulto?
Desta, pues, compañía
Rómulo capitán, temiendo el día
de tu mudanza, a fin de resguardarse,
trató fortificarse,
para cuyo seguro,
el surco de un arado lineó muro,
con ley tan inviolable, que su extremo
asaltarle costó la vida a Remo.
Éste fué (¡oh tú, otra vez, varia fortuna,
condicional imagen de la luna!)
el origen, que altiva te conserva
crecida, a imitación de mala yerba;
pero ya tu castigo
llega, pues llega mi valor conmigo.
Y así, antes que sus armas se prevengan
(vengan los batidores, o no vengan),
entremos en sus lindes desde luego
publicando la guerra a sangre y fuego.   (584b-585a)

From Montalbán's second act Calderón has borrowed less than from his own Act I. Even in the trial scene where the handling corresponds closely with that of Montalbán, he breaks completely from Montalbán's language. A fairly close rendering of a short passage in a speech of Aurelio seems to be the full extent of Calderón's appropriation. Occasionally a commonplace phrase or idea which occurs in Montalbán has been perpetuated, as for example: "¿Un hijo dije? Llámole un cuidado" in "Bien dijo quien dijo que era / en las personas humanas / muchos cuidados un hijo". In Act III, on the other hand, Calderón relaxed his efforts and, as we have seen, was sometimes content to revise; more often than not he adopts the same stanza form as Coello. Yet, where he is closest to his source, Calderón enriches the original with new and colourful imagery. Here, for example, is a passage from Veturia's pleading with Aurelio to ask for a truce, which has no counterpart in *El privilegio de las mujeres*:

> que no hay víbora, por más
> que en flores se disimule,
> que no escupa la triaca
> contra el veneno que escupe,
> ni en las mismas flores hay
> que no den, rojas o azules,
> tósigo a la araña amargo
> y miel a la abeja dulce.
> Y pues virtudes y vicios
> de una causa se producen
> ¿qué mucho que de una misma
> voz ser la lengua resulte
> víbora para los vicios
> y flor para las virtudes?   (608a-b)

Even when borrowing actual lines of the source he added to and revised the imagery:

El privilegio de las mujeres.

> Roma, tu patria infeliz,
> humilde a tus plantas yace,
> o por instantes viviendo,
> o muriendo por instantes.
> ¿Ves ese soberbio muro
> que intrépido y arrogante
> con la frente abolla el cielo,
> con el bulto estrecha el aire?
> ¿Ves ese olimpo de piedras,
> ese monte de pilares,
> esa columna de acero,
> ese encelado de jaspe?
> Pues no muro, pues no olimpo,
> no columna ni gigante
> es ya; monumento sí,
> que entre sus cenizas yace,
> pues son de los hijos suyos
> sepulcro todas las calles.   (1378a)

Las armas de la hermosura.

¿Es posible, cuando yace
(aquí quedasteis los dos)
Roma en el último trance,
o por instantes muriendo,
o viviendo por instantes,
no te conmuevas al ver
que esa fábrica admirable,
ese cáucaso de bronce,
ese obelisco de jaspe,
ese penacho de acero,
ese muro de diamante,
que hizo estremecer la tierra,
que hice embarazar el aire,
atemorizado a ruinas,
está titubeando frágil,
como que ya panteón
de tanto vivo cadáver,
sólo falta resolver
si se cae o no se cae?   (616a)

But many of the play's associations are new. Rome is compared by Calderón with the Lernaean hydra. The distorted sense of values of the patricians has made of her a monster and led to bloodshed, whether in private vengeance or in war. It is appropriate, therefore, that the patrician flag should be red and contrasted with the white flag of the *plebs*. But violence and war, whether the organized resistance of Rome to the Sabine attacks or the spontaneous revolt of the people in support of Coriolano, lead only to chaos and confusion:

ASTREA.	...el confuso estruendo...	(586b)
VETURIA.	...en el ciego, el confuso tumulto...	(593b)
CORIOLANO.	Oye, por si algo entendemos de una confusión grande.	(614a)
CORIOLANO.	De tanto confuso estruendo ¿qué has entendido?	(614b)

The point is illustrated by the many reversals of fortune, by Astrea's mistaking the Roman lines for her own and by the death of Flavio. Calderón is deliberately associating moral *confusión* with the confusion of war, of which it is the cause. Rome is the theatre in which Aurelio, Coriolano, Veturia and others play their parts and shape their own and their city's destiny.

Except in Act III Calderón normally avoided the stanza forms of the source:

El privilegio de las mujeres.			Las armas de la hermosura.	
Act I:	1.	silva	1.	quintilla
		romance U-A		romance E-A
		—	2.	silva
		—		romance E-O
	2.	romance E-O	3.	redondilla
		silva		romance E-O
		romance I-O		redondilla
Act II:		—		romance I-O
	1.	silva	1.	romance A-A
		romance A-E	2.	redondilla
		redondilla		romance E-O
	2.	silva	3.	romance E-O
		romance I-O		—
Act III:	1.	silva		—
		redondilla		—
	2.	romance U-E	1.	romance U-E
	3.	—	2.	silva
		décima		décima
		romance A-E		romance A-E
		silva		—
		romance E-E		romance E-E

He adopts the same stanza form only in two places in Act I and nowhere in Act II. In Act III, on the other hand, bearing in mind the transposition of scenes, he follows Coello closely.

Though a court play, written presumably for production in the theatre of the Buen Retiro, *Las armas de la hermosura* required no complicated machinery and could easily have been performed on the apron stages of the Príncipe or the Cruz. For its two 'discoveries' —Coriolano in prison early in Act II, and later in the Act the setting up of the throne—the inner stage could have served as well as the 'foro'. In the *corrales* the sideboards and table of the opening setting could have been carried on to the main stage or revealed in the inner stage. Even so, *Las armas de la hermosura* lends itself to far more elaborate staging than the source-play, assuming the facilities are available, and the directions of extant texts call for the use of perspective scenery and quite complicated sets for the crowd scenes, combined doubtless with lavish costumes. The directions for the opening set, as recorded in the earliest extant text (1679), are:

> *Córrese la cortina, y vense todos los bastidores del*
> *teatro transmutados en aparadores de piezas de plata,*
> *y en medio una mesa llena de vasos y viandas, y sen-*
> *tados a ella hombres y mujeres, y en su principal*
> *asiento* CORIOLANO *y* VETURIA *y los músicos de-*
> *trás, arrimados al foro, y* PASQUÍN *y otros sirviendo la*
> *mesa* (84r).

and for the investiture in Act II:

> *Con esta repetición, las chirimías y atabalillos, salen*
> *todas las mujeres y hombres, y se abre todo el foro,*
> *y en un trono* CORIOLANO, *con laurel, manto y bastón;*
> *y a sus lados,* AURELIO, LELIO, ENIO *y* RELATOR (98v).

Neither situation has an exact parallel in the source-play.

But *Las armas de la hermosura* is more markedly a court play in its use of music, which is combined with poetry and allegory in a manner akin to that of the *auto*:

> Alegoría, poesía
> y música, ya es preciso
> que resulte de esta unión
> el numeroso artificio
> de un auto sacramental.
>
> (Pando y Mier, V, 5)

Music and song have a serious purpose in Calderón's plays. His conception of music is basically Platonic and, as J. W. Sage has shown, it is often used to symbolize the harmony of the universe, and the harmony of mankind living in accordance with God's purpose. [1] This is its function in *Las armas de la hermosura*. In scene i the love of Coriolano and Veturia is emphasized by the singing of the two choruses; but the peace and order are soon disturbed by the cries of war:

> ROMANOS. ¡Qué asombro!
> ROMANOS. ¡Qué confusión! (580a)

It is only at the end of the play and after many changes of fortune that Coriolano and Veturia are reunited, and their love and forthcoming marriage are again celebrated by music. Elsewhere, musicians are used to give voice to the sentiments of the Roman people, to

---

[1] J. W. Sage, 'Calderón y la música teatral', *BHi*, LVIII (1956), 275-300.

applaud, for example, Coriolano's victory, and in Act III to ask for peace-terms. In the final scene the chorus reiterates the theme which underlies the whole play:

> ¡Viva quien vence!
> Que es vencer perdonando
> vencer dos veces.   (618b)

This operatic conception has no precedent in the source.

The superiority of *Las armas de la hermosura* over *El privilegio de las mujeres* is due primarily to its greater cohesion and unity. Though Calderón's characters are the same as those of the source, they have been conceived anew in terms of the theme of mercy, and the related themes of love and honour. The structure is basically the same, but new incidents have been added to provide the link between cause and effect. Calderón's play shows, too, with greater force than the source-play how, by their inhuman conduct, the Roman patricians bring Rome to near-disaster, and how she is saved only by the intervention of a woman. All the characters in the play are well-intentioned and it is appropriate that it should end happily. But Calderón shows how the peace and joy of his last scene are the consequences of Veturia's plea that mercy is superior to revenge. *Las armas de la hermosura* is at once a great work of art and a moral lesson of universal application.

IV

LÓS CABELLOS DE ABSALÓN[1]

CRITICS who have taken Calderón's borrowings from earlier plays as proof of the poverty of his imagination and of his desire to purloin the works of others have, not unnaturally, fastened upon *Los cabellos de Absalón,* for here—as everyone knows—he took over almost word for word a complete act of Tirso de Molina's *La venganza de Tamar.* No other example is known in Calderón's work of appropriation on this scale. For *El médico de su honra* and *Las armas de la hermosura* he borrowed the general structure and the main characters of the source-plays and yet completely transformed the originals, taking over only a few lines in all. For the remaining plays he diverged much further from his sources. Even in *Los cabellos de Absalón* the copying does not extend beyond a single act, an act which is part of a completely different dramatic structure.

Los cabellos de Absalón is not coextensive with *La venganza de Tamar.* The story of both plays is the familiar one of Amnon, Tamar and Absalom, recorded in Samuel II, 13: Amnon, who seduces his half-sister Tamar, is murdered at Baalhazor by Absalom. Tirso devoted the whole of Act I of *La venganza de Tamar* to Amnon's falling in love with Tamar. This material is omitted by Calderón, who begins his play at the point at which Tirso begins his Act II. Thus Act I of *Los cabellos de Absalón,* dealing with the circumstances leading to Tamar's seduction, is coextensive with Act II of *La venganza de Tamar.* Then Act II, showing Absalom's revenge

---

[1] Texts used:
   La venganza de Tamar
      Tercera parte, 1634.
      Ed. Cotarelo y Mori, NBAE (Madrid, 1906). Vol. 1, 407-33.
      Ed. J. E. Hartzenbusch, BAE, IX, 401-20.
   Los cabellos de Absalón
      Ed. Vera Tassis, VIII, 1684.
      Ed. J. J. Keil, 193-217.
      Ed. J. E. Hartzenbusch, BAE, IX, 421-41.
      Ed. Astrana Marín, pp. 925-59. (Madrid, 1945, 3.ª ed., revisada.)
   Quotations are from the BAE edition of *La venganza de Tamar* and Astrana Marín's edition of *Los cabellos de Absalón.*

upon Amnon, is a copy of Tirso's Act III, and Act III deals with
Absalom's conspiracy against his father David and his death. The
relationship is as follows:

La venganza.	Los cabellos.	
Act I	—	Amnon falls in love with Tamar.
Act II	Act I	Circumstances leading to Tamar's seduction.
Act III	Act II	Tamar avenged: death of Amnon.
—	Act III	Death of Absalom.

The third act of *Los cabellos de Absalón* is new, and the first a
complete recasting of Tirso's second.

Why did Calderón take over intact Tirso's Act III? That he was
neither a plagiarist, nor careless, nor lacking in imagination, is clear
from his inspired and meticulous recastings of other plays, to say
nothing of the first act of *Los cabellos de Absalón* itself, totally
rewritten within the same general limits as Tirso's Act II. It seems
highly improbable, too, that his procedure can be explained as a
momentary lapse into laziness. Some critics, like Cotarelo y Mori,
have suggested that Act III of *La venganza de Tamar* came so
near to perfection that Calderón felt he could not improve upon
it, that his appropriation is a tribute to the supreme achievement
of Tirso:

> "*La venganza de Tamar*, tragedia de intensa y sombría grandeza por
> la que se ve que ni aún los asuntos más escabrosos y difíciles degeneraban
> en manos de Téllez. Así lo entendió Calderón al colocar el acto tercero de
> *La venganza* como segundo y preparatorio del desenlace de su drama *Los
> cabellos de Absalón*, sin atreverse a retocarlo." [1]

But, as I hope to show, even a few minor revisions would have
cleared up the inconsistencies entailed by the adoption of Tirso's
act. Don Angel Valbuena looks for the reason in the subject matter.
He accepts the view of Otto Rank that Calderón, though curiously
attracted by the theme of incest, found its consummation repugnant,
and that in *Los cabellos de Absalón* he avoided the issue by copying
out Tirso's lines verbatim:

---

[1] *Comedias de Tirso de Molina*, I, lviii.

Calderón se siente a la vez atraído y repelido por conflictos parecidos en *La devoción de la cruz* y en *Las tres justicias en una,* pero en ambas obras el incesto no llega a consumarse, ya por la fuerza milagrosa de la cruz, ya porque en la misma pasión había un confusionismo que no daba paso a la pasión ilícita. En cambio, en la historia de Tamar y Amnón (Amón escribían Tirso, Calderón, y, en general, toda la época) se encuentra con que en la misma Biblia se describe el abominable pecado. ¿Qué hará el poeta? ¿Escenificarlo? ¿No terminar la obra planeada? La solución se la da la comedia de Tirso. Para la consumación del incesto se limitará a incluir, completo, un acto del mercenario. [1]

It is true that Tirso himself was very careful to keep close to the Biblical text in writing the act in question. [2] But one of the two violent scenes between Amón and Tamar comes in Calderón's Act I, where he was careful to rewrite and, incidentally, to tone down the brutality of Tirso's scene. And the greater part of the Act which Calderón copied is in no way concerned with incest. At most, Valbuena's explanation can account for one brief scene.

None of the arguments advanced to explain Calderón's incorporation of a whole act of Tirso are, to my mind, satisfactory. Setting *Los cabellos de Absalón* against *La venganza de Tamar* throws light on this as well as upon other points. The play has been surprisingly little studied; most critics exhaust the space allotted to it by pointing to Tirso's contribution. Menéndez y Pelayo remarked, with unwonted terseness, that 'la obra de Calderón no tiene de bueno más que lo que tomó de Tirso'. [3] Schack, on the other hand, though perhaps not altogether clear as to what Calderón had taken from Tirso, accords it the highest honours:

Esta magnífica tragedia ocupa lugar preferente entre las obras de nuestro poeta..., ¿a qué señalar sus perfecciones aisladas, cuando este drama, en la construcción simétrica de tan escogidos materiales, forma un todo perfecto? [4]

The truth, I believe, lies midway between these two judgements.

The Biblical story of Amnon and Tamar—a story of offence and revenge—is simple and complete, though the narrative is enlivened

---

[1] *Calderón* (Madrid, 1941), pp. 131-32.

[2] Cf. J. C. J. Metford, 'Tirso de Molina's Old Testament Plays', *BHS*, XXVII (1950), 153.

[3] *Estudios y discursos de crítica histórica y literaria,* III (1941), p. 172.

[4] Op. cit., IV, 395, 397.

with touches of dialogue, such as Amnon's conversation with Jonadab and with his father David, and with vivid details of the seduction and desolation of Tamar and of Absalom's revenge. Tirso preserved the pattern of the Old Testament story: Act I shows Amón's love for Tamar, Act II the circumstances leading up to his rape of Tamar, and Act III Tamar's dejection and the revenge of Absalón. He was obliged, of course, to supplement the Biblical material, but he draws little upon the rest of the Book of Samuel. His play is in the main a character study of Amón, and the scenes follow Amón in every stage of his fatal passion for Tamar. It opens with him home from war, impatiently ordering his servants to rid him of the last vestiges of uniform, his spurs and boots. He is a soldier, but not by choice like his father. Nor is he a young gallant like his brothers Adonías and Absalón. Whilst Absalón goes to keep an appointment with a lady and Adonías to gamble, Amón finds solace only in poetry. But he is curious about his father's wives and concubines, guarded by high walls; curiosity leads to resolution and, once resolved, he is deaf to all warnings. The scene follows him to the royal garden where, unwittingly, he falls in love with his half-sister Tamar, and under cover of darkness converses freely and shamelessly with her. Only on the following morning does he discover that the girl who has won his love is his own sister. Vainly he tries to resist his passion, then reckless and despairing—one who himself in the first scene has been shocked by Absalón's designs upon his father's wives—he sets out, masked, to declare his love. At Josefo's house he escapes after kissing the hand of Tamar. This whole act, which Calderón was to omit, is a detailed portrait of Amón—strange, sensitive, sensual and weak.

Tirso's emphasis remains virtually the same in Acts II and III. Act II shows Amón depressed, uncertain of himself and impatient with others, giving orders and cancelling them a moment later. He asks for music and company, only to dismiss everyone who dares come near him. Doctors annoy him, his servant Eliacer bores him and the fatuous fencing master makes him angry. Having dressed against the advice of his servants, he upbraids them for what they have not done and brands them liars when they protest. He alone fails to greet his father when he returns triumphant from Rabbah, and answers his loving inquiries with bitterness. He then invents the story of his love for an Ammonite princess, persuading Tamar to soften the blow of her absence and presumed death by consenting to act her part; and he promptly charges her with perfidy for allowing her lover Joab to kiss her hand. In a final act of desperation, he confesses his incestuous love to Jonadab, adopts his sinister plan and, in the last scene of Act II, assaults Tamar. Acts I and II have shown Amón drifting inevitably, despite himself, towards his terrible crime. Every scene has been focussed upon him. Tirso has departed considerably from the Biblical story to underline the human aspect, to show Amón caught up in a chain of circumstances which leads ultimately to incest. His picture is one of understanding and sympathy. He presents the incident from Amón's viewpoint, not to justify his conduct but to show how, given such a psychological make-up and such circumstances, the crime came to be committed; this, I believe, is the secret of the pathos of the play.

Act III shows the tragic consequences. Absalón takes it upon himself to revenge his sister's rape, invites Amón to the country and brutally murders him. But whereas Acts I and II are largely an elaboration of the record of the Book of Samuel to fill out the portrait of Amón and to provide motives for his crime, Act III shows a serious departure from the Old Testament story, which is relevant to Calderón's later reworking of Tirso's play. In the Biblical narrative and in the play David, because of his love for Amnon, cannot bring himself to injure him, and it is Absalom, Tamar's brother, who sees the dishonour cleared. In the Book of Samuel Absalom's motive is revenge. In Tirso's play, a second and more powerful motive is Absalón's ambition. Already in the first scene Absalón has boasted of his physical beauty. Then early in Act III, before hearing of Tamar's disgrace, he confesses his designs upon the throne and presses his claims against those of Adonías. Thus the dishonour of Tamar presents Absalón not merely with an occasion for revenge but with a chance to satisfy his ambition:

> Con su muerte cumpliré
> la justicia y mi ambición.   (415c)

More than that: Tirso anticipates Absalón's later conspiracy against his own father in a scene in which, coming upon the king's crown, he fits it upon his own head and muses with himself:

> Bien me estáis: vendréisme ansí
> nacida, y no digo mal,
> pues nací de sangre real,
> y vos nacéis para mí.　(415c)

Tirso, that is, departed from the Biblical story to make ambition the motive behind Absalón's espousing the cause of Tamar.

Absalón's death is foretold on no less than three different occasions in *La venganza de Tamar*. When David expresses his anxiety about the safety of Amón, Absalón replies:

> Si hiciere venganza en él
> plegue a Dios que me haga guerra
> cuanto el sol dora y encierra,
> y contra ti rebelado
> de mis cabellos colgado
> muera entre el cielo y la tierra.　(416a)

Laureta the flower girl warns him:

> Pues tened, Absalón, cuenta
> con él, y no os queráis tanto,
> que de puro engrandeceros
> estimaros y quereros,
> de Israel seáis espanto.
> Vuestra hermosura enloquece
> a toda vuestra nación:
> Narciso, sois, Absalón,
> que también os desvanece.
> Cortáos esos hilos bellos;
> que si los dejáis crecer,
> os habéis presto de ver
> en alto por los cabellos.　(418b)

Misinterpreting the words of Laureta, Absalón repeats them to his sister in his last words in the play:

> todo Israel me ha de ver
> en alto por los cabellos.　(419c)

The stark horror of the scene showing the murdered Amón, with Absalón and Tamar coldly congratulating themselves, serves to emphasize the brutality of the revenge. And we note even that Tirso makes Absalón himself, not his servants, kill Amón. Set against this scene is that in which David, overcome by paternal affection for Amón and conscious of his own grievous sins, leaves without a word of reprimand. And if Amón's encounter with the disguised Tamar shows that he is unrepentant, in the final scene of the play David curses Absalón and bitterly laments Amón's death.

By showing the death of Amón to have been the means of furthering Absalón's ambition rather than the avenging of the honour of Tamar, Tirso enlisted the audience's sympathy for his protagonist. The Spanish code of honour was explicit and unambiguous in its insistence upon revenge. But just as Calderón shows the superiority of mercy over vengeance in *Las armas de la hermosura,* so Tirso in *La venganza de Tamar* clearly commends the pardon of a loving father and points to the untimely death of Absalón. But the theme of Absalón's ambition, whilst it serves the purpose of transferring the audience's sympathy from avenger to avenged, necessarily remains undeveloped in Tirso's play and actually detracts from its dramatic impact. In this respect Tirso's play invited recasting. It may well be that Tirso himself had a sequel to the play in mind, or even wrote such a sequel. One recalls too that Mira de Amescua invites his audience to a second part of *El arpa de David* which might have embraced similar material. The essential difference, at all events, between *Los cabellos de Absalón* and *La venganza de Tamar* is Calderón's presentation of the story in terms of the ambition of Absalón, pursuing it to its logical conclusion with Absalón's death.

Tirso is believed to have written *La venganza de Tamar* before 1624, but it was first published ten years later in his *Tercera Parte.* [1] Calderón may well have begun *Los cabellos de Absalón* soon afterwards. [2] His new conception of the story sprang from a theme of Tirso's play which was left undeveloped, and the primary structural change required was a further act after Amón's death showing the fate of Absalón. Tamar's demand for revenge provided a convenient opportunity for Absalón to rid himself of the chief obstacle to his own claims to the throne, and Calderón's new Act III contains an attempt on the life of the King himself. New material was at hand in Samuel II, 14-18, which records the events from David's recall of Absalom from exile to his conspiracy and, finally, his death at the hand of Joab. Calderón devoted a whole new third act to these developments. He was obliged, therefore, to

---

[1] Cf. Metford, op. cit., pp. 160-63.
[2] Hilborn dates it c. 1634, op. cit., p. 25.

So, at the very beginning of his play, long before the rape of Tamar, Calderón shows Absalón's designs upon the crown. Tamar's dishonour will provide him with a heaven-sent opportunity of furthering his ambitious designs by the removal of the heir apparent. Moreover, Calderón gives to David words which are relevant both to Absalón and to Amón:

> ...imperio tiene
> el hombre sobre sí propio,
> y los esfuerzos humanos,
> llamado uno, vienen todos.
> No te rindas a ti mismo,
> no te avasalles medroso
> a tu misma condición...   (927b)

Absalón will be as much a slave to his ambition as Amón to his incestuous love.

Still keeping close to the pattern of Tirso's act, Calderón shows Tamar's visit to Amón and her consenting for a while to act the part of his beloved. But Calderón insists upon the confusion of Amón who, with his reason blinded by his incestuous passion, is associated with darkness:

> AQUITOFEL. ...enfado de la luz del sol recibe,
> con que entre sombras vive;
> y aun está sin abrir una ventana,
> ni ver la luz hermosa y soberana.   (926b)
>
> DAVID. ¿tanto a una pasión se rinde,
> tanto a una pena, que absorto,
> confuso, triste, afligido,
> no les permite a sus ojos,
> la luz del día, negando
> la entrada a sus rayos de oro?   (927a)

Later, Amón seeks to exculpate himself by claiming that his will has been enslaved from birth:

> Deste atrevimiento mío
> no tengo la culpa yo,
> porque en mí sólo nació
> esclavo el libre albedrío.
> No sé qué planeta impío
> pudo reinar aquel día...   (930b)

In *La venganza de Tamar* Joab is Tamar's lover. Tamar calls off the love-game with Amón on account of Joab, and Amón confesses his incestuous love to Jonadab out of jealousy when he sees Joab kiss Tamar's hand. But Joab's love has no effect on later developments and is not referred to again. Calderón dispensed with this unnecessary complication; Tamar sees the futility and danger of acting the part of Amón's beloved, and Jonadab discovers his master's secret by eavesdropping. In both plays, on the advice of Jonadab, Amón asks David's permission for Tamar to come and tend him, and both acts end with the visit of Tamar.

Before the final scene of this first act, Calderón interposes a new scene which is his only departure from the structure of Tirso's act. Salvos are heard off-stage and Absalón comes on to announce the arrival of ships from Tyre. Semel enters and tells of his cargo of cedar trees for the building of God's temple, and of Teuca, the fortune-telling Ethiopian girl who accompanies him. David observes that the cedar trees are premature since he is not worthy of building God's temple, and reprimands Semel for bringing a fortune-teller who is a mouthpiece of the Devil. When David has gone, Teuca angrily predicts what the future holds for Joab, Semel, Aquitofel and Absalón. The interpolation is happily placed, for it allows an interval of time between the granting of Amón's request and the visit of Tamar; the short meeting between Amón and Tamar gains in dramatic effect by being detached. But the primary purpose of the new scene is to anticipate developments in Calderón's new third act and, above all, to direct attention to Absalón. Teuca, as her name suggests, is the widow of Tekoah who will later plead with David to allow Absalón to return from exile. But she is modelled on Tirso's flower-girl Laureta, who in the last act of *La venganza de Tamar* tells the fortune of Amón, Adonías and Absalón. Teuca's predictions for Joab, Semel and Aquitofel foreshadow incidents of Calderón's new Act III as well as their untimely deaths. Joab and Semel will each incur the wrath of David, the one with his lance—by taking the life of Absalón—and the other with his curses:

> que tú lanzas arrojando,
> que tú piedras recogiendo,
> me dais horror, hasta que
> de vuestra muerte herederos
> seáis, siendo vuestra muerte
> cláusula de un testamento.   (933a-b)

and Aquitofel will plot against David and in the end take his own life:

> basta que por tu consejo
> torpe desesperación
> aun te niegue el monumento.   (933b)

More important is Teuca's prophecy for Absalón which follows that of Laureta in Tirso's play:

LAURETA.	Cortaos esos hilos bellos;
	que si los dejáis crecer,
	os habéis presto de ver
	en alto por los cabellos. (418b)
TEUCA.	Ya veo
	que te ha de ver tu ambición
	en alto por los cabellos... (933b)

Absalón alone heeds the words of Teuca, and he misinterprets them as the earlier Absalón misinterpreted those of Laureta in *La venganza de Tamar*:

> Pues siendo así, que yo amado
> soy de todos, bien infiero
> que esta adoración común
> resulte en que todo el pueblo
> para Rey suyo me aclame,
> cuando se divida el reino
> en los hijos de David.
> Luego justamente infiero,
> pues que mis cabellos son
> de mi hermosura primeros
> acreedores, que a ellos deba
> el verme en tal alto puesto;
> y así, vendré a estar entonces
> en alto por los cabellos.   (933b-934a)

Teuca's prediction is ambiguous, and it provides Calderón with an opportunity for dramatic irony; so does the prediction of the old hag in *El príncipe constante*. Absalón assumes from Teuca's words that his vanity and ambition will be satisfied. In fact, they foretell the opposite: Absalón's designs upon the throne will lead directly to his premature and violent death, and death by hanging, entangled by the very hair which he assumes will ensure his succession. Absalón's angry exchanges with Salomón and Joab confirm the error of his ways and foreshadow his death:

SALOMÓN.   que ofensas de un padre, siempre
            las toma a su cargo el cielo.   (934a)

The scene ends with the secret plans between Absalón and his
counsellor Aquitofel:

                ...que no quiero
            hablar ahora en otra cosa
            sino en los designios nuestros.   (934b)

At this point the action returns to Amón's room, and the Act ends,
as does Tirso's, with the assault on Tamar.

After transforming Act II of *La venganza de Tamar* for his first
act, Calderón goes on to copy out Tirso's third act for his second.
In the absence of autograph copies of the two plays, it is not
certain to what extent the variations between the extant texts
indicate changes introduced by Calderón, but his departure from
Tirso can have amounted to no more than a superficial revision.
Certain minor alterations were necessary. Calderón had already
introduced in Act I the fortune-telling girl Teuca who is modelled
on Tirso's Laureta. In this second act, therefore, Tirso's Laureta
becomes Teuca, and a few of her lines which had been included
in Act I are omitted. She appears of course in Calderón's second
act, not wrapped in mystery as in Tirso's play, but as the familiar
character whom Semel has brought with him from Hiram, King of
Tyre. In this same scene too some unimportant lines of Tirso's act
are redistributed to give a small part to Jonadab, and Aquitofel is
included amongst the characters. Calderón was obliged also to make
some minor changes to convert a play-ending into the end of a
second act, carrying forward the interest of the audience to the
developments of Act III. The final words of David in *La venganza
de Tamar*:

            ¡Ay mi Amón! ¡Ay mi heredero!
            Llore tu padre con Jacob diciendo:
            "Hijo, una fiera pésima te ha muerto."   (420c)

are changed in *Los cabellos de Absalón* to:

            ¡Ay mi Amón! ¡Ay mi heredero!
            Búsquese luego a Absalón,
            marchen ejércitos luego
            a buscarle.   (945b)

Our attention is directed from Amón to Absalón and the events of Act III. Calderón rejected also some lines of David's hallucination speech, in which he believes he sees Amón and reaches out to embrace him. Miss I. L. McClelland, who makes some penetrating observations on the differences of technique of Tirso and Calderón in her book on Tirso, has suggested that Calderón wished to omit the 'bothered' effect of David's speech, 'the undisciplined ramblings which in the mouth of Tirso's David are the logical accompaniments to his hallucination'. [1] This may perhaps be true. But Calderón's primary purpose in revising Tirso's text at this point was quite simply to divert the interest of his audience—evidently with as few alterations as possible—from Amón to Absalón. It is interesting to note that Tirso's happy conception of the hallucination is put to further use in Act III of Los cabellos de Absalón when David dreams that Absalón is murdering him.

For the rest, Calderón makes only occasional revisions of language. He omits, for example, the grim but vivid imagery of the despised Tamar:

> Tirano, de aquese talle
> doblar mi agravio procura
> hasta que pueda vengalle.
> Mujer gozada es basura:
> haz que me echen en la calle.
> Ya que ansí me has deshonrado,
> lama el plato en que has comido
> un perro, al suelo arrojado:
> di que se ponga el vestido
> que has roto ya, algún criado.   (413b-c)

The shepherd's songs of Tirso's act, including the fleecing romancillo which is reminiscent of lines in La prudencia en la mujer, have either been reduced or removed; and a song immediately before Amón's murder disappears. To judge by the stage direction of the Vera Tassis text, the earliest extant, the more gruesome details of the scene in which Amón lies sprawled across a blood-covered table with a cup in one hand, a knife in the other and a dagger in his throat, were at some point discarded. The scene directions are:

---

[1] I. L. McClelland, *Tirso de Molina. Studies in Dramatic Realism* (Liverpool, 1948), 50-52, 179.

La venganza de Tamar.

Descúbrese lo interior de la quinta, y vense unos aparadores de plata, caídas las vajillas, y una mesa llena de manjares y descompuesta, con los manteles ensangrentados, y AMÓN *sobre la mesa asentado y caído de espaldas en ella, con una taza en la una mano, y un cuchillo en la otra, atravesada por la garganta una daga. Delante* ABSALÓN *y* TAMAR.

Los cabellos de Absalón.

Descúbrese una mesa con un aparador de plata, y los manteles revueltos; AMÓN *echado sobre ella con una servilleta, ensangrentado, y* ABSALÓN.

Changes of word-order may not all be Calderón's but many are improvements:

La venganza de Tamar.

¡Válgame Dios! ¿Qué voces serán éstas?   (414b)
No quitarán mancha de honra.   (414c)

Los cabellos de Absalón.

¿Qué voces son aquéstas?   (937b)
No quitan la mancha de honra.   (938a)

'Melanconiosa' (416c) becomes   'Tan dolorosa' (941b) and
'La infantica' (416c)   'Ea infanta' (941b)

It is not without significance also that Calderón removed the comic relief which Tirso, so characteristically, provided in the form of shepherd's dialect and song. For example:

BRAULIO.   Que á la hé que quillotráis
desde ell alma á la asadura
a cuantos viéndôs están
y que para mal de muchos
el dimuño os trujo acá.   (416c)

In the absence of autograph copies of the plays, this is perhaps as much as one can say in collating the two texts.

I have referred earlier to Cotarelo's view that Tirso's act came so near to perfection that Calderón felt incapable of improving it. Tirso handled his material well, but there can be no doubt that, in the structure of *Los cabellos de Absalón*, his text could have been improved even by an inferior dramatist. It contains, for example, the remnants of the part for Eliazar, Amón's servant. Most of Eliazar's lines were lost with the removal of Tirso's first act and the first scene of his second; the few lines that remain in Tirso's third

act, the only reason for his appearance in *Los cabellos de Absalón,*
are quite superfluous. Again Act III of *Los cabellos de Absalón* will
provide considerable rôles for Joab, Semel and Aquitofel; yet
though Calderón has made all three appear in Act I, Joab and
Semel have no part at all in Act II, and Aquitofel appears once
only and then without a word. We have seen that a scene in Calderón's Act I derived, to some extent, from two scenes in Tirso's
third act: from the exchanges between Absalón and Adonías, and
from the prediction of Laureta at Baalhazor. In appropriating
Tirso's third act for his second, therefore, Calderón was in danger of
duplicating his material, and excisions were necessary to avoid
repetition. A few lines were omitted from the scene at Baalhazor,
but not enough; and none were omitted from the earlier scene
between Absalón and Adonías. Thus lines in Act I of *Los cabellos
de Absalón:*

> ABSALÓN.   ...este solo
> desperdicio de su imperio
> en cada un año me vale
> de esquilmos muchos talentos.   (933b)
> De Jerusalén las damas
> me le compran...
> Cuando la hermosura cae
> sobre el valor que yo tengo...   (934a)

are repeated in substance in Act II:

> ADONÍAS.   El cielo ha puesto renta en tu cabeza,
> pues tus madejas a las damas vendes:
> cada año, haciendo esquilmo tu belleza
> cuando aliviarla de tu pelo entiendes,
> repartiendo por tiendas su tesoro
> le compran en doscientos siclos de oro.   (937a)
>
> ABSALÓN.   La guerra, que jubila al sacerdocio,
> en mis hazañas enseñar procura
> qué bien dice el valor con la hermosura.   (937b)

The appropriation of Tirso's act led to an occasional inconsistency.
In Act I Amón's request for food of Tamar's baking is changed to
food prepared by Tamar's servants; in Act II lines referring to the
baking by Tamar have been left unchanged.

Finally, by failing to rewrite Tirso's act, Calderón was unable
to provide his play with a consistent scheme of images. Both Act I

and Act III contain many familiar Calderonian associations. There is the sun image, for example, and the wider imagery of light and darkness of which it is part. Absalón is compared by Tamar to a new sun and linked thereby to Phaethon, who symbolizes ambition:

> Póngase el sol caduco, pues que nace
> joven otro que da rayos más bellos
> con el crespo esplendor de sus cabellos.   (951b)

But his ambition and presumption lead to murder and treachery, and he finds his death in an *espesura*, his hair entangled in an oak-tree:

> ¡Que en las copadas encinas
> se me enredan los cabellos!   (958b)

The gloom and the entanglement mirror his moral confusion. And Tamar, who has supported his conspiracy against David, goes to bury herself in utter darkness:

> iré a sepultarme viva,
> en el más oscuro centro...   (959b)

Similarly, in the first act Amón shuns the light of day. At the end of the play we find too the association of war with confusion, reflecting, as in *Las armas de la hermosura*, the distorted values of those responsible for it:

> Los traidores y leales,
> mezclados confusamente,
> no se distinguen...   (953b-954a)
>
> ...con un acero
> vendré a morir en confusión tan rara...   (957b)

Because of Tirso's act, any satisfactory sequence of images was impossible.

The evidence of the third act of *Los cabellos de Absalón* adds weight to the view that, after a very careful recasting of Tirso's work for Act I, Calderón lost interest in his new play or, working against time for an *autor*, was obliged to appropriate what he could of the rest of *La venganza de Tamar*. It is taken up with Absalón's rebellion against his father and his murder by Joab, events which are foreshadowed in the first two acts. Joab arranges for Teuca to come in disguise to David to intercede on behalf of the exiled Absalón. Absalón is pardoned and allowed to return. But he begins at once to plot with Aquitofel to overthrow his father, and finally leads an army against him. David, warned by Cusay, escapes with his life; and just as he had pardoned the crime of Amón, so now he pardons Absalón and insists that he be spared. In the battle which follows, however, Absalón is killed by Joab as he hangs by his hair from an oak-tree. Though this material is not found in Tirso's play, [1] Calderón follows closely the five relevant chapters of the Book of Samuel, and the result is an act which is disproportionately long, with many incidents which might well have been omitted. Every phase of Absalón's conspiracy against his father is presented in action: Teuca's interview with David at the instigation of Joab, Absalón's return and pardon, the evil counsel of Aquitofel who is later supplanted by Cusay, the capture of Jerusalem, David's escape, and finally Absalón's death. In addition, Calderón shows the death of the treacherous servant Aquitofel by his own hand, the sentence to death and reprieve of Jonadab, Tamar's joining the conspiracy of Absalón against her father, the curses of Semel, and the conversion of Teuca. Many of the scenes are, in themselves, excellently handled and very moving: that between Absalón and his father, for example, and the final scene of the play. But the material is excessive, the dramatic arrangement imperfect and the tone quite different from that of Acts I and II.

The title of Calderón's play suggests that its unity is to be sought in the person of Absalón. He supplants Amón as protagonist. The reconstruction of *La venganza de Tamar* involved the rejection of the first part of Tirso's play which was concerned almost exclusively with Amón, and contained the greater part of his lines. This major

---

[1] Cotarelo y Mori refers to the adaptation by Godínez, in which the death of Absalom is incorporated: 'Una refundición de esta comedia parece hizo el Doctor Felipe Godínez, a cuyo nombre se publicó: *La Venganza de Tamar. En Sevilla, por Francisco de Leefdaal, en la casa del Correo Viejo*; 4.º, sin año (hacia 1730), 32 páginas con el *Entremés gracioso del Morogueco* (de Benavente), que lleva al fin. Lo más importante de esta refundición es el final, donde el poeta introdujo también la muerte del rebelde Absalón, qué ocurrió mucho después de la del primer hijo de David'. *Comedias de Tirso de Molina*, II (Madrid, 1907), pp. XLb - XLIa. Godínez's play, which I have consulted in the Bibliothèque Nationale, is largely a cut and defective copy of *La Venganza*, with some additional lines. But Godínez rewrote the last scene: Absalón escapes after killing Amón, David enters swearing revenge, and Joab bring news of Absalón's death. The 'discovery' then reveals, on one side Amón dead upon a table, on the other Absalón hanging by his hair.

omission removed much of Amón's part and scarcely affected that of Absalón. And a whole new act concerned primarily with Absalón follows after Amón's death. Absalón's part in the new play was expanded mainly at the expense of that of Amón. At the same time, Calderón conceived his material in terms of the quality which Absalón personifies, ambition. At the beginning of Act I exchanges between Absalón and Tamar reveal Absalón's designs upon the crown, and before the act ends Teuca prophesies his violent and untimely death. Act II, reproduced from Tirso's play, contains the famous scene in which Absalón fits the crown upon his head, and shows the revenge of Tamar as a means of removing the heir apparent. Act III rounds off the story. Absalón is now led to revolt against his own father, and tragedy overtakes him. His death is the punishment of unbridled ambition. Such is the new completeness of Calderón's play presented in terms of Absalón. Amón's stature is correspondingly reduced. Tirso's careful study of the circumstances which led him to incest were dispensed with, and when Calderón's play opens Amón is already a victim of his passion. Even so, it is still Amón's incestuous love for Tamar that compels our interest. The reason, I suspect, is quite simply that Amón is necessarily the more sympathetic of the two characters. Both are bad in that they pursue ends—in the one case pleasure and the other power—by means that are illicit. Both offend against the natural law and commit offences that are punishable. But Amón's is a sin of the flesh, Absalón's of the spirit. Amón is overtaken by a passion which blinds him and deprives him of his will; Absalón is clear-sighted and calculating. So Amón is the object of sympathy, Absalón of scorn. To this extent Calderón's reorientation, for all the drastic structural change, is only in part effective. If Absalón's ambition detracts from the dramatic force of Tirso's *La venganza de Tamar*, Amón's incestuous love detracts from that of Calderón's *Los cabellos de Absalón*.

It is, however, David who dominates *Los cabellos de Absalón* and to a less extent *La venganza de Tamar*. He it is, with the quality which he represents, who gives Calderón's play the degree of unity which it possesses. When in Act III Teuca comes to persuade him to pardon Absalón she argues that justice should be tempered by prudence, and David observes:

> pues cosa es cierta
> que hace más el que perdona
> su dolor, que el que se venga.   (947b)

Later when Jerusalem falls to Absalón, and David is obliged to flee to the mountains, he asks that Absalón, for all his conspiracy, shall be forgiven:

> ¡Ay Absalón, hijo querido mío,
> cómo procedes mal aconsejado!
> No lloro padecer tu error impío,
> mas lloro que no seas castigado
> de Dios; a él estas lágrimas envío
> en nombre tuyo, porque perdonado
> quedes de la ambición que a esto te indujo.   (956b)

and orders his supporters to spare his life.

> Pues que mi honor te fío,
> advierte que Absalón es hijo mío:
> guárdame su persona; no el despecho
> de la gente matármele pretenda,
> que es todo el corazón de aqueste pecho
> destos ojos la más amada prenda.
> Mírame tú por él, porque sospecho
> que moriré si hay alguien que le ofenda.   (957b-958a)

David's mercy towards Absalón has been anticipated by his pardon of Amón in Act II. Both Amón and Absalón are murdered against the express orders of David, whose love for his sons outweighs the crimes of incest and rebellion. David himself has sinned, and his sin significantly is that of Amón, though in his case it led not to incest but to homicide. Yet God in his mercy has forgiven him, as he forgives Amón:

> Adulterio y homicidio
> siendo tal, me perdonó
> el justo Juez, porque dije
> un pequé de corazón.
> Venció en Él a la justicia
> la piedad; su imagen soy:
> el castigo es mano izquierda,
> mano derecha el perdón,
> pues ser izquierdo es defecto...   (939b)

Earlier in the play he had urged his children to be merciful:

> Con esto
> que aprendáis a ser piadosos,
> hijos míos, os advierto... (933a)

David is a truly tragic figure who moves our sympathies; the humanity of Tirso's portrayal has been caught and even enhanced by Calderón. It is David too who exemplifies the positive aspect of the play. If passion and ambition are punished, mercy is commended. In this respect, *Los cabellos de Absalón* is related to *Las armas de la hermosura*, with which it shows resemblances of language:

Los cabellos de Absalón.

TEUCA.   que es grande Dios el que sabe
          medir castigos y premios. (959b)

Las armas de la hermosura.

RELATOR.   "¡Viva Senado que sabe
          unir castigos y premios." (602a)

The role of Tamar is similar in the two plays, but as with Amón Calderón sacrifices much of Tirso's fine character study. He dispensed with the details of Tirso's Act I which contributed so much to the earlier portrait of Tamar, in particular the warmth and tenderness which are made to contrast with her later severity and insistence upon revenge. It is this latter side of Tamar which is to the fore in Calderón's new Act III. Tamar, who was privy to Absalón's designs on the crown, now supports his conspiracy against David; and at his death, though recognizing that he has brought his fate upon himself, mourns him and retires from the world in despair. Calderón scarcely extends the parts of either Adonías or Salomón, though both are made to defend their father against Absalón. Salomón, 'prudente', reveals to Absalón his folly, and Teuca hints at his auspicious future; for Adonías, on the other hand, she predicts a violent death. Calderón's recasting entailed also changes in the minor characters. His new Act III required the widow of Tekoah, the two counsellors of Absalom, Ahitophel and Cusai, and Shimei who cursed and stoned David. Teuca, as we have seen, takes over the rôle of Tirso's Laureta. Calderón dispensed with the three wives of David, who could serve no useful purpose in his play, and with Tamar's servant Diana, though not with Eliacer. The part of Jonadab, the evil adviser of Amón, is extended and, though sentenced to death in Act III, he is reprieved. Aquitofel, on the other hand, the confidant of Absalón, whose imprudence is shown from the play's first scene, dies by his own hand. Joab is no longer Tamar's lover but he assumes greater importance with Calderón's extension. Throughout the play he is associated with Salomón and is a loyal supporter of David against the treachery of Absalón; and though it is predicted that his disobedience and vengeance, like the curses of Semel, will be punished by death, he is pardoned by David.

Some of the characters of Los cabellos de Absalón, in particular Absalón and Amón, are typically Calderonian in so far as they are shown to be responsible for the disasters which overtake them. Yet the play as a whole lacks the familiar pattern of Calderón's best work. The Biblical story itself, perhaps too revered to admit of drastic changes, was refractory. The characters of Adonías and Salomón are unsatisfactory, for although Teuca predicts a violent death for the one and happiness for the other, they are given only minor parts and little is made of the contrast between their conduct. Even Tamar, with her essential rôle in the story, is enigmatic, enlisting our sympathy when assaulted by Amón and then forfeiting it by her support for Absalón in his rebellion against David. By dispensing with Tirso's first act, moreover, Calderón leaves Amón's passion for Tamar unmotivated and unexplained. But it is in respect of David himself that the Biblical material was most unyielding.

Amón's incest and murder, and Absalón's conspiracy and death, are two different, though related, stories. David alone and the theme of forgiveness could have given unity to the play, and this was perhaps Calderón's intention since he includes a number of passages commending forgiveness. But the story itself, far from illustrating the efficacy of mercy, would seem to prove its futility and folly. David pardons Amón but only that he may be brutally murdered by Absalón, and his pardon of Absalón leads to civil war and Absalón's death at the hands of Joab. David then pardons Joab, but a violent death is predicted for him. At the beginning of the play David is shown as having dealt terrible vengeance upon the Ammonites at Rabbah:

> A Rábata, murada y guarnecida
> ciudad del fiero Amón, dejo vencida,
> sus muros excelentes
> demolidos, sus torres eminentes
> deshechas y postradas,
> y sus calles en púrpura bañadas.   (926a)

and he claims that it is because of his bloodstained hands that he is forbidden to build God's temple:

> pues el gran Dios no permite
> que yo fabrique su templo,
> porque manchadas las manos
> de sangre idólatra tengo.   (933a)

Yet his forgiveness of his sons leads only to murder and violence. Unlike *Las armas de la hermosura*, therefore, where the mercy of Coriolano brings peace and joy to Rome, *Los cabellos de Absalón* must end—assuming fidelity at least to the main outline of the Biblical story—with war and confusion.

Act I of *Los cabellos de Absalón*, the only one which permits of a detailed comparative study, provides a particularly fine illustration of Calderón's recasting within narrow limits; since in his second act he takes over Act III of *La venganza de Tamar* complete he is obliged to carry the action forward to precisely the same point and present it in such a way that Tirso's work will harmonize with it. Calderón's aim, therefore, conforms closely to Tirso's; and all the scenes except one have their exact counterpart in *La venganza de Tamar*. Yet not so much as a single line of Tirso's has been borrowed. Details of handling testify to the diligence with which Calderón was rewriting and to his superior craftmanship. In *La venganza de Tamar*, for example, Amón invents the story of a love-affair with an Ammonite who has been killed at Rabbah, and asks Tamar to mitigate his grief by taking her part. Calderón includes the same request but without the Ammonite story. Instead, he brings the dialogue round to the point where Amón addresses Tamar as his beloved. For the termination of the love-game, whereas in *La venganza de Tamar* Tamar, to dispel the suspicions of Joab, is obliged to repeat what the audience already knows, in Calderón it is the overplaying of the game which brings it to an end. One may compare too the handling of Amón's interview with David. Tirso, it would seem, gave little thought to the scene: David is sent for, Amón bluntly makes his request for Tamar to tend him and it is readily granted. Calderón, on the other hand, provided a motive for David's return and anticipated it in an earlier scene:

> (Ap. Por volver
> a hablarle a solas, lo otorgo;
> que quizá no se declara
> por estar delante todos.)   (927b)

David, therefore, enters unsummoned, and the conversation between the two is so arranged that Amón's request seems not only reasonable but natural. At the same time, as Miss McClelland has observed, Calderón uses the scene to elaborate upon the humanity of Tirso's David. [1] Once again, we find Calderón surpassing the source dramatist in poignancy and human feeling.

The two acts provide interesting material for a comparative study of the language of Tirso and Calderón. The very first scene in which David, accompanied by his general Joab, returns to Jerusalem after his victory at Rabbah typifies Calderón's transformation of his source material. Tirso begins with some eighty lines of high-sounding octaves in which David describes the successful assault on Rabbah and then formally greets those who have come to welcome him. They include all his household except Amón: his wives, Micol, Abigail and Bersabé, and his children Tamar, Absalón and Adonías. The three wives have no part of importance in the action of the play, yet it is to them that David devotes much of his speech. The subsequent exchanges, in contrast to the long discourse, have all the apparent spontaneity, capriciousness and triviality of ordinary conversation. The scene, unfortunately, is too long to quote. Contrast the style of Calderón:

SALOMÓN. Vuelva felicemente,
de laurel coronado la alta frente,
el campeón israelita,
azote del sacrílego moabita.

ADONÍAS. Ciña su blanca nieve
de la rama inmortal círculo breve
al defensor de Dios y su ley pía,
horror de la gentil idolatría.

---

[1] I. L. McClelland, op. cit., 179-82.

ABSALÓN. Himnos la fama cante
con labio de metal, voz de diamante,
de Jehová al real caudillo,
de Filistín al trágico cuchillo.

TAMAR. Hoy de Jerusalén las hijas bellas,
coronadas de flores y de estrellas,
entonan otra vez con mayor gloria
del Goliat segundo la victoria.

DAVID. Queridas prendas mías,
báculos vivos de mis luengos días,
dadme todos los brazos.
Renuévese mi edad entre los lazos
de dichas tan amadas.
¡Ay dulces prendas, por mi bien halladas!
Adonías valiente,
llega, llega otra vez. Y tú, prudente
Salomón, otra vez toca mi pecho,
en amorosas lágrimas deshecho.
Bellísimo Absalón, vuelve mil veces
a repetirme el gusto que me ofreces
en tan alegre día.
Y tú no te retires, Tamar mía;
que he dejado el postrero
tu brazo, ¡ay mi Tamar!, porque no quiero
que el corazón en gloria tan precisa,
viendo que otro le espera, me dé prisa.
A Rábata, murada y guarnecida
ciudad del fiero Amón, dejo vencida,
sus muros excelentes
demolidos, sus torres eminentes
deshechas y postradas
y sus calles en púrpura bañadas:
gracias primeramente
al gran Dios de Israel, luego al valiente
Joab, general mío,
de cuyo esfuerzo mis aplausos fío.   (925b-926a)

The octaves of Tirso's scene and the informal exchanges which
follow it have been replaced by a passage which is balanced,
symmetrical and stylized. On the one side David; on the other his
four children. The latter speak first, each with four lines of *silva*,
each with telling phrases and images which epitomize their father's
glorious past. David then replies: first a formal greeting, then a
word for each of his children, and finally a brief account of his
triumph at Rabbah. One notes too the remarkable economy of
Calderón's writing. The three wives have gone, allowing him to
concentrate upon the four children, all of whom are prominent in

the later action. At the same time, the attack upon Rabbah which Tirso described at some length both in David's opening speech and in his remarks about Joab is dealt with in six lines. The single-mindedness of Calderón in admitting only what was relevant to the theme and story he was dramatizing contrasts sharply with the discursiveness of Tirso. Calderón incidentally excised here the reference to the Ammonite crown which, according to the Biblical narrative, David won at Rabbah—a reference which might have lessened, and certainly did not enhance, the effect of the later situation in which Absalón tries on his father's crown. And the echo of Garcilaso's famous sonnet serves to foreshadow the play's ending when death will have robbed David of two of his sons.

In the following scene David goes to visit Amón; I quote both dramatists at length:

La venganza de Tamar.

AMÓN. — *Dichos*

DAVID. ¿Qué es esto, amado heredero?
Cuando tu padre dilata
reinos que ganarte trata
por ser tú el hijo primero,
¡dejándote consumir
de tus imaginaciones,
luto al triunfo alegre pones,
que me sale á recebir!
Diviértante los despojos
que toda tu corte ha visto:
todo un reino te conquisto:
alza á mirarme los ojos.
Llega á enlazar á mi cuello
los brazos: tu gusto admita
esta corona que imita
el oro de tu cabello.
Hijo, ¿no quieres hablarme?
Alza la triste cabeza,
si ya con esa tristeza
no pretendes acabarme.

ABSALÓN. Hermano, la cortesía
¿cuándo no tuvo lugar
en vuestro pecho, a pesar
de cualquier melancolía?
Mirad que el Rey, mi señor
y padre, hablando os está.

ADONÍAS. Si Adonías causa da
a conservar el amor
que en vos mostró la experiencia,

por él os ruego que habléis
a un monarca que tenéis
llorando en vuestra presencia.

SALOMÓN. No agüéis tan alegre día.

TODOS. ¡Ah Príncipe!, volvé en vos.

DAVID. ¡Amón!

AMÓN. (*Alza la cabeza muy triste.*)
        ¡Oh! ¡Válgame Dios!
¡Qué impertinente porfía!

DAVID. ¿Qué tienes, caro traslado
de este triste original?
que en alivio de tu mal
de todo el hebreo estado
la mitad darte prometo.
Gózale y no estés ansí:
pon esos ojos en mí,
de todo mi gusto objeto.
No se oscurezca el Apolo
de tu cara: el mal despide.
¿Qué quieres? Háblame, pide.

AMÓN. Que os vais y me dejéis solo.

DAVID. Si en eso tu gusto estriba,
no te quiero dar pesar;
tu tristeza ha de causar
que yo sin consuelo viva.
Aguado has el regocijo
con que Israel se señala;
pero ¿qué contento iguala
al dolor que causa un hijo?
¡Qué! ¿No mereciera yo,
aunque fingiéndolo fuera,
una palabra siquiera
de amor? Dirásme que no.
Príncipe, ¡un mirarme solo!
Crüel con mis canas eres.
¿Qué has? ¿Qué sientes? ¿Qué quieres?

AMÓN. Que os vais y me dejéis solo.

ABSALÓN. El dejarlo es lo más cuerdo,
pues persuadirle es en vano.

DAVID. ¿Qué vale el reino que gano,
hijos, si al príncipe pierdo?   (409b-c)

Los cabellos de Absalón.

Salen DAVID, ADONÍAS, ABSALÓN, SALOMÓN, TAMAR, JOAB
        y AQUITOFEL.

ABSALÓN. Éste es de Amón el cuarto;
        [ya has llegado
más del afecto que del pie guiado.

DAVID.   Abrid aquesta puerta.

(Ábrenla, y se ve a AMÓN *sentado en una silla, arrima-
do a un bufete, y de la otra parte* JONADAB.

JOAB.   Ya, señor, está abierta,
y al resplandor escaso que por ella
nos comunica la mayor estrella,
al príncipe se mira
sentado en una silla.

TAMAR.   ¿A quién no admira
verle tan divertido
en sus penas, que aun no nos ha sentido?

DAVID.   ¡Amón!

AMÓN.   ¿Quién me llama?

DAVID.   Yo.

AMÓN.   ¡Señor!, pues ¿tú aquí?

DAVID.   ¿Tan poco
gusto te deben mis dichas,
mi amor afecto tan corto,
que aun no llegas a mis brazos?
pues yo, aunque tú riguroso
me recibas, llegaré,
hijo, a los tuyos. Pues ¿cómo,
empezando en mí el cariño,
aun no obra en ti el alborozo?
¿Qué tienes, Amón? ¿Qué es esto?
Que aunque tus tristezas oigo,
pensé que al verme templaras
de su violencia el enojo.
¿Aun parabién no me das,
cuando vuelvo victorioso
a Jerusalén? Mis triunfos
¿aun no vencen tus enojos?
Un príncipe que heredero
es de Israel, cuyo heroico
valor resistir debiera
constante, osado y brioso
los ceños de la fortuna
y del hado los oprobios,
¿tanto a una pasión se rinde,
tanto a una pena, que absorto,
confuso, triste, afligido,
no les permite a sus ojos
la luz del día, negando
la entrada a sus rayos de oro?
¿Qué es esto, Amón? Si de causa
nace tu pena, no ignoro
que podré vencerla yo:
tuyo es mi imperio todo,
dispón dél a tu albedrío,
desde un polo al otro polo.

Y si no nace de causa
conocida, sino sólo
de la natural pensión
deste nuestro humano polvo,
aliéntate: imperio tiene
el hombre sobre sí propio,
y los esfuerzos humanos,
llamado uno, vienen todos.
No te rindas a ti mismo,
no te avasalles medroso
a tu misma condición:
mira que el pesar es monstruo
que come vidas humanas
alimentadas del ocio.
Sal deste cuarto, y pues vienen
a él tus hermanos todos
hoy conmigo, habla con ellos.
Llegad, pues, llegad vosotros,
ya que las ternezas mías
pueden con Amón tan poco.

ADONÍAS.   Príncipe...

ABSALÓN.   Hermano...

SALOMÓN.   Señor...

TAMAR.   Amón...

AMÓN.   (Ap.)   A esta voz respondo.

TAMAR.   ¿Qué tienes?

SALOMÓN.   ¿Qué sientes?

ABSALÓN.   ¿Qué
te aflige?

ADONÍAS.   ¿Qué te da asombro?

DAVID.   ¿Qué apeteces?

TODOS.   ¿Qué deseas?

AMÓN.   Sólo que me dejéis solo.

DAVID.   Si en eso no más estriban
tus deseos rigurosos
vamos de aquí. (Ap. Por volver
a hablarle a solas, lo otorgo;
que quizá no se declara
por estar delante todos.)
Venid. Ya solo te quedas.
¡Ay infeliz, qué de gozos,
qué de gustos, qué de dichas
desazona un pesar solo!   (927a-b)

Tirso's writing is extraordinarily effective in its simplicity: the tender pleading of a father to a dejected son, Amón's stubborn silence until the sharp call from his father, his bitter retort, another appeal, his blunt demand to be left alone, a final appeal and a repetition of the demand. Some of the poignancy of Tirso's scene is sacrificed to casuistry in *Los cabellos*. Characteristic of Calderón is the logical reasoning. 'Either the cause of your sadness is known or unknown. If known... if unknown...'[1] And David interlards his pleadings with some gentle philosophizing: a prince should accept the frowns of fortune, man has authority over himself, sadness is a monster whose sustenance is idleness. Tirso's David pleads with tears, Calderón's more coolly rationalizes. But Calderón does not lose sight of the human David who admits in an aside that he will return to visit Amón alone. The association of Amón's moral blindness with darkness is new, and David's reminder of man's authority over himself is, as we have seen, relevant to the subsequent experiences of both Amón and Absalón.

The whole act offers material for a detailed comparison of style which cannot be undertaken here. Against the simple directness, for example, of Tirso's language in the scene in which Tamar first visits Amón, can be set the ingenious arguments of Calderón's scene. There is ingenuity also in Tirso's writing but it expresses itself most often in word-play. Amón, mortally sick from his love for Tamar, forces a parallel between their two names:

> AMÓN. ...en tu nombre y en el mío
> hermana, mi mal consiste.
> ¿No te llamas tú Tamar?
>
> TAMAR. Ese apellido heredé.
>
> AMÓN. Quítale al Tamar la T,
> y dirá *Tamar*...
>
> TAMAR.   *Amar*.
>
> AMÓN. Ese es mi mal. Yo me llamo
> Amón; quítale la N.
>
> TAMAR. Serás *amo*.
>
> AMÓN.   Porque pene,
> mi mal es amar: yo amo.
> Si esto adviertes, ¿qué preguntas?
> ¡Ay, bellísima Tamar!
> Amo, y es mi mal amar,
> Si á mi nombre el tuyo juntas.   (410a)

[1] For Calderón's casuistry, see J. M. de Cossío, 'Racionalismo del arte dramático de Calderón', *CR*, XXI (1934), 39-70 and E. W. Hesse, 'La dialéctica y el casuismo en Calderón', *Est*, IX (1953).

Calderón's ingenuity, on the other hand, manifested itself rather in skilful and subtle argument. Thus, in the conversation between Amón and Tamar, Amón is made to reveal to the audience, but conceal from Tamar, that she is the object of his love. In the violent scene with which the act ends, Tirso is grimly direct. Amón, desperate now, shows no trace of tenderness; he dismisses his servants and bluntly declares his intentions. Tamar appeals to him in vain; her feeble protests are as firmly and finally overpowered as the two or three syllables beginning a line are interrupted and capped by the five or six which end it:

AMÓN.	Ansí te amo.
TAMAR.	*(Retirándose.)* Sosiega...
AMÓN.	No hay sosegar.
TAMAR.	¿Qué quieres?
AMÓN.	Tamar, amar.
TAMAR.	Detente.
AMÓN.	Soy, Amón, amo.
TAMAR.	¿Si llamo al Rey?
AMÓN.	A amor llamo.
TAMAR.	¡A tu hermana!
AMÓN.	Amores gusto.
TAMAR.	¡Traidor!
AMÓN.	No hay amor injusto.
TAMAR.	Tu ley...
AMÓN.	Para amor no hay ley.
TAMAR.	Tu rey...
AMÓN.	Amor es mi rey.
TAMAR.	Tu honor...
AMÓN.	Mi honor es mi gusto. (413a-b)

Calderón has tempered the brutality of Tirso's scene. When Tamar enters, Amón is restrained. He tells her quietly that she herself, rather than food or music, can distract him and, when she reminds him that the love-game is over, Amón to the strains of music confesses tenderly and pitifully that he is in love with her. A musician answers Tamar's call for help, but Amón dismisses him. Tamar strives to defend herself and wounds Amón with his own sword before the scene ends. Calderón toned down the violence of *La venganza de Tamar,* and by means of the wounding of Amón incorporates a foreboding of his death.

Tirso's language is often subtle and difficult; but the second act of *La venganza de Tamar,* like the first, is above all the study of a person who comes alive by the naturalness and the truth of the dialogue. This is the key, I think, to the deeply human, tragic force of Tirso's act, and to his play as a whole. Calderón's language is more stylized. It is at once formal, more economical and more ingenious than Tirso's, just as there is more attention to shape, more economy and more ingenuity in the handling of the action. Yet Calderón succeeded in preserving the deeply human appeal of Tirso's play, and at times in enhancing it.

As in *El médico de su honra* and *Las armas de la hermosura,* Calderón seems deliberately to have avoided Tirso's stanza-forms, as the following table shows:

La venganza de Tamar, Act II	*Los cabellos de Absalón, Act I*
redondilla (song)	—
octava	silva 4
redondilla	romance O-O
soneto	décima
redondilla	romance E-O
soneto	—
redondilla (song)	
—	romance E-O (song)
décima	romance E-O (song)

The *décima*, the only form common to the two acts, is not used in the same place. Calderón introduced no novelties of staging. It is interesting to note that, although he interpolated a whole new scene in this act, he maintained continuity of action. Immediately before the ships from Tyre are announced, Amón leaves with Jonadab, but David remains on stage—or can do so—and, hearing the clarion, asks:

> ¿Qué nueva salva es aquésta...?   (932b)

and we are carried straight into the new scene. The end of Calderón's interpolation is similarly interlocked with the main action. Instruments are played off-stage, and Absalón explains to Aquitofel that this is music to cheer Amón. The interval between their leaving the stage and the entrance of Jonadab and Amón is bridged by the musician's song. No one character remains on stage throughout Calderón's act, but he interlinks the various phases of the action; there is no instance of a cleared stage. In both acts Amón is 'discovered' in the inner stage; and, although Calderón includes in the text a reference to a door:

> ABSALÓN. Este es de Amón el cuarto; ya has llegado
> más del afecto que del pie guiado.
> DAVID. Abrid aquesta puerta.

the fact that Joab is made to explain:

> Ya, señor, está abierta. (927a)

suggests that it was simply the usual curtain. The stage direction
of the earliest extant text, that of Vera Tassis, reads:

> *Corriendo una cortina, se descubre Amón...*

The inner stage is used for the two 'discoveries' of Act II—the
work of Tirso—and for the two new 'discoveries' which Calderón
supplied in Act III.

Tirso had recourse to music in *La venganza de Tamar,* particularly in the first scene of his second act in which musicians come
to divert Amón; but since *Los cabellos de Absalón* begins only after
this point, it contains no parallel scene. Calderón, however, uses
music for a very different purpose in the final scene of his first act.
Musicians accompany Tamar as she comes to Amón's room and
their song discloses that love is the cause of his malady. Later a
musician answers Tamar's call for help, but Amón passes it off as
a request for more music and this drowns her further cries:

> AMÓN. Tu voz ya no es de provecho,
> con esa dulce armonía.
> TAMAR. Pues daré voces al cielo. (935b)

The rôle of music is here in striking contrast to that of, say, the
first scene of *Las armas de la hermosura.* There two choruses echoed
the reciprocated love of Veturia and Coriolano; here, by drowning
the cries of Tamar, the musicians favour the incestuous lust of Amón.
This is an example of what, for Calderón, was false music which,
however beguiling, is of the Devil. He contrasts it with true music
which revealed God to man:

> aquella [armonía]
> que áspid del aire en flores escondido,
> la fragancia que envía
> hubo quien dijo della
> que era un hermoso estiércol del oído. [1]

---

[1] Sage, op. cit., 284.

A comparison of *Los cabellos de Absalón* with its source shows the precise contribution of Calderón and at the same time sets into relief its greatness and its shortcomings. Act I is a model of recasting and an example of Calderón's best work; but the appropriation of an act of Tirso for Act II, and the imperfect, if vigorous, dramatization of the Biblical narrative for Act III, suggest that Calderón lost interest in the play. One can only surmise the reason for this. If, as Valbuena has suggested, Calderón found the subject repulsive he can hardly have been blind to its implications when he began his play, and he survived the experience of re-writing one of the most troublesome scenes. Perhaps he found his material unwieldy and realized that it could not be moulded into a unified play; yet again these difficulties must have been clear from the start. Only a lack of interest, probably after work on it had begun, can account, in my opinion, for the unsatisfactoriness of the play as a whole and for the wholesale appropriation of Tirso's act. It is possible that, in this instance, the recasting of Tirso's play was commissioned by a stage manager and Calderón may even have been asked only for a third act in order to round off the story of Absalón and a first to compress in a single act the first two acts of Tirso. The subject was one of immediate appeal, yet Tirso's *La venganza de Tamar* was so obviously incomplete. The new play, in other words, may have been conceived from the start as the combined effort of two dramatists, and not unnaturally Calderón would have been less interested in it than in a play of his own. Or, if the reason for the commission was that a play was required at short notice, Calderón would have been writing against time, and he may have been obliged to take over Tirso's act in order to comply with the conditions of his contract. This would account for the apparent loss of interest after Act I. *Los cabellos de Absalón* contains some excellent scenes and some fine poetry; and, as Shelley, Schack and others have remarked, David is one of the most human and tragic of his characters. But it lacks the unity and the attention to detail of his best work.

V

EL MAYOR ENCANTO AMOR[1]

El mayor encanto amor is a mythological play and concerns the encounter of Ulysses with Circe. It was first performed in 1635. Most of Calderón's mythological plays were written after he was ordained a priest in 1651. They were intended, amongst other things, as fine spectacle, and were often commissioned for royal performances in the open air theatre of the gardens of the Buen Retiro. Music and song were an essential part of these plays, and in time Calderón evolved the musical and semi-musical *zarzuela*. But spectacle was by no means all that the mythological play offered. Since the time of the Stoics the ancient myths had been interpreted allegorically. M. Seznec, in *La survivance des dieux antiques* (The Warburg Institute, London, 1940) has shown how their moral and allegorical interpretation was the means by which the pagan world of the ancients could be reconciled with the Christian world of the Middle Ages. This, naturally enough, was the interpretation which particularly commended itself to Counter-Reformist Spain. Jupiter, for example, symbolized God, Pluto Lucifer and Pan Christ. The Circe episode in the story of Ulysses was no exception. Erasmus, after claiming in the *Enchiridion* that:

> Immo fortasse plusculo fructu legetur fabula poetica allegoria, quam narratio sacrorum librorum, si consistas in cortice (Seznec, op. cit., p. 90).

cites the story of Circe as one of his examples.

Pérez de Moya who, like Fray Baltasar de Victoria, published a Spanish mythography after the manner of the famous Italian manuals of Boccaccio, Gyraldi, Comes and Cartari, gave his *Philosophia*

---

[1] Texts used:
                    Polifemo y Circe.
                        Ed. J. E. Hartzenbusch, BAE, XIV, 413-28.
                    El mayor encanto amor.
                        Segunda parte, 1637, QC, Q.
                        Ed. Vera Tassis, II, 1682.
                        Ed. J. J. Keil, I, 282-306.
                        Ed. J. E. Hartzenbusch, BAE, VII, 385-410.
Quotations are from the BAE editions.

secreta (Madrid, 1585) the sub-title 'Donde debajo de historias fabulosas se contiene mucha doctrina provechosa a todos estudios, con el origen de los ídolos o dioses de la gentilidad', and devoted Book V to 'fábulas para exhortar a los hombres huir de los vicios y seguir la virtud' and Book VII to 'fábulas para persuadir al hombre al temor de Dios, y a que tenga cuenta con la que ha de dar de su vida, pues según esta fuere, así recibirá el galardón.' His interpretation of the Ulises/Circe episode is the following:

> Circe es aquella pasión natural que llaman amor deshonesto, que las más veces transforma a los más sabios y de mayor juicio en animales fierísimos y llenos de furor, y algunas veces los vuelve más insensibles que piedras, acerca de la honra y reputación que conservaban con tanta diligencia antes que se dejasen cegar desta fierísima pasión. Y porque el que mucho se deleita de holgarse con las comunes y sucias mujeres, es comparado al puerco, por esto fingieron los sabios haber Circe convertido los compañeros de Ulises en estos animales. Con ninguno otro se dice haber tenido que ver Circe, sino con Ulises. Por Ulises se entiende la parte de nuestra ánima que participa de la razón. Circe es la naturaleza. Los compañeros de Ulises son las potencias del alma, que conspiran con los afectos del cuerpo y no obedecen a la razón. La naturaleza, pues, es el apetecer las cosas no legítimas, y la buena ley es detenimiento y freno del ingenio depravado. Mas la razón, entendida por Ulises, permanece firme sin ser vencida, contra estos halagos del apetito.
>
> [Ed. E. Gómez de Baquero (Madrid, 1928), II, 219].

The even more popular compilation of Fray Baltasar de Victoria, *Teatro de los dioses de la gentilidad,* appeared with a preface by Lope de Vega (dated Madrid 1619) in which he too called particular attention to the allegorical interpretation of myths and to the philosophy which underlies them. Of Ulysses, Baltasar de Victoria writes:

> Andando Ulises por sus navegaciones, aportó al promontorio Circeo, y todo lo que se dice de haber ella convertido sus compañeros en bestias fieras, es teología mitológica, como lo da a entender San Agustín.
>
> [Ed. Barcelona, 1702, I, 638].

Cervantes saw in Homer's portrait of Ulysses "un retrato vivo de prudencia y de sufrimiento" *(Don Quixote,* I, xxv), and Gracián regarded the *Odyssey* as "la peregrinación de nuestra vida por entre Scilas y Caribdis, Circes, Cíclopes y Sirenas de los vicios" *(Agudeza y arte de ingenio,* LVI).

For Calderón, as for his compatriot Gracián, the voyages of Ulysses symbolized the journey of life, and his encounter with Circe

9

the human conflict between duty and passion, between reason and lust. In the *auto Los encantos de la culpa* Calderón interprets the story theologically: Ulysses is Man, Circe Guilt and Antistes Understanding. Unlike the *auto*, the play presents the story in human terms. Yet, even here, though Calderón has no intention of making his characters abstractions, Ulysses is Everyman, and his temporary submission to Circe the victory of passion over reason. It is this human conflict which gives unity to the play. The spectacle, music and poetry of the mythological plays in general, and of *El mayor encanto amor* in particular, have blinded critics until recently to their serious and significant themes. Schack commends above all their poetry, and his comments on *El mayor encanto amor* are sympathetic but somnolent:

> Así como los compañeros de Ulises se encuentran encadenados por la belleza de Circe, y por su isla, semejante al Paraíso, así también el lector se siente adormecido por las alas del deleite, creyéndose trasladado a una isla maravillosa, desde la cual ve, en lo profundo, a la mar azulada o a sus riberas encantadas formando graciosas bahías, y a sus suaves colinas, que parecen respirar amor. [1]

Menéndez y Pelayo believed even the poetry, not to mention probability, to have been subordinated to spectacle:

> el poeta queda siempre en grado y en categoría inferior al maquinista y al pintor escenógrafo..., más se atendía al prestigio de los ojos que a la lucha de los afectos y los caracteres, ni a la verdad de la expresión. [2]

Dr. Johnson was no less at fault when he defined the Jacobean Mask, which has so much in common with these mythological plays, as 'a dramatic performance written in a tragic style, without attention to rules or probability.' Valbuena Prat was the first in recent years to lay stress on the allegory of the Ulysses story and to cite the evidence of contemporary mythographers, [3] and he has been followed by Don Eugenio Frutos and W. G. Chapman, who recently published a preliminary study of Calderón's mythological plays. [4] An examination of *El mayor encanto amor* in conjunction with its source-play demonstrates the validity of the new approach.

---

[1] Op. cit., IV, 409-10.
[2] *Calderón y su teatro* (Madrid, 1910), p. 381.
[3] Ed. *Autos sacramentales*, II (Madrid, 1942), lviii ff.
[4] E. Frutos Cortés, *Calderón* (Barcelona, 1949), p. 124 and W. G. Chapman, 'Las comedias mitológicas de Calderón', *RLit*, V (1954), 34-67.

El mayor encanto amor was first printed by Calderón's brother
Don José in the *Segunda parte* in 1637. Two interesting documents
have survived which throw light on the play's conception. The first
is the copy of a manuscript, formerly in the possession of the *Biblioteca Nacional,* in which a play on the subject of Ulysses and
Circe is envisaged. The second is a letter dated 30 April 1635 in
which Calderón criticizes a *memoria* of Cosme Lotti on the grounds
that he is intruding into the sphere of the dramatist. Cotarelo y
Mori assumed that the first document referred to an actual performance of an earlier version of *El mayor encanto amor,* which has
since been lost. [1] But Dr. N. D. Shergold has recently demonstrated
that the document is the very *memoria* of Cosme Lotti against which
Calderón protests in his letter. [2] *El mayor encanto amor* was first
performed on 25 June 1635. Calderón adopted some of Lotti's
suggestions, but he modelled his play on an earlier work of which
he was part-author with Mira de Amescua and Pérez de Montalbán: *Polifemo y Circe.*

Mira de Amescua wrote the first of the three acts of *Polifemo
y Circe,* Pérez de Montalbán the second, and Calderón the third. [3]
The story is that of Ulysses' encounter with Polyphemus and Circe,
told in Homer, *Odyssey,* X and Ovid, *Metamorphoses,* XIV, and
more immediately in Góngora's *Polifemo* (1613) and Lope de Vega's
La Circe (1624). In Act I, the work of Amescua, Ulises disembarks
in Sicily near the palace of Circe. His followers are promptly
transformed into animals, but he is himself protected by magic
flowers sent by Juno. He is vulnerable, however, to the charms of
Circe, and at the end of the act he succumbs to her beauty: deaf to
the alarums of battle he falls asleep in her arms. Montalbán's
second act directs attention to Polifemo and his love for Galatea.
Acis, one of the followers of Ulises, comes to the aid of Galatea,
but Acis is killed and Galatea turned into a nymph. Meanwhile,

---

[1] Cf. Casiano Pellicer, *Tratado histórico sobre el origen y progresos de la comedia y del histrionismo en España* (Madrid, 1804), II, 146, and Cotarelo y Mori, op. cit., p. 165.

[2] Cf. N. D. Shergold, 'The First Performance of Calderón's *El mayor encanto amor*', *BHS,* XXXV (1958), 24-27.

[3] For the text of this play I have had to rely on the BAE edition of Hartzenbusch, who explains: 'Se ha reimpreso esta comedia teniendo a la vista dos manuscritos que el señor Don Agustín Durán nos ha franqueado, con su bondad acostumbrada. La parte segunda de *Comedias de varios autores,* en que fue incluido *El Polifemo,* según aparece del índice de Don Juan Isidro Fajardo, no nos es conocida.' (428, nota.)

in the same Act, Ulises has fallen in love with one of Circe's ladies —because of her resemblance to his wife Penelope— and Circe causes an earthquake to separate the two lovers. Calderón's Act III is concerned with the blinding of Polifemo, and the hasty departure of Ulises from Sicily after Acis has appeared to rebuke him for falling a victim to Circe's beauty. Circe, abandoned by her lover, hurls herself into the sea.

The action of *Polifemo y Circe* is contained within the framework of Ulises' stay in Sicily. The scene opens when Ulises and his followers disembark on the Sicilian shore, and closes when they re-embark. Crowded within these limits are the episodes involving the death of Acis and the transformation of Galatea, the blinding of Polifemo by Ulises and Ulises' love for Circe —three distinct stories for the three dramatists who collaborated, and material enough for three plays. To what extent Calderón participated in the general planning of *Polifemo y Circe* is not known. In *El privilegio de las mujeres* he was the author of the first act, in *Polifemo y Circe* of the third. As the author of Act III, it was his task probably to complete the work of his two collaborators, to round off a plot which they had introduced and developed. The story of Acis and Galatea required the episode of the blinding of Polifemo in Calderón's Act III; and Ulises had to be rescued from the clutches of Circe. It may be that Calderón had little or nothing to say in the matter of the play's construction. That within a few years he wrote another play on the subject on quite different structural lines strongly suggests that his own conception of the story did not coincide with that of his collaborators. In any case, whereas in *Polifemo y Circe* he was accommodating himself to a joint plan, probably the conception of the older Mira de Amescua who led off with Act I, in *El mayor encanto amor* he was the sole author, free to develop his story as he chose.

A glance at *El mayor encanto amor* shows the extent of Calderón's structural changes. To begin with, he discarded some two-thirds of his source material. The action involving Polifemo, Acis and Galatea, which takes up the greater part of Acts II and III of *Polifemo y Circe*, is dismissed in a few lines of his first act, in a speech in which Ulises recounts his life-history to Circe:

> Llegué al pie del Lilibeo,
> ese gigante que opone
> al cielo sus puntas, siendo
> excelsa pira de flores,
> donde fui de Polifemo
> mísero cautivo, y donde
> con su muerte rescaté
> mi vida de sus prisiones,
> el trágico fin vengando
> de Acis, generoso joven,
> y la hermosa Galatea,
> hija de Nereo y Doris,
> que, lágrimas de un peñasco,
> al mar en dos fuentes corren,
> cuando... mas deber no quiero
> tan poco a hazaña tan noble,
> que la desluzca en contarla,
> presumiendo que la ignores...   (393c)

Of the three characters Galatea alone survives, and she only for the sake of a brief appearance at the play's end. Calderón's starting point was evidently Mira de Amescua's final scene in Act I of *Polifemo y Circe*. Here Ulises, victim of Circe's beauty, is obliged to choose openly between the rival claims of love and war. On one side stand Turselino and other Greeks urging their master to follow them away; on the other Circe and her nymphs singing the praises of love. Ulises, wavering at first, turns finally from his fellow Greeks to yield to love. Amescua's source for this situation was probably Books XIV-XVI of Tasso's *Gerusalemme liberata* where Rinaldo falls a victim to the beauty of Armida, until his followers succeed in luring him away; his scene, at all events, recalls the parallel incident in Tasso. Calderón constructed his new play on the basis of this situation, with its underlying conflict between *armas* and *amor*.

The rejection of some two-thirds of his source material in order to limit himself to the single conflict between Ulises and Circe confirms —if confirmation is needed— Calderón's preoccupation with the problem of unity. It points certainly to his fundamental criticism of *Polifemo y Circe*. The series of episodes which the play contained are totally unrelated in theme; they are linked only in so far as Ulises and his followers are involved in them, a tenuous thread which Aristotle had argued to be insufficient for dramatic unity. There had been some attempt, it is true, to tie up the episodes of Polifemo and Circe which are quite distinct in the *Odyssey*: Circe's magic is ready at hand to transport her to the cave of Polifemo, and Acis, the victim of Polifemo, is made responsible for Ulises' escape from Circe. But this was inadequate to give unity to such diverse episodes. And there was an excess of material, if not for three dramatists, for a single play. Calderón confined himself to the conflict between Ulises and Circe, and postponed its outcome until the end of the play. The impressive situation at the end of Act I of *Polifemo y Circe*, showing Ulises turning from his followers to the call of love, is reserved until Act III in *El mayor encanto amor*. The whole action leads up to it. This in itself involved the complete reconstruction of the source-play. Much of Amescua's first act in *Polifemo y Circe* was relevant to Calderón's purpose and could serve as the basis of his own first act: the arrival of Ulises in Sicily, his first meeting with Circe, his surviving her enchantments and acceptance of her hospitality. But, by deferring Ulises' submission to her until Act III, Calderón had to provide material for a whole new act. If in *Los cabellos de Absalón* his problem was to compress the action of the source-play into two acts to leave room for a new Act III, in *El mayor encanto amor* it was the more formidable problem of supplying a new Act II which would allow him in Act III to resume the earlier story.

Calderón's solution was to invent three new characters: Ársidas, Lísidas and Flérida. The most important is Ársidas, Prince of Trinacria, a rival for Circe's love and jealous of the favours shown to Ulises. Ársidas makes his first appearance at the end of Act I to declare his love for Circe and to complain of her disdain. Like Ulises, he is immune from her enchantments, but he now pays the price of such immunity by seeing the favours of Circe bestowed upon Ulises. In Act II there is an argument between the two rival lovers as to whether it is easier to affect a love which you do not feel or to dissemble a love which is true. To settle the argument Circe instructs Ulises to pretend to love her and Ársidas to conceal his love; and at the end of the act she tests their reactions by a false alarm of an attack from an army of Cyclops. Ulises rushes to his weapons, Ársidas to Circe. Each lover subsequently seeks to justify his reactions, and swords are drawn; but Circe stops the battle which ensues between Greeks and Sicilians by plunging the scene into darkness. Ársidas retires to the hills to prepare an armed attack and only appears again at the end of Act III as Circe's prisoner. The other new characters are the lovers Lísidas and Flérida, who have been transformed into trees by Circe for the 'offence' of falling in love. They appear in the play's first scene in a passage contained only in the genuine edition (QC) of the 1637 *Parte*, when Ulises draws his sword against Circe and runs it through the two trees. At the end of Act I, at Ulises' request, they are restored to human form. In Act II Circe confides in Flérida her love for Ulises and asks her to make an assignation with him so that she, Circe, may have an opportunity of conversing with her lover incognito. Flérida unfortunately is over-demonstrative in her feigned love and arouses the suspicions of her lover Lísidas, who retreats in high dudgeon to the mountains. Later, Lísidas joins forces with Ársidas and is taken prisoner by Circe. By means of Ársidas, Lísidas and Flérida and new scenes with Ulises and Circe, Calderón provided material enough for a new Act II. With Act III he could revert to the source-play, showing first Ulises' total submission to Circe and later his escape, after being reprimanded by the shade of Achilles.

The correspondence between the characters of the two plays is the following:

Polifemo y Circe.	*El mayor encanto amor.*
Ulises	Ulises
Turselino	Antistes
Chitón	Clarín
—	Lebrel
—	Arquelao
—	Polidoro
—	Timantes
—	Floro
Circe	Circe
Irene	Sirene
Tisbe	Tisbe
—	Casandra
—	Astrea
—	Licia
—	Clori
Polifemo	—
Ácis	—
Galatea	Galatea

Cf. Toro y Gisbert, '¿Conocemos el texto verdadero de las comedias de Calderón?', *BRAE*, V (1918), 411-21.

Polifemo y Circe.	El mayor encanto amor.
—	Ársidas
—	Lísidas
—	Flérida
Iris	Iris
—	Aquiles
—	Brutamonte
—	Dueña
—	Enano

Calderón provides some twenty-four characters against the ten of *Polifemo y Circe*; but this is due solely to the multiplication of minor parts and amounts to no more than a few lines in all. In fact, Calderón retained as parts of importance only three of the six main characters of *Polifemo y Circe*, and added another three.

For a large part of Act I Calderón is following closely the pattern of Act I of *Polifemo y Circe*: Ulises aboard ship off the Sicilian coast, the disembarkation near the palace of Circe, the transformation of his followers into animals and his own protection from Circe's enchantment by the flowers sent by Juno. Yet, at the very outset, he points to the fundamental human conflict which underlies the myth. In a speech which has no parallel in *Polifemo y Circe*, Antistes tells Ulises of the discovery of Circe's palace and of his own escape after his friends have been transformed. The speech of Antistes does more than inform us of the fate of his friends; it foreshadows that of Ulises. After relating how his friends were deceived by the beautiful damsels who attended Circe, Antistes comments:

> Mintió el deseo; mas ¿cuándo
> dijo verdad el deseo?   (391c)

and he emphasizes that, if his friends were physically overcome by the poisoned drink, the real poison was beauty. By falling a victim to passion, Ulises will in the same way succumb to the beauty of Circe. Antistes ends by urging his master to flee the island, since only by escaping can he hope to survive:

> ...que en efecto,
> el que se sabe librar
> de los venenos más fieros
> de una hermosura, es quien sólo

niega los labios a ellos.
Esto en fin me ha sucedido,
y vengo a avisarte dello,
porque desta esfinge huyamos...   (392a)

Ulises' disregard of the warning and advice of Antistes is a clear enough hint at what will follow. But Calderón is more specific a few lines later. Iris, the messenger of Juno, explains that the flowers she bears, though effective against the enchantments of Circe, provide no protection against love:

Toca con él sus hechizos,
desvanecéranse luego,
como al amor no te rindas...   (392b)

And when, at this point, Calderón borrows a song from the earlier play, his new reading of the last two lines is perhaps significant:

Polifemo y Circe.	El mayor encanto amor.
En hora dichosa venga	En hora dichosa venga
a los palacios de Circe	a los palacios de Circe
el rayo de los troyanos	el siempre invencible griego
el discreto y fuerte Ulises. (414a)	el nunca vencido Ulises. (392c)

The speech of Antistes, describing the disaster which has befallen his friends, prepares the audience for the scene in which Circe proffers Ulises the poisoned cup. Calderón could therefore dispense with the many asides of the corresponding scene in *Polifemo y Circe* which make the point that the drink is poisonous. In the source also the audience waits for the effects of Circe's nectar upon Ulises; that there are none is proof that the flowers have removed the poison. Calderón provides positive and immediate proof of the effectiveness of the flowers, making a flame issue forth from the goblet. And his long speeches for Ulises and Circe are no mere digressions as in the source. In *Polifemo y Circe*, Circe is able still to prevent Ulises from leaving; in *El mayor encanto amor* she must plead and plot to make him stay. Calderón here includes a reference to Aquiles who in Act III will appear to Ulises to remind him of his heritage and responsibility:

> Heredero de las armas
> de Aquiles fui, porque logren,
> si dueño no tan valiente,
> dueño a lo menos tan noble...   (393b)

Ulises rashly assumes that, having survived the poisonous nectar, he has nothing to fear from Circe, and seeing an opportunity of freeing her many victims, he accepts her invitation to stay awhile as her guest:

> No fuera Ulises, si ya
> que a estos montes he venido,
> la libertad no trajera
> a cuantos aquí cautivos
> tiene el encanto. Hoy seré
> de aquesta Esfinge el Edipo.   (394c)

Like Oedipus, he will ultimately triumph; and like the Sphinx, Circe will destroy herself. But his decision to stay, motivated though it is by his sense of duty, is imprudent, and before his final escape he will be enslaved by passion. Antistes warns him of Circe's guile:

> Señor, no de sus lisonjas
> te creas, porque es fingido
> su halago.   (394c)

and the prophetess Casandra comments in an aside upon his recklessness:

> ¡Ay de ti! porque no sabes
> a lo que te has atrevido.   (394c)

Yet such is his confidence that he will even feign love for Circe in order to achieve his purpose. These unmistakable references to the temerity and indiscretion of Ulises foreshadow later developments.

At this point Calderón shows the release of Lísidas and Flérida, who are required above all for his new Act II. This opens with Circe's confession to Flérida of her love for Ulises, followed immediately by Ulises' admission that he is in love with Circe. Thanks to an ingenious device, however, Calderón makes it possible for both lovers to conceal their feelings. Flérida has been asked by Circe to dissemble her love for Lísidas and to pretend to be in love with Ulises in order that Circe may secretly be able to take her place and talk with Ulises. Later, inspired by her own predicament, Flérida suggests as a topic of discussion the problem of whether it is easier to feign or dissemble, provoking an argument between Ulises and Ársidas. Circe intervenes and requires them to demonstrate in their behaviour towards her the position they hold to be the easier. By this means Calderón is able to keep Ulises and Circe together through much of his second act without either discovering the feelings of the other. At the end of the act Ársidas, who is no longer required by Calderón, is removed to the mountains, and Ulises is left alone with Circe. These events of Calderón's new Act II advance the action and are an integral part of the play's structure. At the same time, the new characters, Ársidas, Lísidas and Flérida, all three involved in affairs of love, are by no means out of place in a play whose central conflict is the love of Ulises for Circe.

Ársidas is a rival of Ulises, and his jealousy and the disdain shown to him by Circe call attention to the favours bestowed on Ulises. Ársidas and Ulises, alone amongst those who have come to the island, are invulnerable to the magic of Circe, and throughout the Act they have parallel parts. Ársidas confesses that he came to Trinacria 'de mis afectos traído'. He is a victim of his passion; and, after vainly seeking to win Circe's love, prepares an armed attack upon her. Even in this he is ineffective and at the play's end he is Circe's prisoner. Ársidas serves as a warning to Ulises; he shows the consequences of succumbing to Circe's charms. But his part in Act II is disproportionate to his importance to the play and to his contribution to the underlying theme; he is all too obviously a stop-gap. Lísidas and Flérida are also lovers, and because they have dared to declare their love for each other they have been transformed into trees. They are restored to human form at the request of Ulises, and his lines:

> Sólo pido
> que estos dos árboles, que hoy
> a lástima me han movido,
> porque fue mi acero causa
> de aumentarles su martirio,
> en pago de aquesto, sean
> a la luz restituidos.   (394c)

refer to the earlier incident, omitted from modern editions, in which, after drawing his sword against Circe, Ulises ran it through the two trees. In Act II Flérida, acting upon the orders of Circe, affects a love for Ulises and incurs the wrath of Lísidas. At the end of the play Lísidas discovers the reason for Flérida's action, and the two lovers are reunited. The fact that Lísidas and Flérida became trees when others became wild beasts is perhaps intended by Calderón to indicate the purity of their love for each other; chastity, like Daphne, was traditionally converted into a tree. It is possible also that they owe something to Acis and Galatea whose love in *Polifemo y Circe* is shown to be chaste and honourable:

GALATEA.	¿Es amor honesto?
ACIS.	Sí: los rayos del sol compite en pureza.
GALATEA.	¿Es grande?
ACIS.	Tanto, que con el cielo se mide.
GALATEA.	¿Serás firme?
ACIS.	Esas montañas no están al cierzo más firmes. (416c)

Calderón seems to have intended the 'amor honesto' of Lísidas and Flérida to be set against the 'amor deshonesto' of Ulises and Circe, but the contrast is little developed.

Considerable space is devoted to the *graciosos* in this second act. Clarín's escapades with the giant Brutamonte were undoubtedly inspired by Chitón's meeting with Polifemo in *Polifemo y Circe*, though there is little resemblance between the two scenes. But, like another Clarín in *La vida es sueño* (written at about the same time), he has more than a comic rôle: his fate is made to symbolize the fate of Ulises himself. From the beginning of the play Clarín has been closely associated with his master. When the Greeks leave to explore the land in the first scene, Clarín remains behind with Ulises, so that only he and Antistes witness the appearance of Iris, and their master's drinking without injury the magic cup of Circe. Clarín, alone with Ulises, remains on stage throughout the first act. In Act II, when Circe overhears him denigrate her, he acts as if Lebrel were responsible, and believing that he has deceived her goes on her instructions to get his reward. The giant Brutamonte produces a box which for Clarín has only a duenna and a dwarf, though Lebrel finds it full of jewels. After his meeting with Brutamonte, Clarín is transformed by Circe into a monkey, and only half-way through Act III, when he happens to look into a mirror, is he restored to human form. Calderón clearly intended a parallel between Clarín and Ulises. Just as Clarín, believing that he has deceived Circe, finds himself deceived, so Ulises confident of defeating Circe is himself defeated. If the effrontery of the servant leads to his being transformed into a monkey, so his master pays for his temerity by being converted into someone who bears no resemblance to his former self. The scene in which Clarín becomes a monkey immediately precedes that in which Ulises, alone with Circe on a hawking expedition, admits defeat by her beauty, and declares his love. Clarín leaves the stage as Ulises enters, and his final words are clearly directed to Ulises:

> ¡Hombres monas!, presto habrá
> Otro más de vuestra especie.   (401c)

We shall see later how the restoration of Clarín forestalls in the same way the recovery of Ulises. New and apparently incidental material is relevant to the main action of Calderón's play.

The final scene of this new Act II is made both to foreshadow and motivate the great scene of Ulises' submission in Act III. Circe's testing of Ulises and Ársidas by the false alarm of an attack from the Cyclops, and her magical intervention to stop the battle which follows, provides good spectacle, inspired probably by the spectacular earthquake at the end of Act II of *Polifemo y Circe*. But what is significant is the manner in which Ulises has reacted to the news of an attack upon Circe. Whatever his motives, at the sound of drums he calls for arms and rushes off to repel the attackers. Later he defends his behaviour by claiming that, far from having deserted Circe, he has for her sake taken up arms to meet the enemy; he was prepared to fight for love. But only Ulises himself knows that his love is real; to the others it is a feigned love imposed by Circe. It is hardly surprising, therefore, that Ulises' friends mistake his reaction as proof of his response to war, and it is this which leads them to adopt the particular ruse in Act III to draw Ulises away from the company of Circe. Antistes there explains:

> Yo pues viéndonos perdidos,
> hoy he pensado una traza
> con que a su olvido le acuerde
> de su honor y de su fama:
> y es, que pues el otro día
> cuando oyó tocar al arma
> se olvidó de amor, y fue
> tras la trompeta y la caja...　(404b)

Calderón has not, I think, succeeded in disguising the fact that much of what happens in Act II is, strictly speaking, superfluous. Not only are the characters of Ársidas, Lísidas and Flérida dispensable as far as the basic story of Ulises and Circe is concerned, but many passages of writing, remarkable in themselves, suggest that he is padding: the subtle and carefully balanced arguments of Ulises and Ársidas, the greater part of Clarín's encounter with Brutamonte, and above all Ulises' description of a heron-hunt in which the elaborate account of falconry in *Casa con dos puertas* is turned into a sustained narrative simile. [1] At least Calderón attempted to integrate his new material into the action of his play, and made it serve a dramatic purpose, to advance the action, to anticipate developments in Act III or to give emphasis to the play's theme. It would seem too that he deliberately linked together the different scenes to give continuity of action. For the first half of the act Circe remains on the stage; only when she is with Ulises is the scene specified:

> CIRCE.　En este hermoso jardín...　(397b)
>
> En esta tejida alfombra...　(397b)

With Brutamonte and Clarín the scene has shifted to the mountains:

> CLARÍN.　Engañada Circe bella
> (que en efecto las mujeres,
> que saben más en el mundo,
> se engañan más fácilmente),
> agradecida me dijo
> que a este monte me viniese...　(399b)

and Hartzenbusch labels the beginning of Clarín's speech 'Monte' to indicate the scene change from the garden. But Calderón has

---

[1] Cf. Sloman, A. E., 'Calderón and falconry: a note on dramatic language', *RPh*, VI (1953), 299-304.

already, without a break in the action, transported his characters to the mountains:

> y así, al bien y al mal atento,
> Flérida, ausentarme intento
> de aqueste monte cruel... (399b)

With Lebrel's entrance Calderón refers again to the location:

> Huyendo vengo a este monte... (400b)

With the arrival of Ulises and Circe on a hawking expedition we are in a 'Sitio apacible':

> CIRCE.   ...he de esperar
> entre estos álamos verdes... (401b)
>
> De la caza cansada,
> a este apacible sitio retirada... (401c)

and the situation is confirmed in lines of Ársidas:

> Siguiéndote, señora, con tu gente
> por la florida margen desta fuente
> vine; que ella pautada de colores,
> las señas de tu pie daba con flores. (402b)

Thus, without an abrupt change of scene, we have moved from the 'monte cruel' to a sheltered glade, the setting of the scene ending. For all the shifting scene the action of Act II is continuous.

In Act III Calderón reverts to the material of the source-play, and his handling can again be compared with that of the earlier dramatists. His first scene corresponds more or less exactly with the last scene of Act I of *Polifemo y Circe*. There Ulises had just made the acquaintance of Circe, and Turselino and other Greeks, seeing him caught up with her charm, call to him to embark, and counter the songs of love by the call to war. Circe wins, and the scene ends with the testing of Ulises' love by feigning to have been transformed into a statue. Calderón greatly extended the scene, in part to make room for a long speech by Antistes to explain his stratagem to lure Ulises away, and to include some exchanges between the *graciosos* Lebrel and Clarín; though his new second act, devoted almost exclusively to Ulises' love, rendered superfluous Circe's test of Ulises' sincerity. His scene, however, has a quite different impact if only because of its new position in the play's structure. Amescua uses the situation to round off a first act; Calderón makes it the climax of a whole play. The Ulises who in *El mayor encanto amor* openly rejects the summons of his followers in order to remain in the embraces of Circe is one who has ignored the counsel of Antistes and the warnings of Juno's messengers and who has dared even to play the part of Circe's lover. The proud, all-conquering warrior, who has inherited the weapons of Aquiles, turns from his arms and admits defeat by love.

Having restricted his play to the Circe/Ulises story, Calderón could elaborate also upon the conflict between reason and passion. Mira de Amescua, it is true, did not fail to pass judgement upon Ulises' behaviour; his submission to Circe was, in Turselino's words, 'infame pasatiempo' and Ulises himself was 'sin valor/o ya encantado o ya preso'. But Acts II and III of *Polifemo y Circe* show both the constancy and the valour of Ulises. He tells Circe of his wife Penelope and makes her jealous by preferring to her one of her maidens, Irene, who reminds him of Penelope; and he sees vengeance done to Polifemo for the deaths of Acis and Galatea. Calderón allowed no place in his play for the Polifemo episode and he omitted all references to Penelope. Ulises' behaviour is represented as unworthy of a man of honour. His mind, like Cipriano's in *El mágico prodigioso*, is clouded by passion, and he is oblivious of his obligations:

> Ulises pues sin recelo,
> sólo de sus gustos trata,
> siempre en los brazos de Circe...   (404a)

Antistes devises a scheme:

> con que a su olvido le acuerde
> de su honor y de su fama...   (404b)

Ulises himself admits:

> No soy sin duda el que fui,
> pues a delicias süaves
> entregado ¡ay de mí! estoy
> y tras los ecos no voy
> más belicosos y graves...   (405c)

By exposing himself to passion and abandoning reason Ulises is but a shadow of his former self; and he has so degraded himself that he is no better than the vicious Circe in whose embraces he lies. Calderón here includes two sonnets in which Ulises and Circe declare their love for each other. Ulises explains how he has been able to resist the enchantments of Circe but not her tears; and Circe admits that, hoping to ensnare Ulises by her physical beauty, she has herself become infatuated by him. Both sonnets end with the line:

> Luego el amor es el mayor encanto.

The lure of passion is the play's subject, and at this point in the action the parallel sonnets link the two victims.

The other important scene of Act III, in which Aquiles appears to Ulises, also derives from the source-play. Between them Calderón has interpolated some new material. First, Flérida brings to her mistress news of the approach of an army headed by the disgruntled Ársidas, and Circe leads off a contingent of women against it. The scene ends with the battle between the two parties. This is another dispensable scene, and the long speech of Flérida, with lines reminiscent of earlier plays of Calderón describing the enemy fleet slowly coming into view, suggests that one of its purposes was to fill out the play. But the attack upon Circe accounts for her absence from her palace and presents Ulises with an opportunity to escape.

The taunting of Ulises by Aquiles was inspired by a situation in Calderón's own third act of *Polifemo y Circe*. Towards the end of the act, when Ulises goes to drink in a stream, he is stopped by a voice. A rock opens and reveals the bloodstained Acis, who recalls for Ulises his glorious past and reprimands him for his dishonour and infamy. Made aware of the depths to which he has sunk, Ulises escapes to his ships. Calderón, who had dispensed with the part of Acis in his new play, happily replaced him by Aquiles whose arms Ulises had inherited. Already in the source-play Calderón had referred to Aquiles:

> ¡Tú, Ulises valeroso,
> a quien ampara el sol en esta ausencia,
> Júpiter generoso
> da su sangre, Mercurio su elocuencia
> y sus armas Aquiles,
> así te vences de lisonjas viles!   (427b)

10

The scene in *El mayor encanto amor* gains considerably by following so closely upon that in which Ulises has openly admitted defeat by love; the full extent of his humiliation has just been witnessed by the audience. But the replacement of Acis by Aquiles, whose shade had appeared to Agamemnon, accounts in itself for much of the new effect. The arms of Aquiles, representing all the past glory and achievements of the Greeks, are brought on and laid at the feet of Ulises whilst he sleeps. Ulises' own words of insult and abuse reveal the extent of his degeneration:

> ...Mas ¿qué veo?
> el grabado arnés ilustre
> de Aquiles a mis pies yace,
> torpe, olvidado e inútil.
> Bien está a mis pies, porque
> rendido a mi amor se juzgue,
> y segunda vez en mí
> amor de Marte se burle.
> Tarde, olvidado trofeo
> del valor, a darme acudes
> socorro contra mí mismo;
> que aunque contra mí ayudes,
> hoy colgado en este templo
> quedarás, donde sepulten
> sus olvidos tus memorias.   (408c)

It is fitting that Aquiles himself shall appear to rebuke him and remind him of his high calling and responsibility. The choice is a clear one between duty and its dereliction, or between right and wrong. Humiliated and ashamed by this vision, Ulises summons his companions and flees to his ships. In this reconstruction and rewriting of the earlier scene. Calderón has far surpassed his own modest achievement in *Polifemo y Circe*.

In the same scene, immediately before the appearance of Aquiles, Calderón shows the restoration of Clarín to human form when he looks at himself in a mirror, anticipating the restoration of Ulises to his former self. Again, as in Act II, Calderón includes a clear pointer to the bond between Clarín and Ulises. Lebrel is searching for the monkey whose disappearance mysteriously coincides with the appearance of Clarín. At this point Antistes enters with the Greeks in search of Ulises:

> ANTISTES. Dime, Lebrel, ¿dónde está...
> LEBREL.   ¿La mona? No sé: ¡ay de mí!

ANTISTES.   Ulises, te digo.

CLARÍN.   Allí.

(Descúbrese un trono, donde está Ulises durmiendo.)

(408b)

Lebrel's mistake confirms the link between Clarín in the form of a monkey and the degenerate Ulises. And the parallel is maintained after the appearance of Achilles by the interventions of Clarín and Lebrel. Just as Clarín is restored to his former shape by seeing himself in a mirror, so Ulises, mirrored as it were in the words of Aquiles, is made aware of his degeneracy and recovers his former stature. Tasso's Rinaldo, we recall, escaped from Armida after seeing himself in his diamond-studded shield. [1] It may be that in writing *El mayor encanto* Calderón had in mind also Tirso de Molina's mythological play *El Aquiles* with which it has some curious parallels. At the beginning of Tirso's play, for example, Ulises prefers love to duty when he feigns madness in order not to leave Penelope. But the principal episode of *El Aquiles* is Achilles' own effeminacy: he refuses to take part in the Trojan War so that he can stay with Deidamia. The parallel between Calderón's Ulises and Tirso's Aquiles is close: both are infatuated by a woman, both prefer this infatuation to duty and both are subsequently disillusioned. The disillusionment itself provides the closest parallel. There are two stages in the process of Aquiles' rehabilitation. First a voice reveals to him his present degradation and the true path of honour. Then Aquiles looks into a mirror and sees for himself what he has become. Calderón's play, it will be observed, has both the voice and the mirror devices, but the latter is reserved for the *gracioso* Clarín.

Polifemo y Circe and *El mayor encanto amor* have similar endings. Ulises returns to his ships and Circe, in despair, takes her own life. But the storm which Circe threatens to cause in the source-play materializes in Calderón's. The audience sees fire rising from the troubled waters. Suddenly the sea is calmed by the nymph Galatea, who appears in a triumphal car drawn by two dolphins and surrounded by tritons and sirens bearing musical instruments. In *Polifemo y Circe* Circe dies off stage; in *El mayor encanto amor* her palace sinks dramatically into the sea and a volcano appears belching

---

[1] Cf. *Gerusalemme liberata*, XIV, 77; XVI, 30.

forth flames. These divergencies from the source were impelled primarily, it would seem, in the interest of spectacle.

Ulises' escape represents the victory of reason over passion, a passion which, if not incestuous like Amón's or even adulterous like Prince Enrique's—Calderón suppressed at least all references to Penelope—flagrantly conflicts with his duty. Unlike Coriolano's love for Veturia, Ulises' love for Circe is irreconcilable with his obligations; and these he shirks to remain in her embraces. His conduct is morally reprehensible. But he comes to recognize his degeneracy: the rebuke of Achilles opens his eyes and he abandons Circe to join his followers. His final speech to Circe is taken over from the source-play, but it has the significant additional lines:

> del mayor encanto amor
> la razón me sacó libre. (409c)

Ulises is Everyman, and the clash between his attachment for Circe and his duty to his fellows is the conflict between passion and reason, ultimately between the senses and the spirit. Circe herself is vicious; she uses flattery and guile to ensnare her victims and indulge her passion, and when rejected by Ulises dies by her own hand. In essentials Calderón's story of Ulises and Circe differs little from that of the source, but by concentrating on this single conflict, he was able to clarify and elaborate the allegory. The other characters of importance have parts relevant to it. The clearest example is Antistes. In a long speech early in Act I he warns his master of the danger of Circe and urges him to flee the island; later in the act he repeats his warning. In Act III he exposes the degeneracy of Ulises and devises the ruse to rescue him from Circe. Though this first plan fails, he succeeds finally with the arms of Aquiles. Calderón modelled Antistes on the earlier Turselino, but he extended and confirmed his rôle as the good counsellor. It differs little from that of *El Entendimiento* in *Los encantos de la culpa*.

The only other important character who has an obvious counterpart in the source-play is the *gracioso* Clarín. Clarín's antics with the giant Brutamonte were inspired by those of Chitón with Polifemo, though they have little in common. But Calderón, as we have seen, linked Clarín with Ulises: his transformation into a monkey and restoration to human form symbolize the degeneration and ultimate recovery of his master. The remaining characters of importance are new. Ársidas is linked with Ulises in that these two alone have the means of resisting Circe's poisoned cup; and he is a rival for Circe's love. Ársidas is enslaved by passion, and his effeminacy and ineffectiveness are intended as a warning to Ulises. Lísidas and Flérida are also lovers, but their love is rational and is reciprocated. Like other visitors to Sicily they are the victims of Circe, but they are transformed into trees, which symbolize their chastity. Their pure love seems to be set against the impure love of Ulises, Circe and Ársidas. They arouse the sympathy of Ulises and are restored to their former selves, and in the last scene they are reunited.

The new structure of *El mayor encanto amor,* involving an original second act and the rearrangement of material common to the two plays in Acts I and III, allowed Calderón little opportunity for the rewriting of individual scenes or the appropriation of actual lines. Only in two instances, in the first and last scenes of the play, are corresponding passages written in the same stanza-form. Calderón, like Amescua, opens his play with *silva,* but he appears to have taken over no more than half-a-dozen lines in all from the earlier scene. More often he restates the same thought in his own words:

> *Polifemo y Circe.*
> ¿No ves en varios puestos
> escuadrones de pájaros funestos
> que gimen y no cantan,
> y de los rayos de la luz se espantan?   (413b)

> El bruto humildemente
> la melena ha postrado de su frente,
> y con piadosas señas
> las guedejas sacude entre las peñas.   (413c)

> *El mayor encanto amor.*
> Y si las copas rústicas miramos
> destos funestos ramos,
> no pájaros süaves
> vemos, nocturnas sí, agoreras aves.   (391a)

> Y el rey de todos ellos,
> el león, coronado de cabellos,
> en pie puesto, una vez hacia las peñas,
> y otra hacia el mar, cortés nos hace señas.   (391b)

The only other passage in which Calderón uses the same stanza-form is found in the last scene of the play. Here the source lines were his own, and it is not surprising that he drew on them more freely. A number of lines, if not exactly reproduced, are merely revised and adapted, as for example:

> *Polifemo y Circe.*
> Altos montes de Sicilia,
> cuya hermosura compite
> con el cielo, pues sus flores
> con las estrellas se miden,
> yo soy de vuestros engaños
> triunfador, Teseo felice
> fui de vuestros laberintos
> y muerte de vuestra esfinge.   (427c)

> *El mayor encanto amor.*
> Ásperos montes del Flegra,
> cuya eminencia compite
> con el cielo, pues sus puntas
> con las estrellas se miden,
> yo fui de vuestros venenos
> triunfador, Teseo felice
> fui de vuestros laberintos,
> y Edipo de vuestra esfinge.
> Del mayor encanto, amor,
> la razón me sacó libre
> trasladando esos palacios
> a los campos de Anfitrite.   (409c)

And the hendecasyllabic couplet which at intervals breaks into the *romance:*

> ...para hacer mejor camino
> agua (en) mis ojos, viento (en) mis suspiros.

occurs in both plays.

Elsewhere, in scenes common to the two plays, Calderón seems to have been working with his source in front of him. This is certainly true, of the first meeting of Ulises and Circe. Nearly the whole of Circe's magnificent speech was inspired by the corresponding speech of the source-play. The opening lines of *Polifemo y Circe:*

> Prima nací de Medea,
> aquella que para el curso
> de los astros y penetra
> esos cóncavos profundos
> del mar...   (415b)

have been elaborated in a long feminist passage in *El mayor encanto amor,* the first six lines of which bear the stamp of Calderón:

> Prima nací de Medea
> en Tesalia, donde fuimos
> asombro de sus estudios,
> y de sus ciencias prodigio;
> porque enseñadas las dos
> de un gran mágico, nos hizo
> docto escándalo del mundo
> sabio portento del siglo...   (394a)

Other lines of the source-play have been systematically expanded, as for example:

> Aquí al terminar el día,
> del sol considero el curso,
> y el de la luna contemplo
> en el silencio nocturno...   (415b)

each pair of lines extended to four:

> No te digo que del sol
> los veloces cursos sigo
> siendo cambiante cuaderno
> de tornasoles y visos;
> no que de la luna observo
> los resplandores mendigos,
> pues una dádiva suya
> los hace pobres o ricos...   (394a)

Yet the structure of the speech and the devices it employs, above all its parallelisms, are characteristically Calderonian. And, as if deliberately to emphasize the fact that he was rewriting and not copying, for the *redondillas* of the first part of the source he uses *décimas,* for the *octavas* of Ulises' speech *romance* O-E, and for the *romance* in U-O of Circe's *romance* in I-O. Similarly in rewriting the scene in which Ulises yields publicly to Circe and Acis comes to rebuke him, he replaces *romance* and *silva* by *redondillas.*

Some of Calderón's images have their origin in the source, but he extended and elaborated them into an intricate network. In the third act of *Polifemo y Circe,* for example, he had compared Ulises' rejection of Circe with the escape of Theseus from the labyrinth of the Minotaur and to Oedipus' solution of the riddle of the Sphinx.

The passage is preserved in *El mayor encanto amor* with only slight revision:

> *Polifemo y Circe.*
> Teseo felice
> fui de vuestros laberintos
> y muerte de vuestra esfinge.   (427c)

> *El mayor encanto amor.*
> Teseo felice
> fui de vuestros laberintos,
> y Edipo de vuestra esfinge.   (409c)

But Calderón associates Circe with the Sphinx on no less than three other occasions in *El mayor encanto amor*:

> desta esfinge huyamos   (392a)

> Hoy seré
> de aquesta Esfinge el Edipo   (394c)

> esa esfinge así se lo mandaba   (407b)

Elsewhere she is compared to a monster and a beast:

> aunque yo fiera y monstruo
> tan dada soy a los vicios   (395a)

> perezca hoy la memoria desta fiera   (407b)

There are other references also to the labyrinth in which Ulises finds himself:

> por diversos laberintos   (391c)

Circe's purpose, we are told early in the play, is to:

> hacer los hombres brutos   (392a)

This is true in both a literal and a metaphorical sense. Ulises' followers are converted into animals; Clarín becomes a monkey. But Ulises himself, by submitting to Circe, is similarly degraded, not physically but morally. Calderón directs our attention to his degradation by means of images, many of which have been referred to in earlier chapters. Here are some of the more prominent associations:

TORPIDITY.	torpes mis sentidos tuve	(406a)
BLINDNESS.	ciego estuve	(406a)

DEAFNESS.	sordo estuve	(406a)
DUMBNESS.	acuérdele mudo él	(408b)
SLEEP.	desvelado	
	se da Ulises por vencido	
	a la deidad de Morfeo,	
	a cuyo letal trofeo	
	las potencias ha rendido	(405c)
LETHARGY.	en mudo letargo yace	(407b)
OBLIVION.	para que despertador	
	de tantos olvidos sea	(408b)
SLAVERY.	esclavo tuyo he de ser	(406b)
POISON.	yo fui de vuestros venenos	
	triunfador	(409c)
DARKNESS.	bien	
	que estaban sin luz presumen	
	mis sentidos, pues sin sol	
	aun todo el cielo no luce	(408c)
IMPRISONMENT.	las prisiones romperé	(406a)
DEATH.	sepultado en blando sueño	(407a)

This succession of images driving home the degeneracy of Ulises
is without parallel in the source. At the same time Calderón
anticipated the moral confusion of Ulises by giving more emphasis
in the very first lines of the play to the inauspiciousness of his
arrival in Sicily. The land is desolate:

> No parece habitable
> En lo inculto, intrincado y formidable.   (391a)

The streams are like those of the underworld:

> Sólo se ve de arroyos mil surcado,
> cuyo turbio cristal desentonado
> parece, a lo que creo,
> desperdiciado aborto del Leteo.   (391a)

There are birds of ill-omen:

> No pájaros süaves
> vemos, nocturnas sí, agoreras aves.   (391a)

The woods are intricate and confusing:

> ¡Qué bosque es de confusión tan rara
> Aqueste que pisamos!   (391b)

> Por diversos laberintos.   (391c)

We have already referred to the spectacle of *El mayor encanto amor*. *Polifemo y Circe* itself required fairly elaborate staging; Ulises and his followers arrive in Sicily by a ship which is represented on the stage; and the same ship is 'discovered' at the end of the play to take them away. Early in Act I a lion enters and makes signs to Ulises. The nymph Iris appears suspended in the air, and the same machine presumably whisks Ulises away in the earthquake at the end of Act II:

Vuela la reja con Ulises...

In Act III a rock opens and reveals Acis:

Ábrese un peñasco y sale ACIS *ensangrentado.*

Some of these details are perpetuated in Calderón's play: the ship and animals, and the appearance of Iris. A counterpart for the rock episode is the reversion of Lísidas and Flérida from trees to human form:

Ábrense dos árboles y salen FLÉRIDA *y* LÍSIDAS.

Calderón makes considerable use of trapdoors to add more spectacle: for a table which rises from below and subsequently disappears with the two *graciosos* on it, for the sleeping Ulises (though this could have been a 'discovery') and for the appearance of Aquiles. Another innovation, apparently, was the use of fire: fire issues from the goblet in Act I when Ulises applies to it the magic flowers, flames herald the appearance of Aquiles, and a volcano rises in the place of Circe's palace. And since Calderón's play was for production on an open-air stage which was an island on a lake, for his final scene Galatea could be drawn across the water in a real boat:

> Serénase el mar y sale por él, en un carro triunfal, Galatea, tíranle dos sirenas, y alrededor muchos tritones con instrumentos.   (Parte, 24 v.)

> Serénase el mar y sale por él, en un carro triunfal, tirado de dos delfines, Galatea, y alrededor muchos tritones y sirenas, con instrumentos.
> (Vera Tassis, II, 49b)

Circe destroys herself in a manner described at length in the text:

> estos palacios
> que mágico el arte finge
> desvanecidos en polvo,
> sola una voz los derribe.
> Su hermosa fábrica caiga
> deshecha, rota y humilde;
> sean páramo de nieve
> sus montes y sus jardines.
> Un Mongíbelo suceda
> en su lugar, que vomite
> fuego, que a la luna abrase,
> entre humo, que al sol eclipse.   (410c)

and the scene ends with a ballet of Tritons and Sirens.

Elaborate though *El mayor encanto amor* is, it is clearly less elaborate than the production envisaged by Cosme Lotti. Here, for example, is Lotti's proposed opening:

Formaráse en medio del Estanque una Isla fixa, levantada de la superficie del agua siete pies, con una subida culebreante, que vaya á parar á la entrada de la Isla, la qual ha de tener un parapeto lleno de desgajadas piedras, y adornado de corales, y otras curiosidades de la mar, como son perlas, conchas diferentes, con precipicios de aguas, y otras cosas semejantes. En medio de esta Isla ha de estar situado un monte altísimo de áspera subida con despeñaderos y cabernas, cercado de un espeso y obscuro bosque de árboles altísimos, en el qual se verán algunos de los dichos árboles con figura humana, cubiertos de una corteza tosca, y de sus cabezas y brazos saldrán entretexidos, y verdes ramos, de los quales han de estar pendientes diversos trofeos de caza y guerra, quedando esta forma de Teatro alumbrado de luces, ocultas en poca cantidad, y dando principio á la fiesta, en la qual se oirá un estrepitoso murmurio y ruido, causado de las aguas, y se verá venir por el Estanque un grande y soberbio carro plateado y argentado, el qual han de tirar dos monstruosos pescados, de cuyas bocas saldrá continuamente gran cantidad de agua, creciendo la luz del Teatro como se fuere acercando, y en la superficie de él ha de venir sentada con magestad y bizarría la Diosa Agua, de cuya cabeza y curioso vestido saldrán infinita copia de cañitos de ella, y asimismo se verá salir otra gran cantidad de una urna en que la Diosa ha de ir inclinada, que caerá mezclada con diversidad de peces, que jugando y saltando en el precipicio de la misma agua, y culebreando por todo el carro, vendrán á caer en el Estanque. Esta máquina admirable ha de venir acompañada de un coro de veinte Ninfas de ríos y fuentes, las quales han de ir cantando y tañendo á pie enxuto por encima de la superficie del agua en el Estanque, y quando pare esta hermosa máquina en presencia de S. M. la Diosa Agua dará principio á la escena representando la Loa, y acabada ésta se oirán diversidad de instrumentos, volviéndose á salir del Teatro con el mismo acompañamiento y música. Y apenas habrá desaparecido, quando se oirá un estrepitoso son de clarines y trompetas bárbaras, y haciendo salva de mosquetes y artillería, es oirá decir *tierra, tierra,* y se descubrirá una grande hermosa, y dorada

nave, adornada de flámulas, gallardetes, estandartes, vanderolas, que con
hinchadas velas llegará a tomar puerto recogiéndolas, y echando las áncoras
y amarras, donde se descubrirán Ulises y sus compañeros... [1]

Calderón pointed out that he would incorporate only those
suggestions of Cosme Lotti which were consistent with his own
conception of the story:

> Yo evisto vna memoria q cosme loti delteatro yapariencias que ofrece
> hazer asu Mgd. en la fiesta de Lanoche de S. Juan; yavnque esta trazada
> con mucho ynjenio; La traza de ella no es Representable por mirar mas
> alaynbencion de las tramoyas que algusto dela Representacion = Yaviendo
> Yo Señor de escriuir esta comedia no esposible guardar el orden que en ella
> semeda pero haciendo elecion de algunas de sus apariencias las que yo abre
> menester de aquellas para loque tengo pensado son las siguientes. [2]

This letter in itself would suggest the need for revising the judgement
of Menéndez y Pelayo that Calderón was interested only in the
spectacle of the mythological plays.

In one respect, at least, Cosme Lotti's *memoria* is relevant to
our study. He refers to a *gracioso* who, though transformed like his
friend into a pig, is allowed to stand upright and speak like a man.
The *gracioso* took a fancy for a lady whom Circe, in a fit of jealousy,
transforms into a monkey; and he is made to remain transformed
longer than his friends as penance for his misdemeanour. Cosme
Lotti comments:

> de lo qual resultará una alegoría gustosa y entretenida, pues la dama vién-
> dose transformada en mona, y teniendo por esta causa gran discordia con el
> cochino, le reprehenderá debaxo de esta metáfora los vicios y torpezas de
> los hombres, y el cochino con otra alegoría semejante debaxo de la metáfora
> y transformación de mona reprehenderá los de las mugeres.
>
> [Pellicer, pp. 154-55]

Though Calderón did not adopt the details of Lotti's proposal, it is
clear that, like Lotti, he intended the *gracioso's* part to be symbolical.
The *memoria,* moreover, goes on to describe how Virtue appears
to Ulises to reprimand him for his effeminacy and then leads him
to a fountain:

> donde mirándose como en un espejo, y viéndose tan otro de su antiguo valor
> y ser, con fixa resolución se determinará á dexar á Circe.
>
> [Pellicer, p. 164]

---

[1]   Casiano Pellicer, op. cit., II, 146-49.
[2]   L. Rouanet, 'Un autographe inédit de Calderón', *RHi*, VI (1899), 197-98.

This reference to a mirror in connexion with Ulises confirms that Calderón intended to point the parallel between Clarín's restoration to human form and Ulises' recovery from his moral degradation.

Music, and doubtless expensive costumes, went hand in hand with spectacle, and it is no surprise that the lines of song in *El mayor encanto amor* run to around forty. In many instances Calderón is simply following the example of the source dramatists and in particular of Mira de Amescua. Like Mira he uses musical accompaniment for the appearance of Iris, possibly to drown the noise of the machine. For the first meeting of Ulises and Circe he borrows the actual words of Mira for the musicians' song which is heard, with one variation, no less than three times:

> *En hora dichosa venga*
> *A los palacios de Circe*
> *El rayo de los troyanos*
> *El discreto y fuerte Ulises.*

Ulises' effeminacy and imprudence are set in relief by this reminder of his true self, a paragon of discretion and valour. In Act II, the lines of a quatrain of song, which are distributed amongst Ulises, Circe, Lísidas and Flérida, establish a link between the two pairs of lovers. But the most remarkable use of music occurs in the scene in which Ulises is tested; the spiritual conflict is represented by two choruses, one chanting *Amor, amor* and the other *Guerra, guerra.* Here we have a clearer example of what has already been noted in *Los cabellos de Absalón.* Music is used to further the ulterior motives of Circe:

> ¿Qué blandas voces süaves,
> repetidas en los vientos,
> son con sonoros acentos
> dulce envidia de las aves?
> ¡Qué bien el amor me suena!   (406a)
>
> ¡Qué blanda, qué dulcemente
> suena esta voz repetida!   (406a)

It is pleasing in sound but, far from serving the purpose of God, it lulls Ulises into moral torpor.

El mayor encanto amor, though based demonstrably on *Polifemo y Circe,* is a new play. Calderón rejected two of the three separate episodes of the source, and totally recast the material that remained. The fine lyrical passages and the imagery, which are distinctive features of the play, are original. So is the brilliant handling of the scenes in which Ulises yields to Circe and later is upbraided by Aquiles, though both were inspired by the source. By limiting himself to the single issue between Ulises and Circe, Calderón was able to penetrate to and develop the symbolic meaning of the Ulises episode, to concentrate upon the human conflict between reason and passion and to conceive the whole story anew in terms of this conflict. But, in order to give his play the required dimensions, he was obliged to supply a good deal of new material, concerned primarily with Ársidas, Lísidas and Flérida. There is no doubt that he took pains to make these characters and the incidents in which they are involved relevant to the theme of his play. Yet, despite this, they seem to be only imperfectly integrated into the play's structure, and Act II remains all too obviously an interpolation.

VI

LA NIÑA DE GÓMEZ ARIAS

THE story of the villainous Gómez Arias, who eloped with and
seduced the maiden who loved him and then disposed of her by
selling her to the Moors, was immortalized in a famous ballad; but
the source of Calderón's play *La niña de Gómez Arias*,[1] was an
earlier play of the same title by Luis Vélez de Guevara. Guevara's
text, unfortunately, has long been inaccessible. It was available
evidently to Schack who included in his history a sympathetic and
accurate account of its plot[2] and to Ramón de Mesonero Romanos
in 1858 when he edited the plays of dramatists contemporary with
Lope de Vega;[3] Don Ramón indeed provides in that volume a
list of the *dramatis personae*, an outline of the plot and the text of
its most important scene. Whether or not the play was seen by
Menéndez Pelayo is unknown; the inaccuracy of his statement that:

de [la comedia de Guevara] aprovechó Calderón no sólo el argumento, sino
escenas enteras y largas tiradas de versos.[4]

suggests that it was not. More recently, Guevara's text has been
presumed lost,[5] though it was known to F. E. Spencer.[6] In fact,
it is extant in two *sueltas* in the British Museum and in one in the

---

[1] Texts used:

Source: Suelta (Madrid, 1700?).
          Suelta in Chorley, *Colección*, II (British Museum).

Calderón: *Cuarta parte*, 1672.
          Ed. Vera Tassis, IV, 1682.
          Ed. J. J. Keil, X, pp. 388-413.
          Ed. J. E. Hartzenbusch, BAE, XIV, 23-43.
          Ed. Astrana Marín, pp. 355-89. (Madrid, 1945, 3.ª ed.
          revisada.)
Quotations are from the second *suelta* and from Astrana Marín's edition.
[2] Op. cit., IV, 353-55.
[3] BAE, LXIV (Madrid, 1858).
[4] M. Menéndez y Pelayo, op. cit., p. 288.
[5] e. g. A. Valbuena Prat, *Literatura dramática española* (Barcelona, 1930), p. 222.
[6] F. E. Spencer and R. Schevill, *The Dramatic Works of Luis Vélez de Guevara*
(Berkeley, 1937).

Schaeffer library. [1] Guevara's play is concerned with the exploits of Gómez Arias and his sister Doña María. The action begins in Córdoba not long before the fall of Granada. Act I shows Gómez's advances to 'la niña' Gracia, and his sister's advances to his soldier-friend Juan de Guevara, the brother of Gracia. Brother and sister conveniently court sister and brother, and the servant Perico bears notes to both Gracia and Juan from their respective lovers. Act II presents the elopement of Gracia with Gómez Arias and of María with the person she takes to be Juan, actually a rival lover Luis. Its most famous scene, reproduced by Mesonero Romanos, is that in which Gómez disposes of Gracia to Avenjafar, the *alcaide* of the. Moorish fortress. Gómez now attaches himself to a party of brigands; and when he discovers María fleeing from her seducer Luis, he obliges Luis to marry her and then has him hurled to his death from a cliff. At this point Vélez includes a reference to his famous *bandolera* play, *La serrana de la Vera*:

> ...por mí has de tener
> más fama que la Serrana
> de la Vera, y juntamente
> la niña de Gómez Arias.   (10r b)

In Act III Queen Isabel comes to Córdoba, and an expedition is sent to attack Benamejí. It encounters and defeats the brigands led by Gómez Arias, releases their prisoners, Juan and María, and later rescues Gracia. Gómez and María are sentenced to death; but, thanks to the pleas of mercy of Gracia and Juan, they are pardoned by the Queen.

It was probably during the thirties that Calderón chose to recast Vélez de Guevara's play. [2] He kept the same title but renamed 'la niña' Dorotea, linking her—perhaps deliberately—with the heroine of Cervantes. There are other echoes of *Don Quixote* in the play, as in the words of Ginés:

---

[1] I have consulted both the *sueltas* in the BM. One reads 'Madrid?, 1700?' The other is part of Chorley's made-up volumes, *Colección de comedias sueltas con algunos autos y entremeses de los mejores ingenios de España desde Lope de Vega hasta Comella*, volume II.

[2] Hartzenbusch dates it before 1651, and Hilborn c 1637-39. Veléz's play is undated. It is not discussed by Professor Bruerton in 'La ninfa del cielo, La serrana de la Vera and related plays', *Hom. Huntington* (Wellesley, 1952), 61-97 nor in 'Eight plays by Vélez de Guevara', *RPL*, VI (1952-53), 248-53. I have not, unfortunately, seen the unpublished edition of Vélez's play prepared by Ramon Rozzell, Ohio State University, 1947. Rozzell, it would appear, dates it 1608-1615. Cf. *El embuste acreditado*, ed. A. C. Reichenberger (Granada, 1956), p. 79.

Ya los caballos, señor,
atados quedan, con harta
queja de los tres, diciendo
en rocinantes palabras...   (368a)

Acts I and II of Calderón's play show Gómez Arias involved in two different love-affairs, first with Beatriz, who has a rival lover Félix, and second with 'la niña' Dorotea. Gómez Arias elopes with Dorotea at the end of Act I, and early in Act II abandons her at the foot of the Alpujarras. She is captured by the Moor Cañerí, but is rescued shortly afterwards. Later, by chance, she finds herself again alone with Gómez Arias, who this time resolves to sell her to the Moors. So in Act III we have the familiar episodes of the disposal of 'la niña' and later her recovery by the Queen and the sentence of death passed upon Gómez Arias; and Calderón has the sentence carried out. It will be apparent that Calderón's debt to Vélez de Guevara is considerable. The two central figures Gómez Arias and Dorotea derive directly from the source, as well as some other characters with whom they are involved: Gómez's servant, 'la niña''s father, the Moorish Commander and the Queen. The main episode follows the same general course: Gómez Arias induces 'la niña' to elope with him, seduces her and—after an unsuccessful attempt at desertion—disposes of her by selling her to the Moors; later she is rescued by forces of the Queen who sentences Gómez to death. And certain scenes, in particular that in which Gómez's intention becomes known to Dorotea and she pleads for mercy, are obviously modelled on the source text. Calderón does introduce new characters, but none to rival Gómez and 'la niña', in importance. It is probable that he looked no further than Vélez de Guevara's play. [1]

Yet, as our summary of the two plots reveals, there are structural differences between the plays. In the first place, Calderón has dispensed entirely with the character of María and with the intrigues in which she is implicated. The source-play had two plots, one centring on Gómez Arias and the other on María. Calderón has removed the secondary plot and concentrated upon the single conflict between Gómez Arias and 'la niña', a conflict to which

---

[1] The problem of the genesis of the *cantar* and legend of Gómez Arias is considered by Ramon Rozzell, 'The song and legend of Gómez Arias', *HR*, XX (1952), 91-107.

11

neither María nor her lover was relevant. Whatever interest resides in María in Vélez de Guevara's play is at the expense of Gómez Arias and the main issue. The paths of brother and sister do cross from time to time, but that did not by any means guarantee dramatic unity; and Calderón evidently did not see the means whereby the two plots could be combined, since he dispensed with the one altogether. This first change of Calderón was one entailing the omission of a large body of material of the source-play; the second involved an important rearrangement of what remained. In the story of Gómez Arias the key scene is that in which 'la niña' pleads with her lover not to carry out his threat to dispose of her to the Moors. This is the very core of the legend containing the famous lines:

> Señor Gómez Arias
> duélete de mí.
> Soy niña y muchacha
> nunca en tal me vi.

In Guevara's play the scene comes in the second act. Calderón postponed it until early in Act III, so that it takes place at the climax of a chain of events which both prepare for it and anticipate it. Once past, the play moves swiftly to its close. The scene is made to assume its rightful place in a structural pattern to which Calderón adhered with remarkable consistency: exposition in Act I, development in Act II, climax and dénouement in Act III.

The consequences of these two changes were considerable. By the removal of the María affair Calderón was discarding about one-third of his source material, as well as the characters of María herself and her lovers Juan and Luis. Then, by postponing until Act III the sale of 'la niña' to the Moors, he had to fill his first two acts with material which in the source-play occupied little more than one. His procedure was to replace María and her two suitors by a new lady Beatriz and two new men Don Félix and Don Juan Iñiguez. Whereas María was a second centre of interest diverting attention from Gómez Arias, Beatriz like Dorotea is in love with Gómez and her part in the play is primarily concerned with him. Don Félix and Don Juan are rivals of Gómez Arias, the one in love with Beatriz and the other with Dorotea. Three characters in Guevara's play about whom revolves a second plot give way to three new characters, who are inseparable from Gómez Arias and Dorotea, and who provide new and related manifestations of human behaviour. The relationship between the characters of the two plays is as follows:

Vélez de Guevara	Calderón
Gómez Arias	Gómez Arias
Perico	Ginés
Sancho	—
Arias Gómez	—
Doña Gracia, la niña	Dorotea, la niña
Quiteria	Juana
Laureano	Don Luis
Avenjafar	Cañerí
Celín	—
La reina Isabel	La reina Isabel
Doña María	—
Don Juan	—
Beltrán	—
Don Luis	—
Don Pedro	—
Adamuz	—
El conde de Palma	—
—	Doña Beatriz
—	Celia
—	Don Diego
—	Don Félix
—	Fabio
—	Don Juan Íñiguez de Haro
—	Floro

The first act of Vélez de Guevara's play is taken up with the overtures of Gómez Arias to Gracia 'la niña', and those of his sister María to Juan. Gómez Arias, fleeing from the siege of Granada on account of a dispute, comes to Córdoba and renews his acquaintance with Juan, who has a secret affair with his sister María. Gómez immediately falls in love with Juan's sister Gracia. Rival lovers of Gracia and María, Pedro and Luis, are succesfully shaken off. Calderón's act bears little superficial resemblance to that of Vélez. Both historical and geographical settings have been changed. Granada has now fallen and the story is set in the latter part of the reign of the Catholic Monarchs when *morisco* communities garrisoned in the Alpujarras are making raids on the neighbouring towns. The action takes place, not in Córdoba, but in Granada and Guadix. I shall comment later on the reason for these changes. In Calderón's play Gómez Arias has just fled from Granada after an exchange of blows with a rival lover Félix, whom he has discovered in the house of his lady Beatriz. Félix, wrongly accused of cowardice by Beatriz, is persuaded to seek revenge upon Gómez and leaves Granada in pursuit. Beatriz's father, Don Diego, comes with news of his appointment as captain of the expedition against the stronghold of the Moorish raiders, and at the same time he informs Beatriz that she must marry Juan Íñiguez de Haro.

Though Calderón's scene is new, it was probably suggested by a passage in Vélez's play in which Gómez tells why he has left Granada:

> Obligóme a dexar su Vega, llena
> de triunfos, y despojos vn agrauio
> con harta culpa, y con deuida pena,
> y al contrario afrentado es de hombre sabio
> huir la cara, ya que de la suya
> fueron mis cinco dedos lengua, y labio,
> y no es bien que a soberuia se atribuya
> este desman, que la ocasion fue tanta
> que no ay cosa en contrario que me arguya
> que vn hombre como yo jamas leuanta
> la mano sin razon, mas assi es justo
> que el compas lleue a quien infamias canta
> que viendole entonar a mi disgusto,
> le hize facistol la infame cara,
> aunque se precia de jayan robusto...   (1r-1v)

The function of the scene is to prepare for and anticipate later developments. By accusing Félix of cowardice, Beatriz drives him to seek revenge on Gómez Arias, and sets in motion the train of events which follows. The significance of her action is brought out in the exchanges between her and her servant, in which Calderón foreshadows the tragedy which is to come:

> CELIA.   ¡Qué mal, señora, has andado
> en haber ocasionado
> nuevos empeños!
>
> BEATRIZ.   No estuve
> en lo que dije, ni hube
> la voz apenas formado,
> cuando en ella reparé.

CELIA.   ¡Oh, cuántas veces, señora,
          un acaso causa fué
          de mil desdichas!
BEATRIZ.   No ahora
          me aflijas. Si confesé
          que hice mal, ¿qué he de decir?
          No me des más que sentir,
          pesar juntando a pesar;
          que harto tengo que llorar
          que padecer y sufrir.   (356b)

Again, the play will end with a successful assault on the *morisco* fortress of Benamejí. So, in this first scene, Calderón presents the person who will command the Christian forces, and he includes an announcement of the Queen's visit to Granada and the assault to be made on Benamejí. Mention is also made of the Moorish leader El Cañerí, and the reference to the brigandage of the *moriscos* and their failure to honour their pact with the Catholic monarchs anticipates his ultimate fate:

          que rebeldes a los pactos
          piadosos con que los reyes
          los admitieron vasallos,
          en toda Sierra Nevada
          bandidos y rebelados,
          tienen a la Andalucía
          llena de ruinas y estragos
          siendo el Cañerí, un adusto
          monstruo etíope africano,
          cabeza de sus motines
          y caudillo de sus bandos.   (357a)

In the first scene Calderón does no more than refer to Gómez. For scene II the action shifts to Guadix where Gómez has fled with his servant Ginés. Here, in a dialogue between master and servant, attention is called to the main traits of Gómez's character. Ginés complains that his master is poor, a soldier and gambler and, worst of all, a lover. Most of the discussion arises out of Ginés' observation that, though he can understand that a man should fall once or even twice in love, his master's habit of being infatuated with every girl he sets eyes upon is beyond his comprehension. Gómez defends his conduct by means of a syllogism; and when he goes on to refer to Dorotea ('la niña'), the latest object of his affection, Ginés confidently predicts her fate:

GINÉS. ...y favorecido, tú
la olvidarás.

GÓMEZ. No haré.

GINÉS. Deja
que medio mates a otro
y nos vamos a otra tierra;
y verás, en viendo a otra,
cómo désta no te acuerdas. (359b)

This scene has a close parallel in Vélez de Guevara's play where half way through the first act Gómez Arias welcomes Perico back from the court and informs him of his sudden infatuation for Gracia. Features such as Gómez's poverty and his being little disposed towards marriage are common to both texts. Calderón's scene, though running to twice its length, was certainly inspired by Guevara's. In the source-play, however, we have already witnessed Gómez Arias' first meeting with Doña Gracia, and the scene does little more than review what has happened and underline certain facets of Gómez's character. In Calderón's play this is the first appearance of Gómez Arias, and the information about Dorotea is news as much for the audience as for Ginés. Calderón, moreover, makes Gómez a self-confessed *burlador*, whose affair with Beatriz we have already heard about; and the words, of Ginés forecasting the fate of Dorotea anticipate the play's dénouement.

At this point in Calderón's play, Dorotea makes her first appearance, visited at her house by Gómez Arias, when her father Don Luis is absent at the *Ayuntamiento*. Her father returns unexpectedly in the company of Félix, and both Gómez and Dorotea overhear in hiding Félix's charges against Gómez for his conduct towards Beatriz. Félix leaves, but Gómez and Dorotea are again obliged to hide when the father returns a second time, on this occasion with Juan Iñiguez who, to avoid a marriage of convenience with Beatriz, asks for the hand of Dorotea. Gómez is later discovered, swords are drawn and he escapes when the lights are extinguished by Dorotea. The act ends with Gómez and Dorotea eloping together amidst the general confusion. This spontaneous flight of Dorotea with Gómez Arias after the accumulation of events at her father's house is quite different from the pre-arranged elopement of Gracia. Calderón's scene, with the carefully manipulated situation of the lovers in hiding which is so conveniently resolved when the lights are extinguished, seems appropriate rather to comedy than to tragedy.

Yet a serious purpose underlies it. Before the end of Act I it reveals the character and motives of both Gómez and Dorotea. Hitherto we have known of Gómez's philosophy only from the conversation between him and Ginés; here we witness first-hand his resourcefulness and his unscrupulousness. The remarks of Félix disclose that Gómez has abandoned Beatriz after promising to marry her, and Gómez observes in an aside:

> ¡Qué buen
> desengaño, si no fuese
> tan tarde! (362b)

Like the 'burlador de Sevilla' he revels in his deceit. By degrees, Calderón is preparing his audience for the extreme villainy which Gómez will be shown to be capable of later.

The scene is perhaps still more important for the light it throws on Dorotea. Her elopement with Gómez is manifestly imprudent. But whilst Calderón does not justify what she does he shows at least the motives for her action. In the first place she is jealous of Beatriz, her rival for Gómez's love; and since Gómez Arias now knows that his suspicions regarding the intruder in Beatriz's house were unfounded, Dorotea has reason to fear that he may return to Beatriz. Secondly, she learns that Gómez's life is in danger, both from Félix and from her own father whose help he has enlisted. Finally, she discovers that Juan Íñiguez is seeking her hand in marriage and overhears her father's assurance that she will become his wife. If her jealousy makes her fear that she may lose Gómez, her threatened marriage to Don Juan and the price upon Gómez's head seem to demand immediate and desperate action. Dorotea's elopement is impulsive and unpremeditated. Passion blinds, as Ginés suggests:

> ¿Estáis ciegos? (367a)

and the error and bewilderment of Dorotea are symbolized by the extinguishing of lights and the resultant confusion. The final lines of the act epitomize the central conflict of the play:

> DOROTEA. Amor, ¿qué no haré por ti?
> GÓMEZ. ¿Qué no haré por ti, deseo? (368b)

On the one hand Gómez, wanton in his affections and utterly

unscrupulous, on the other Dorotea sincerely and passionately in love.

In this final scene, too, Calderón points to the responsibility of the characters other than Gómez and Dorotea. Reference is made to the 'necia ignorancia' of Beatriz and to the credulity and irresponsibility of women like her:

> ...como las más mujeres
> bozales indias de amor
> plumas y colores creen
> más que el oro de la dicha...   (362b)

> ¡Ah, cielos, y cuántas veces
> de las mujeres destruyen
> los fáciles pareceres
> la más asentada fama,
> hablando en lo que no entienden!
> Que como ellas, ignorantes,
> no saben cuánto contiene
> en sí una fácil palabra
> a no decirla no atienden.   (363a)

But Félix himself is wrong to pay attention to Beatriz's accusations, as Don Luis observes:

> ...no es bien que os despeñe
> tanto la necia ignorancia
> de una mujer.   (363b)

Finally, the fathers of Beatriz and Dorotea decide to marry their daughters against their will. These are the circumstances, arising in every case from serious human shortcomings, which lead to the situation in which Dorotea finds herself at the end of Act I, and which account in some measure for her rash decision.

Though Dorotea elopes with Gómez Arias at the end of Act I, her sale to the Moors, which follows immediately afterwards in the source-play, is postponed by Calderón until Act III. The material of Act II, therefore, is original. When the curtain rises, three days have passed since Dorotea fled with Gómez, and the two find themselves at the foot of the Alpujarras. Dorotea refers to the promise she has received from Gómez to marry her, and recalls the sequence of events which led her to elope. Then, when she has fallen asleep, Gómez makes a hasty getaway with Ginés. Dorotea sees in a vision her lover deserting her and awakes to find herself

a captive of the Moor Cañerí. Shortly afterwards she is rescued by
Don Diego, whose forces are already in action against the Moorish
raiders. Calderón's new scene hinges upon a very moving human
situation. Dorotea, despite her vision, does not suspect that she has
been abandoned, and when the Moor informs her that a young man
has been killed close by, she assumes that Gómez is dead and
tenderly mourns the loss of one who, the audience knows, has
cruelly deserted her. Never for a moment does she doubt the
sincerity of Gómez, and she pleads that, should he still be alive,
he may be released in order to arrange for her ransom:

> y no temáis que haga falta
> quedándome yo, porque
> me adora, me estima y ama
> de manera, que es lo mismo
> partir sin mí que sin alma...   (371a)

The scene prepares us also for Gómez's sale of Dorotea to the
Moors in Act III. The very enormity of Gómez's crime is, as Menéndez y Pelayo rightly observed, a serious difficulty for the dramatist:

> Consideradas las cosas rectamente, su asunto más propio parece de una no-
> vela, en que, con la conveniente preparación y el gradual desarrollo, pueden
> entrar hasta las aberraciones morales y los fenómenos patológicos, donde
> siempre será repugnante espectáculo el de un galán que por vil codicia
> vende su dama a los musulmanes, que es lo que hace Gómez Arias con su
> niña. [1]

Dorotea has sacrificed everything for her lover:

> No digo yo haber dejado
> por ti mi madre y mi casa,
> mas los imperios del mundo,
> cuando por ti los dejara,
> aun me parecieran poco
> trofeo para tus plantas.   (368a)

everything except her honour, which she naively believes is
safeguarded by Gómez's promise to marry her. Gómez, in contrast,
having satisfied his lust, finds Dorotea repugnant and is utterly
unscrupulous:

---

[1] M. Menéndez y Pelayo, *Calderón y su teatro*, 4th ed. (Madrid, 1910), p. 288.

> No me hubiera ella creído,
> que entonces yo la adorara;
> pero ya, ¿para qué es buena,
> pues no hay cosa que más valga
> que una hermosura, ni menos
> que una hermosura gozada?   (370a)

To set Gómez's behaviour in relief Calderón has recourse to the *gracioso* Ginés. Ultimately Ginés is cowardly, and when his master offers him the choice of accompanying him or of immediate death he chooses the path of safety. But he is shocked to learn of Gómez's intentions:

> Aunque eso en tu condición
> poca novedad me haga,
> me hace mucha novedad
> la ocasión en que lo tratas.   (369b)

and he censures his cruelty:

> GINÉS.   Repara,
> señor, en que es tu crueldad
> mayor que...   (370a)

Ginés is very like Catalinón in *El burlador de Sevilla*, just as his master has much in common with Don Juan; and though his warnings are less persistent and specific he serves the same purpose. Gómez's observation:

> ¿Ahora me sacas
> moralidades?   (370a)

is reminiscent of Don Juan's:

> ¿Predicador
> te vuelvas, impertinente?

And the comment of Ginés on Dorotea:

> ¡Mal haya
> mujer que a hombre enamorado
> de otra cree!   (370a)

recalls the belated comments of Don Juan's victims:

> ¡Mal haya la mujer
> que en hombres fía!

For the second part of Act II Calderón required a situation in which Gómez would again be obliged to rid himself of Dorotea, a difficult requirement since Gómez will hardly choose to elope with her a second time. Gómez goes to Granada to follow up his love-affair with Beatriz. Félix returns to Beatriz, believing that he has killed his rival in the exchange of blows at Guadix; so also does Juan, reverting to Beatriz now Dorotea has disappeared. Meanwhile Don Diego, whose absence has not gone unnoticed by Beatriz's suitors, has rescued Dorotea, and returns unexpectedly to his house; and Don Luis, the father of Dorotea, goes there in search of his daughter. Every important character in the play converges on the house of Beatriz. Gómez, in hiding and unaware of the presence next door of Dorotea, rushes in at the disturbance caused by Don Luis, and in the darkness carries off the lady crying 'Padre, Señor', believing that she is Beatriz. Dorotea in turn assumes that she is being rescued by Don Diego, who has just delivered her from El Cañerí. So it is that the act ends with Gómez's involuntary escape with Dorotea. For this scene Calderón derived some help perhaps from Vélez de Guevara, whose sub-plot offered the kind of situation needed. When the earlier María invites her lover Juan to visit her, her note is delayed; and in the darkness she leaves with a rival lover Luis. The elopment of Gómez Arias with Dorotea whom he takes to be Beatriz resembles the elopment of María with Luis whom she takes to be Juan. But the scene itself has no parallel in the source-play. The extraordinarily complicated situation, typical of the *capa y espada* play, is engineered by Calderón only at the expense of a whole series of coincidences. And it is strangely similar to the final scene of Act I, even to the extent of having Ginés as the decoy.

This curious scene supplies new material to fill out Act II and provides the situation of Gómez's eloping a second time with Dorotea. It also sheds more light on the conduct of the various characters. Gómez's depravity, if further proof is needed, is clear from his exchanges with Ginés on Beatriz:

> GÓMEZ.   De Beatriz enamorado
> a Beatriz pienso adorar.
> GINÉS.   Y si, aunque tan fino estás,
> te desagrada al gozarla,
> ¿qué has de hacer della?
> GÓMEZ.   Dejarla
> en otro monte...   (373a)

and the father of Dorotea later refers to him as one:

> de quien contó la fama
> que en vicios sólo su vivir emplea...   (377b)

Dorotea admits to her 'desacierto de amor' (378a), Félix confesses that in returning to Granada and entering Beatriz's house he is 'atrevido' (372b); and Beatriz maintains that:

> fué movido
> de mi desdén y sus celos...   (373b)

and acknowledges that her earlier accusation against him were 'cólera' and 'desacuerdo' (374b). But the confusion which leads to Dorotea's abduction is, significantly, caused by her own father who brands her 'hija aleve', and tries to kill her. It is Don Luis's desire for vengeance and Dorotea's own cries for help which place her at the mercy of Gómez. At the same time, Gómez's mistaking Dorotea for Beatriz, improbable though it may be, emphasizes the parallel between the two rivals for Gómez's love.

Most of the scenes of Calderón's third act have their counterparts in Guevara's play. His first scene concerned with the disposal of Dorotea derives from the second half of Vélez de Guevara's Act II, and the rest of the act, showing her recovery and Gómez's sentence, from the final scene of Guevara's Act III, though some new material was still required to round off the Beatriz affair. For Gómez's sale of 'la niña', Calderón follows Guevara closely. The two scenes have much in common. Gómez and 'la niña' are accompanied by a servant to within sight of the Moorish stronghold of Benamejí. Rejected by Gómez, 'la niña' herself suggests, in her plea to him not to abandon her, the way in which he ultimately disposes of her. Signals are made to the Moorish Commandant, who comes in person to make the purchase. 'La niña' first pleads with Gómez to accept her as slave if not as wife, then cries out for revenge, and, before being taken away, asks vainly for a final embrace. The servant who protests against his master's action is himself sold. Both dramatists incorporate the famous lines of 'la niña':

> Señor Gómez Arias,
> duélete de mí,
> no me dejes presa
> en Benamejí...   (382a)

and the servant parodies the lines when he is sold. All these are features of both scenes. Yet, for all this similarity, the effect is wholly different. The brutal action of Gómez gains something from the careful anticipation and preparation of Calderón, though it is at the expense of remarkable coincidences. In Vélez's play Gracia is disposed of by the lover with whom she has just eloped. In Calderón the episode comes at the end of a far more complicated chain of circumstances. Dorotea, finding herself in Act II a captive of the Moors, assumes that Gómez is dead and has no suspicion of his treachery. When rescued by Don Diego she continues to mourn for him. Then, after the confusion at Beatriz's house, she suddenly finds herself alone with her lover. The violence of what follows could scarcely be greater. Amidst her joy at the reunion she discovers that Gómez had abandoned her in the mountains and that he is with her now only because he has taken her for Beatriz. Even so, her love remains unshaken, and she is willing to forgive. But Gómez taunts and insults her, and caps his cruelty by selling her to Cañerí. The pathos of Vélez de Guevara's scene has been remarkably enhanced.

But the most striking contrast between the two scenes is provided by the language. Vélez de Guevara begins with Gracia's rather ingenuous questions to Gómez Arias about his changed attitude to her:

> GRACIA. Señor Gómez Arias
> del cuerpo gentil,
> ojos matadores,
> que saben fingir.
> Palabras de azúcar,
> y principio, y fin
> de los pensamientos
> que viven en mí.
> ¿Qué tristeza es esta,
> que apenas salís
> de gozar mis braços
> quando os miro ansí?
> ¿Qué se han hecho tantas
> finezas que oí,
> que fueron hechizos
> con que me rendí?
> Habladme, miradme,
> mi bien, ¿qué decís?
> porque de sospechas
> me vendré a morir.

> Señor Gómez Arias,
> duélete de mí,
> que soy niña, y muchacha,
> y nunca en tal me vi.   (7va)

When she learns that he does not love her, she appeals to him to accept her as a slave:

> Y quando no quieras
> de veras cumplir
> de esposo la fe
> que te merecí,
> yo seré tu esclaua,
> que quiero seruir
> más a tus criadas
> que verme sin ti.
> Hiérrame esta cara
> ponme aqui y alli
> clauo y S, y luego
> podrás escriuir:
> Soy de Gómez Arias,
> que mejor que alli,
> amor en el alma
> lo supo esculpir.
> Para esclaua tuya,
> mi gloria, nací,
> véndeme.   (7vb-8ra)

This is precisely what Gómez Arias does, and Gracia is allowed only a very few more lines before she is sold. The whole scene is remarkable for its directness, simplicity and economy. It is intensely moving primarily because it rings true. The short lines of the *romancillo* metre, which are used throughout, suggest the frailty and helplessness of the maiden, and contribute considerably to the emotional effect.

Contrast the manner of Calderón. First, there is an outburst from Gómez when he realizes that he has carried off Dorotea for Beatriz. Dorotea's reply calls attention to the disorder which Gómez's behaviour has caused:

> Siempre el vivo al muerto vi
> temer; siendo aquesto cierto,
> ¿cómo al contrario lo advierto,
> pues en trance tan esquivo
> se asombra el muerto del vivo
> y agasaja el vivo al muerto?   (379a)

Yet, for all his treachery and unfaithfulness, she offers to forgive him. He replies only to mock her, and claims that if she eloped out of love for him she has only herself to blame, and if she did not love him she can scarcely expect him to love her. Now for the first time Dorotea sees Gómez as he really is:

> ¿Qué monstruo airado
> que bárbaramente aleve
> no hay precepto que le dome,
> que helado cadáver come,
> que caliente coral bebe,
> a una queja no se mueve?   (380a)

Gómez makes to abandon her, and when she pleads with him and hurls herself at his feet he thinks of the idea of selling her to the Moors. Signals are made, Cañerí appears on the walls of the fortress, and Dorotea is offered for sale as a slave. At this point Calderón holds up the action with three *décimas* of Cañerí introduced by the lines:

> Pues ¿cómo dudas si quiero
> comprarla, que un mundo entero
> daré, cristiano, por ella?   (380b)

Nothing is too much, he reflects, to give for the beautiful Dorotea. Against the cruelty of Gómez, anxious only to be rid of Dorotea, the Moor Cañerí offers everything he has.

The *décimas* of Cañerí are a prelude to the monumental speech of Dorotea which follows. This is the crowning point of the play. The victim at once of the cruelty and lust of Gómez Arias and of her own irresistible love, Dorotea gives expression in some two hundred lines both to her own love and to a bitter denunciation of Gómez. She begins with a series of brilliant images inveighing against his monstrous tyranny:

> Monstruo ingrato, bruto fiero,
> pasmo horrible, asombro vil,
> fiera inculta, áspid traidor,
> crúel tigre, ladrón neblí,
> león herido, lobo hambriento,
> horror mortal, y hombre, en fin,
> por decirte de una vez
> cuanto te puedo decir...   (381a)

and leads up to her appeal to heaven for revenge, anticipating explicitly the *dénouement:*

> Véngueme el cielo de ti.
> El sol te niegue sus luces,
> su aliento el aire sutil,
> el agua su azul esfera,
> la tierra su verde abril.
> Bañado en tu misma sangre,
> un verdugo dividir
> veas, por traidor, tu cuello...   (381b)

But her love for Gómez overcomes her, and switching abruptly from invective to entreaty, she implores him lovingly, passionately, to take pity upon her:

> Pero ¿qué digo? ¡Ay de mí!
> Mi señor, mi bien, mi esposo,
> tu esclava soy, es así...   (381b)

She appeals to Gómez to spare her life, even if he cannot accept her as wife, and begs to be allowed to retire to a convent, or to renounce any claims to him before Beatriz, or even to be his slave. Then, as Cañerí approaches, Dorotea makes her final appeal, incorporating both a prediction of Heaven's revenge and a variant upon the traditional lines:

> Ea, señor, dueño mío,
> mi cielo y mi bien, en ti
> vuelve por ti mismo, y sea
> el mirarte arrepentir
> mérito ya, y no delito:
> porque de no hacerlo así
> cielo, sol, luna y estrellas,
> sin alumbrar ni lucir;
> hombres, aves, fieras, peces,
> sin obrar ni discurrir;
> montes, peñas, troncos, fieras,
> sin albergar ni servir;
> agua, fuego, tierra y viento,
> sin animar ni asistir,
> atentos a acción tan fea,
> se volverán contra ti,
> viendo que de tantas veces
> no te enternece el oír:
> Señor Gómez Arias,
> duélete de mí,
> no me dejes presa
> en Benamejí.   (382b)

In this magnificent climax to Dorotea's speech, Calderón again
anticipates the play's *dénouement*. The rest of the scene remains
fairly close to that of Vélez de Guevara. Ginés reproves Gómez
for his latest outrage and is himself sold to the Moors. The earlier
Perico's parody of the famous quatrain becomes in Calderón an
elaborate parody of Dorotea's final lines. And there is another
reminiscence of Tirso's *El burlador de Sevilla* in Gómez's:

> ¡Sermoncito escuderil
> tenemos!   (383a)

Vélez de Guevara's play, where Gracia is allowed only sixteen
lines when she is informed that she will be sold:

> Mi vida, ¿qué culpa
> graue cometí,
> que merezca pena
> que es más que morir?
> Pues daros el alma
> fue agrauio, ¿que ansí
> la tratáis agora
> sin más aduertir
> mi honor ni mi amor?
> ¿No miráis que os di
> de entrambos las llaues?
> ¿No habláis? ¿Qué dezís?
> Señor Gómez Arias,
> duélete de mí,
> que soy niña y muchacha
> y nunca en tal me vi.   (8ra)

has nothing to correspond to Dorotea's outburst. Calderón places
this scene as the climax of a subtly and carefully prepared dramatic
movement, of which Dorotea's speech is the culminating point; and
he marshals all the rhetorical devices at his command to make it so.
It is one of the most brilliant pieces of virtuosity in the whole
Spanish theatre. There can be no doubt about the superiority of
Calderón's handling of the play's action, and of the enhanced
dramatic effect of his scene for this reason alone, despite the
improbability of Gómez's mistaking Dorotea for Beatriz. As to the
scene itself, and in particular its language, one can say only that
Vélez's and Calderón's lines both in their own way achieve remarkable effects, and that the difference between them is above all one
of manner. Vélez, as Spencer remarked, adheres more closely to the

poignant spirit of the ballad; but to state, as he does, that Vélez's simplicity is greater art [1] is simply a reflexion of his repugnance to the poetic language of Calderón.

Calderón so constructed his play as to leave room for little action after this great scene. About half an act remains to show the consequences of Gómez's behaviour. In three short scenes Calderón presents the rejection of Gómez by Beatriz at Granada, the arrival of the Queen and the order for an immediate attack on the fortress of Benamejí, and the recovery of Dorotea and the sentence passed on Gómez. The climax of his play past, the story moves swiftly to its close. This does not happen in the source-play. After the selling of 'la niña', Vélez de Guevara has still to account for part of Act II and the whole of Act III. Some of the action is concerned with Gómez's being a bandit and with the episodes involving María and her seducer; for the rest Vélez de Guevara portrays the various stages of the attack on the fortress of Benamejí and the capture of Gómez. Not once, but twice, is Doña Gracia saved in the nick of time by the opportune appearance of the Christian forces. There was material enough and to spare for Calderón, and to a large extent he is handling afresh and rewriting parts of the source-play. The brief scene in which Gómez returns to Granada for a final meeting with Beatriz is, of course, new. Like Dorotea, Beatriz has been infatuated with Gómez, and it is her good fortune that Gómez mistook Dorotea for her at the end of Act II. In this new scene Beatriz discovers from her father the truth about Gómez, and when he comes to visit her she obliges him to confess. Dorotea's fate serves as a lesson to Beatriz:

> Si es su ruina un ensayo
> de cuerdos avisos llenos,
> y si me ha avisado el trueno
> ¿por qué he de esperar el rayo?   (385a)

and in four final *décimas* she roundly castigates Gómez for his treachery.

The second scene, showing the Queen's interview with the maiden's father and her order for an immediate assault on Benamejí, corresponds to the long first scene of Vélez de Guevara's third act;

---

[1]   Op. cit., p. 72.

and details such as the letter of 'la niña' to her father and the Queen's resolve not to sleep before 'la niña' has been recovered, derive from this and other parts of Guevara's play. But, as early as the first scene of his play, Calderón had anticipated the Queen's arrival in Granada and the attack upon the fortress of Benamejí, and had shown the appointment of Beatriz's father as captain of the Queen's forces. He is able, therefore, to compress his scene into a hundred lines or so. Dorotea in her letter admits to her own moral error:

> Yo erré, de un hombre engañada... (386a)

but her father insists upon the extent of the wickedness of Gómez:

> y vamos, digo otra vez,
> al mayor, al más indigno
> que pudiera imaginar
> el más depravado juicio
> de los hombres, el más fiero
> más cruel y más inicuo... (386a)

And Dorotea herself makes the point that, not only has Gómez compromised her honour and endangered her life, but has jeopardised her faith:

> Trata de mi libertad,
> y dame después castigo,
> que no, señor, la deseo,
> por no morir a los filos
> de tu acero, mas porque
> de la esclavitud que vivo,
> si no peligro en la fe,
> en la persuasión peligro. (386b)

At the same time, lines of the Queen call attention to the offences of the Moors:

> Las leyes despreciando,
> que el grande, que el Católico Fernando,
> tu rey y señor mío,
> les dió, ha sabido atropellar su brío.
> Esta justa venganza,
> de quien una tan gran parte me alcanza
> a ti me trae ahora,
> porque segunda vez hoy vencedora
> me vea tu campaña,
> a quien riega el Genil y el Darro baña. (385b)

The scene forestalls the punishment of both Gómez and El Cañerí.

The fast-moving last scene of Calderón's play derives from scenes which occupy most of Vélez de Guevara's third act. Calderón has preserved but the barest outline of the original; the resistance of 'la niña' to the advances of her Moorish captor, the capture of the fortress by Christian forces and the Queen's sentence upon Gómez. Some details are carried over; just as in Vélez de Guevara the musicians' song before the Queen concerns the maiden and contains the famous lines: 'Señor Gómez Arias...', so in Calderón the musicians of Cañerí entertain Dorotea with a version of the same quatrain. But hundreds of lines of the original have given way to one short new scene. Calderón here made two significant changes in the story: Gómez Arias and the Moor El Cañerí die. In Guevara's play both Gómez and his sister are sentenced to death:

> *Pregonan dentro.*
>
> Esta es la justicia,
> que mandan hazer
> los católicos reyes
> Fernando, y Isabel,
> a este hombre, y a esta muger,
> por salteadores,
> y otros inormes delitos
> mandan que mueran asaeteados
> en dos palos. Quien tal haze
> que tal pague.   (16ra)

But the Queen listens to the appeal of the father of Gómez Arias and orders a stay of execution; and at the request of 'la niña' who asks that Gómez should be spared to marry her, and a similar request of Juan in respect of María, both are pardoned. Gómez humbly submits:

> Esto ha permitido el cielo,
> mi bien, para dicha vuestra,
> y para descanso mío,
> y porque la vida os deua.   (16vb)

Calderón follows the lead of Vélez de Guevara in showing the maiden's plea for mercy, and in order that her honour may be restored Gómez is made to accept her hand in marriage. But the Queen refuses pardon, and Gómez is led off to his execution, his head being placed at the spot where Dorotea was sold. And whereas Avenjafar in the source-play escapes, El Cañerí is condemned to death and dies at the Queen's feet.

Calderón set the story of Gómez Arias against the background of the raids of the *morisco* garrison at Benamejí. In the play's first scene Don Diego had referred to the failure of the *moriscos* to fulfil their obligations; in return for the generosity of the Catholic monarchs they indulged in raids, plunder and murder. El Cañerí, as leader of the garrison, must bear responsibility for these attacks and he is made to confess:

> porque ya sabes que- anda
> (temerosa de los robos,
> muertes, iras y venganzas
> que hacemos) corriendo el monte
> la milicia de Granada...   (370b)

As a person El Cañerí is more sympathetic than the earlier Avenjafar who is prevented from assaulting the maiden and later murdering her only by the attack on Benamejí. But the *morisco* community which he heads failed to honour its pact with the Queen and was a threat to the lives and souls of her subjects, and he must die. The Queen's sentence is explicit:

> Tú, bárbaro, rebelado
> a mis preceptos, que píos
> por vasallo te admitieron,
> hoy morirás, en castigo
> de aquestas comunidades
> que osado has introducido.   (388b)

Calderón's change of setting of *La niña de Gómez Arias* was no mere whim. By postponing the action of the play until after the fall of Granada he was able to provide a close thematic link between it and the subsidiary plot. In this respect the play has an exact parallel in Lope's *Fuenteovejuna*. The sub-plot showing the rebellion of the Order of Calatrava against the state is for most of the play independent of the story of Fernán Gómez's crimes against the village of Fuenteovejuna; but treason and rape are both forms of rebellion against the social order, the one individual, the other general. Similarly, in *La niña de Gómez Arias,* the two actions represent different aspects of the same theme: El Cañerí by his crimes against the state, and Gómez by his crime against Dorotea, are both rebels against society. And both pay for their rebellion with their lives.

It is appropriate that 'la niña' shall intercede for Gómez; this is consistent with her behaviour throughout the play. She forgives him for abandoning her in Act II, she forgives him for selling her in Act III; and by marrying him her honour is restored. But, as the Queen makes clear, this cannot be the end of the matter:

> Aguarda, que si los dos
> estábamos ofendidos,
> tú estás vengado y yo no.   (389a)

and she orders Gómez to be executed:

> En cualquier delito, el rey
> es todo. Si parte has sido
> tú y le perdonas, yo no,
> porque no quede a los siglos
> la puerta abierta al perdón
> de semejantes delitos.   (389b)

It is not simply that any relenting on Gómez's part can only be taken as insincere and his pardon as an opportunity for further deception, as Ginés observes:

> Por Cristo,
> que si éste se sale sólo
> con casarse por castigo,
> que desde mañana vendo
> cuantas hallare.   (389a)

Gómez's crimes are the rebellion of an individual, but he has rebelled against not only Dorotea but her family and society as a whole. Dorotea herself may forgive, but the Queen must punish. It is a complete evasion of the moral problem to allow Gómez to survive unscathed, and this is a serious weakness of Vélez's play. Vélez here fell a victim to the temptation to produce the romantic, happy ending which he, so rightly, resisted in *La serrana de la Vera*.

The story of Gómez Arias is a variant on the familiar theme of honour, and our play has an affinity with the famous wife-murder plays and with *El alcalde de Zalamea*. But it differs from them in that the villain of the piece is the leading character. Gómez Arias is one of the very few evil protagonists in the whole of Calderón's repertoire. He is far more than the victim of a violent passion; he personifies lust and villainy. Whereas even the incestuous Amón, enslaved by his love for Tamar, wins our sympathy, Gómez is

despicable. He betrays the trust of Dorotea, rejects her as soon as
he has seduced her, and sells her to the Moors when he can find
no other means of disposing of her. He is a self-confessed *burlador*
who has no shame about what he has done; and he predicts the
same fate for Beatriz once she has submitted to him. Set against
his lust is the love of Dorotea. Dorotea does voluntarily elope with
Gómez, and her harrowing experiences, like those of Cervantes'
Dorotea, are in part the punishment of her ingenuousness and
indiscretion; she fails to see the consequences of her action and to
this extent is morally guilty. But she is blinded by a love which is
both sincere and legitimate, and she is the daughter of an authoritarian father. At the play's end she readily forgives the brutal outrage
of Gómez, and in the assault on Benamejí shows exemplary initiative
and courage. Dorotea's intentions are good; she deserves to be
rescued and to see her honour cleared.

The only other characters of importance who derive directly
from the source are El Cañerí and Ginés. El Cañerí, as we have
seen, is associated with Gómez Arias. If Gómez was a 'Judas de amor'
who failed lamentably in his obligations towards Dorotea, El Cañerí
and the *moriscos* he leads failed in their obligations to the Catholic
monarchs and thereby endangered the lives and spiritual welfare of
Christian subjects. Like Gómez, El Cañerí dies for his treachery. The
servant Ginés is also fitted into the play's pattern. His part is much
larger than the earlier Perico's, and though he contributes some
humour to the play, he is used primarily to set in relief the character
of his master. Like Catalinón in *El burlador de Sevilla* he is the
voice of protest, condemning Gómez's desertion of Beatriz in Act I,
his abandonment of Dorotea in Act II and her sale in Act III. His
sympathy for Dorotea in Act III underlines the callousness of Gómez
and he is made to share her fate. In the relief of Benamejí his
opportunism sets in relief the courage and integrity of Dorotea. And
throughout the play he is often made to comment on the behaviour of
the other characters.

The remaining characters are mostly new. The most important of
them is Beatriz who has much in common with Dorotea. Like
Dorotea, she is beautiful and in love with Gómez; and, her mind
clouded by passion, she is imprudent, not only in her relations with
Gómez whom she naively trusts, but with Félix. Beatriz indeed is

shown to be the first cause of the play's tragedy. By accusing Félix of cowardice, she drives him to seek revenge upon Gómez. More than once her reckless, irresponsible talk is censured. The parallel between her and Dorotea is emphasized by the similar situations at the end of Acts I and II, by Gómez's remark that Beatriz's fate will be the same as Dorotea's, and by Gómez's mistaking Dorotea for Beatriz. But Beatriz learns her lesson from Dorotea's misfortune and is undeceived. The four male parts are not extensive. The two fathers are honourable and courageous; but both have some responsibility for what happens to their daughters since both choose husbands for them without consulting them. A. A. Parker has drawn attention to Calderón's attitude towards fathers, particularly in respect of *La devoción de la cruz*:

> ...vió que la cuestión de la autoridad paterna tenía matices complicados, y en su teatro el trastorno moral que podría ocasionar en el hijo el abuso de esta autoridad llegó a ser un problema fundamental que le preocupó mucho. [1]

and we have noted in our chapter on *El médico de su honra* Mencía's reference to the abuse of parental authority:

> y mi padre atropella
> la libertad que hubo en mí.   (189a)

Dorotea's father, moreover, by seeking revenge rather than forgiving his daughter, is directly responsible for Gómez's carrying her off a second time. Of the two *galanes*, Don Juan has but a few lines, and is shown to be blinded by the beauty of Dorotea. In the same way, Félix is infatuated with Beatriz, and his jealousy leads him to bribe Beatriz's servant in order to enter her house. He is persuaded against his better judgement to seek revenge upon Gómez, and later is reckless enough to enter Beatriz's house a second time. Though a man of honour, he succumbs to jealousy and fails to win the lady he loves.

Calderón's total reconstruction of the source-play left little opportunity for detailed rewriting. His first act, though obviously inspired by the work of Vélez, has only an occasional parallel situation. He comes closest to the source in the exchange between

---

Gómez Arias and his servant, but although he uses the same stanza form, romance in E-A, he does not borrow a single line. His second act was entirely new. Only in Act III, with the disposal of 'la niña', the plans for an attack on the *morisco* fortress and finally the recovery of Dorotea and Gómez Arias' punishment, did he have occasion to rewrite scenes within the same general limits as those of Vélez. He did so, to judge by the details that have been borrowed, with the source text in front of him. Yet, despite the features in common, he recast and completely rewrote all these scenes and used a new metre.

Calderón's imagery owes little to Vélez. Many of the associations will be familiar from the plays we have discussed earlier. The moral confusion of Dorotea which makes her elope with Gómez is connected with the darkness and confusion of the final scene of Act I:

> la extraña
> confusión de aquella noche.   (368b)

She is deserted in a wood which shuts out the rays of the sun and is labyrinthine:

> En el verde laberinto
> destas peñas y estas ramas,
> defendido aún a los rayos
> del sol.   (368a)

and her dishonour is associated with madness and sleep. Calderón emphasizes the link between Gómez Arias and El Cañerí by applying to them the same epithets and images; both are monsters and wild beasts:

Gómez

¿Qué monstruo airado,	
que bárbaramente aleve	(380a)
el más fiero,	
más cruel y más inicuo	(386a)
Gómez Arias, un hombre	
fiero, alevoso y esquivo.	(386b)

El Cañerí

el fiero Cañerí	
adusto bárbaro alarbe	(375b)
Cañerí, ese monstruo fiero	(381b)
al fiero Cañerí.	(386b)

Little can be said about the staging of the two plays. Calderón's was first printed in the *Cuarta parte,* whose date of approval is June 18, 1672 but it was certainly written many years earlier, and the extant text may not represent the form in which it was first performed. The complicated situations at the end of Act II would seem to have required doors which would open and shut, lock and unlock. For the scene in which Dorotea is deserted by Gómez and discovered by El Cañerí, the *moriscos* first appear on the gallery and then descend by a staircase leading down to the main stage:

> CAÑERÍ. Bajad con silencio, que
> de aqueste monte en la falda
> caballos y gente he visto
> entre esas espesas matas.
> . . . .
> Baja
> con silencio, no nos sientan.   (370b)

The staircase may or may not have been in full view of the audience; the insistence upon the descent in the dialogue itself suggests perhaps that it was not. The first scene of Act III contains a similar situation; to judge by the stage directions, the *moriscos* first appear at the summons of Gómez on the gallery and then leave, coming on to the main stage by the normal entrance after Dorotea's long speech. In the source-play, according to the 1700 text, signals are made to the upper gallery, representing the fortress's walls, but the Moors come on to the main stage. At the end of Act III the stage directions of Calderón's play provide evidence of a spectacle which had no parallel in the source. Don Luis, the Christian Commander, and El Cañerí, grappling with each other in single-handed combat, fall from above, presumably from the gallery, before the assembled forces of the Queen:

> *La caja y clarín toca siempre, y salen la reina y todos los soldados que puedan al tablado, y caen desde lo alto abrazados* CAÑERÍ *y* DON LUIS (Vera Tassis, 308b).

The recasting of *La niña de Gómez Arias* is curiously similar to that of *Polifemo y Circe:* a large part of the source has been rejected and new material provided to replace it. But it diverges further from the source; only Act III has much in common with that of Vélez. Calderón reconstituted the whole play to concentrate on the issue between Gómez and the maiden; the parts of both have been extended and their characters more clearly delineated. The new characters, Beatriz, Don Félix and Don Juan, Don Luis and Don Diego, as well as the borrowed characters of Ginés and El Cañerí, are all carefully woven into the play's pattern; they are linked to or contrasted with Gómez and Dorotea, and they exemplify different facets of human conduct. And Calderón reverses the outcome of Vélez's play to provide a *dénouement* both dramatically and morally appropriate. Gómez and El Cañerí are characters whose conduct is evil, and they pay with their lives. The others by contrast have good intentions, but they too in pursuit of good fall short of the required standard of behaviour and to that extent contribute to the tragic outcome of the play. Calderón transformed the play of Vélez de Guevara into a work which is artistically superior and thoroughly his own.

VII

EL PRÍNCIPE CONSTANTE

C ALDERÓN'S *El príncipe constante,* [1] written towards the end of
the year 1628, is the story of Prince Ferdinand of Portugal, who
died a captive in the hands of the Moors. The historical facts are
the following. In 1415 the Portuguese wrested from the Moors
the town of Ceuta. Some twenty years later, in 1437, they sought
to strengthen their foothold on the African mainland and sent an
expedition against Tangier; in charge was Henry the Navigator,
accompanied by his younger brother Ferdinand. The expedition
failed. The Moors, forewarned of the attack, brought up strong
reinforcements and surrounded the Portuguese; and they consented
to spare them only if they would surrender Ceuta. Henry agreed,
and left Ferdinand behind as royal hostage. Back in Portugal,
however, the Portuguese were unwilling lightly to abandon Ceuta,
and although various attempts were made to come to different terms
with the Moors, Ferdinand remained in captivity. He died at Fez
in 1443. Fellow-prisoners of Ferdinand, who included his biographer
João Álvares, brought back relics of his body on their release
in 1451. His remains were finally recovered when Tangier fell to
the Portuguese in 1471, and were buried in state in the Monastery
of Batalha.

El príncipe constante, then, is historical, and I have studied at
length elsewhere the whole chain of testimony which reaches back

---

[1] Texts used:
  Source:
> *Comedias de Lope,* Parte 23, Osuna 132.
> *La fortuna adversa,* ed. A. E. Sloman in *The Sources
> of Calderón's 'El príncipe constante'* (Oxford, 1950).
  Calderón:
> *Primera parte,* 1636, 1640.
> *Comedias escogidas de los mejores ingenios,* VI, 1654.
> Ed. Vera Tassis, I, 1682.
> Ed. J. J. Keil, op. cit., pp. 260-81.
> Ed. J. E. Hartzenbusch, op. cit., I, 245-62.
> Ed. A. A. Parker (Cambridge, 1938).
> Ed. Astrana Marín, op. cit., pp. 895-924. (Madrid, 1945,
> 3.ª ed., revisada.)
> Ed. P. Pou Fernández (Zaragoza, 1950).
  Quotations are from my own text of the source and Astrana Marín's edition of
Calderón's play.

from Calderón's play to the biography of João Álvares. [1] I suggested in that study that Faria y Sousa's *Epítome de las historias portuguesas*, published in Madrid in 1628, with its disproportionate stress on the personal tragedy of Prince Ferdinand, probably led Calderón to choose this theme. But his immediate source was a play, *La fortuna adversa del infante Don Fernando de Portugal*, attributed to Lope de Vega, but possibly the lost *El príncipe constante* of the Valencian dramatist Tárrega, written perhaps 1595-98. By this time, nearly two hundred years after his death, Ferdinand had become a legendary figure. No longer the victim of circumstances, a pawn in the protracted negotiations between Portuguese and Moor, he was taken as having refused freedom for the sake of Ceuta, choosing to die a martyr that it might remain in Christian hands. Ferdinand was acclaimed the Spanish Regulus. *La fortuna adversa* was the last of a long line of chronicles and interpretations. Schack first called attention to *La fortuna adversa* in the *Nachträge* appended to second edition of his *Geschichte der dramatischen Literatur und Kunst in Spanien* in 1854. But neither Valentin Schmidt [2] nor K. L. Kannegeiser [3] refers to it, and Krenkel [4] and Maccoll, [5] editors of critical editions of *El príncipe constante*, merely repeat the observations of Schack. Yet, except for minor details taken from Faria y Sousa's *Epítome*, it was Calderón's exclusive source.

La fortuna adversa is modelled on the first Spanish biography of Ferdinand published at Medina in 1595, Román's *Historia y vida del religioso Infante don Fernando*. Written probably within a few years of the publication of Román's book, it follows Román closely. Act I opens at the Portuguese court with preparations for the attack on Tangier. The scene then moves to Africa, first to the Moorish court at Fez and later to Tangier where the Portuguese disembark. The act ends with the Portuguese defeat, their acceptance of the Moorish demand for Ceuta's return and Fernando's remaining behind as hostage. In Act II the scene moves back to the Portuguese Court where news arrives from Fernando who, whilst asking to be

---

[1] *The Sources of Calderón's 'El príncipe constante'*, with a critical edition of its immediate source, *La fortuna adversa del Infante don Fernando de Portugal* (a play attributed to Lope de Vega) (Oxford, 1950).
[2] *Die Schauspiele Calderons* (Elberfeld, 1857).
[3] *Der standhafte Prinz* (1861).
[4] *Klassische Bühnendichtungen der Spanier*, 1 (Leipzig, 1881).
[5] *Select Plays of Calderón* (London, 1888).

rescued, insists that on no account shall Ceuta be relinquished. The rest of the act is taken up with Fernando's experiences as a prisoner in Fez, in particular his suffering at the hands of the Moorish Vizir Lazaraque. Act III shows the breakdown of Fernando's health and his death in captivity. His body is restored to Portugal by the Moorish general Muley, whose life Fernando had spared at Tangier; Fernando's spirit comes to assist him and to provide him with an opportunity of killing Lazaraque. A sub-plot running throughout the play centres on the Moorish Queen, who competes with Arminda for the love of Muley and who makes advances to Ferdinand.

Calderón's *El príncipe constante* has the same general shape as *La fortuna adversa*. Act I is concerned with the assault on Tangier and the capture of Fernando, Act II with Fernando's treatment as a captive, and Act III with his death in captivity and the restoration of his remains. It carries over too the most important characters: Fernando himself, his brother Enrique, his nephew Alfonso who recovers his body, the King of Fez and the Moorish general Muley. And the Princess Fénix owes something to the Moorish Queen. *El príncipe constante* is coextensive with *La fortuna adversa*. Yet Calderón's handling of the action is so different that none of his scenes corresponds exactly with scenes in the source-play and few even have counterparts. Similarly, thirty-six characters of the earlier play have been reduced to fourteen, and even those which have survived have little in common with their originals. They are compared below:

La fortuna adversa.	El príncipe constante.
Don Fernando	Don Fernando
Don Enrique	Don Enrique
El rey niño	El rey Alfonso
El rey Eduardo	—
Alencastro	—
Mariscal	—
Ruygómez de Silva	Don Juan Coutiño
Diego	Brito, *gracioso*
Pedro	Cautivos
Juan	—
Luis	—
Julio	—
El rey moro	El rey de Fez, *viejo*
Lazaraque	—
Muley	Muley, *general*
—	Tarudante

La reina mora	Fénix
Arminda	—
Iataf	Celín
Gómel	Rosa
Gazul	Zora
Amete	Estrella
Cartero	Celima
Moro	—
Nuestra Señora	—
San Antonio de Padua	—
San Miguel	—
Pobres I-IV	—
Maceros I-II	—
Marineros I-II	—
Soldados	—
Criado	—
Un judío	

The total transformation of *La fortuna adversa* was required by Calderón's new conception of the story of Prince Ferdinand and in particular of the character of Ferdinand himself. The historical Ferdinand was a pious, sickly Prince who spent long hours in prayer and fasting, and ministered to the needs of the poor. In the assault on Tangier he took second place to Henry, and when it failed he was left behind to satisfy the demands of the Moors for a royal hostage. His death in captivity was due primarily to the Portuguese refusal to fulfil the promise made at Tangier. Ferdinand's greatness lay in his exemplary patience in adversity and his courage in face of hardship, ill-health and finally death. But his subordination to Henry and his essentially passive rôle in captivity did not lend themselves easily to dramatic treatment. Yet the portrait of Fernando in *La fortuna adversa* is more or less historical. In the play's first scene he appears as a prayerful and saintly figure who distributes clothes and food to the poor. At Tangier he is subordinate to Enrique, and he disembarks with the sea contingent whilst Enrique advances upon the town by land. The source dramatist to this extent keeps close to the record of Román, though he shows on stage only the section under the charge of Fernando. Calderón admits no trace of the diffident Ferdinand in his play; from the very outset he makes him tower above the other characters. Calderón was prepared even to reverse historical fact to achieve his purpose. Dispensing entirely with the material of the first scene of *La fortuna adversa*, he introduces him to his audience, in a speech of Muley, as a renowned soldier like Enrique:

> Enrique y Fernando, gloria
> deste siglo, que los mira
> coronados de victorias.
> Maestres de Cristo y de Avis
> son, los dos pechos adornan
> cruces de perfiles blancos,
> una verde y otra roja.   (899a)

and at his first appearance, in the landing scene at Tangier, he is in charge of the expedition.

Prince Ferdinand's renown rested above all upon his behaviour as a prisoner, and the greater part of both the source-play and *El príncipe constante* is necessarily concerned with his endurance of the hardships and suffering of captivity. But Calderón takes advantage of the battle at Tangier in the first act to portray the active side of Fernando as a prelude to his resistance and endurance later. Elsewhere I have shown how his conception of Fernando corresponds closely with St. Thomas's definition of the virtue of Fortitude. [1]

1. Aggressive side:
    (a) *Magnanimitas* (opposed to *Praesumptio, Ambitio, Inanis Gloria* and *Pusillanimitas*).
    (b) *Magnificentia* (opposed to *Parvificentia*).
2. Enduring side:
    (a) *Patientia*.
    (b) *Perseverantia* and *Constantia* (opposed to *Mollities* and *Pertinacia*).

Fernando's behaviour at Tangier is quite different, certainly, in the two plays. The humble Prince who in *La fortuna adversa* is under the charge of his brother and kneels in prayer on the beach, is converted into a bold, confident commander. He scorns ill-omens and insists on being the first to disembark, though he avoids at the same time the excesses of presumption, ambition and vain-glory. He exemplifies *magnanimitas*. Nor is this the only aspect of Fernando, the man of action. Seizing upon a brief incident of the source-play, Calderón makes him generous in victory. In *La fortuna adversa* Fernando wounds and captures the Moorish general Muley, and in

---

[1] Op. cit., pp. 72 ff. For Calderón's thought, see the excellent studies of A. A. Parker, *The Allegorical Drama of Calderón* (Oxford, 1943) and Don Eugenio Frutos, *La filosofia de Calderón en sus autos sacramentales* (Zaragoza, 1952).

a spontaneous act of clemency spares his life and releases him. The source dramatist disposed of the episode in two *coplas reales:*

> Sale MULEY *herido, y tras dél* DON FERNANDO.
>
> MULEY. Ten, esp[a]ñol, bueno está;
> no me mates.
>
> FERNANDO. No ayas miedo,
> que tu muerte no me da
> la gloria que ganar puedo.
> Queda a Dios.
>
> *(Vase.)*
>
> MULEY. Ve con Alá.
> ¡O valor inacessible
> de aquella fuerça terrible!
> ¡O hidalguía notable
> de aquel contrario visible!
> Que después de parecer
> fuego por adonde passa
> con la espada y su poder,
> al rendido es blanda masa.
> ¡Cómo te he de encarecer,
> valeroso cauallero,
> de tus christianos azero!
> Ya la muerte en mí endereça,
> porque me hirió en la cabeza
> en el encuentro primero.   (963-981)

Calderón, recalling Narváez's generosity towards Abindarráez, incorporates Góngora's famous *romance Entre los sueltos caballos*, and expands the few lines of the original into a long and moving scene; and he insists upon the liberality of Fernando:

> que a quien liberal ofrece,
> sólo aceptar es lisonja.   (904a)
>
> Generosa acción es dar,
> y más la vida.   (904a)

By means of this scene Calderón supplies what St. Thomas had shown to be the second part of the aggressive side of Fortitude, *magnificentia.*

Calderón's presentation of Fernando as a fearless Christian crusader and his elaboration of the incident of Muley's release account for the principal divergencies between the first acts of *El príncipe constante* and *La fortuna adversa.* Fernando is transformed into an intrepid man of action, the embodiment of the aggressive side of Fortitude. By this means Calderón postponed until the end of Act I the fundamental problem posed by his story, namely that it concerned a passive hero, remarkable not for what he does but for what he endures. Whatever liberties he might take with it, endurance had necessarily to be an essential feature. To some extent, the difficulty was met by the traditional view of Fernando as a Spanish Regulus, who was taken to have volunteered to remain a hostage at Tangier and to have refused freedom at the price of Ceuta. But the significance as drama of this active resistance seems to have gone completely unrecognized by the source dramatist. Fernando's volunteering to remain behind at Tangier, for example, is passed over in *La fortuna adversa* in a few lines:

FERNANDO.	Pues, hidalgos, ¿qué haremos?
MENESES.	Todos que la des queremos.
FERNANDO.	Pues vamos tratarse ha.
	¿Quién ha de yr por rehenes?
ALENCASTRO.	Escoge a tu parecer,
	pues aquí a todos nos tienes.
FERNANDO.	Ninguno ha de yr; yo é de ser.
MORO.	¡Gran bondad, gran valor tienes!
RUYGÓMEZ.	Yremos los tres contigo.
FERNANDO.	No haréis: solos mis criados
	quiero 'que vayan conmigo.
ALENCASTRO.	¡Señor!
FERNANDO.	Viuid descuydados;
	¡Alto, vamos, moro amigo! (1101-13)

His decision to reject freedom at the expense of Ceuta is first made known by King Eduardo:

Él me auisa, y es bien cierto
que esto su valor lo puede,
que no dé a Ceuta, aunque quede
por ello en África muerto...   (1134-37)

and is confirmed by Fernando's letter; in both instances it is presented indirectly. Later, after a scene concerned entirely with the sub-plot, Fernando points out that he is a hostage, not a captive:

Aconséjate mejor,
que yo no vine cautivo.   (1635-36)

that only the Portuguese King has the right to surrender Ceuta:

> Si es la ciudad de mi rey...   (1685)

and that the pact at Tangier was a legitimate stratagem:

> Fué de la guerra ambición.   (1693)
> por excusar mayor daño
> quando su perdición vieron.   (1718-1719)

And he offers money for his freedom:

> ¿Y si dineros te dan,
> acaso? (no bastarán?)   (1747-48)

Now for the first time he is allowed a note of defiance which anticipates his attitude in *El príncipe constante:*

> ...hazed aquestos tiranos
> con crueldad embrauecer.
> Morir es gloria infinita
> entre esta gente por vos...   (1818-21)

The only stage in the progressive deterioration of Fernando's position as a captive which is the result of any positive decision or action on his part is his rejection of the advances of the Moorish Queen and consequently of her offer of help.

Fernando's refusal to accept freedom at the expense of Ceuta, which in *La fortuna adversa* is made known only through the words of the Portuguese King and by letter, in *El príncipe constante* is the issue round which Calderón has built one of the two great scenes of the play. He recognised the dramatic significance of this momentous decision of one whose story is essentially one of passivity. Portugal was willing to sacrifice Ceuta to liberate its Prince, and Eduardo's will stipulated that the exchange should be made. Mere acquiescence on Fernando's part meant freedom; but freedom on terms which Fernando regarded as dishonourable. His courageous decision, therefore, was both crucial and aggresive, and Calderón devoted infinite care to its preparation to secure the maximum dramatic effect. It was partly perhaps with this scene in mind that he simplified the issue at Tangier at the end of Act I. Historically, and in *La fortuna adversa*, the Portuguese contingent is spared on condition that Ceuta shall be returned to the Moors; and Fernando remains behind as a hostage. In *El príncipe constante* Fernando is a prisoner of war who surrenders to the Moorish King after a hand-to-hand fight; and the King makes this release conditional upon the return of Ceuta. Whereas in the source-play the issue is between Ceuta's return and the liberation of the Portuguese forces—and having been liberated, the Portuguese were under a moral obligation to return Ceuta, irrespective of the attitude of Fernando—in *El príncipe constante* Ceuta is quite simply the price of Fernando's freedom. Fernando, that is, can legitimately weigh his own freedom against the retention of Ceuta in Christian hands.

In face of the sudden reversal of fortune at the end of Act I, Fernando does not despair. He accepts defeat with equanimity and cheers Enrique. And if Muley misconstrues his words:

> Iré a la esfera cuyos rayos sigo (905b)

Fernando's meaning can only be that he willingly bows to what he believes to be the divine will. At the same time it is dramatic irony envisaging his martyrdom and ascent to Heaven. His patience, allowing him to be cheerful in the face of adversity, is a foretaste of his behaviour in Acts II and III. And Calderón is already hinting at Fernando's decision in the great scene in Act II. The Moorish King states clearly the choice to be made, Fernando or Ceuta:

> Pero dile a Duarte, que en llevalle
> será su intento vano,
> si a Ceuta no me entrega por su mano.   (905b)

and Fernando's words to Enrique call attention to the dilemma:

> Dirásle a nuestro hermano
> que haga aquí como príncipe cristiano
> en la desdicha mía.   (905b)

What does a Christian prince do? Sacrifice his own brother or a Christian town? Enrique understands Fernando to mean that Ceuta should be surrendered, and he agrees:

> Pues ¿quién de sus grandezas desconfía?   (905b)

and this is what King Eduardo will do. Fernando then repeats his injunction:

> Esto te encargo, y digo
> que haga como cristiano.   (905b)

Fernando's words imply that Enrique has misunderstood him, but he does not say so directly, nor does he make any specific request to the King his brother:

> Dirásle al Rey... Mas no le digas nada,
> si con grande silencio el miedo vano
> estas lágrimas lleva al Rey mi hermano. (906a)

Professor Wilson sees in the ambiguity of Fernando's words human frailty and moral uncertainty, which make his later saintliness all the more convincing. [1] Fernando does not lose hope, but his hesitation contrasts with his resoluteness and determination in Act II. Whereas at the end of his act the earlier dramatist devoted only a few inconsequential lines to Fernando's fate, Calderón points to the fundamental issue at stake and hints at later developments.

In *La fortuna adversa* Fernando is ill-treated by his captors from the first. Act II opens with news of his arduous journey to Fez, and in the second scene he is already in chains and imprisoned in a dungeon. Calderón in contrast shows him receiving the treatment due to a royal prisoner. The Moorish King is confident that Ceuta will be returned and invites him to a tiger fight; and Fernando cheers his fellow captives and keeps alive their hopes of an early release. By this means Calderón is able to show the dramatic effect of Fernando's later defiance, an abrupt change from the conditions appropriate to a royal person to those of a slave, as well as from the prospect of liberation to the slender hope only of escape. The great scene itself owes almost nothing to the source-play. There, news of King Eduardo's death does not come until Act III and Eduardo is made to oppose the return of Ceuta; Fernando's opposition, as we have seen, is shown only indirectly by letter and in lines of the King. Moreover, the argument of the Moors is that Ceuta is theirs by right, since the Portuguese were spared at Tangier. It is true that Fernando's arguments against Ceuta's return in *El príncipe constante* are similar to those contained in his letter in the source, and his contemptuous attack on Mohammedanism may well have been suggested by the reference to the 'fea y sucia seta de Mahoma'. But details scattered through a number of scenes of *La*

---

[1] E. M. Wilson and W. J. Entwistle, 'Calderón's *El príncipe constante*: two appreciations', *MLR*, XXXIV (1939), 208.

fortuna adversa, and many that are new, are concentrated in one great impassioned speech. In neither play is Fernando a mere passive hero. His captivity and death are not imposed on him by circumstances beyond his control, but are self-chosen, deliberately and advisedly, to prevent the sacrifice of a Christian town. But the source dramatist failed utterly to make dramatic capital out of Fernando's choice, a failure which is all the more grave since the opportunity was almost unique in the story of one whose greatness lay in endurance. Calderón's achievement was to use the occasion to the full. Fernando's stopping short the speech of Enrique emphasises the prompt and decisive action required; the aggressiveness of his words mirrors perfectly his aggressive action; and his tearing up the documents to effect the exchange is a fitting climax to his heated outbursts. His action brings upon him at once a change of estate; he is stripped and bound with chains and subjected to the cruelty and hardship of a common slave.

This scene, with its tremendous dramatic impact and its brilliant rhetoric, has no counterpart in the source. It was Calderón's first and most important occasion to present Fernando the captive as an active hero, by exploiting to the full his refusal to accept freedom at the price of a Christian town. At the end of Act II Calderón devised a second situation which demanded the same active resistance. After Enrique's departure there remains for Fernando, as for all captives, the hope of escape, and his hopes are raised by Muley who awaits an opportunity of repaying the debt he owes to his deliverer. As early as Act I, before taking leave of Fernando, Muley remarks:

> *(Dentro.)* Espero que he de pagarte
> algún día tantos bienes. (904a)

and he reiterates these sentiments immediately after Fernando's defiance of the Moorish King:

> *(Ap.)* Ya ha llegado la ocasión
> de que mi lealtad se vea.
> La vida debo a Fernando,
> yo le pagaré la deuda. (911a)

These words anticipate Muley's plan, disclosed at the end of Act II, to secure Fernando's escape. Fernando is grateful to Muley; but as soon as the King makes Muley personally responsible for his safe-keeping, Fernando refuses his offer. The situation was suggested to Calderón probably by the few lines in *La fortuna adversa* in which the Moorish Queen offers to help Fernando if he will return her love; and in the same scene in the source-play a Jew is caught plotting to rescue him. But the source dramatist again had failed to use his material to any dramatic advantage. For Calderón this was an opportunity for a second positive and critical decision by Fernando. Having rejected freedom for the sake of Ceuta, Fernando now rejects all hope of escape for the sake of the honour of his friend. It is fitting that at this point there is a reference to his constancy:

> ...porque yo,
> por mi Dios y por mi ley,
> seré un *príncipe constante*
> en la esclavitud de Fez.   (915b)

Any hope of Fernando's liberation on terms other than the surrender of Ceuta are dashed early in Act III in the interview between Alfonso and the Moorish King. In *La fortuna adversa* Fernando is condemned finally to solitary confinement without the comfort of his fellow captives. He dies on stage, and the Virgin Mary, St. Anthony and St. Michael descend from above to be present at his death-bed. Here at least was some kind of spectacle, although there could be nothing very dramatic about Fernando's last show of humility. For the death-bed scene Calderón substitutes a final act of defiance. Reduced now to a loathsome wreck Fernando still clings to life in order to praise God; and when Muley, who provides him with food, is sent away, he begs from the King himself and is provoked to his moving outburst. This famous speech of Fernando is characteristic of the great declamatory orations of Calderón's plays; its brilliant rhetoric and imagery owe nothing to the source-play. It is intended as a final statement of Fernando's convictions. One who has chosen captivity rather than sacrifice a Christian town or a friend's honour now faces death itself with courage and confidence. And, although in face of the Moorish King's inclemency, no initiative is required of Fernando, his final act of endurance is given expression in a speech which is magnificently aggressive and dramatic. It has no counterpart in *La fortuna adversa*.

Neither *La fortuna adversa* nor *El príncipe constante* ends with

Fernando's death. In both his spirit returns to inspire those who undertake to restore his body to Portugal. The source dramatist follows a fictitious story of the recovery of Fernando's remains recorded by Román, in which the Moorish King's nephew, wrongly accused of plotting against his uncle, decides to be revenged by removing Fernando's body from the gates of Fez and bringing it in person to Portugal. Muley is there responsible for transporting Fernando's body to Lisbon, thus repaying a debt of gratitude; and Fernando's spirit returns to assist Muley and his companions, and to pursue the cruel Lazaraque and allow Muley the chance of killing him. Calderón took the idea of Fernando's reappearance from *La fortuna adversa,* but he made the dénouement more impressive and significant by reverting to the authentic story of the recovery of Fernando's remains by King Alfonso after the capture of Tangier in 1471. Fernando reappears not simply to assist his fellow captives to carry his bones to Portugal but to inspire and encourage a new Portuguese assault on Africa and to dispel the misgivings of the fearful Enrique, as he had done at Tangier. Alfonso's troops avenge the earlier defeat, and Fernando's spirit is made to appear a second time at the head of the victorious Portuguese forces which enter Fez. The Moorish King admits defeat, and hands over the remains of Fernando in exchange for his daughter Fénix and Tarudante, whom Alfonso has taken captive. The play ends when the coffin has been lowered to the Portuguese from the walls of Fez and is borne off to the Portuguese ships. Calderón's final scene shows the triumph of the Portuguese; Fernando's military defeat at Tangier is avenged by Alfonso's victory. It shows too the granting of Fernando's last wish that his body should be restored to Portugal for Christian burial and that he should be interred in the mantle of his order. Even death has not put an end to Fernando's grievances, for his body hangs at the walls of Fez, exposed to insults and mockery. Alfonso delivers Fernando's body from this final affront and assures it Christian burial.

Far more important is the symbolical significance of this final scene. It asserts the invincibility of Fernando's spirit, the triumph of his personal faith. When in Act II Fernando rejects freedom at the expense of Ceuta he reproves Enrique for words which, he claims, would be unworthy even on the lips of a pagan:

> ...aun de un hombre lo fueran
> vil, de un bárbaro sin luz
> de la fe de Cristo eterna.   (909a)

and he goes on to ask:

> ¿fuera católica acción...
> que los templos soberanos,
> atlantes de las esferas,
> en vez de doradas luces,
> adonde el sol reverbera,
> vieran otomanas sombras;
> y que sus lunas opuestas
> en la iglesia, estos eclipses
> ejecutasen tragedias?   (909a-b)

This association of the Christian faith with light runs through the whole play. Fernando's persecution is linked with darkness; the dungeon, for example, to which he is committed is wet and dark:

> ...en mazmorras
> húmedas y oscuras duerma,   (911a)

Yet he remains constant in his faith, and his constancy is related to light. Muley tells the King how Fernando's friends carry him into the sun:

> Pasando la noche fría
> en una mazmorra dura,
> constante en su fe porfía,
> y al salir la lumbre pura
> del sol, que es padre del día,
> los cautivos (¡pena fiera!)
> en una mísera estera
> le ponen...   (916a)

And, in his last appearance on the stage. Fernando thanks God for the sun's light and heat:

> ...yo bendigo al día
> por la gracia que nos da
> Dios en él; pues claro está
> que cada hermoso arrebol
> y cada rayo del sol
> lengua de fuego será
> con que le alabo y bendigo.   (919a)

> Cuando acaban de sacarme
> de un calabozo, me dais
> un sol para calentarme:
> liberal, Señor, estáis.   (919a)

These implied associations become explicit in the climax of Fernando's last speech:

> ...y aunque sea
> mi esfera esta estancia sucia,
> firme he de estar en mi fe;
> porque es el sol que me alumbra
> porque es la luz que me guía,
> es el laurel que me ilustra.   (921a)

His death coincides with the setting of the sun, and the Moorish King tells Alfonso:

> sabe, Alfonso, que a la hora
> que Fénix salió ayer tarde [1]
> con el sol llegó al ocaso,
> sepultándose en dos mares
> de la muerte y de la espuma,
> juntos el sol y el Infante.   (924a)

But his spirit lives on, and he appears bearing a flaming torch. Fernando emerges from the darkness of suffering and death to light.

Fernando's faith allows him to remain constant; it is also a beacon of light to others. When the Portuguese return to Africa to rescue him it is dark and Enrique is afraid:

> Mira que ya la noche,
> envuelta en sombras, el luciente coche
> del sol esconde entre las sombras puras.   (922b)

But Alfonso, like his uncle Fernando, is fortified by faith:

> Pelearemos a oscuras;
> que a la fe que me anima,
> ni el tiempo ni el poder la desanima.   (922b)

And Fernando's spirit comes in person to light them on their way:

> ...con esta luciente
> antorcha desasida del oriente
> tu ejército arrogante
> alumbrado he de ir siempre delante,
> para que hoy en trofeos
> iguales, grande Alfonso, a tus deseos,
> llegues a Fez, no a coronarte agora,
> sino a librar mi ocaso en el aurora.   (922b-923a)

---

[1] Parte, *le vió* for *salió*.

This is no empty rhetoric. Inspired by Fernando's faith, which is symbolized by the torch, the Portuguese are assured of victory. Later, Fernando appears at the head of the triumphant Portuguese army:

> En el horror de la noche,
> por sendas que nadie sabe,
> te guié; ya con el sol
> pardas nubes se deshacen.   (923b)

The image is the same, and the echoes of St. John of the Cross would seem to confirm that Calderón intended to point to more than the military success of the Portuguese army. By the light of faith Fernando has triumphed over the darkness of death, and he inspires others to the same spiritual victory.

The author of. La fortuna adversa was content to accept the general arrangement of Fernando's story, which he found in the biography of Román, in so far as it could be accommodated within the framework of a play. Calderón conceived the story anew. He saw Fernando as the exemplary Christian crusader and the embodiment of Fortitude, and he recognized that, if Fernando's greatness rested primarily upon his endurance, his story could be presented satisfactorily on the stage only by exploiting those instances of active resistance which occurred in the source-play, and by devising new ones. The supreme moments of El príncipe constante are Fernando's rejection of freedom at the expense of Ceuta, his refusal of Muley's offer of escape and his final defiant outburst against the Moorish King.

The new conception of Fernando necessarily affected Enrique who had to take second place. But Calderón saw in Enrique the means of setting Fernando into relief by contrast, and the renowned Henry the Navigator, whose very recklessness was probably the primary cause of the Tangier disaster, is converted into one who is diffident and defeatist. He trips on landing in Africa and frets over this and other ill-omens. Fernando, on the other hand, by his presence of mind, turns bad omens into good, and reprimands his brother for falling into the error of the infidel. Many of Fernando's exhortations are addressed to Enrique in person:

> Pierde, Enrique, a esas cosas el recelo
> porque...   (900b)
> ¡Ea, Enrique, buen principio
> esta ocasión nos ofrece!
> ¡Ánimo!   (901b)

Historical truth was incompatible with what was dramatically appropriate only to the extent that Enrique should be subordinate to Fernando. But, for the sake of contrast, Calderón reverses the facts of history. One wonders if his audience did not find this particular 'suspension of disbelief' a little disconcerting. The contrast between Enrique and Fernando is maintained throughout *El príncipe constante*. When, at the end of Act I, Fernando is captured by the Moorish King, he addresses his words of cheer to Enrique:

> Enrique,
> tu voz más sentimiento no publique;
> que en la suerte importuna
> éstos son los sucesos de fortuna.   (905b)

In Act II it is Enrique who comes to Africa with the humiliating documents to effect the exchange of Fernando for the Christian town of Ceuta, and who is reprimanded by Fernando:

> No prosigas, cesa,
> cesa, Enrique; porque son
> palabras indignas ésas,
> no de un portugués infante,
> de un maestre, que profesa
> de Cristo la religión,
> pero aun de un hombre lo fueran
> vil, de un bárbaro sin luz
> de la fe de Cristo eterna...   (909a)

Historically, Enrique had no part in the recovery of the body of Fernando, and the source dramatist dispensed with him after Act II. But Calderón allows him to accompany Alfonso to Africa in Act III, and in a second landing-scene, which parallels the landing-scene in Act I, he is again fearful and diffident, expressing his misgivings about the time and place of Alfonso's assault. Enrique's diffidence, as I pointed out in my earlier study, is the caution of one who looks for no help from Providence; Fernando's confidence is the faith of the Christian crusader. Alfonso, on the other hand, mirrors his uncle Fernando. In *La fortuna adversa* he appears only in the final scene to be crowned King of Portugal and to welcome Muley with the relics of Fernando. Calderón has amplified the part. Alfonso comes in disguise to Fez to offer money for Fernando's ransom and his words before leaving anticipate his return at the head of the new Portuguese expedition. In the landing scene in Act III he shows the same crusading zeal as Fernando, and like Fernando he rebuts the fears of Enrique. In this way, Calderón couples Alfonso with Fernando whose remains he is to restore to Portugal, and both are set in relief by Enrique.

Calderón's new *dénouement* employing the authentic account of the recovery of Fernando's body by Alfonso rather than the fictitious 'nephew' story would seem to have been responsible for Fénix, the one important new character of *El príncipe constante*. Alfonso V of Portugal captured Arzila and Tangier in 1471, and by a treaty signed with the Governor of Arzila, Mawlay Sayh (Muley Xeque), exchanged the Governor's wives and son, who had been taken prisoner, for the relics of Fernando. This ending for Calderón's play required some person or persons to be exchanged for Fernando, a new requirement since in *La fortuna adversa* Fernando's body is stolen from Fez and transported to Portugal by Muley. The rôle is filled by Fénix, daughter of the Moorish King. Fénix owes something to the Moorish Queen of *La fortuna adversa*. The Queen competes with Arminda for Muley's love and, when worsted by Arminda, turns her attention to Fernando. The vulgar amours of the Moorish Queen give way to a more delicate and aristocratic love-affair centring on the lady Fénix, for whose love Muley competes with Tarudante, Prince of Morocco. But what is a detachable sub-plot in *La fortuna adversa* with a considerable amount of action is scarcely developed by Calderón; Tarudante, one of the two lovers, first appears in Act III and exchanges only a very few lines with Fénix; and the relationship between Muley and Fénix is never clearly stated, consisting of a series of misunderstandings which are brushed aside when at the play's end Alfonso asks that the two shall marry. The source dramatist had linked the Moorish Queen with Fernando by making her offer to help him provided he returned her love. Calderón does not perpetuate this idea: Fernando is made to favour the suit of Muley and any fears of Muley that he might be another rival for Fénix's love are unfounded. Yet, for all that, Fénix is closely connected with Fernando.

Fénix's principal contribution to Calderón's play was perhaps suggested by the circumstances which required her part. At the end of the play she must be exchanged for Fernando's remains. This situation of a lady who is bartered for a corpse would have recalled for Calderón the stock antithesis between Beauty and Death and inspired, I suggest, the conception of Fénix as a beautiful lady obsessed with death. From the very first scene emphasis is laid upon the *hermosura* of Fénix. Zara refers to her in the third line as 'Fénix hermosa', all the other maidservants call attention to her beauty and Fénix's own first words are 'El espejo' and 'De qué sirve la hermosura'. Throughout the play, the various characters with whom Fénix is concerned—the King her father, her lover Muley, Tarudante and Fernando himself—all without exception preface their remarks with references to her beauty. And the old hag who foretells her fate states specifically that 'this beauty' will be the price of a corpse:

> ¡Ay infelice mujer!
> ¡Ay forzosa desventura!
> ¿Que en efecto esta hermosura
> precio de un muerto ha de ser?   (906b)

Fénix serves to accentuate the qualities and the stature of Fernando. Like Fernando, she is beset with misfortune. In the first scene she explains that she is sad without knowing the reason of her sadness:

> ...de la pena mía
> no sé la naturaleza;
> que entonces fuera tristeza
> lo que hoy es melancolía.
> Sólo sé que sé sentir;
> lo que sé sentir no sé;
> que ilusión del alma fué.   (896a)

The distinction between *tristeza* and *melancolía* and the play of words in the last three lines admirably convey to the audience the confusion of Fénix. [1] It derives in part at least from her love for Muley, and is soon aggravated by her father's announcement that she must marry Prince Tarudante of Morocco, and by Muley's jealousy. Finally, she is visited by an old hag who predicts that she will be bartered for a corpse. Like the beautiful Mariene of *El mayor monstruo, los celos,* whose death is predicted by a Jewish astrologer,

---

[1] Cf. E. M. Wilson, op. cit., 213.

Fénix becomes obsessed by evil forebodings and falls a victim to melancholy. Her words are one long bewailing of her fate.

Fernando and Fénix are first brought together in the second part of Act II. Before this, the contrast between them has been established in the first scene of the Act where Fernando's cheering of his fellow-captives follows immediately upon Fénix's interview with Muley; against Fénix's melancholy are set the patience and compassion of Fernando. When later the two meet, the contrast is clear. This scene with its famous parallel sonnets has rightly been praised by critics as one of the most beautifully lyrical scenes in the Spanish theatre. But it is more than a lyrical interlude; it has an important dramatic purpose. For Fernando the flowers symbolise the fate of man; they reveal the transience of time and the inevitability of death, facts of life which Fernando accepts with resignation. Fénix, having requested flowers to distract her, discovers in them yet another warning of facts from which she is trying to escape. She dislikes both flowers and stars which remind her that she, like them, must die. The interview brings out the contrast between the two characters and the constancy of Fernando, which safeguards him from sorrow in the face of hardship and death. When in Act III Fénix pleads with the King on Fernando's behalf it is because of his repugnant condition:

> Horror da a cuantos le ven
> en tal estado... (916b)

Afraid of death, she is terrified to look upon the dying Fernando; and later, when she sees him after his last act of defiance, her only words are exclamations of horror and she rushes off panic-stricken: ·

> Horror con tu voz me das
> y con tu aliento me hieres.
> ¡Déjame, hombre! ¿Qué me quieres?
> Que no puedo sentir más. (921b)

In the play's last scene she denounces her father for abandoning her to the Portuguese and, like him, despairs:

> FÉNIX. ¡Ay de mí! Ya mi esperanza
> de todo punto se acabe.
> REY. Ya no me queda remedio
> para vivir un instante. (924a)

Fénix is a pitiful character, well-intentioned, charitable, but obsessed by the terror of death and lacking the Christian constancy of Fernando. She is humiliated at the end of the play when she is exchanged for Fernando's bones. The contrast between Fernando and Fénix is wholly without precedent in the source-play. [1]

The other main characters of *El príncipe constante*, though changed, owe rather more to their opposite numbers in *La fortuna adversa*. The King of Fez derives from two earlier characters. The source dramatist, following closely the biography of Román, included in his play both the Banū Marīn King, 'Abd-al-Haqq' (Adulaque) and his vizier Al-Azrak (Lazaraque); it was Al-Azrak who was made responsible for the cruel treatment of Fernando and at the end of the play was stabbed to death by Muley. Calderón has fused Adulaque and Lazaraque into a single character, 'el rey de Fez', who alone is responsible for Moorish policy and in particular for the treatment of Fernando. In place of the weakling puppet Adulaque and the treacherous intriguing vizier who held the reins of Government, Calderón presents a King who is respected by his subjects and feared by his enemies. The King first appears as an authoritarian father, obliging Fénix to accept the hand of Tarudante. When informed of the Portuguese expedition against Tangier he is resourceful and resolute. At Tangier he is personally responsible for the capitulation of the Portuguese by defeating their commander Fernando in single combat. He generously spares all but Fernando himself and his conditions for his ransom are unexceptionable. In Act II he is courteous to his royal captive; he invites him to a tiger fight and formally expresses his condolences with him when news arrives of Eduardo's death. But his attitude changes when Fernando rejects freedom at Ceuta's expense and delivers a contemptuous attack upon Mohammedanism. He at once reduces Fernando to the state of a common slave, and inflicts upon him hardship and suffering which lead to his early death in captivity. He is obdurate in the face of the appeals of Fénix and Muley, and merciless to

---

[1] There may well be some significance in the fact that both Fénix and the town of Ceuta are associated with beauty. William M. Whitby, for example, in *BC*, VIII (1956), 1-4, suggests a parallel between the love triangle of the subordinate action, Muley-Fénix-Tarudante, and the triangle of a different kind in the main action, Fernando–Ceuta–Moorish King. But Fénix is a major character who cannot be relegated to a sub-plot; like Rosaura in *La vida es sueño*, she belongs to the whole play, not to a part of it. And the rigid equation of Fénix with Ceuta in my view obscures rather than illuminates the play's final scene.

Fernando on his death-bed. In defeat he despairs, overcome by the sudden reversal of fortune, and is prepared to sacrifice the life of his own daughter. The King's treatment of Fernando is legitimate but cruel. Fernando, certainly, provoked him with his abuse of Islam, and alone stands between him and the return of Ceuta which in Christian hands is a permanent insult to the Moors; only when thwarted by Fernando does the King resort to cruelty to break down his resistance. Yet both Muley and Fénix are made to protest against the treatment of Fernando, whose own last defiant speech is primarily an attack on cruelty, above all in kings whose hall-mark is clemency. But it is against the King's cruelty that Fernando sets his Christian fortitude, a conflict to which Calderón refers again and again in the latter half of the play:

REY.   ...que yo
              rigor tengo.
FERNANDO.   Y yo paciencia.   (911a)
REY.   Veré, bárbaro, veré
            si llega a más tu paciencia
            que mi rigor.   (911a)
FERNANDO.   Mayor que su rigor es mi paciencia.   (911b)

Muley is the character of Calderón's play who approximates most closely to his counterpart in the source. The earlier Muley, spared in the fighting at Tangier, shows his gratitude by risking his life to bring Fernando food; later he steals his body and bears it to Portugal. He is involved also in a sub-plot in which the Moorish Queen and the girl Arminda compete with each other for his love. Calderón, by his significant extension of the scene in which Fernando spares Muley, attached more importance to the friendship between them; but his principal addition is the attempt by Muley to allow Fernando to escape. As well as shedding light on the character of Fernando, this new episode underlines Muley's sense of obligation to a friend. In Act III Muley is made to plead on Fernando's behalf with the King, and it is he who brings Fernando food. The conduct of Muley is inferior to that of Fernando. On more than one occasion his anxiety and fears are set against Fernando's hope and cheerfulness. Perhaps the difference between them is suggested by the 'light' or 'sun' which inspires them. Muley's 'sun' is Fénix, Fernando's is God; and Calderón makes Muley

14

misunderstand the words of Fernando when he is captured by the Moorish King:

> Iré a la esfera cuyos rayos sigo.   (905b)

But Muley strives to repay the generosity of one who spared his life, and is a true friend to him in his misfortune. His chivalry is ultimately rewarded when he wins the hand of Fénix:

> D. ALFONSO.   te pido
> que aquí con Muley la cases,
> por la amistad que yo sé
> que tuvo con el Infante.   (924b)

The most important of the remaining characters is Don Juan, who replaced the four officers who accompanied Fernando and Enrique to Tangier in *La fortuna adversa.* Don Juan, as I have shown elsewhere, [1] is D. Juan Coutiño, Count of Miralva, a historical character taken from Faria y Sousa's *Epítome de las historias portuguesas.* The Count is reputed for his bravery during the assault on Arzila in 1471, which cost him his life. Although like King Alfonso he is a generation younger than Fernando, Don Juan appears in *El príncipe constante* as his contemporary. He is a member of the expedition to Tangier and Fernando's faithful companion in captivity, bearing witness both to his hardships and to his constancy. He risks punishment to bring Fernando food, and when his master dies stays like a faithful watchdog to take care of his body:

> D. JUAN.   Un hombre, que, aunque me maten,
> no he de dejar a Fernando,
> y aunque de congoja rabie,
> he de ser perro leal
> que en muerte he de acompañarle.   (923a)

Juan symbolizes loyalty. Although, like Muley, he falls short of the saintliness of Fernando, his loyalty is recognized before the curtain falls by the friendly greeting of King Alfonso:

> D. ALFONSO.   Don Juan, amigo,
> ¡buena cuenta del Infante
> me habéis dado!   (924b)

---

[1] Op. cit., p. 60.

Prince Tarudante has only a minor part; he makes his first appearance in Act III and is ineffective both in his advances to Fénix and in his support of the Moorish King. He is compassionate to Fernando, but when in the final scene Fénix is given to Muley he is allowed no opportunity even to express his feelings. He was conceived probably as a reflection of the Moorish King, as Alfonso was a reflection of Fernando. The *gracioso* Brito is the counterpart of the jargon-speaking Iataf of *La fortuna adversa;* but the part is considerably reduced and he contributes only two items of humour. This is the only relief in the whole play to the mood of impending tragedy. *Gracioso*-like, he is frightened of water and cowardly in battle, but he loyally serves Fernando in captivity and, like Don Juan, wins freedom.

Calderón reduced the thirty-six characters of the source to fourteen; and of these fourteen, five—Celín, Rosa, Zara, Estrella and Celima—have no more than a line or so in the entire play. The remaining nine all have distinctive rôles. Fernando dominates the stage throughout the play, remarkable in Act I for his valour and generosity in battle and in the remaining acts for his patience and constancy in adversity. Mirroring Fernando is the young King Alfonso who comes to Africa to recover Fernando's remains. The other main characters throw Fernando into relief. As Parker has said, all the characters in the play pursue ends which are in themselves good by means sanctioned by the law. But the Moorish King by his cruelty, Enrique by his diffidence, Fénix by her despair, even Muley and Juan, are all inferior to Fernando. They lack his faith and Christian constancy. They are human; Fernando is a saint. [1]

Calderón's transformation of the earlier Fernando into the aggresive figure who rejects freedom at the expense of a Christian town and the honour of a friend, and who defies his captors even when faced with death itself, his far-reaching changes in the remaining characters and his new version of the restoration of Fernando's relics, necessitated new second and third acts which bear little resemblance to those of *La fortuna adversa.* Certain facts, it

[1] *MLR.* XLVII (1952), 254-56. I take this opportunity of acknowledging my debt to Professor Parker for his constructive review of my book on *El príncipe constante.*

is true, survive in *El príncipe constante* : Fernando's concern for his fellow-captives and his insistence on sharing their hardships, the whole idea of Fernando as the Spanish Regulus, the threats of his captors, Muley's resolve to help him, his working unrecognized as a slave, the vain appeals for mercy, the hanging of Fernando's body at the gates of Fez, and the appearance finally of his spirit. But not a single scene in Acts II and III of *El príncipe constante* has an exact counterpart in *La fortuna adversa*. The first act alone bears some structural resemblance to that of the source, with the landing scene at Tangier, Fernando's sparing of Muley, and the defeat of the Portuguese. Yet the different intentions of the two dramatists render pointless any comparative study of details of handling.

Calderón's arrangement of his material as a single dramatic movement centring on Fernando, to whom all the other characters of the play are subordinated, resulted both in the elimination of much that was unessential in *La fortuna adversa* and in a remarkable tightening of the action. In place of the looseness of plot of the source-play with its superabundance of *tramoyas*, Calderón provides an action that is stripped of everything except the essential. The source dramatist was simply dramatizing, with a few changes, the story which he found in Román's biography of Fernando, transferring incidents, characters and even turns of expression from book to play. Calderón penetrated beneath the multifarious incidents of Fernando's life-story to a single theme which is both profound and universal. His singleness of purpose, here as in all his best plays, made possible a unity and cohesion entirely lacking in the source. Other factors contribute to the play's compactness. One notes, for example, that the action is fixed in Africa. The source dramatist opened his play in Portugal, moved to Africa for the battle of Tangier and returned to Portugal for his first scene in Act II. From the middle of Act II the action is principally in Africa, except for a brief bridge-scene in Portugal in Act III, and for the final lines of the play. Calderón dispensed entirely with the scenes in Portugal. Even for the scenes in Africa he gives the impression of continuity of action by allowing it seemingly to remain in one place, an ungeographical Fez which is on the sea; we recall the Jerusalem-on-Sea in *El mayor monstruo los celos*. Hence no abrupt shift of scene is required when the action moves from the King's palace to Tangier in Act I, or from Fez to the landing-place of Enrique in Act II and of Alfonso's expeditionary force in Act III. Similar concentration may be seen in respect of time. The expedition to Tangier took place in 1437, Fernando died in captivity in 1444 and his body was recovered by Alfonso in 1471. The source dramatist once again remains close to Román's biography; Muley in the play's last scene informs us that Fernando spent six years in captivity, and Alfonso, a generation younger than Fernando, is shown as a boy-king. Calderón is deliberately vague about time, and events which dragged over some thirty-four years are compressed in what appears to be a single continuous action. Alfonso is presented as Fernando's contemporary, and Enrique accompanies his expedition as he had done the previous one, historically thirty-four years earlier.

Music and spectacle have a place in both *El príncipe constante* and its source. If *La fortuna adversa* was written, as I have argued elsewhere, between 1595 and 1598,[1] and if its extant text approximates fairly closely to the form in which it was first produced, it required more elaborate staging than most plays of that date. For the conversion of Iataf a font is made to appear, presumably through a trap-door:

> *Parécese vna fuente, [de] que sale vn chorro.*   (2527)

The play contains no 'discovery', but before his death Fernando is carried into the inner stage, which is curtained off or covered when he dies:

> *Música: cúbrese la apariencia.*   (2770 ff)

Fire is kindled on a rock, which opens and reveals Fernando's spirit:

> *Enciéndese fuego en la peña, y con ruydo se abre, y aparécese Fernando con vn vestido blanco de la hechura del con que murió, y con vna cruz y vn hacha en la mano.*   (3072 ff)

Immediately before this, the Virgin Mary, St. Anthony of Padua and St. Michael have been lowered on to the stage on a machine to the accompaniment of music:

> *Suena música, y aparécese Nuestra Señora y San Antonio de Padua y San Miguel; baxan por inuención.*   (2710 ff)

---

[1]   Op. cit., p. 115.

For the landing-scene at Tangier the source dramatist made use
of the voices off of two sailors, and the Portuguese enter bearing
oars and *espuertas*. In Act III a gun is discharged off stage. Here
are the stage directions for the play's opening:

> *Salen E[duardo] Rey, don Enrique y don Fernando, con cruzes en los
> pechos, Enrique con la de Christo y Fernando con la de Alcántara; y
> Ruygómez de Silua, y Meneses, y Alencastro, y el Mariscal, los quatro con
> vnas cañas en las manos, en lugar de báculos, trayendo Enrique vn estan-
> darte rojo con las armas de Portugal, de la vna parte, y de la otra vna
> cruz de hábito de Christo, con vna letra que diga: IN HOC SIGNO VIN-
> CIS. Ha de auer puesto vn dosel con la silla real, y vna mesa con vna
> fuente y en ella vna corona, y vn bastón de general; y van saliendo los
> caualleros por su orden, y pone Enrique el estandarte junto a la corona; y
> aurá sillas.*

In contrast, the staging of *El príncipe constante* is simple. Calderón omitted all the *tramoyas* of the source, although he gave his
play a more spectacular ending by having the coffin of Fernando
lowered from the walls of Fez. Throughout the last scene the upper
gallery represents the town's walls, and the coffin is lowered by
means of ropes:

> *Bajan el ataúd con cuerdas por el muro.*   (924b)

Fernando's spirit appears twice with a flaming torch but it does
not emerge from a burning rock. On the other hand, Fernando's
final appearance on stage alive, to judge by Muley's description of
him as a corpse on a dunghill, borders on the horrific. Like so many
other plays of this period *El príncipe constante* seems to require
two doors, but these could have been merely curtained openings.
The only other features are the noises off: a gun early in Act I,
'ruido de desembarcar' for the landing scene, and from time to
time trumpets and drums. The opening scene has four lines of song:

> *Al peso de los años*
> *lo eminente se rinde*
> *que a lo fácil del tiempo*
> *no hay conquista difícil.*   (895b)

The exchanges between Zara and the Christian slaves, as Wilson
remarked, [1] point to the very essence of slavery in a play which
centres on a captive; the song itself contributes to the mood of the

---

[1] Op. cit., p. 212

play and hints at the subsequent development of the action and at the conduct required of the persons involved.

In no instance is Calderón simply rewriting a scene of the source-play. Lines of *El príncipe constante,* naturally enough, sometimes echo lines in *La fortuna adversa,* and elsewhere I have listed parallel passages. [1] Rarely, however, do they amount to more than a single phrase, and more often than not Calderón would seem to be deliberately shunning the use of the same word or expression. One may compare for example:

La fortuna adversa.

Traelde vn capote viejo,
que hasta que mude el pellejo
entre hierros y cadenas,
no se han de librar sus penas,
pues da contra mí consejo.
Carga de hierro sus pies;...   (1660-65)

and:

boluí, señor, hazia Arcila
los ojos desde esse cerro,
y no vi el cielo con poluo
y con gente no vi el suelo.
Vi gran multitud de lanças,
de cuyos luzientes hierros
si acaso al sol le faltaran
sus rayos, los dieran ellos.   (793-99)

with:

El príncipe constante.

              al cuello
y a los pies le echad cadenas;
a mis caballos acuda
y en baño y jardín, y sea
abatido como todos;
no vista ropas de seda
sino sarga humilde y pobre...   (911a)

and:

a la falda de ese monte
vi una tropa de jinetes,
que de la parte de Fez
corriendo a esta parte vienen

---

[1] Op. cit., pp. 52 ff.

> tan veloces, que a la vista
> aves, no brutos, parecen.
> El viento no los sustenta
> la tierra apenas los siente;
> y así, la tierra ni el aire
> saben si corren o vuelen.   (901b)

The imagery of *El príncipe constante* is quite original. I have had occasion to comment, for example, on the association of Fernando's suffering and death with darkness and his faith with light. The idea of the appearance of Fernando's spirit with a lighted torch derives from *La fortuna adversa:*

> *aparécese Fernando con vn vestido blanco de la hechura del con que murió,*
> *y con vna cruz y vn hacha en la mano.*   (3072)

but an isolated incident of the source is in *El príncipe constante* but one of a series of associations running through the whole play. The versification also is new: to cite the more important parallel situations, for the landing scene Calderón uses *tercetos* instead of the earlier *quintillas* and *romance;* for the sparing of Muley *romance* instead of *quintillas;* and for the appearance of Fernando's spirit *silva* and *romance* instead of *redondillas.*

The author of *La fortuna adversa* adapted, hurriedly it would seem, to the dimensions of the stage the biography of Fernando which he found in Román's *Historia.* The play, despite a certain level of competence, is anecdotal and superficial. *El príncipe constante,* in contrast, is unified and profound. Calderón succeeded in extracting from the story of one whose greatness lay in endurance rather than action the stuff of drama, and in penetrating beneath the story itself to a theme that is significant and universal. Prince Ferdinand is made to symbolize Christian Fortitude, intrepid in battle, magnanimous in victory, but above all patient in adversity and constant even unto death. Other characters of *La fortuna adversa* are fitted to this dramatic pattern, reflecting the qualities of the Prince or throwing them into relief by contrast; the remainder are discarded and, where necessary, replaced. Already by 1629 Calderón was a consummate dramatic craftsman.

VIII

EL ALCALDE DE ZALAMEA

O F the eight plays considered in these pages only *El alcalde de Zalamea* [1] had until recently been compared in any detail with its source, a play of the same title attributed to Lope de Vega. The first *Alcalde* survives in two MSS and in a *suelta* at the British Museum. It was unknown evidently to Valentin Schmidt, [2] though Schack had drawn attention to it in 1854. [3] Ten years later, when a manuscript copy of the play belonging to Durán passed to the Biblioteca Nacional, Hartzenbusch briefly compared it with Calderón's play. [4] In 1887 Krenkel published the source-play as an appendix to his scholarly edition of Calderón's *Alcalde;* he printed also the study of Hartzenbusch and added comments of his own on further parallels between the two plays. [5] Menéndez y Pelayo provided a second text of the source in the Academy edition of the works of Lope de Vega and included a short comparative study in the introduction. [6] Subsequent editors of Calderón's play have, in the main, echoed the comments of these scholars. Krenkel and Menéndez y Pelayo both accepted the source-play as the work of Lope, but Hartzenbusch suggested that it was a rewriting of a Lope play

---

[1] Texts used:

Source: Suelta (?), BM.
Ed. Menéndez y Pelayo, Acad. XII (Madrid, 1901).

Calderón: *El mejor de los mejores libros*, 1651.
Ed. Vera Tassis, VII (1682).
Ed. J. J. Keil, op. cit., IV, pp. 88-110.
Ed. J. E. Hartzenbusch, op. cit., III, pp. 67-86.
Ed. M. Krenkel (Leipzig, 1887).
Ed. J. Geddes (New York, 1918)..
Ed. Ida Farnell (Manchester, 1921).
Ed. Astrana Marín, pp. 511-41. (Madrid, 1945, 3.ª ed., revisada.)
Ed. A. Cortina (Madrid, 1955).

Quotations are from the Menéndez y Pelayo text of the source, and from Astrana Marín's edition of Calderón's play.

[2] *Die Schauspiele Calderóns...* (Elberfeld, 1857).

[3] *Geschichte der dramatischen Literatur und Kunst in Spanien,* 2nd ed., *Nachträge,* Spanish translation, IV, p. 206, n. I.

[4] *Memoria leida en la Biblioteca Nacional,* 1864. Cf. Krenkel, op. cit., pp. 371-88.

[5] Max Krenkel, *Klassische Bühnendichtungen der Spanier,* III (Leipzig, 1887).

[6] *Acad.* XII (Madrid, 1901), ed. Menéndez y Pelayo.

by another and lesser dramatist. [1] Morley and Bruerton agree that in its present form at least, it is not the work of Lope. [2] The play's date is uncertain also, but it can be roughly dated by its versification. Whether or not it is by Lope, the eight hundred lines of *quintilla* amounting to almost thirty-five per cent of the total, the nine per cent of *sueltas* and the few lines of *redondilla* (only one hundred and fifty six) suggest a period before 1610, although the thirty-six per cent of *romance* is typical of rather later plays. [3] Calderón's *El alcalde de Zalamea* is extant in the 1651 volume of *El mejor de los mejores libros*, and is thought to have been written in the 1640s. The probable date of the play attributed to Lope is such that it could not be later than Calderón's. A collation of the two texts confirms this relationship. [4]

The first *El alcalde de Zalamea* is concerned with a peasant whose daughters were seduced by two captains who pass through Zalamea on their way to Portugal in 1580. It was based probably upon an actual incident which occurred at that time in Zalamea, though Krenkel has shown its resemblance to the forty-seventh tale of the *Novellino* of Masuccio Guardati of Salerno. Two army companies are billeted in Zalamea. In Act I the protagonist, Pedro Crespo, is elected *alcalde*, and though slow to accept responsibility he is soon vigorously demonstrating his courage and integrity. Meanwhile his two daughters, Inés and Leonor, flirt shamelessly with the captains of the companies, Don Juan and Don Diego, and at the end of the first act prepare to elope with them. Crespo thwarts the attempt and arrests an army sergeant. In Act II Crespo decides to punish the sergeant and, despite the arrival of the notorious Don Lope de Figueroa, stands by his decision. To the captains' indignation, Don Lope listens to Crespo's explanation and even commends his action. In revenge, the captains persuade Inés

---

[1] 'Parece que, antes que manejara Calderón este asunto, algún autor, no de los primeros por cierto, refundió el primer *Alcalde de Zalamea*', cf. Krenkel, op. cit., p. 377.

[2] *Chronology of Lope de Vega's Comedias* (New York, 1940), 251-52.

[3] Cf. Courtney Bruerton, 'La versificación dramática española en el periodo 1587-1610', *NRFH*, X (1956), 337-64.

[4] I have referred earlier to the suggestion by Don Angel Valbuena in his *Historia del teatro español* (Barcelona, 1956), which reached me after the completion of this book, that the *Alcalde* attributed to Lope is later than Calderón's. But, in the face of the overwhelming evidence of Morley and Bruerton, Don Angel assumes that the play is by Lope, and he ignores the fact that the versification points to a date, not in the thirties but in the early 1600s. He is obliged also to advance the date of Calderón's play from the 1640s to the 1620s. The present chapter will, I hope, dispose at least of his claim that the play attributed to Lope is more unified and formally superior to Calderón's.

and Leonor to elope with them, seduce them and abandon them. In Act III, Inés and Leonor seek the help and protection of the *alcalde*, their father, and they produce the written promises of the captains to marry them. Crespo surprises Don Juan and Don Diego at a nearby farm and obliges them to honour their promises; and when Philip II arrives in Zalamea and asks to see them, he draws a curtain and shows them hanging by their necks. Crespo has been satisfied with nothing less than the captains᾿ death; and since, he explains, Zalamea's executioner has no experience of beheading, the captains have suffered the disgrace of hanging. The King excuses Crespo's action and makes him *alcalde* for life; Inés and Leonor are sent to a convent.

In outline, Calderón's play is similar to its source. Soldiers are billeted upon the peasants of Zalamea. Their captain is infatuated by Crespo's daughter, seduces her and refuses to marry her. Crespo takes the law into his own hands and executes the seducer. Philip II makes Crespo mayor for life. The relationship between the characters is the following:

SOURCE	CALDERÓN
Pedro Crespo	Pedro Crespo
Inés	Isabel
Leonor	—
—	Juan
—	Inés
Ginesillo	—
El rey Felipe II	El rey Felipe II
Don Lope de Figueroa	Don Lope de Figueroa
El capitán Don Diego	Don Álvaro de Ataide
El capitán Don Juan Galindo	—
Galindo	Rebolledo
—	La Chispa
Juan Serrano	—
Bartolo	—
El escribano	Un escribano
—	Don Mendo
—	Nuño

Critics have duly noted these and other similarities. But, despite a superficial resemblance, the two plays have surprisingly little in common. Their plots follow divergent courses until the last scene, and even the characters, which owe most to the source dramatist, have been transformed. Don Lope de Figueroa alone survives intact; Pedro Crespo has been ennobled and most of his part is new; Isabel and the Captain, though inspired by their models, are quite different characters; and the rest are wholly original. Calderón's conception of Crespo's story required him, in fact, to discard the major part of the source material, and his debt to the source has been greatly exaggerated. Schack can hardly have read the first *El alcalde de Zalamea* to make the outrageous claim:

> También en *El alcalde de Zalamea* aprovechó Calderón una comedia del mismo título, de Lope de Vega... apropiándose la traza entera de la fábula, los caracteres de los personajes y las escenas más conmovedoras, de suerte que sólo la dicción poética quedó propiedad suya [1]

Even Menéndez y Pelayo, who edited the source-play and recognised the injustice of Schack's remarks, could write:

> Lo que Calderón debe a Lope en *El alcalde de Zalamea* no es cualquier cosa accidental o secundaria, sino la idea poética fundamental, el conflicto dramático, el plan, los principales personajes, las situaciones culminantes, y además algunos versos enteros y una porción de frases literalmente copiadas.

and went on to comment:

> Que todo lo enmendó y mejoró no tiene duda, ni podía esperarse otra cosa de un poeta de su talla que se pone a refundir una obra ajena: pero *facilius est inventis addere...* [2]

Easy, perhaps, but Calderón was doing infinitely more. This notion that Calderón in *El alcalde de Zalamea* was merely modifying and perfecting an earlier play survives even in the work of Don Angel Valbuena, who brackets it with *El médico de su honra* and writes:

> ...la labor personal consiste en la perfecta arquitectura de la comedia, en el redondeamiento de la expresión, en la concisión sabia. [3]

The striking novelty and originality of Calderón's conception have not hitherto been recognized.

Calderón's *dénouement*, moreover, has prompted certain critics to regard the play as revolutionary. Krenkel, for example, assuming that it was not well received by the Madrid public of the time,

---

[1]   Op. cit., IV, p. 209a.
[2]   Introduction to Lope de Vega, *Obras, XII* (Madrid, 1901), clxiv.
[3]   *Literatura dramática española* (Barcelona, 1930), 224.

points to the final scene as the explanation. A common peasant, he argues, sentences an officer and gentleman to death, further dishonours him by having him garrotted, and is exonerated, indeed rewarded; this was surely enough to blind the audience to the play's poetry. Menéndez y Pelayo, though clear that the play was written in no tone of protest, suggests that it reflects the vitality of the local councils of the day and that it might nowadays be taken as championing municipal liberty. [1] This was the interpretation of López de Ayala: amongst the various personages who appear before the bust of Calderón in *La mejor corona* is the *alcalde* of Zalamea, and his opening lines are:

> ¡Vive Cristo! que ha llegado
> a Zalamea el rumor
> de esta fiesta, y he querido
> también presenciarla yo,
> que soy alcalde perpetuo
> por el rey nuestro señor;
> y más perpetuo por obra
> de Don Pedro Calderón,
> que de un rústico labriego
> hizo el alcalde mejor.
>   Yo soy el poder civil,
> el derecho y la razón
> de pecheros oprimidos
> contra su duro opresor.
> Soy la justicia ordinaria,
> soy la virtud sin blasón,
> y frente al hombre de guerra
> yo soy el hombre de pro. [2]

No-one, I suspect, would have been more astonished by this interpretation than Calderón himself. Now it so happens that the one scene which Calderón borrowed was the last. But he retained it at the expense virtually of the whole of the remaining material of the source-play; until the second half of Act III the two plots have in fact little in common. What changes did Calderón make in borrowing it? What is its effect in its new context? To my knowledge no critic has had recourse to the source for the elucidation of Calderón's scene.

---

[1] Op. cit., p. clxxi.
[2] Adelardo López de Ayala, *Obras completas*, IV (Madrid, 1884), p. 312.

The first Pedro Crespo arrests the captains who have seduced
and abandoned his daughters, and obliges them to honour their
promise of marriage; then he executes them. The King in person
excuses his action and makes him *alcalde* for life. Does the captains'
behaviour justify their execution? They deliberately deceive Crespo's
daughters; and, although they later agree to honour their promises,.
they make plans to abandon their victims at the earliest opportunity.
They violate other girls too, and plunder the peasants' farms.
Certainly the captains are culpable. But Crespo's daughters must
share part of the blame since they have been ingenuous enough to
think that they will win noble husbands, and they voluntarily elope.
As far as they are concerned restitution has been done when the
captains consent to marry them, and both they and their father are
unaware that the captains plan to abandon them again. The offence of the captains, therefore, has been cleared before Crespo has
them hanged. All this, to say the least, is unsatisfactory in the
source-play. That it was unsatisfactory to Calderón is clear by his
changes. Isabel, unlike Inés and Leonor, is the very embodiment of
virtue; and, far from eloping with the captain, she is forcibly
abducted. Moreover, the captain rejects Crespo's plea that he
should marry Isabel to restore her honour. Calderón's captain, unlike
those of the source-play, bears full responsibility for the dishonour
to Crespo's family and acknowledges no obligation to marry Isabel.
So much for the moral law. What of the procedural law of the state?
A peasant *alcalde* passes sentence of death upon an army captain
and has him hanged or garrotted like a common criminal. Calderón
allows no room for doubt that by so doing Crespo has exceeded his
powers as *alcalde*. The captain himself protests on a number of
occasions that he can be tried only by court martial:

> ¿Qué tiene que ver conmigo
> justicia ordinaria?   (534b)
>
> ...que en la justicia, es forzoso
> remitirme en esta tierra
> a mi consejo de guerra:
> con que, aunque el lance es penoso,
> tengo mi seguridad.   (534b-535a)
>
> ...si por justicia ha de ser,
> no tenéis jurisdicción.   (536a)
>
> Sobre mí no habéis tenido
> jurisdicción: el consejo
> de guerra enviará por mí.   (536b)

In the last two instances he addresses himself directly to Crespo, and it is significant that Crespo declines to answer. When Crespo has carried out his plan, he at once admits in the King's presence that he has transgressed the law. His excuse is simply that, since the captain merited his death, his own transgression matters little:

> ...¿qué importa errar lo menos
> quien ha acertado lo más?   (540b)

The distinction which Calderón makes between the moral law and the law of the state, between *derecho* and *ley*, is fundamental to his play. Crespo's execution of the captain is illegal; the law of the state required that a captain should be tried by court-martial and that he should be beheaded, not hanged. But it is not morally wrong; on the contrary, it is unequivocally in accordance with moral law. Crespo breaks the regulations of the state in order to ensure that justice be done.

The first *El alcalde de Zalamea* begins with Pedro Crespo's election as *alcalde* and with the lines which explain the *alcalde's* rôle; and from this point on, it is devoted principally to Crespo's successful fulfilment of his duties. He has pledged himself to be the servant of the town, and throughout he is scrupulously impartial. He orders his own friend the town clerk, under threat of banishment, to put an end to his illicit love-affair, and acts at once when a farmer comes to complain of the shopkeeper who denies receiving a sum of money deposited with him. The clerk and constable provide a running commentary on his well-doing. It is they who bring news of his appointment, and the clerk observes:

> Al malhechor haréis daño,
> porque sois (y no me engaño)
> propio para Alcalde vos.   (567a)

Act II opens with this tribute from the constable, Juan Serrano:

> No ha tenido el lugar mejor Alcalde:
> ¡Que esto tenía escondido Pedro Crespo!   (576b)

and later in the act the clerk reaffirms:

> El cielo
> le enseña: pudiera ser
> de muchos jueces ejemplo.   (580b)

And Crespo's reputation as *alcalde* is exemplified in action on the stage by his warning to the clerk, his punishment of the shopkeeper, his order that his own debts should be paid, and his going at once to the aid of the farmer whose stock is being robbed by soldiers. Although the main incident of the play concerns his own family, Crespo acts in his capacity as *alcalde*. His daughters are considered as two more of Zalamea's citizens who come under his jurisdiction. When in Act I Crespo discovers that the captains are flirting with his daughters, it is as *alcalde* that he warns them, and on behalf of the whole town. He is careful to mention no names:

> ...son justas las querellas
> pues vienen con libertad
> á infamar á dos doncellas
> de esta honrada vecindad.   (569b)

As *alcalde* again, he later repeats the warning to the Captains servant Galindo, and this time he even lies, claiming to refer to the daughters of a friend of his:

> Que no inquieten los vecinos
> del lugar, porque otra vez
> á quejárseme han venido
> hijas de un amigo mío.   (574b)

Soldiers and civilians alike come under Crespo's jurisdiction. and the sergeant, like the lying shopkeeper, is sentenced to be flogged. The sergeant protests, and members of the town council, though admiring Crespo's efficiency, have doubts about the legality of his action:

> SERRANO.   sólo temo
> que quiera perseguir á los soldados
> con tanto extremo: ¡plegue á Dios que sea
> el agua limpia! Y más, este sargento
> no sé en qué ha de parar; los capitanes
> sospecho que andan medio amotinados.   (576b)

Don Lope de Figueroa questions at first Crespo's authority in respect of soldiers:

> D. DIEGO.   Pues ¿de qué modo
> puede él prender soldados?
> D. LOPE.   Pues sabrémoslo,
> que bien sé que no puede...   (577b)

But he is convinced by Crespo's arguments, and admits:

> Está bien hecho...   (579a)

When at the play's end he accompanies the King to Zalamea, he refers to Crespo with the words:

> ...es hombre de humor
> su Alcalde; es hombre extremado.
> Tendrá Vuestra Majestad
> gusto en verle, que el villano
> tiene cierta autoridad
> de más de juez cortesano.   (593a)

The captains, on the other hand, resent Crespo's interference and their behaviour towards his daughters is directly motivated by his treatment of their sergeant:

> D. JUAN.   En el alma escribo
> de tu padre villano,
> la ofensa hecha por su misma mano.
> D. DIEGO.   Afrentóme el sargento,
> y yo en su mismo honor tomar intento
> la venganza, de suerte
> que sienta menos la penosa muerte.   (582a)

Their affront is aimed at Crespo the *alcalde*. And Crespo punishes them as *alcalde*. He takes pains, for example, to see that the soldiers who are causing trouble are within his area of jurisdiction:

> LABRADOR.   Señor, en el cortijo de las Peñas,
> que es de mi amo el cura Antón Hidalgo...
> ALCALDE.   Pienso que viene á ser este cortijo
> nuestra jurisdicción.   (587a)

He does not yet know that they include the two captains, and the expedition against them is not in pursuit of the girls' offenders but in answer to the complaints of a farmer.

Crespo received his dishonoured daughters as *alcalde*, not as their father:

> ...¿No veis
> que agora soy juez severo?   (588a)

and promises that he will plead their cause before the King; but, having arrested the captains, he decides to redress their wrong himself. Before carrying out the sentence he is concerned about the money he owes to a certain Martín Alonso. His own scruples serve to emphasize the kind of conduct he will expect from others:

> que no es de hombres honrados y cristianos
> comer con gusto ni dormir sin pena,
> cuando el pobre á quien debe, por ventura
> no tiene un pan que dalle á sus hijuelos.
> No entendí tal de Pedro Crespo: ¿ahora,
> á la vejez, no paga lo que debe?...   (587a)

Just as he takes responsibility for his own debts and obligations, so he will ensure that others take theirs:

> D. DIEGO.   ¿Quién eres, feroz villano,
> que á caballeros te atreves?
>
> ALCALDE.   Que no lo eres es muy llano,
> pues no pagas lo que debes.   (592a)

The captains are obliged to marry his daughters. Don Lope de Figueroa does not protest at the captains' arrest, and the King receives the news that they have been hanged with remarkable calmness; he questions only the manner of their death, excuses and commends Crespo's action and makes him *alcalde* for life. Crespo might well wish so lenient a King to outlive Methuselah! Irregular or not, his action as *alcalde* has been upheld.

The first *El alcalde de Zalamea* is essentially a play about an *alcalde*. It shows Pedro Crespo solemnly and conscientiously dealing with grievances of Zalamea's citizens. The grievance of his own daughters is but one more problem which comes his way in his capacity as *alcalde* and, though it affects him personally and is more serious and far-reaching in its consequences, it is dealt with in the same way. But the momentous decision to execute the captains is illegal; a play conceived as the story of a peasant *alcalde* ends with his grossly exceeding his powers! Yet Crespo must be an *alcalde* if the brilliant *coup de théâtre* was to be preserved in Calderón's recasting. His solution was ingenious. He delayed Crespo's election until well into Act III so that, whilst retaining the *dénouement* of the source-play, he avoided writing a play about an *alcalde*. The postponement of Crespo's election is not, as critics have claimed, a mere change of arrangement in the interest of dramatic effect. It is the outcome of a different view of Pedro Crespo, one which is clear from the change in the *dramatis personae*. 'El alcalde Pedro

Crespo' becomes 'Pedro Crespo, labrador'. This new approach to the Crespo story rendered superfluous much of the material of the first *Alcalde*. The earlier Crespo is involved in many of its incidents only as *alcalde*: the shopkeeper episode which sprawls over much of Act I, the arrest and punishment of the sergeant, the payment of his debts to a mason, the farmer whose stock is raided by soldiers. The source dramatist was concerned to show that Crespo was impartial, that his attitude to the captains was the same as that towards other offenders against the law. Calderón dismisses this whole issue, which accounts for so much of the source-play, in a few lines. To Don Lope's taunt:

> Éste es el alcalde, y es
> su padre.

Crespo replies:

> No importa en tal
> caso, porque si un extraño
> se viniera a querellar,
> ¿no había de hacer justicia?
> Sí; pues ¿qué más se me da
> hacer por mi hija lo mismo
> que hiciera por los demás?...   (540a)

Calderón's principal debt to the source dramatist was for the outlines of his main characters. Pedro Crespo himself owes much to his model. The earlier Crespo is a peasant of independence and integrity who is elected *alcalde,* his daughter is abducted by an army captain and he redresses the dishonour by having him executed. But honour is only of secondary importance in the source, and there is surprisingly little insistence upon the conflict between *villano* and *noble*. Crespo's daughters admittedly take pride in the prospect of captains as husbands; naive enough to take them at their word, they realize when it is too late that they are despised as peasant girls, unequal to the rank and status of their suitors. Only at this point in Act II do the captains scoff at the girls as *villanas,* daughters of a *villano* father:

> D. DIEGO.   ¡Villana! ¡Vive el cielo
> que deje con tu muerte ejemplo al suelo!
> ¿Tu marido me llamas
> cuando mi nombre con tu nombre infamas?   (582a)

and Leonor pleads:

> ...porque tiene heredada
> villana sangre, pero sangre honrada. (582b)

This issue is raised again when Crespo resolves that the captains shall die for their action:

> Nadie de ayudarme trate,
> que honor la ocasión alcanza
> para que solo los mate.
> Tomaránla aquestas manos
> de dos cortesanos fieros,
> porque entiendan cortesanos
> que, á agravios de caballeros,
> hay justicia de villanos. (591b)

But the most significant passage in this connexion is found in the scene in which Crespo surprises the captains and makes them promise to marry his daughters:

> Hacer fuerza bien sabéis,
> que fué siempre de villanos;
> luego no es bien que os pintéis
> caballeros cortesanos,
> si agravio a mi honra hacéis;
> y pues villanos quedáis
> con las obras que mostráis,
> en nada os ofendo aquí,
> si bajándoos hasta mí,
> con mis hijas os casáis. (592b)

The conflict between nobleman and peasant, which was only incidental to the source, is fundamental to Calderón's play. He presents Crespo less as *alcalde* than as a man of honour. At the same time he ennobles him. The protagonist of the source was an unlearned rustic; from his anxiety over his daughters' recklessness he turns to discuss his newly-acquired ox. At times he is even a comic figure, as when he assumes his cloak of office:

> ¡Yo alcalde! ¡Quién tal pensara!
> ¡Por Dios, que me asienta bien! (567b)

He cannot read; and though a cut above Cervantes's candidates at Daganzo and Tirso's Berrocal, he seems hardly fitted for the tragic rôle to follow. True, as the play progresses, he grows in self-confidence and never fails to rise to the occasion. But Calderón's

Crespo is of finer cloth. Like Peribáñez, he is well-to-do, the richest peasant in Zalamea. [1] He has poise and self-confidence, and when ultimately he is elected *alcalde* he accepts the appointment as one who is worthy of it. Just as Tamar was expelled from the kitchen, so Crespo is no longer involved in the buying of bullocks. And Calderón filled out the earlier portrait with many features that are new: his extraordinary shrewdness and cunning, and his paternal qualities. The family scenes, showing Crespo as a loving and responsible father, are without parallel in the source.

To complete the picture of peasantry, and to give emphasis to the theme of honour, Calderón makes use of two other characters. The story required a daughter through whom the peasant's honour was compromised. But it is misleading to state that for Isabel Calderón merely reduced the two daughters of the source-play to one. Rather he has discarded the earlier girls and substituted one who is new. Like Inés and Leonor, Isabel is motherless, is raped by a captain and enters a convent: that is the full extent of the parallel. She is virtually everything that Inés and Leonor are not: modest, retiring, virtuous. There is certainly considerable pathos in the earlier character studies. Inés and Leonor are ingenuous; more reckless and light-hearted even than Tirso's Tisbea, they are duped by their captain suitors. At least they are honest about it, and their only complaint is that they have been deceived. By their naiveté and ambition they bring their fate upon themselves. Isabel, in contrast, is both virtuous and prudent. Her repugnance to the advances of Don Mendo and her retirement when soldiers come to Zalamea are contrasted with the forwardness of her cousin Inés, who inherits not a little from the daughters of the source-play. Before Crespo declares his intention of hiding her in an attic, Isabel has come to the same decision herself. When finally she is forcibly abducted and seduced, she pleads with her father to take

---

[1] Even so, Lope allowed Peribáñez some rustic speech, and presented him as:

> un villano
> que ayer al rastrojo seco
> diéntes menudos ponía
> de la hoz corva de acero,
> los pies en las tintas uvas,
> rebosando el mosto negro
> por encima del lagar,
> o la tosca mano al hierro
> del arado...

2356-2404

her life so as to remove the stain from the family honour. Calderón required the innocence of Isabel in order to place full responsibility for the family dishonour on the shoulders of the captain, and it is doubtful whether he owes anything to some lines of the source which anticipate her character:

> ¿Dónde iré a cobrar mi honor?
> ¡Cielos, que me atemoriza
> ya de Leonor y de Inés
> la libertad que publican!
> Si por fuerza las sacaran,
> estando ellas recogidas,
> en el poder más lascivo
> vivieran castas y limpias,
> que la torre del honor
> sobre voluntad estriba.   (581a)

Like Crespo, Isabel embodies the peasants' sense of honour, and it ⌐ to her that Calderón entrusts the monumental speech at the beginning of Act III. The whole action has been moving towards this point since the sergeant's words to the captain:

> SARGENTO.   ...porque en Zalamea
>   no hay tan bella mujer...
>
> CAPITÁN.   Di.
>
> SARGENTO.   Como una hija suya.   (513a)

The plot hinges on the seduction of Isabel. Yet unless we recognize the intimate link between Isabel and her father—the common front that they present to the captain—the speech will appear to be a serious reorientation of the play's interest, for it is Crespo rather than Isabel whom Calderón has set against the Captain. Not only is he the guardian of the family honour, but the events of the play are presented in the main from his standpoint. Contrast, for example, *La niña de Gómez Arias* which is presented from the point of view of the injured daughter Dorotea. Isabel's seduction is shown primarily as the defeat and humiliation of Crespo; but it is a personal affront and it is appropriate that at this point she should be made the spokesman of the Crespo family.

Isabel has an opposite number in the source; Crespo's son Juan is an addition. In the earlier play Crespo seems to be the only honourable person in Zalamea. His daughters willingly elope with soldiers, his town clerk is reprimanded for keeping a mistress, the

local shopkeeper cheats a farmer and Crespo himself has succeeded
a mayor who turned a blind eye to the offences of his friends. We
have Crespo's own word for it that:

> Agora todo es maldad
> en la más pequeña villa.   (566a)

Hardly the preparation for Crespo's complaint to the captains!

> vienen con libertad
> á infamar a dos doncellas
> de esta honrada vecindad.   (569b)

In Calderón's play Crespo's son and daughter complete the picture of
integrity and honour represented by Crespo himself, just as the
citizens of Fuenteovejuna and Ocaña complete that of Frondoso and
Laurencia, and of Peribáñez and Casilda. The scenes between Juan
and his father are unquestionably among the play's best, showing us
Crespo endeared to a family whose honour he is resolved to
defend. Juan is a younger, immature and more impetuous version
of Crespo. At times his reactions correspond exactly with those of
his father, as on the occasion of Don Mendo's advances to Isabel or
of the captain's serenading. At others, the two are contrasted with
each other. Juan, for example, aspires to the rank of a noble, and
when he resents having soldiers billeted in the house he has to be
reminded of his peasant stock. It is Juan also who draws from his
father his two significant statements on honour. In the attic scene
at the end of Act I Juan's impulsiveness and indiscretion are set
against the self-control and prudence of Crespo. In Act III he
assumes responsibility for the family honour and attacks and wounds
the captain for the abduction of Isabel; in this at least he has his
father's approval. But whilst Crespo recognizes the innocence of
Isabel and pardons her, Juan assumes that her dishonour requires
her death, and Crespo arrives only just in time to expose his error.
For Juan as for the audience the events of the play are an object-
lesson.

Against Pedro Crespo Calderón set Don Álvaro de Ataide, a
nobleman scorning peasantry. The rôle of the captain derives from
the source-play, but Don Álvaro bears little resemblance to the
earlier captains. Don Diego and Don Juan are cowards, weaklings
and imposters. They flatter Crespo's daughters in conventional

language and when surprised by Crespo run for their lives. Impudent as long as Crespo is their prisoner, they meekly accede to his demands when arrested and pin their hopes of escape on fraud rather than on courage. They are contemptible characters and virtually indistinguishable one from the other. Calderón substituted a single finely-drawn character who, despite his behaviour towards Isabel, is not unsympathetic. The captain has a weakness for women, and his sergeant, significantly, has arranged for him to be billeted in the house with the prettiest girl in Zalamea. At first the captain treats the news with contempt; but Isabel's retirement rouses his curiosity and a glimpse of her fires his passion. From this point on he is presented as enslaved by passion:

> Este fuero, esta pasión,
> no es amor sólo, que es tema,
> es ira, es rabia, es furor.   (521b)

> Es una furia, un delirio
> de amor.   (530a)

More serious still is the captain's false conception of honour. For him honour is the prerogative of a nobleman. Being of noble birth himself he assumes that he is *ipso facto* honourable. A peasant, on the other hand, can have no sense of honour, and he expects the Crespo family to accede at once to his will:

> ¿Qué opinión tiene un villano?   (519b)

> ¡Que en una villana haya
> tal hidalga resistencia,
> que no me haya respondido
> una palabra siquiera
> apacible!   (522a)

But throughout the play he retains his captain's pride. He refuses to marry Isabel, and can only mock at Crespo's threats of violence, standing by his rights to be tried by court martial. He does not weaken under arrest, and threatened with death he is merely exasperated by Crespo's impudence:

> ¡Ah villanos con poder!   (537a)

Alvaro is convincing as a captain, which his models never were.

Don Lope de Figueroa is the only character whom Calderón carried over unchanged from the source-play. Although he has a part in only one scene in the first *El alcalde de Zalamea,* he is so vividly drawn that he assumes an importance quite disproportionate to his part; the scene in question is one of the genuinely great moments of the play. That the character of Don Lope admirably served the purpose of Calderón is evident from the very considerable extension of his rôle. He appears first in Act I for a clash of words which keeps close to the scene in the source-play. Calderón then makes him replace the captain at Crespo's house, and in Act II we have the famous supper-scene in which Crespo and Don Lope show their deep respect and admiration for each other; and Crespo's own peasant son Juan enlists under Don Lope. In Act III the two quarrel again and the play ends, one feels, with Don Lope's temper a little high. Don Lope often resembles Crespo, although Crespo embodies the virtues of the peasant, Don Lope those of the army officer. If Crespo is set against the captain, he is deliberately coupled with Don Lope. And the disorder created by the captain's misdemeanours is thrown into relief by the order and harmony of the supper scene in Act II, when Don Lope and Crespo have come to terms. Assuming correct behaviour, soldiers and peasants were perfectly reconcilable. Don Dámaso Alonso has pointed out that in the parallel phrases of Pedro Crespo and Don Lope de Figueroa the correlation is what he has called 'identificativa'; that is, the two characters say the same things in different words. [1] This in itself suggests that Calderón wishes to emphasize what the two characters have in common rather than their differences. Don Lope is essentially the same character as his namesake in the source; but Calderón enlarged his rôle and made him an essential part of the play's pattern.

Two other characters fill out the picture of soldiery, Rebolledo and La Chispa. Both are new. There is nothing in the source to compare, say, with the opening scene of Calderón's *El alcalde de Zalamea;* the earlier companies had been in Zalamea for several days when the play opened. Rebolledo is a figure peculiar neither to Spain nor to the sixteenth-century; wherever there is a uniform there is a Rebolledo, the spokesman of the rank and file, in the know, ever-complaining, boasting in the 'you see if I don't' kind of way. He is nonetheless a likeable character who, with La Chispa, is

[1] D. Alonso, 'La correlación en estructura del teatro calderoniano', in *Seis calas en la expresión literaria española* (Madrid, 1951), 115-86.

the life and soul of the party, grousing when not distracted and enjoying a lark; he is the ideal stooge for the captain's plan to find Isabel. But he is quite unscrupulous when threatened with a beating, and both he and La Chispa are ready at the play's end to tell all they know rather than risk torture. Rebolledo and La Chispa lend colour to the soldier scenes, motivate some exits and entrances, and provide light relief when the tension is high. They also exemplify a standard of behaviour which is inferior to that of the other characters of the play.

Apart from Philip II, whose rôle is formal and follows closely that of the source, Calderón admitted two other characters, the *hidalgo* Mendo and his servant Nuño. Don Mendo represents a type familiar enough to readers of Spanish literature: the penniless squire keeping up a show of honour and position whilst horse, hounds, servant and himself starve. Hitherto, critics have tended to concentrate rather upon Don Mendo's antecedents than upon his rôle, which is perhaps as he would have wished! His purpose is obvious enough. In a play whose protagonist declares:

> que honra no la compra nadie...　(516b)
>
> Yo no quiero honor postizo...　(516b)

Calderón includes a person for whom honour is no more than a label. Mendo is the type of *hidalgo* addressed by the devil in Quevedo's *Las zahurdas de Plutón:*

> ...en la chancillería del infierno arrúgase el pergamino y consúmense las letras, y el que en el mundo es virtuoso, ése es el hidalgo, y la virtud es la ejecutoria que acá respetamos, pues aunque desciende de hombres viles y bajos, como él con divinas costumbres se haga digno de imitación, se hace noble a sí y hace linaje para otros.

Without even the means of feeding himself, let alone others, he prides himself on his *ejecutoria* which exempts him from having to billet soldiers. Crespo, on the other hand, welcomes the chance of being host to soldiers and takes pleasure in being what he is, a *villano*. As a rival for Isabel's love, Mendo is linked with the captain, and the two share the same opinion of peasantry. But Mendo's spinelessness is in marked contrast with the captain's courage and determination. He makes only an idle declaration of love at Isabel's window and, whenever danger is near, runs away. The play gains a good deal of humour at the expense of Mendo and Nuño, and they help to maintain continuity of action. In Act I we move with them from the scene between the sergeant and captain to Crespo's house; in Act II they bridge the interval between the incidents at Crespo's house and the company's leaving Zalamea.[1] Calderón's dispensing with Don Mendo in Act III, when the action accelerates, is perhaps deliberate, to indicate his futility and ineffectiveness.

Calderón's new approach to the Crespo story rendered useless, as I have said, the greater part of the material of the first *El alcalde de Zalamea*. He was able to utilize the characters of Crespo, his daughter, the captain and Don Lope, but with the exception of Don Lope they are transformed; and they are supplemented by the important new characters of Juan and Mendo, as well as the minor ones of Inés, Rebolledo and La Chispa. It was not until the very last scene of his play that he could draw substantially upon a situation from the source. Elsewhere the nearest approach to his model comes at the end of Act I in the encounter between Crespo and Don Lope. Act I of the source-play is largely taken up with Crespo's duties as the newly-elected *alcalde*. At the end of the act Crespo's daughters attempt to elope with their captain suitors, and an army sergeant is arrested. The first scene of Act II contains the famous clash between Crespo and Don Lope de Figueroa who comes to protest against the threatened punishment of the sergeant. The greater part of Calderón's Act I is entirely new: the company's arrival in Zalamea and their billeting, the antics of Mendo and Nuño, the exchanges between Crespo and Juan, the removal of Isabel, the captain's arrival at Crespo's house and the ruse to discover Isabel. The scene at the end of the act, however, owes something to the single scene of the earlier play in which Don Lope has a part. Calderón's indebtedness is clear from the similarity of details:

SOURCE

D. LOPE.	(¡Pese á la pierna,
	no viniera un demonio y la llevara!) (577b)
D. LOPE.	Juro á Dios echar un bando,
	que no parezca en el pueblo
	hoy, so pena de la vida,
	ningún soldado! (579a)

---

[1] Cf. Albert E. Sloman's 'Scene division in Calderón's *El alcalde de Zalamea*', *HR*, XIX (1951), 66-71.

CALDERÓN

D. LOPE.   ¿No me basta haber subido
            hasta aquí, con el dolor
            desta pierna, que los diablos
            llevaran, amén, sino
            no decirme: "aquesto ha sido?"   (520a)

D. LOPE.   Hola, echa un bando, tambor,
            que al cuerpo de guardia vayan
            los soldados, cuantos son,
            y que no salga ninguno
            pena de muerte, en todo hoy.   (520b)

In both plays Don Lope is 'renegado' and Crespo 'testarudo'.

In Calderón's play, of course, the clash between Don Lope and Crespo occurs in quite different circumstances. The captain, we recall, affects a quarrel with Rebolledo in order to find Isabel, and chases him upstairs. Crespo, hearing the alarum, is confronted with the captain for the first time in the play in his daughter's bedroom, though with considerable self-control he makes a show of accepting his explanation. But Juan accuses the captain to his face, and just as swords are drawn Don Lope appears. The situation is admirably planned. The formidable gout-ridden general is faced with a disturbance as soon as he arrives in Zalamea and has to climb to a room at the top of the house to investigate it. And the encounter between Don Lope and Crespo provided Calderón with the perfect act-ending. We know already of Crespo's pride and sense of honour, but not until these dramatic exchanges are we shown the full measure of his stature. The redoubtable general finds his match in an equally redoubtable peasant, who is prepared to go to any lengths to defend his honour:

> A quien se atreviera
> a un átomo de mi honor,
> viven los cielos también,
> que también le ahorcara yo.   (521a)

And here appropriately, after various hints and suggestions earlier in the act, Calderón explicitly anticipates the play's *dénouement*. Setting the text of Calderón's scene against the original reveals an interesting detail. In the earlier play Crespo arrested the army sergeant and gave orders for him to be flogged in the presence of the captains. Don Lope, though not suspecting that the captains are responsible for the outrage, reprimands one of them for not having dealt with the matter personally:

> Mejor fuera, caballero,
> que el capitán castigara
> delitos que son tan feos,
> y más en los oficiales:
> y no alboratar el pueblo,
> dando lugar á que digan
> que es el capitán como ellos. (579a)

Calderón allows Don Lope similar lines in his play but in a very different context. His Don Lope knows that the captain is responsible for the disturbance in Crespo's house; yet it is Crespo, not the captain, whom he reprimands:

> CRESPO.   Ved ahora
> si hemos tenido razón.
> D. LOPE.   No tuvisteis para haber
> así puesto en ocasión
> de perderse este lugar.
> Hola, echa un bando, tambor,
> que al cuerpo de guardia vayan
> los soldados, cuantos son,
> y que no salga ninguno,
> pena de muerte, en todo hoy. (520b)

The point is perhaps significant. Responsibility for the disturbance in Isabel's room rests squarely upon the captain. But Don Lope suggests that Crespos themselves are not blameless. Although they have been provoked, they are by their action on the point of endangering the peace. That Don Lope is not simply being perverse is clear from his reaction to Crespo's famous definition of honour where, for all his anger, he admits:

> ¡Vive Cristo, que parece
> que vais teniendo razón! (521b)

Calderón's second act has, if anything, even less in common with the source than the first. The earlier dramatist, after the affair of the sergeant, devoted the rest of his act to the elopement and desertion of Inés and Leonor. Calderón carried his action forward to the abduction of Isabel, but he delayed the news of her fate until Act III. His whole act breaks completely with that of the source, and his two great scenes, first between Don Lope and Crespo on the

terrace of Crespo's house and second between Juan and his father,
are without precedent. A remark of Don Lope's echoes lines of the
earlier Don Lope:

SOURCE

D. LOPE.   ¿Es posible que no viene un demonio
             a llevarse esta pierna?

D. JUAN.   ¡Bravo miedo
             le ha cobrado el villano!

ALCALDE.   ¿Tiene gana
             de estar sin pierna, y no llama más de uno?
             Llame treinta demonios ó cuarenta,
             que se la arranquen presto.   (578a)

CALDERÓN

CRESPO.   Dios, señor, os dé paciencia!

D. LOPE.   ¿Para qué la quiero yo?

CRESPO.   No os la dé.

D. LOPE.   Nunca acá venga
             sino que dos mil demonios
             carguen conmigo y con ella.   (524a)

and the breaking up of the serenading party may have been suggested by the foiled elopement in the source. This, as far as I can
discover, is the extent of Calderón's indebtedness in this act. How
could Menéndez y Pelayo possibly claim that the source dramatist
provided Calderón with the plan of his play?

Act III opens with Isabel lamenting her dishonour, whilst her
father is tied to a tree. The general situation and a few of the lines
have a parallel in the source:

SOURCE

INÉS.   Puesto os han infames lazos
             porque nuestra infamia vean
             vuestros ojos, sin que sean
             furioso estorbo los brazos.
             Temiendo que no nos deis
             la muerte, os habrán atado...   (584b)

CALDERÓN

ISABEL.   No me atreveré, señor,
             a contarte mis desdichas
             a referirte mis penas;
             porque si una vez te miras
             con manos, y sin honor,
             me darán muerte tus iras...   (532a)

But the details of the situation are quite different. Leonor and Inés, having voluntarily eloped with the captains, merely lament their deception, and conscious of their guilt dare not approach their father. Isabel, on the other hand, is innocent; she releases her father and, overcome by the shame which through her has come upon the family, pleads with him to take her life. Crespo spares Isabel and swears revenge on the captain:

> Que el ansia mía
> no ha de parar, hasta darle
> la muerte.   (534a)

It is at this point that he learns that he has been elected *alcalde*, and that his first duties are to welcome the King to Zalamea and see punishment done to one who has wounded an army-captain. This postponement of Crespo's election allowed Calderón to change completely the impact and significance of the story's *dénouement*. Resolved on violating the law by personal revenge on the captain, Crespo is by virtue of his election suddenly made responsible for the law's observance:

> CRESPO.   (Ap.) ¡Cielos!
> ¡Cuando vengarse imagina,
> me hace dueño de mi honor
> la vara de la justicia!
> ¿Cómo podré delinquir
> yo, si en esta hora misma
> me ponen a mí por juez,
> para que otros no delincan?   (534a)

and he remarks appositely:

> (Pero cosas como aquéstas
> no se ven con tanta prisa.)   (534a)

The situation does indeed call for careful thought. He must and will clear his family's honour, but it has to be done in a manner compatible with his position as *alcalde*.

This now becomes the preoccupation of Calderón's protagonist. The earlier Crespo is intent upon fulfilling his duties as *alcalde* and wishes to ensure that the captains are within his area of jurisdiction. Calderón's Crespo is concerned above all with his family's honour, and is anxious only that he shall not compromise his position as *alcalde*. His first step is to ask the captain to marry Isabel, the only peaceable way in which his honour can be cleared. Alone with Don Álvaro, he lays aside his staff of office and pleads with him as Isabel's father to marry her. But humility is met by insolence. Don Álvaro, unlike Fernando in *Don Quixote*, refuses to make amends or even to recognize the error of his ways. So, his plea rejected and his patience exhausted, Crespo assumes again his authority as *alcalde* and has the captain arrested. This magnificent scene with its pathos and drama has no counterpart in the source-play. The first Pedro Crespo merely arrests the captains and proclaims:

> y pues villanos quedáis
> con las obras que mostráis,
> en nada os ofendo aquí,
> si bajándoos hasta mí,
> con mis hijas os casáis.   (592b)

Calderón's Crespo, commanding far greater respect than his model, buries his pride and kneels before his daughter's seducer:

> No creo
> que desluzcáis vuestro honor,
> porque los merecimientos
> que vuestros hijos, señor,
> perdieren con ser mis nietos,
> ganarán con más ventaja,
> señor, por ser hijos vuestros.   (536a)

Only after the captain has refused to marry Isabel does he order his arrest.

The scene then switches to Crespo's house. Crespo arrives in time to prevent Juan from taking his sister's life and arrests him for wounding the captain; and he insists that Isabel's accusation against the captain be presented in writing. Crespo's behaviour, not surprisingly, bewilders both Juan and Isabel. And it has bewildered scholars; Krenkel, with the source-play in mind, observes that he does not feel that Calderón's Crespo is acting with the same impartiality as the earlier Crespo.[1] The code of honour clearly stipulated that a dishonoured person should die and that a family's dishonour should be kept secret. Yet Crespo foils Juan's attempt

---

[1] Op. cit., 76-77.

upon his sister's life and insists on making public the offence against her. Crespo is certainly no less determined now than before to clear the family honour, and since the captain has refused to marry his daughter this can only be done by killing him. But, recognizing Isabel's innocence, he spares her life:

CRESPO.	¿Qué es esto?
D. JUAN.	Es satisfacer, señor, una injuria, y es vengar una ofensa, y castigar...
CRESPO.	Basta, basta; que es error que os atrevéis a venir...
D. JUAN.	¿Qué es lo que mirando estoy?
CRESPO.	...delante así de mí hoy, acabando ahora de herir en el monte un capitán. (538a)

Juan is arrested and committed to prison, though this is to ensure his safety: [1]

> (Ap.) Aquesto es asegurar
> su vida, y han de pensar
> que es la justicia más rara
> del mundo.   (538a)

As *alcalde* Crespo follows the procedure of the law to punish the captain:

> ...no basta sabello
> yo como yo; que ha de ser
> como alcalde, y he de hacer
> información sobre ello.
> Y hasta que conste qué culpa
> te resulta del proceso,
> tengo de tenerte preso.   (538a)

If later he exceeds his powers as *alcalde,* at least he uses his authority to have a full investigation of the captain's behaviour, to summon witnesses and to pass judgement.

At this point Don Lope arrives. His voice off-stage brings the play's tension to breaking point, for Crespo has flagrantly denied the

---

[1] Cf. *Las armas:*

> y también
> porque preso, asegurada
> su persona esté...

rights of a soldier. The suspense is aggravated by Don Lope's first words taking Crespo into his confidence about the mayor who has dared to arrest his captain; and when he learns the truth the storm bursts. In the exchanges which follow Calderón reverts again to the single scene containing Don Lope in the first *alcalde*:

SOURCE

D. LOPE.	No puedo responderos de cólera...	(577a)
D. JUAN.	¿Hay desvergüenza mayor que la que tiene este villano?	(577b)
D. DIEGO.	Soldados: éste es el tiempo de nuestra venganza. ¡Mueran estos villanos!	(578a)

CALDERÓN

D. LOPE.	Que estoy perdido, os confieso de cólera.	(538b)
D. LOPE.	La desvergüenza es mayor que se puede imaginar...	(538b)
D. LOPE.	Esta es la cárcel, soldados...	
SOLDADOS.	Mueran aquestos villanos.	(539b)

But the situation is quite different; and the clash is so arranged that it anticipates the full extent of Crespo's audacity in the prison-scene, with which the play ends. Here Calderón almost certainly had the source text in front of him. The arrival of the King, the revelation of the captain's dead body, Crespo's cross-examination, his excuses, his appointment as *alcalde* for life, his daughter's retirement to a convent: all this stems directly from the source. And there are close parallelisms of expression:

SOURCE

ALCALDE.	Forzar doncellas, ¿no es causa digna de muerte?	(595b)
REY.	Pero si son caballeros, era justo ver también que habíais de degollarlos, ya que os hicisteis su juez.	
ALCALDE.	Señor, como por acá viven los hidalgos bien, no ha aprendido á degollar el verdugo.	(595b)
REY.	Y á vos, por lo bien que hacéis vuestro oficio os hago alcalde perpetuo.	(596a)

CALDERÓN

CRESPO.   Este proceso, en quien bien
probado el delito está,
digno de muerte, por ser
una doncella robar,
forzarla en un despoblado...   (540a)

REY.   ¿Por qué, como a capitán
y caballero, no hicistes
degollarle?

CRESPO.   ¿Eso dudáis?
Señor, como los hidalgos
viven tan bien por acá,
el verdugo que tenemos
no ha aprendido a degollar.   (540b)

REY.   Vos, por alcalde perpetuo
de aquesta villa os quedad.   (541a)

But the differences are significant. In the source the angry exchanges between Don Lope and Don Crespo on the subject of an *alcalde's* powers occur early in Act II; in Act III the King and Don Lope make only a polite inquiry about the captains. In Calderón's play Crespo's arrest of the captain is his first action as *alcalde*, and the King and Don Lope come expressly to protest against it. Crespo's reply is to this specific protest:

Este proceso, en quien bien
probado el delito está,
digno de muerte, por ser
una doncella robar,
forzarla en un despoblado
y no quererse casar
con ella, habiendo su padre
rogádole con la paz.   (540a)

The scrupulous care he has taken in investigating the case as *alcalde*—the securing of witnesses, the arrest of Juan, and Isabel's complaint in writing—has prepared him for Don Lope's taunt:

Éste es el alcalde, y es
su padre.   (540a)

He answers:

No importa en tal
caso, porque si un extraño
se viniera a querellar,
¿no había de hacer justicia?

Sí; pues ¿qué más se me da
hacer por mi hija lo mismo
que hiciera por los demás?
Fuera de que, como he preso
un hijo mío, es verdad
que no escuchara a mi hija,
pues era la sangre igual.
Mírese si está bien hecha
la causa, miren si hay
quien diga que yo haya hecho
en ella alguna maldad,
si he inducido algún testigo,
si está escrito algo de más
de lo que he dicho, y entonces
me den muerte.   (540a)

The King concludes that the case against the captain is proven:

Bien está
sentenciado...   (540a-b)

and only when he denies the authority of Crespo to carry out the sentence is the captain's body revealed. Calderón's timing is admirable. Having just extracted from the King confirmation of the justness of his sentence upon the captain, Crespo can only be charged with carrying it out, and with hanging a nobleman rather than beheading him. He may well ask:

Y ¿qué importa errar lo menos
quien ha acertado lo más?   (540b)

Justice has been done, even if the law of the state has been broken. In the source-play the King readily accepts the *alcalde*'s explanation and comments 'Muy bien'; he objects only to the manner of the captain's death. It is interesting to note that Crespo is not so exonerated in Calderón's play. There is neither 'honrado juez' from the King nor 'justo juez' from Don Lope as in the source. Instead, Crespo is reprimanded for his audacity:

Pues ¿cómo así os atrevistes?...   (540b)

and told that a court exists to deal with such matters. For the last few lines of the play the centre of interest is Don Lope. His captain has been hanged, his law flouted, his authority challenged. It is appropriate that the King should turn to him in pardoning Crespo's act:

Don Lope, aquesto ya es hecho.
Bien dada la muerte está;
que errar lo menos no importa
si acertó lo principal.   (540b)

The King's verdict silences further criticism. But Calderón does not,
like the earlier dramatist, leave it at that. When the King leaves,
Don Lope quietly observes to Crespo that he might well be grateful
for the King's arrival and that, had he consulted him, his daughter's
honour might have been safeguarded:

¿No fuera mejor hablarme,
dando el preso, y remediar
el honor de vuestra hija?   (541a)

In the remaining lines Crespo maintains his strict insistence on the
letter of the law in respect of his son; Juan has committed a
punishable offence and he is released only at the request of Don
Lope.

Calderón's *El alcalde de Zalamea* is deservedly famous for its
fine characterization, in particular for the portraits of the rugged,
independent Crespo and the testy, gout-ridden general Don Lope.
All the characters, with the possible exception of Isabel, emerge as
persons of flesh and blood: the know-all soldier Rebolledo, his
mistress La Chispa, Don Mendo's servant Nuño, even the *Escribano*.
Though the plot derives from an earlier play, Calderón was apparently drawing upon personal experience of the army. And the
play is outstanding for its magnificently conceived human situations:
the farewell scene between Crespo and his son, Isabel's reunion
with her father after the seduction, and Crespo's pleading with the
captain to marry his daughter. But critics have perhaps overstated
the extent to which this play is exceptional. Like all the best plays
of Calderón, *El alcalde de Zalamea* presents a complicated picture
of human behaviour in terms of a single theme. Its peculiarity, I
suggest, is that, though in all his plays Calderón necessarily
presented his themes in terms of human experience, he has here
taken more care to keep the intellectual aspect subordinate to the
human; his characters and situations are less bookish and have the
appearance at least of having been drawn from life.

The play has the cohesion and unity of Calderón's best work.
Like *El médico de su honra* it is remarkable illustration of his use

of hints and suggestions to foreshadow his *dénouement*; as the play advances, the suggestions accumulate and become more explicit. But above all we see Calderón's idea of moral responsibility and the strict causal sequence which resulted from it. Don Álvaro is responsible for Isabel's dishonour: regarding honour as the pre-rogative of noblemen, he is conspicuously dishonourable himself and contemptuous of the honour of the Crespos; and he is blinded by his passion for Isabel. Crespo is the embodiment of the sense of honour of a peasant and his philosophy is immortalized in the famous lines:

> Al rey la hacienda y la vida
> se ha de dar; pero el honor
> es patrimonio del alma,
> y el alma sólo es de Dios.   (521a)

By hanging the captain he breaks the laws of the state and his action is illegal. But it is 'errar lo menos'. By his breach of a military regulation Crespo ensures that natural justice is done. The conduct of Isabel is exemplary; her virtue is beyond reproach and she lives to see her honour cleared. Juan, with the best intentions, is impetuous, and he holds the conventional view of honour and revenge. Don Mendo is a person for whom honour is a mere label and his conception of honour is set against that of Crespo. Don Lope de Figueroa, on the other hand, is intended as a match to Crespo, and he represents the highest traditions of the army. Calderón's play is the supreme vindication of the peasant man of honour. The captain pays for his crime with his life, and Philip II, recognizing that moral justice has been done, excuses the illegality of Crespo's action. Crespo removes the offence against his family's honour and receives the commendation of the King. With good will and prudent behaviour soldier and peasant can live together in peace, as do Don Lope and Crespo in Act II. Such at least is the interpretation suggested by a comparison of the play with its source.

Calderón broke completely from the language of the source-play and parallelisms are few and far between. I can find no single passage of length in which he is demonstrably rewriting a passage of the original; and in the few lines which are close to the source only occasionally is there identity of phrase. The imagery is new and typically Calderonian. As in other plays of this type, honour is associated with light. Crespo tells Juan:

> eres de linaje limpio
> más que el sol...   (528b-529a)

and assures the captain that by marrying Isabel:

> No creo
> que desluzcáis vuestro honor...   (536a)

Don Mendo's comparing Isabel with the rising sun and a second dawn are intended, of course, to appear exaggerated and absurd, but they have their place in a general scheme of imagery. Isabel *is* like the sun both in her beauty and her shining honour. Later, abducted and raped by the captain, she shuns the light and pleads with the sun not to rise. Once again the scene of dishonour is a dark, tortuous wood:

> Aqueste intrincado, oculto
> monte, que está a la salida
> del lugar fué su sagrado...

and Isabel comments:

> ¿cuándo de la tiranía
> no son sagrado los montes?   (532b)

The captain's infatuation is *ira, rabia, furor, furia, delirio*. He himself compares it with four forms of fire in his important scene with the sergeant early in Act II:

> De sola una vez, a incendio
> crece una breve pavesa;
> de una vez sola un abismo,
> sulfúreo volcán, revienta;
> de una vez se enciende el rayo
> que destruye cuanto encuentra;
> de una vez escupe horror
> la más reformada pieza;
> ¿de una vez amor, qué mucho,
> fuego de cuatro maneras,
> mina, incendio, pieza y rayo,
> postre, abrase, asombre y hiera?   (522b)

The insistence upon violence and destructiveness suggests the consequence of his own lust, and foreshadows his own death. The captain is the squall which, as Crespo feared, carries off his grain:

> ¡Oh, quiera Dios que en las trojes
> yo llegue a encerrarlo, antes
> que algún turbión me lo lleve
> o algún viento me lo tale! (516a)

The ineffective Don Mendo, on the other hand, is a mere *fantasma,* as unsubstantial as mist:

> Isabel
> es deidad hermosa y bella,
> a cuyo cielo no empañan
> los vapores de la tierra. (521b)

Calderón's verse-forms are quite different from those of the source dramatist. For the clash between Pedro Crespo and Don Lope, in place of *romance* in E-O he has *romance* in Ó in Act I and *redondillas* in Act III; and for the last scene in place of *romance* in É romance in Á. Different too is his use of music and songs. The first scene of Calderón's second act, for instance, contains an interesting example of contrasting types of music. The concord between Pedro Crespo and Don Lope and the peace as they sup together in the open air are symbolized by the rippling brook and the wind playing in the vines:

> Sentaos, que el viento suave
> que en las blandas hojas suena
> destas parras y estas copas,
> mil cláusulas lisonjeras
> hace al compás desta fuente,
> cítara de plata y perlas,
> porque son, en trastes de oro,
> las guijas templadas cuerdas.
> Perdonad si de instrumentos
> solos la música suena
> sin cantores que os deleiten
> sin voces que os entretengan,
> que como músicos son
> los pájaros que gorjean,
> no quieren cantar de noche
> ni yo puedo hacerles fuerza. (523a-b)

But this peace is about to be broken by the captain and his party who come to serenade Isabel; their music is the strumming of guitars and the singing of a *jácara*. Calderón changed even the staging of the final *coup de théâtre*. The source dramatist sets the 'discovery' in the upper gallery:

> CRESPO.   Descubrid ese balcón;
> aquí mis yernos veréis.   (595b)

and shows the captain's hanging. Calderón's 'discovery' is in the inner stage: a curtain is drawn or alternatively doors are opened, and the captain is shown garrotted on a chair:

> CRESPO.   Si no creéis
> que esto, señor, es verdad,
> volved los ojos y vedlo,
> aquéste es el capitán.   (540b)

Calderón transformed a play about an *alcalde* into a study of a peasant's honour. He owed to the source dramatist the basic facts of his story and, in particular, its striking *dénouement* and the outlines of the four main characters, notably Pedro Crespo and Don Lope de Figueroa. But the rest of the play's material, its handling and its language, are new and original. It is no longer a question of a detailed recasting of the source-play scene by scene which the new conception of *El médico de su honra* and *Las armas de la hermosura* allowed, nor even of part of the source-play. The structure of the source has been demolished to its foundations and a new one substituted; and of the material itself only a small proportion was salvaged.

IX

LA VIDA ES SUEÑO

THE sources of *La vida es sueño* [1] have often been investigated. But Farinelli, Olmedo and other scholars have been concerned above all with antecedents for the play's theme 'Life's a dream', and for the story of the awakened sleeper. Calderón's debt to an earlier play has until recently been completely overlooked, and still remains unstudied. The play in question is *Yerros de naturaleza y aciertos de la fortuna*, written by Calderón himself in collaboration with Antonio Coello. *Yerros* is preserved in a manuscript dated 1634, at the end of which, in a hand different from that of either Calderón or Coello, one reads: 'Vea esta comedia don Germo. de Villanueva —En Madrid a 4 de mayo de 1634', and after it 'Esta comedia está escrita como de dos grandes ingenios, puédese representar. Germo. de Villanueva'. Act I contains on its cover the play's title and the name of Don Antonio Coello, and is written in one hand, probably Coello's. Act II shows a second hand which has been identified as Calderón's, and begins with the familiar formula 'Jhs. María Joseph'. The first hand reappears at the beginning of Act III with forty-two lines of *romance* in í. Calderón then resumes and writes the next four folios, ending abruptly in the middle of a scene with Rosaura's line: 'Esto mi padre desea'. From this point the first hand continues to the end.

Yerros remained in manuscript until 1930, and was apparently unknown to Schack, Schmidt, Krenkel, Maccoll, Menéndez y Pe-

---

[1] Texts used:

    Source:
        Ed. Astrana Marín, op. cit. (Madrid, 1945, 3.ª ed., revisada.)
    Calderón:
        Primera Parte, 1636, 1640.
        Ed. Vera Tassis, I (1682).
        Ed. J. J. Keil, op. cit., I, 1-25.
        Ed. J. E. Hartzenbusch, op. cit., I, 1-19.
        Ed. M. A. Buchanan (Toronto, 1909).
        Ed. Astrana Marín, op. cit. (Madrid, 1945, 3.ª ed., revisada.)
        Ed. M. de Riquer (Barcelona, 1954).
    Quotations are from the Astrana Marín edition.

layo, Viel-Castel, Farinelli and Olmedo. Northup seems to have been the first to ·call attention to the relationship between it and *La vida es sueño* in 1910. [1] His essay is primarily concerned with a ·description of the manuscript of *Yerros* and with a summary of its plot, but he devotes a page or so to the parallel between the two plays, and inclines to the view that *La vida es sueño* was written first:

> I see no positive proof that the Coello-Calderón play was written after *La vida. es sueño,* although it is highly probable that such was the case.

Northup was misled by his assumption that *La vida ·es sueño* was written before 1634, when *Yerros* was licensed, and by the idea, which was then current, that in order to keep pace with the demand for plays Calderón rehashed material which he or others had already used. He regards *Yerros* as 'a mere pot-boiler written for profit and for nothing more'. Cotarelo exposed the error of Northup. [2] There is no evidence for dating *La vida es sueño* before 1634. For this play, as for *Las armas de la hermosura* and *El mayor encanto amor,* Calderón recast an earlier play of which he was part-author. Juliá Martínez agrees with Cotarelo, though he suggests that Calderón was already engaged on *La vida es sueño* before *Yerros* was completed:

> Dado lo que en otros casos ocurriera, fácil es suponer que *Yerros* reclame la prioridad, pero seguramente que en los días en que fué escrita, habían tomado forma ya en la fantasía del poeta los personajes de su más aplaudida producción. Y es posible que, cuando Coello trazó la última jornada estuvieran escritos bastantes folios de la obra genuina de su colaborador. [3]

Neither Cotarelo nor Juliá Martínez, nor to my knowledge any subsequent critic, has gone beyond the recognition that *Yerros* was a precursor of *La vida es sueño.* And some continue to discount the fact. Schevill could still write in 1933:

> *Los yerros de naturaleza y aciertos de la fortuna* is manifestly a poor *Machwerk* composed after *La vida es sueño,* and the resemblances in plot seem wholly insignificant. *(HR, I, 1933, 191.)*

---

[1] Cf. G. T. Northup, '*Los yerros de naturaleza y aciertos de la fortuna,* by Don Antonio Coello and Don Pedro Calderón de la Barca', *RR,* I, (1910), 411-25.
[2] Op. cit., p. 150n.
[3] Op. cit., p. 23.

And, more recently, Hilborn has dated *La vida es sueño* 1631-32, at least two years earlier than the dated manuscript of *Yerros*. [1]

I do not claim that the following pages have any significant contribution to make to the interpretation of *La vida es sueño*. They will, for example, throw little light on the meaning attached by Calderón to the phrase 'Life's a dream', though they confirm in many details the recent interpretations of E. M. Wilson and Leopoldo Palacios. [2] They do establish, however, that *Yerros* was Calderón's starting point for *La vida es sueño*, and they show how, by extending the idea underlying the source, Calderón was able to build upon its principal characters the structure of a new and original play.

Yerros is set in Poland. King Conrado has just died and is survived by his twin children Polidoro and Matilde; Polidoro, born after his sister, is by the Salic law the rightful successor. Nature's principal error—*yerro de naturaleza*—is that, though in appearance Polidoro and Matilde are indistinguishable, it is Matilde rather than Polidoro who has the virile qualities of a King. Matilde, at all events, has designs upon the throne. She resolves to remove her brother secretly and replace him by assuming his name and costume; and she discloses her plan to Filipo, the King's *privado*, who appears to support her. It is first reported that Matilde has been drowned; Matilde then removes her brother and gives orders for him to be killed. Filipo harbours a grievance against Polidoro, but instead of killing him he imprisons him in a tower. Later Filipo's son, Segismundo, anxious to avenge the insult to his father, breaks into the palace and stabs to death the person he takes to be Polidoro. So by a stroke of fortune Matilde is dispatched, and Polidoro is brought out of hiding and restored to the throne. Polidoro, chastened by his prison experience, pardons his enemies and offers his hand to Rosaura.

On the surface Calderón's *La vida es sueño* has little in common with *Yerros*. Both plays are set in Poland and both involve characters by the names of Segismundo and Rosaura; that would seem

---

[1]   Op. cit., p. 18.

[2]   E. M. Wilson, '*La vida es sueño*', *Revista de la Universidad de Buenos Aires*, 3a época, Año IV, Nos. 3 and 4 (1946), 61-78, and Leopoldo Eulogio Palacios, '*La vida es sueño*', *Finisterre*, II (1948), 5-52. (For the elucidation of Calderón's play the reader is referred to these important studies, to which the present chapter owes much.

to be the full extent of the resemblance. The basic story, however, is the same in both plays: a Prince, the legitimate heir to the throne, regains the rights that have been denied him. Matilde in *Yerros*, regarding herself better qualified to rule than her brother Polidoro, usurps his throne. Similarly, Basilio in *La vida es sueño* imprisons Segismundo because of the horoscope which makes him, in his view, unfit to succeed. Both plays are concerned with what appears to be an error of nature: Polidoro and Segismundo seem to lack the qualities required of a King. Both show the intervention of man, Matilde and Basilio, to correct that error. But the error proves to be man's not nature's, and in the play's *dénouement* the designs of both Matilde and Basilio are thwarted. Matilde dies a violent death, and Basilio owes his life to Segismundo's mercy.

The idea which underlies *Yerros* is that a man's life is his own and that he has an inalienable right to freedom; intervention by other men which jeopardizes or denies that freedom is illegitimate and ineffective. When the play ends, Matilde —admittedly by a startling coincidence— has been punished and Polidoro reinstated. This is one of the ideas which underlies *La vida es sueño*: Segismundo finally is acknowledged Prince and heir, and Basilio is humiliated. But Calderón's play not only exposes the fallacy and futility of one person intervening in the fate of another; it develops the complementary idea of a man working out his own salvation, discovering through disillusion the path of prudence. It shows the error of Basilio and also the exemplary achievement of Segismundo. The achievement of Segismundo, moreover, is made the dominant issue, and Segismundo himself the play's protagonist. Hence the obvious differences between Polidoro and Segismundo. Polidoro has an essentially passive rôle as the victim of Matilde. Segismundo, on the other hand, is the central figure of *La vida es sueño*, who achieves by his own will what Basilio has lamentably failed to achieve.

Calderón replaced the brother-sister relationship of *Yerros* by one of father and son. The plot of *Yerros* depends upon the stock device of indistinguishable twins: Polidoro is secretly deposed only because Matilde is his exact likeness; similarly, Matilde is killed only because she is mistaken for Polidoro. Had Calderón merely wished to dispense with the conventional device of twins and to substitute a father and son, he would have required new circumstances for the son's removal and reinstatement. But he was obliged to reject the plot of *Yerros* in order to extend its basic idea; he needed new incidents and situations to show a Prince's conversion. And it is in this respect that he made his most striking innovation. The crucial experience of Segismundo is his day's sojourn at the palace and the delusion that it was all a dream, a delusion which led him to the fundamental truth that life itself is as transient as a dream. Calderón saw precisely what he needed in the story of the awakened sleeper, deeply rooted in Spanish, and ultimately in Eastern, tradition. The palace experience of Segismundo has no precedent in *Yerros*; but it overlies a situation which is common to both.

Nor is this all. Though there is no precedent in *Yerros* for the important horoscope motif, the awakened-sleeper situation is quite clearly anticipated. Matilde, it will be remembered, is killed by Filipo's son who assumes that he is being revenged upon Polidoro. Filipo, discovering the error, sees the opportunity of clearing his son and of restoring the rightful ruler. Since Matilde is believed to have been drowned, he has only to remove her body and set Polidoro in her place. But Polidoro has to be restored in secret; he must be made to carry on as if he had not been imprisoned. So, without a word of explanation, he is led blindfold from the tower and left alone. He removes the bandages from his eyes and finds himself in the familiar surroundings of the palace. The circumstances in themselves clearly resemble those in which Segismundo awakens first in the palace and later back in his prison-cell in Act II of *La vida es sueño*. Listen also to Polidoro's words:

> Aguarda, verdad o sombra
> de mi dicha y mi desgracia,
> de mi vida y de mi muerte,
> que me obligas y me agravias.
> Aguarda. ¡Válgame el cielo!
>
> *(Quítase el lienzo de los ojos.)*
>
> ¿Adónde estoy? ¡Qué mudanza!
> El centro oscuro que fué
> mi albergue, en aquestas salas
> me trocó. ¿Si estoy soñando?
> ¿No es de mi cuarto esta cuadra?
> ¿No estoy en palacio yo?

> Sí, que bien me desengañan
> estas señas, si no es ya
> que es de mi desdicha maña
> o falsedad de mi pena
> fingirme glorias pasadas.   (1349a)

They correspond to these of Segismundo :

> ¡Válgame el cielo, qué veo!
> ¡Válgame el cielo, qué miro!
> Con poco espanto lo admiro,
> con mucha duda lo creo.
> ¿Yo en palacios suntuosos?
> ¿Yo entre telas y brocados?
> ¿Yo cercado de criados
> tan lucidos y briosos?
> ¿Yo despertar de dormir
> en lecho tan excelente?
> ¿Yo en medio de tanta gente
> que me sirve de vestir?
> Decir que sueño es engaño :
> bien sé que despierto estoy.
> ¿Yo Segismundo no soy?
> Dadme, cielos, desengaño.   (227b)

> ¡Mas, ay de mí! ¿Dónde estoy?...
> ¿Soy yo, por ventura? ¿Soy
> el que preso y aherrojado
> llego a verme en tal estado?
> ¿No sois mi sepulcro vos,
> torre? Sí, ¡válgame Dios,
> qué de cosas he soñado!   (236a)

Polidoro's lines were apparently written by Coello, not by Calderón; but that they occur in such a situation in *Yerros* suggests that we have here the germ of *La vida es sueño*. This perhaps was the spark that suddenly illumined Calderón's mind, which revealed the potentialities of the theme that was only partially developed in *Yerros*, and the manner in which it might be given dramatic expression.

We have noted how, for *El príncipe constante* and *El alcalde de Zalamea*, Calderón was obliged to reject many of the incidents and situations of the source-plays; his principal debt was in respect of characters. This is truer still for *La vida es sueño*. It will be clear already that there is some kind of correspondence between Segismundo and the earlier Polidoro and between Basilio and the earlier Matilde. And these are by no means the only parallels. Five of the seven characters of *La vida es sueño* derive directly from *Yerros*. The relationship is shown below:

YERROS	LA VIDA ES SUEÑO
Polidoro	Segismundo
Matilde, *sister to Polidoro*	Basilio, *father of Segismundo*
Filipo, *viejo*	Clotaldo, *viejo*
Rosaura, *daughter of Filipo*	Rosaura, *daughter of Clotaldo*
Policena, *servant*	—
Segismundo, *son of Filipo*	
—	Astolfo
—	Estrella
Tabaco, *servant*	Clarín, *servant*
Fisberto	—
Federico, *privado*	—

Segismundo hails primarily from Polidoro. Both characters are the victims of tyrants; both are deprived of their rights of succession to the throne and imprisoned; both live to see their oppressors vanquished and their rights restored. For most of *Yerros* Polidoro is the innocent victim of the tyranny of his twin sister, and at the play's end his triumph is a mere stroke of fortune. After his imprisonment, however, he is a different person. Awed by the workings of Providence, he pardons his enemies and makes amends for his wrongs to the family of Filipo. This, I believe, was Calderón's point of departure for *La vida es sueño*, and I must quote Polidoro's final speech in full. First he reads the note which Filipo has left:

FILIPO.	Y junto al cuerpo, una carta está en el suelo.
POLIDORO.	¿A quién dice? La carta mostrad; alzadla.
FILIPO.	"Avisos de Polidoro".
POLIDORO.	Si son avisos ya tardan. "Ningún delito se huyó (*Lee*) del castigo; Providencia piadosa, en tu breve ausencia, castigos te conmutó. Quien por ti a reinar entró, en tu delito tropieza; sustituyó su cabeza la tuya por ser tan una, enmendando la fortuna lo que erró Naturaleza". (1350b-1351a)

He then goes on:

Bien dice que avisos son
que el cielo los da por señas
a mis años. Pues, vasallos,
bien es que yo los entienda;
corte de Polonia, amigos,
bien miráis la providencia
con que el cielo me ha guardado,
y esta espantosa tragedia
bien podéis adivinar
el misterio que en sí encierra.
Ambición fué de Matilde,
que el cielo dejó deshecha;
y, aunque es verdad que conozco
que ella sola no pudiera
ser todo en aquesta hazaña,
y que hay cómplices en ella,
nada desto se averigüe,
quédense en todos suspensas
estas cosas, pues tomó
del cielo la providencia
este instrumento, este brazo
por castigo y por enmienda
de la ambición de Matilde
y en mí de mis años. Fuera
de que también yo obligado
me reconozco a la ofensa,
pues ya me guardó la vida
quien de mi reino me lleva;
y así, en albricias de todo
y de todo en recompensa,
volved vos a mi privanza,
Filipo a mi gracia vuelva,
y por soldar el desaire
que os hice, Rosaura, sea
hoy mi esposa, y Segismundo,
que de Polonia hizo ausencia,
vuelva a gobernar mis armas
para que con esto vean
que, ya que el reino me quitan
yerros de Naturaleza,
pues pudo fingir Matilde
que era yo, agora lo enmiendan
aciertos de la fortuna;
pues por mí el golpe le acierta
de la muerte, porque acaben,
en mi dicha y su tragedia,
los males de Polidoro,
de Matilde la soberbia,
y los yerros de dos plumas
que en deseos sólo aciertan.   (1351a-b)

Polidoro has profited by his experiences: he recognizes his offence against the family of Filipo, he restores Filipo to favour, he pardons Filipo's son and accepts his daughter as his wife. This may well have inspired Calderón's conception of Segismundo, a person who, though victimized, is himself in need of, and capable of, regeneration. Calderón's new play could thereby end with the tyrant's punishment and the victim's conversion. And the victim replaces the tyrant as the play's protagonist.

Polidoro is involved in the action of the source-play first as the brother of Matilde and second as the lover of Rosaura. In his relations with Matilde his rôle is exclusively passive. His twin sister resents his succeeding to the throne when she was born first and has, she believes, all the qualities of a ruler; and without any provocation on his part, she removes him. At the end of the play it is by sheer accident that Matilde is killed and Polidoro restored. Polidoro, like Segismundo, is committed to prison but the play does not appear on stage. This passive rôle of Polidoro vis-à-vis his contains no prison scene; between his departure and return he tyrant sister was completely changed by Calderón. The spotlight is now fixed on Segismundo; we see him in his prison cell, we watch his behaviour at the palace, we witness his disillusionment and conversion. In this respect Segismundo owes little to Polidoro. Polidoro's affair with Rosaura offered Calderón more scope. Returning from the field of battle, Polidoro dares to come unannounced to Rosaura's room, and when surprised and reproved by her father Filipo he strikes him in the face. Matilde has mentioned humility as the main trait of Polidoro, one who commands the love and affection of the people:

> ...al contrario, Polidoro,
> tan humilde, tan modesto,
> de valor tan abreviado,
> de corazón tan estrecho,
> de condición tan humilde,
> que sólo fundó su intento
> en dejarse hollar de todos,
> en ser amado del pueblo,
> tanto que, ya su llaneza,
> sin diferenciar sujetos,
> casi ya en indignidad
> tocó peligroso extremo...   (1321b-1322a)

But in the honour episodes of the play Polidoro shows himself to be singularly imprudent. He is impetuous and quick-tempered in his relations with Filipo and is unable to control his jealousy towards Fisberto, a rival for Rosaura's love:

> ¡Ay celos,
> no entréis con tanta violencia
> que me declaréis!   (1331b)

Northup claimed even that there was much inconsistency in the portrayal.[1] Polidoro, at least, is self-critical. He admits to his audacity in entering Rosaura's room:

> ...aunque él me dió la ocasión,
> sabe Dios cuánto me pesa;
> mas la paciencia irritada
> es furor y no es paciencia.   (1330b)

and recognizes that she has reason to be offended:

> Rosaura de mi ofendida
> la razón no he de negarle...   (1335b)

and he refers on more than one occasion to his anger:

> una cólera tan necia...   (1331a)

> mi cólera fiera...   (1332a)

> aquel ciego furor...   (1335b)

These qualms of conscience and confessions prepare us for the salutary effect of his prison experience.

Segismundo's character is in many respects the opposite to that of Polidoro. He is the personification of pride, and for the first two acts of *La vida es sueño* he represents man at his most abject, one whose fate was predicted as:

> ...sería
> el hombre más atrevido
> el príncipe más cruel
> y el monarca más impío
> por quien su reino vendría
> a ser parcial y diviso,
> escuela de las traiciones
> v academia de los vicios...   (222b)

---

[1] Op. cit., 417.

In the prison-tower he is presented as a monster, half-man half-animal, and at the palace in Act II he is utterly reckless and proud: he attempts to kill Clotaldo, he insults Astolfo, he threatens Estrella and Rosaura and vilifies the King. In all this he recalls not his counterpart Polidoro but Matilde; and in one incident at least he is clearly modelled upon her. During her brief period of rule Matilde, exasperated by the *gracioso* Tabaco, threatens to hurl him over a balcony:

> ¿Esto sufro? Si en tu vida
> me entras aquí, ¡vive el cielo,
> que te eche por un balcón!   (1340a)

Segismundo will carry out the threat in *La vida es sueño*. But Segismundo progresses from extreme pride in Act I to humility at the play's end. The process is by no means sudden, as Wilson has shown. In Act I he takes pity on Rosaura, in Act II at the palace he makes rational and enlightened observations; after his disillusionment at the end of Act II he first spares Clotaldo, then champions the cause of Rosaura and finally pardons his own father and surrenders Rosaura to Astolfo for the sake of her honour. For most of *Yerros* Polidoro is contrasted with his proud, unscrupulous sister; but he is a victim of anger, jealousy and impetuousness in the honour scenes and he learns prudence only after his prison experience, when he makes a public apology and reparation for his affront to Filipo. There is no precedent in *Yerros* for the moral and psychological development of Segismundo, but Polidoro's recognition of his offence against Filipo inspired, I believe, Calderón's conception. *Yerros*, at all events, like *La vida es sueño*, shows a person who is involved with a tyrant and with a girl, a girl whose name is the same in both plays. Although, as we shall see, Calderón changed in some respects the rôle of Rosaura, he was able to accommodate her and her father in his new play. However small the ultimate resemblance between Segismundo and Polidoro —and of all the characters perhaps he owes least to *Yerros*— Segismundo undoubtedly derives from Polidoro, and is primarily involved with two other characters who are in outline the same in both plays.

I have mentioned the influence of Matilde upon Segismundo. But Matilde's opposite number in *La vida es sueño* is, of course, Basilio. Calderón, we have seen, dispensed with the indistinguishable twins of *Yerros* and substituted a father and son; a father replaces a sister. Yet Basilio's behaviour has something in common with Matilde's. Matilde is a blend of pride and ambition. She confesses:

> Criéme yo, aunque mujer,
> con tan varonil esfuerzo,
> con fama tan ambiciosa,
> con natural tan sediento
> de reinos, de monarquías,
> de coronas y de imperios,
> que, a pesar de los adornos
> mujeriles, al estruendo
> de Marte me alborotaba...   (1321b)

Envious of her brother's succession to the throne, she is prepared even to have him murdered to achieve her designs. She resolves to reveal her plan to Filipo:

> Salga ya, salga, ¿qué dudo?,
> esta ambición de mi pecho;
> llueva esta nube en granizos,
> gima esta esfera en incendios,
> brote esta tormenta en rayos
> y hable aqueste rayo en truenos.
> Ea, Filipo famoso,
> pues que por padre te tengo,
> pues me debes tanto amor
> y pues tanto amor te debo,
> hoy he de hacer con tu ayuda,
> pues ya me ayuda tu esfuerzo,
> la más invencible hazaña,
> el mayor atrevimiento,
> la resolución más grande
> que en el humano denuedo
> pudo caber...   (1322b-1323a)

And when he leaves she admits:

> pues la ambición me conduce
> al más peligroso intento.   (1323a)

Filipo later refers to the plot as:

> estos delirios que piensa
> de su vanidad dictados
> creídos de su soberbia...   (1334a)

At the same time, Matilde is infatuated by a certain Fisberto and she refers herself to her twin passions of ambition and love:

> Ambición y amor, ¿qué es esto?
> ¿Cómo han de hacer en mi vida,
> desconcertado instrumento,
> consonancia y armonía
> dos destemplados intentos:
> amor, que suena a un vasallo,
> y ambición, que suena a un reino?
> Yo, en mi majestad altiva
> y humillada en mis deseos,
> cuándo ambiciosa en la esfera
> y cuándo amante en el centro,
> cuando yo coronas piso...   (1323b)

Matilde's death is the punishment of pride and ambition and was predicted in the words of Tabaco:

> ...¿cuándo no murió
> despeñada la soberbia? [1]   (1333b)

Ambition and passion could have no place in Calderón's conception of Basilio. But proud he certainly is: proud of his learning and ability to read the stars' prediction, proud in the belief that he can change the course of fate predicted for his son:

> Pues dando crédito yo
> a los hados, que divinos
> me pronosticaban daños
> en fatales vaticinios
> determiné de encerrar
> la fiera que había nacido,
> por ver si el sabio tenía
> en las estrellas dominio.   (222b)

And, like Matilde, he fails. At the play's end he recognizes his error:

> ¡Qué bien (¡ay cielos!) persuade
> nuestro error, nuestra ignorancia,
> a mayor conocimiento
> este cadáver que habla
> por la boca de una herida,
> siendo el humor que desata

---

[1] These lines appear in a passage which, according to the Juliá edition, is crossed out in the MS.

sangrienta lengua que enseña
que son diligencias vanas
del hombre cuantas dispone
contra la mayor fuerza y causa!
Pues yo, por librar de muertes
y sediciones mi patria,
vine a entregarla a los mismos
de quien pretendí librarla.   (246b-247a)

Like Matilde, too, Basilio is responsible for the fulfilment of the very thing which he tried to avoid. In *Yerros*, intent on murdering Polidoro, Matilde saves his life; by taking his place she it is who is the victim of the revenge of Filipo's son. This is dramatically foreshadowed early in the play in one of Matilde's own speeches:

...porque, sabe
que, a pesar de todo el reino,
hoy tengo de hacer, Filipo
que mi hermano... Mas ¿qué es esto?
(Dentro.)
¡Viva Polidoro, viva
de Polonia el heredero!   (1323a)

In *La vida es sueño* Basilio imprisons Segismundo in order to prevent what the stars have predicted. Yet his very action, by depriving his son of the upbringing and associations of the normal person, inclines him to behave as the stars predicted:

Mi padre, que está presente,
por excusarse a la saña
de mi condición, me hizo
un bruto, una fiera humana:
de suerte, que cuando yo
por mi nobleza gallarda,
por mi sangre generosa,
por mi condición bizarra,
hubiera nacido dócil
y humilde, sólo bastara
tal género de vivir,
tal linaje de crianza,
a hacer fieras mis costumbres:
¡qué buen modo de estorbarlas!   (247b)

The genesis of Basilio is unmistakable. Yet the differences between him and Matilde are significant. Matilde is evil by any standards. She coldly and brutally plots against her brother's life and is tyrannical as a ruler. Only once, at the end of Act I, does her conscience prick her:

> Pavor me ha dado pensar
> que entre mis exequias reino,
> y que hay tan poca distancia
> entre una viva y un muerto.   (1341b)

It is right that she should die a violent death. Basilio, on the other hand, is well-meaning; he is misguided rather than evil. Discovering and believing his son's horoscope, he removes him —as he thinks— for the good of his country; and, far from plotting his death, he arranges for his upbringing. Later he comes to question the wisdom of his action and allows his son a trial period in the palace to test the stars' verdict. And he so arranges matters that, should Segismundo fail, he can find himself back in the tower as if it had all been a dream:

> Si él supiera que es mi hijo
> hoy, y mañana se viera
> segunda vez reducido
> a su prisión y miseria
> cierto es de su condición
> que desesperara en ella;
> porque sabiendo quien es
> ¿qué consuelo habrá que tenga?
> Y así he querido dejar
> abierta al daño la puerta
> del decir que fué soñado
> cuanto vió.   (226b)

In this Basilio is motivated by paternal love. And he recognizes the existence of the individual will, though he acts as if it were inoperative in the case of his son. The words of the dying Clarín open his eyes to his error. He sees the futility of running away from the victorious rebels and, more important, of his attempt to change the fate of his son:

> Quien piensa huir el riesgo, al riesgo viene:
> con lo que yo guardaba me he perdido;
> yo mismo, yo, mi patria he destruído.   (240b)

Disabused, he is generously spared by Segismundo. Matilde is never made aware of her evil machinations, and her punishment is the result simply of a startling coincidence. Nothing that she has done, however evil, provokes Segismundo to kill her. Basilio's defeat and humiliation, on the other hand, are the direct effect of his own mistakes. Finally, whilst there is no development in the character of Matilde, Basilio changes as the play advances. His decision to bring Segismundo to the palace is itself a revision, if not a reversal, of his earlier decision. And when the experiment fails we watch the whole process of his doubts and disillusionment until he is made to see his error by the words of the dying Clarín. The differences between Basilio and Matilde are a measure of Calderón's achievement in *La vida es sueño*.

Calderón allowed Rosaura to retain the same name as her opposite number in *Yerros*. The first Rosaura is the daughter of the chief minister Filipo and the object of the affections of Prince Polidoro. A rival for her love is Fisberto, who in turn is loved by Matilde. Early in the play Prince Polidoro goes to Rosaura's room to declare his love and, when surprised and reprimanded by her father Filipo, strikes him. Filipo himself does not feel aggrieved; he claims that a Prince cannot give offence and that Polidoro's action is only a mark of disrespect. His loyalty is such that he will not be revenged and he even takes it upon himself to ensure Polidoro's safety rather than be a party to Matilde's plot. Rosaura, however, feels deeply the insult to her father; her own love for Polidoro has turned to anger and she swears that vengeance will be done:

> ROSAURA.   No niegues, señor, tu agravio;
> que yo, aunque le tuve amor
> al Príncipe, en odio, en ira,
> ya mi amor se convirtió;
> y si mi hermano no venga
> en él este agravio, yo,
> aunque soy mujer...
>
> SEGISMUNDO.   Espera.
> ¿Qué es agravio?
>
> ROSAURA.   El que le dió
> el Príncipe, que a mi padre...;
> pero no acierta el valor
> a pronunciar tal afrenta,
> cuando sangre tuya soy.
> Mírale al rostro y sabráslo,
> que él te lo dirá mejor
> con esas señas que en él
> el Príncipe le imprimió.   (1327b)

But Rosaura's brother takes it upon himself to clear the dishonour,

and succeeds finally in entering the palace and stabbing the person
he takes to be the Prince. By chance, he is the instrument of Polidoro's restoration; and Polidoro accepts the hand of Rosaura in
marriage. Calderón's Rosaura is also the daughter of the King's
minister, and the centre of the honour episode. But the episode
itself is new and different and it does not directly involve the play's
protagonist. In *La vida es sueño* Rosaura's lover is Prince Astolfo,
who abandons her in Russia and comes to Poland to marry his
cousin Estrella. This time it is Rosaura herself, rather than her
father, who is aggrieved, though once again the family honour is
at stake. And Calderón was able to dispense with her brother, thereby leaving the name Segismundo available for his protagonist.
The relationship between the two Rosauras is self-evident. *La vida
es sueño* contains also a reference to an incident of the source-play.
At the end of Act I, Clotaldo assumes at first that Rosaura is his
son; and when she tells him that Astolfo is responsible for her
dishonour he points out:

CLOTALDO.   ...Si moscovita has nacido,
el que es natural señor,
mal agraviarte ha podido:
vuélvete a tu patria, pues,
y deja el ardiente brío
que te despeña.

ROSAURA.   Yo sé
que, aunque mi príncipe ha sido,
pudo agraviarme.

CLOTALDO.   No pudo,
aunque pusiera atrevido
la mano en tu rostro.   (224b-225a)

This is precisely what Polidoro has done to Filipo:

POLIDORO.   ¿Esto oyó
mi honor? A tal desvergüenza
este castigo le doy.
                    (Dale un bofetón.)
FILIPO.   ¡Ay de mí!
ROSAURA.   ¿Qué es lo que has hecho?
FILIPO.   ¿Aqueste agravio a mi honor?
POLIDORO.   No agravio, sino castigo
a un viejo.
FILIPO.   Pues sabré yo
dar venganza.   (1327a)

Although Rosaura's love affair with Polidoro in *Yerros* is replaced in *La vida es sueño* by her affair with Prince Astolfo, she is not for that reason unrelated to the play's protagonist. On the contrary, Calderón greatly extended Rosaura's part and associated her throughout his play with Segismundo. I have studied elsewhere the relationship between Rosaura and Segismundo, [1] and shall only summarize here the main points. The parallel is established at the very outset. Each is a victim of misfortune, each respects and pities the other. Mysteriously moved by Rosaura, Segismundo checks his natural impulse to attack her and even pledges his life for her safety when she is discovered. The second scene shows the fates of Segismundo and Rosaura to be interdependent: Rosaura's grievance can only be removed by Astolfo marrying her, but Astolfo will marry Estrella if Segismundo fails to redeem himself during his stay in the palace. The bond of sympathy which unites these companions in misfortune is strengthened in Act II. Both find themselves in the palace, Segismundo as the victim of Basilio's experiment and Rosaura as maid of honour to Estrella. Of all Segismundo's palace experiences, his meeting with Rosaura is the most significant; he feels something more than physical attraction, and back again in the prison-tower he confesses to Clotaldo:

> De todos era señor,
> y de todos me vengaba;
> sólo a una mujer amaba...
> que fué verdad, creo yo,
> en que todo se acabó,
> y esto sólo no se acaba.   (236b)

Rosaura has been responsible for the one occasion when, momentarily at least, Segismundo has curbed his will to revenge, and the incident stands out as the only real experience of his palace stay. His resolve to control his animal nature and to do good follows directly upon his recollection of his meeting with Rosaura.

La vida es sueño comes full circle with the meeting of Segismundo and Rosaura in Act III. Rosaura delivers a long speech in which she recalls the two previous occasions on which they have met, and ends by laying emphasis on their common interests. As

---

[1] Albert E. Sloman, 'The structure of Calderón's *La vida es sueño*', *MLR*, XLVIII (1953), 293-300.

a woman she comes to plead for her honour, as a man whose clothes she wears she pledges to support him against his father. Rosaura, and Rosaura only, can convince Segismundo that his visit to the palace was real and for the first time he knows he is not dreaming. So we reach the final stage in the process of Segismundo's regeneration, when he overcomes his natural impulse to assault Rosaura and decides to champion her honour. In the play's last scene he arranges for Rosaura to marry Astolfo; for the sake of her honour he sacrifices the woman he loves. This, on his own admission, is the greatest and final proof of his conversion:

> Pues que ya vencer aguarda
> mi valor grandes victorias,
> hoy ha de ser la más alta
> vencerme a mí. —Astolfo dé
> la mano luego a Rosaura,
> pues sabe que de su honor
> es deuda, y yo he de cobrarla.   (248a)

Segismundo's undeclared love for Rosaura has its origin in the love between Polidoro and Rosaura in *Yerros*. In both plays the philosophical issue underlying the behaviour of the royal family is linked with an honour episode involving the family of Filipo/Clotaldo. But Calderón strengthened and consolidated the link by making Rosaura the instrument of Segismundo's conversion. At the same time, her part represents a new strand in the complex pattern of human conduct which the play portrays. On more than one occasion she is faced with the conflict between her sense of honour and her duty to her own father; and with exemplary singlemindedness she pursues her aggressor, even when her father cannot help her.

Rosaura's father, Clotaldo, is the character of *La vida es sueño* who owes most to the source-play. He is closely modelled on Filipo, the King's minister. It is Filipo who is entrusted by Matilde with the disposal of Polidoro and who, determined to spare Polidoro's life, is his guardian in prison and finally his deliverer. Clotaldo's duties are similar: he is responsible to Basilio for Segismundo's safety and arranges for his transfer to the palace and his return to prison. Both Filipo and Clotaldo are also involved in their respective plays as fathers, and both are faced with the dilemma of choosing between loyalty to the crown and duty towards their children. In all these points Clotaldo corresponds almost exactly to Filipo in *Yerros*. Filipo is the epitome of loyalty. King Conrado, father of Matilde and Polidoro, who promulgated the Salic law in Poland so that he should succeed to the throne in place of the late King's daughter Clorilene, gave Clorilene in marriage to Filipo, whose loyalty was itself a sufficient guarantee against rebellion:

> Esto consiguió mi padre;
> y, por dar más fundamento
> a su quietud, te dió a ti,
> su mayor amigo y deudo,
> por esposa a Clorilene,
> hija del muerto Manfredo,
> porque fuese tu lealtad
> de sus intenciones freno... (1321a)

In Act I Filipo is insulted by Polidoro; yet his loyalty is such that he tries to keep the insult secret. And when his son Segismundo discovers it and announces that he will be revenged, Filipo brands him a traitor and calls guards to arrest him; Segismundo is fortunate to escape with his life. Filipo, that is, jeopardizes his son's life for the sake of the Prince. Before the insult of Polidoro, Matilde has confided in Filipo her ambitious designs upon the throne; and immediately following it she reveals to him her detailed plan for Polidoro's disposal. Here, it would seem, is a Heaven-sent opportunity for Filipo to be avenged of the Prince. Yet he at once espouses the cause of Polidoro, and offers his services to Matilde in order to ensure Polidoro's safety.

Like Filipo, Clotaldo exemplifies loyalty, and he also makes the point that a Prince can give no offence:

> *Yerros.*

> FILIPO.   Segismundo
> no es agravio el que me dio
> quien es mi Rey; el desprecio
> es el que he sentido yo.
> Los reyes, hijo, no agravian
> que, a semejanza de Dios,
> son los absolutos dueños
> de la vida, y del honor... (1327b-1328a)

> *La vida es sueño.*

> ROSAURA.   Yo sé
> que, aunque mi príncipe ha sido,
> pudo agraviarme.

CLOTALDO.   No pudo,
                aunque pusiera atrevido
                la mano en tu rostro.   (225a)

Like Filipo too he is faced with the dilemma of loyalty to the
King and his duty towards his family; and he does not hesitate
to put loyalty first. In Act I he hands over his own daughter to
the King when it entails, as he believes, her certain death. In Acts II
and III, though deeply concerned about his daughter's grievance,
he is willing to sacrifice his family's honour when it conflicts with
his loyalty to Basilio and his gratitude to Astolfo (who has saved
his life). The following lines of Clotaldo:

                Mi honor es el agraviado,
                poderoso el enemigo,
                yo vasallo, ella mujer:
                descubra el cielo camino...   (225b)

                que al fin el tiempo ha de ser
                quien haga esas diligencias.   (227a)

may be compared with lines of Filipo when presented with a similar
dilemma:

                (Ap.) Mucho tenemos que hablar
                a solas, lealtad y quejas;
                yo prevendré mis razones:
                prevenid también las vuestras.   (1330b)

                ¿Quién, cielos, quién en el mundo
                vió confusión como ésta...   (1334a)

                (Ap.) Mas esto a mi lealtad debo.
                Contigo y conmigo cumplo,
                pues no le mato, y le cierro,
                por si a tantas confusiones
                me abriese camino el tiempo.   (1338b)

Clotaldo evidently deserted the mother of Rosaura, as Astolfo has
deserted Rosaura herself. Yet, in the course of the play, Clotaldo
like his model Filipo is motivated by high principles. Both, by
their prudence and single-mindedness, emerge successfully from the
difficult situations in which they find themselves, and both are
rewarded:

                        Yerros.
                y así, en albricias de todo
                y de todo en recompensa,
                volved vos a mi privanza,
                Filipo a mi gracia vuelva...   (1351b)

> *La vida es sueño.*
> A Clotaldo, que leal
> sirvió a mi padre, le aguardan
> mis brazos con las mercedes
> que él pidiere que le haga.   (248b)

Of the remaining characters, Clarín corresponds to the earlier Tabaco. But whereas Tabaco's part was of little consequence, Clarín has been given a serious as well as a comic rôle, one that helps to give prominence to the play's underlying idea. [1] Tabaco is a braggart and a chatterbox, and his impudent remarks bring upon him a drubbing instead of the thousand *escudos* he was expecting. He is also a coward as is clear when, through his curiosity, he finds himself in the room in which Matilde is murdered. These are all traits of Clarín. He prides himself on his cleverness, and by means of flattery rises to the service of Clotaldo; but he pays for his temerity and impudent words by being made to accompany Segismundo to the prison-tower. At the beginning of Act III he is mistaken for Segismundo, and he confidently plays the part attributed to him. Up to this point Clarín's rôle is not unlike Tabaco's, or indeed that of any *gracioso*. But Calderón here gives the part a tragic twist which has no precedent in *Yerros*. Clarín's behaviour has serious consequences: in the battle between the forces of Basilio and Segismundo, he assumes that by hiding he can avoid danger, and he is the only casualty. Clarín, like Segismundo, Basilio and Astolfo, is undeceived: he learns the folly of his cowardice and over-confidence and pays with his life. His dying words recall those of Basilio's:

> CLARÍN.   Pues no hay seguro camino
> a la fuerza del destino
> y a la inclemencia del hado:
> y así, aunque a libraros vais
> de la muerte con huir,
> mirad que vais a morir,
> si está de Dios que muráis.   (246b)

Just as Basilio tried to avert the catastrophe predicted by the stars, so Clarín tries to avoid his own fate. Clarín owes something to his counterpart Tabaco, but Calderón has made him much more than

---

[1] Cf. Wilson, op. cit., pp. 71-73.

the conventional fool and given him a serious rôle which is relevant to the thesis of the play.

Astolfo was required by the new honour episode. In place of Polidoro's insult to Rosaura's father, in Calderón's play Rosaura herself is wronged by the Prince Astolfo. But Astolfo also is made to illustrate the general idea underlying the play. By his own admission, he fails in his responsibility to Rosaura. He believes that he can avoid the consequences of his action, and aims at satisfying his ambitious designs on the crown by marrying his cousin. Like Basilio and Clarín, he pays for his error. Estrella, finally, is a further character required by the honour episode, with no opposite number in *Yerros*, though the rivalry between Astolfo and Estrella for the throne of Poland reflects the rival claims of Matilde and Polidoro. In both circumstances the Salic law required the choice of the male descendant, not the first-born. The parallel between the following passages is unmistakable:

Yerros.

Manfredo, Rey de Polonia
que, para decir sus hechos
ese monstruo de cien bocas
trabajó con todas ciento,
dejando sólo una hija
que fué Clorilene, al reino
dejó también dividido
en parciales, nó sabiendo
si a Clorilene le toca
por hija del Rey el cetro
o si le toca a Conrado,
mi padre, hermano del muerto
Manfredo, que en ser varón
fundó el derecho más cierto.
Duraron mucho estas dudas,
porque no se hallaba desto
otro ejemplar en Polonia,
hasta tanto que, resuelto
el gran Conrado, mi padre,
hizo escribir su derecho
con caracteres de sangre
en muchas hojas de acero;
porque aclamado y seguido
de la nobleza y del pueblo
y de ti, que le aliviaste
de tanta corona el peso,
promulgó ley en Polonia
para que, desde aquel tiempo,

nunca heredasen las hembras
su corona, recibiendo
la ley sálica, que en Francia
tan injustamente ha hecho
que las mujeres se excluyan
de la sucesión del reino.   (1320b-1321a)

La vida es sueño.

Falleció Eustorgio tercero
Rey de Polonia, quedó
Basilio por heredero
y dos hijas de quien yo
y vos nacimos. —No quiero
cansar con lo que tiene
lugar aquí. —Clorilene,
vuestra madre y mi señora
que en mejor imperio ahora
dosel de luceros tiene,
fué la mayor, de quien vos
sois hija; fué la segunda,
madre y tía de los dos,
la gallarda Recisunda,
que guarde mil años Dios;
casó en Moscovia, de quien
nací yo. Volver ahora
al otro principio es bien.
Basilio, que ya, señora,
se rinde al común desdén
del tiempo, más inclinado
a los estudios que dado
a mujeres, enviudó
sin hijos, y vos y yo
aspiramos a este Estado.
Vos alegáis que habéis sido
hija de hermana mayor;
yo, que varón he nacido,
y aunque de hermana menor,
os debo ser preferido.   (220b-221a)

All the characters of *La vida es sueño*, then, with the exception of Astolfo and Estrella, are based on characters in *Yerros*. And Astolfo and Estrella are required by an honour episode which has a counterpart in *Yerros*; in their rivalry for the Polish throne, they reflect the enmity between Matilde and Polidoro. The characters are involved in new situations and subserve a theme which is more carefully and subtly developed than that of the source. Error is still punished and virtue rewarded, but the outcome depends upon the behaviour of each of the characters involved, not upon an

18

accident of nature. In *Yerros* one can truly say that Matilde was fated to be killed and Polidoro to be restored to the throne. Matilde's guilt had nothing to do with her death at the hands of Segismundo, nor Polidoro's innocence *vis-à-vis* Matilde with his restoration. Contrast what happens in *La vida es sueño*. Here, too, we have a horoscope which is in part fulfilled: as the stars predicted, Poland is plunged into civil war and Basilio prostrated at the feet of his rebel son. The further consequences are unexpected. Basilio is pardoned, and peace and harmony reign. The extent to which the horoscope is fulfilled, moreover, is due not to the intervention of an outside force as in *Yerros*, but to the moral errors of Basilio; and its complete fulfilment is prevented by the forbearance and prudence of the chastened Segismundo. The same is true of the prophecy in *El mayor monstruo los celos*; if Mariene dies at the end of the play as the Jewish astrologer has predicted, it is not because of a fate or destiny which is imposed from without, but because of the moral errors of Mariene herself, of the Emperor Octavia and above all of Herod. All the characters of *La vida es sueño*, Basilio, Segismundo, Clotaldo and Rosaura, Astolfo and Clarín, even (as Wilson has shown) the over-confident servant and the treacherous soldier, deserve and are shown to bring about the fate that overtakes them. As in all the best plays of Calderón, this is the key to its unity, a single pattern of cause and effect in which the action springs from the moral choice of the characters involved. It is the secret also of much of their depth and force, for we see the characters as persons shaping their own destiny. Intellectualized though they are, we can identify ourselves with them and the perennial and fundamental problems of life with which they are faced. Their predicaments are our own, and their choice of vital importance; we are uplifted by their triumphs and we pity their failures.

It would be pointless to attempt a correlation of two plots so radically different. Virtually the only situation which Calderón borrowed from *Yerros* was that in which Polidoro finds himself again in familiar surroundings and wonders whether or not he is dreaming, a situation which may well have been Calderón's starting point for *La vida es sueño*. Reference has already been made to certain details which Calderón carried over from his source. There are others. Calderón adopted the names of Segismundo and Rosaura, names which, to my knowledge, occur together in no other Calderonian play, and only once separately in *Afectos de odio y amor* and *El mejor amigo el muerto*. Both plays refer to a Clorilene. In *Yerros* she was the daughter of the late King Manfredo and the mother of Rosaura; in *La vida es sueño* she was the wife of Basilio:

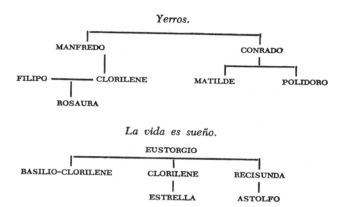

In *La vida es sueño* Astolfo refers to a second Clorilene who, like the Clorilene of *Yerros*, was the daughter of the late King. The duplication results probably from Calderón's fortuitous imitation of the source-play. I have mentioned earlier the face-slap of the source-play to which reference is made in *La vida es sueño* and, conversely, Matilde's threat to hurl a servant over the balcony which becomes a fact in *La vida es sueño*.

Though the language and imagery of *La vida es sueño* owe little to *Yerros*, there are unmistakable echoes, at least of those parts for which Calderón was responsible, namely Act II and the early part of Act III. Like *La vida es sueño*, *Yerros* requires a prison-tower for a person named Segismundo: Filipo's son hides in the tower where Polidoro is imprisoned and awaits an opportunity to clear his father's honour. Fisberto's lines:

> aquella torre que hoy es
> de la soberbia escarmiento...   (1338a)

anticipate the situation with which *La vida es sueño* opens. By a series of metaphors Calderón associated the prison-tower with death. The dominant metaphor 'de un vivo cadáver sepultura' derives directly from the description of the tower in *Yerros*:

De la prisión oscura,
que es de un vivo cadáver sepultura;
del temeroso seno,
de error, de confusión y espanto lleno,
donde preso me tiene mi fortuna,
salgo en el triste imperio de la luna,
porque la suerte mía
no se permite al resplandor del día,
hasta verme vengado,
y así, vivo entre sombras sepultado.
Yacen deste palacio unas ruinas,
memorias de una torre peregrinas,
en retirada parte,
adonde el tiempo, sin estudio ni arte,
brutamente olvidadas,
hoy conserva unas bóvedas cavadas
donde la luz no entra,
porque siempre la sombra al paso encuentra.   (1334b)

The influence of this passage is clear, for example, in the following lines of *La vida es sueño*:

ROSAURA. Sí, pues a sus reflejos
puedo determinar (aunque de lejos)
una prisión oscura,
que es de un vivo cadáver sepultura...   (216b)

BASILIO. hice labrar una torre
entre las peñas y riscos
de esos montes, donde apenas
la luz ha hallado camino
por defenderle la entrada
sus rústicos obeliscos...   (222b-223a)

Again, Segismundo's famous *décimas* on the theme of liberty have their counterpart in *Yerros* in the *décimas* which Matilde speaks when she has taken the place of Polidoro, and are curiously foreshadowed in the repeated final lines:

...aunque nací mujer
nací capaz de reinar.

The debt of *La vida es sueño* to *Yerros* is unmistakable. Critics have failed to notice the remarkable similarity between the two plays because they have approached *La vida es sueño* through its situations rather than through its characters and its theme. In both tyranny is averted and a Prince's rights are restored. The characters closely correspond, and details of incident and language are common to them. Yet for *La vida es sueño,* more than for any of the other plays studied, Calderón diverged completely from the earlier pattern of action; so much so that superficially the resemblance between the plays is slight. The theme of the thwarted tyrant has been made to complement that of man's discovery of himself and of his high purpose in life; the tyrant's victim works out his own salvation. All the characters of *Yerros* which Calderón could accommodate in his new play have been transformed, and all made relevant to the ideas developed. But *Yerros* has at least the distinction of having inspired Calderón's greatest work.

X

CONCLUSION

At the beginning of this book I claimed that these comparative studies might help to elucidate particular plays of Calderón and that, taken together, they might contribute to a better understanding of his dramatic craftsmanship. The foregoing chapters will have justified, I hope, the first of these claims. In this final chapter I shall extract from my findings those points of procedure which seem most relevant to Calderón's work in general. My remarks will necessarily be fragmentary, my conclusions tentative. No comprehensive study of the dramatic art of Calderón could fail to take into account the development in his work, the differences, say, between the plays of the thirties, and the intricate world of fantasy, rhetoric and symbolism of the mythological plays and the sacramental *autos* of the sixties and seventies. It would have to embrace the whole of his dramatic output. This chapter may at least serve to provoke and perhaps to facilitate such a study.

Calderón's source-plays differ considerably from each other, and the procedure he adopted in recasting them varied accordingly. But one point is common to all these recastings: an unswerving and persistent quest for unity. The problem of unity is of course fundamental to all forms of art, and it was one which particularly exercised the minds of the literary theorists of sixteenth-century Italy and Spain. Artistic unity was especially difficult to achieve in the Spanish *comedia*, which sought to imitate the variety of nature and admitted an abundance of action. There was often more than one plot, and every phase in its development was presented upon the stage. 'Spanish audiences are satisfied' wrote Lope de Vega in his *Arte nuevo* 'only if they are taken within the space of an hour or so from the Creation to the Last Judgement.' The history of the Spanish drama in the last decade of the sixteenth century and the first two decades of the seventeenth is largely the history of the development of a *comedia* lacking unity of action to one in which that unity is achieved. Lope's later plays have dramatic unity; so have the best plays of Tirso de Molina and his contemporaries. But most of the plays written between, say, 1590 and 1610 are carelessly and loosely constructed, with an excess of both incidents and characters. Calderón's sources were plays of this kind, and by a variety of means he transformed them.

The clearest examples of Calderón's procedure are provided by his recasting of *Polifemo y Circe* and *La niña de Gómez Arias*. *Polifemo y Circe*, as its title suggests, is concerned with the encounter of Ulises with Polifemo and Circe; it shows the passion of Ulises for Circe, the deaths of Acis and Galatea at the hands of Polifemo and the blinding of Polifemo by Ulises. If the last episode follows upon the second, the only connexion of either with the first is Ulises himself. It is true that Circe's magic is made to transport Ulises to the cave of Polifemo and that Acis is responsible for Ulises' escape, but these slender links could not give unity to such diverse episodes. Calderón's recasting for *El mayor encanto amor* is drastic. He discarded two of the three main episodes, and limited himself to the single conflict between Ulises and Circe. Polifemo and Acis and the action in which they were involved disappear, and Galatea survives only for the sake of a few lines at the play's end. Calderón's treatment of the first *La niña de Gómez Arias* was similar. Vélez de Guevara's play had two plots, one centring on Gómez Arias and the other on his sister María. The experiences of María closely resemble those of Gómez: they have parallel love-affairs in Act I, and in Act II both elope. After Gómez has disposed of 'la niña' to the Moors and María's seducer has been hurled from a cliff, brother and sister attach themselves to a party of brigands. At the end of the play both are sentenced to death and both reprieved. The sub-plot which hinges upon María is irrelevant to the conflict between Gómez and 'la niña', and precisely because it is interesting in itself it draws our interest away from Gómez. In his recasting, Calderón dispensed entirely with María.

For both these plays Calderón was obliged to provide new material and new characters to take the place of what he had rejected. The new characters of *El mayor encanto amor* are Ársidas, Lísidas and Flérida. Only Ársidas has a major part. Like Ulises, he is immune from the enchantments of Circe and is a rival for her love. In Act II he is involved in an argument with Ulises on the subject of love, and in Act III he leads an attack upon Circe and is taken prisoner. The part of Ársidas is clearly relevant to the passion of Ulises for Circe, which is the main subject of the play. However ineffective, he is a rival lover, and his fate is a warning to Ulises. Lísidas and Flérida have only minor rôles: they have been transformed by Circe into trees and are restored to human form by the intervention of Ulises. The story of their estrangement and reconciliation is far too slender to be called a sub-plot. But in a play about love they are lovers, and their pure love is intended perhaps to be set against the impure love of Ulises, Circe and Ársidas. Calderón did not, I think, succeed in disguising the fact that Ársidas, Lísidas and Flérida were appendages, and he was less succesful in this play than elsewhere in bringing out the symbolism of the characters. But at least his intentions cannot be doubted. For *La niña de Gómez Arias* he replaced María and her two suitors by a new lady, Beatriz, and two new men, Don Félix and Don Juan Íñiguez. Beatriz, like Dorotea, is in love with Gómez; Don Félix and Don Juan are rivals of Gómez, the one in love with Beatriz, the other with Dorotea. Three characters of Vélez's play, that is, about whom revolved a second plot, are replaced by three new characters who are an integral part of the main action.

The fundamental differences between *El príncipe constante* and its source *La fortuna adversa* are due in the main to a totally different conception of the story of Prince Ferdinand. Yet here too Calderón's handling of the sub-plot of the source-play is significant. A considerable part of the first two acts of *La. fortuna adversa* is devoted to a love-affair involving Muley and two rivals for his love, Arminda and the Moorish Queen, the complications of which are resolved in the first scene of Act III. This time Calderón did not discard the sub-plot completely. A love episode survives in *El príncipe constante*, but it has been so reduced that it requires scarcely any action. This does not mean that the three characters concerned —Muley, Fénix and Tarudante—are unimportant. On the contrary, both Muley and Fénix have major rôles. They are relevant, indeed essential, to the main issue, and though they are involved in a subsidiary action they cannot be relegated to it. Fénix, for example, though in love with Muley, is promised by her father to Prince Tarudante; yet her significance does not depend upon her relationship with either Tarudante or Muley. Throughout the play her melancholy and obsession with death are contrasted with the Christian fortitude of Fernando and her most important scene is her meeting with Fernando in Act II; in the end, she is exchanged for Fernando's relics. Thus the Moorish Queen of *La fortuna adversa* who is concerned exclusively with a love episode gives way in *El príncipe constante* to Fénix who, though implicated in a sub-plot, is closely and vitally related to the play's protagonist. Muley too is a major character, essential to the play as a whole and associated primarily with Fernando; and even Tarudante, small though his part is, is as much taken up with the problem of Ceuta as with his love.

Calderón's plays have often another kind of sub-plot which, for want of a better word, might be called a background action, usually a major event of history or legend. Sometimes this historical background is merely the setting for the plot, as in *El alcalde de Zalamea*, where the incident at Zalamea is associated with the expedition of Philip II to Portugal in 1580. Elsewhere the background is itself an action which, however slight, develops in the course of the play. We have the war against the *moriscos* in *La niña de Gómez Arias*, the enmity between Peter the Cruel and Henry of Trastamara in *El médico de su honra* and the grievance of the Sabines in *Las armas de la hermosura*. *La niña de Gómez Arias* is of particular interest in this respect since here Calderón departed from the historical setting of the source. Vélez's play takes place at the time of the siege of Granada; Calderón postpones the action until the latter part of the reign of the Catholic Monarchs, when *morisco* communities in the Alpujarras are making raids on neighbouring towns. The leader of the *moriscos* is El Cañerí, and the plays show the assault upon the fortress of Benamejí and El Cañerí's defeat and death. This background action is joined to the main action, since it is to El Cañerí that Gómez sells Dorotea and from whom she is recovered by the Queen's forces. But, far more important than this, is the thematic bond that links El Cañerí with Gómez. Both are rebels against society: El Cañerí by his raids, plunder and murder, Gómez by his crimes against Dorotea. Both betray the trust that is placed in them, both are like beasts in their barbarity and cruelty. At the end of the play both pay for their rebellion with their lives. A single theme unites the background and the main actions.

For *El médico de su honra* and *Las armas de la hermosura* Calderón retained the setting of the sources and took over the actions associated with them. In the two *El médico* plays, the rival lover is Henry of Trastamara, who incurs the hatred of his half-brother and is obliged to leave Seville. There is a formal link between Henry's quarrel with the King and his love for Mencía, since his hasty departure for Seville prompts Mencía to write the fateful letter which brings the suspicions of Gutierre to a head. But Calderón's contribution was to strengthen the thematic link between the two actions which is implicit in the source-play. Just as Gutierre by his cruelty and inhumanity brings tragedy upon his household, so the severity and high-handedness of Pedro lead to his clash with Henry. Gutierre must face a second marriage based on suspicion and hatred, and the King will die at Montiel. In *Las armas de la hermosura* Calderón perpetuates the association in the source-play of the story of Coriolanus with the rape of the Sabines. Again we have a formal link: the subsidiary action concerning the grievance of the Sabines against Rome merges with the main action when the banished Coriolanus accepts the Sabine offer of protection and takes charge of their army. But the main link is thematic. The conception of honour of the Roman patricians which leads them to deny to women their human rights and against which Coriolanus protests is the same conception which led to the rape of the Sabines. Veturia is herself a victim of Rome's abduction; yet in her plea that Coriolanus shall pardon Rome, she is herself pardoning the rape of the Sabines. Veturia, that is, is the embodiment of the Sabine grievance, and she teaches both Coriolano and the Sabines the superiority of mercy over revenge.

Sub-plots occur less frequently in Calderón's plays than in their sources and, where they are found, they are less extensive. It is usual also for Calderón to establish certain formal links between plot and sub-plot so that it would in practice be difficult to disentangle the sub-plot and discard it. What emerges, however, from our studies is the thematic link between the characters of the main action and those of the subsidiary action. Indeed, convenient though it often is to refer to the sub-plot, it is safer not to attempt such a separation. *La vida 'es sueño*, for example, like its source-play *Yerros,* has two

plots: one is concerned with the relationship between Segismundo
and his father Basilio, and the other with Rosaura and her grievance
against Astolfo. Yet the two are so inseparably linked that it is
unwise, and even misleading, to consider them apart. The
characters cannot be neatly assigned, some to the main and some to
the subsidiary plot. Clotaldo is Rosaura's father, but he is also the
King's minister and the tutor of Segismundo. Rosaura comes to
Poland to restore her own honour, but throughout the play her fate
is bound up with Segismundo's. It is Rosaura who makes Segismundo
realise in Act III that he is not dreaming, and who provides him with
the opportunity for the greatest and final proof of his conversion.
Rosaura and Clotaldo and the other characters of the sub-plot, like
Astolfo and Clarín, are part and parcel of the play as a whole; they
are vital to its complex pattern of human behaviour.

The key for the understanding of Calderón's plays, quite clearly,
is not the plot itself, much less the separate episodes of the plot, but
the characters and beyond them the theme which binds them
together. If, as Jonson said, a play is a skein of silk which, taken at
the right end, may be wound off at pleasure, this—the basic theme—
is assuredly the end to pull. The plays studied in these pages are seen
to be the development and elaboration of a basic theme or set of
ideas. An episode or a character of a source-play which detracted
from, or failed to contribute to, the theme underlying the main plot
was rejected. And when, by rearranging the action of the source-
play, or by rejecting source material, Calderón had room for other
characters which could contribute something new to the theme, he
added them. Take, for example, Don Mendo in *El alcalde de Zalamea*.
If we approach the play through its plot he is dispensable. Calderón
makes no attempt to develop the rivalry between Don Mendo and
the captain; Mendo's advances to Isabel are totally ineffective and
he fades out of the picture towards the end of Act II. But his
importance in respect of the theme cannot be disputed. In a play
about true honour Mendo is the perfect foil to the protagonist
Crespo who scorns the kind of honour which can be bought and is
no more than a label. He is fitted into a basic thematic pattern,
and he enriches it. Were Mendo removed from the play, its structure
would not be seriously impaired. It would lose a good deal of
humour and a bridge between some of the scenes. But, above all, it

would lose that important aspect of the idea of honour which Mendo represents.

Calderón's recasting of *La venganza de Tamar* makes it clear that in this instance his principal criticism of the source-play was that it was incomplete. Tirso showed the rape of Tamar and the subsequent death of Amón at the hands of Absalón; but he diverged from the Biblical story by making Absalón's murder of Amón less the avenging of Tamar's honour than an opportunity of ridding himself of a rival to the throne. He gives, in fact, considerable emphasis to the ambition of Absalón, and foretells on a number of occasions his violent death. Yet the theme of ambition necessarily remained undeveloped in a play which ended with Amón's murder; Tirso himself probably had the intention of writing a sequel. Calderón's principal structural change in rewriting Tirso's play was the addition of a new act showing the fate of Absalón; pursuing further his ambitious aims, Absalón conspires against David himself until finally he is murdered by Joab. And to make room for this new act Calderón omits the material of Tirso's Act I. Even if *Los cabellos de Absalón* is, as I have suggested earlier, open to serious criticism, it does at least complete what is incomplete in Tirso.

Calderón's plays are superior to their sources in their unity and in their completeness. At the same time, they are remarkably compact and coherent. A fundamental point in this connexion is Calderón's view of man's moral responsibility which imposed a strict causal sequence upon the different incidents. Man is shown to be responsible for his own fate. His will is free. However strongly disposition and environment may incline, they cannot force. Calderón's characters are not at the mercy of a cruel, implacable fate; they are rather at the mercy of themselves and their fellow men. They shape their own destinies. With reason and judgement to guide them, they must choose between the conflicting loyalties and embarrassing predicaments of life. Catastrophe and tragedy do not spring from some arbitrary change of fortune imposed from outside, but are the consequence of human behaviour which has not measured up to the required standard, whether the motives are good or bad. But man does not live in isolation. He is a member of society; his conduct will affect others and the conduct of others will affect him. Tragedy results not simply from the wrong choice of one person but from a whole series of choices of all the persons involved. Conversely, the averting of tragedy, due to the enlightenment and prudence of a single person, affects not only that person but the whole society in which he or she moves. Calderón presents a world of human error in which there are no innocent victims. This conception of the individual and the corporate responsibility of his characters give his plays their extraordinary cohesion, extraordinary precisely because of the many complicated incidents which are welded together, and at the same time their deep moral significance.

Calderón traces the actions of his plays back to their first cause, and then, stage by stage, shows how all the characters of his play contribute to its development and conclusion. The tragedy of *El médico de su honra*, for example, has its origin in a rash action by Arias and the authoritarian attitude of Mencía's father. Arias imprudently enters the house of Leonor and rouses the suspicions of Gutierre. Gutierre refuses to listen to Arias's explanations. Mencía's father forces his daughter to marry Gutierre. Enrique, knowing that Mencía is married, continues his advances, and Mencía's imprudent remarks encourage him. The rashness of the King and Leonor's indiscretion at Seville lead to Gutierre's imprisonment and give to Enrique the chance of revisiting Mencía. Enrique's reckless disregard for honour, Gutierre's jealousy and cruelty and Mencía's indiscretions lead Gutierre first to suspect and then seemingly to confirm the threat to his honour and to carry through his brutal murder. In a society whose behaviour is determined by a rigorous code of honour the persons involved slowly but inexorably bring their tragic fate upon themselves. In *Las armas de la hermosura* the tragedy which threatens Rome is shown to have its origin in the rape of the Sabine women. Seeking to remove this injustice, the Sabines attack Rome, and the Senate is led to enslave its women by abrogating their rights, assuming that they have made Rome's soldiers effeminate. It is for this reason that Coriolano, defying the Senate's edict, is banished and returns to besiege Rome, threatening it with annihilation. The disaster which threatens Rome, therefore, is the direct result of a decision of the Roman Senate, dictated by a distorted sense of values. Its code of honour has room neither for love nor for mercy. Women are enslaved, Aurelio publicly votes for his son's death, Coriolano will destroy his own city and with it the woman he loves and his best friend. Veturia, in contrast, epitomizes the warmth and tenderness of women. She overcomes Coriolano with her tears and persuades him to pardon.

The contrast between Calderón's plays and those of the source dramatists in this respect is well illustrated by setting *La vida es sueño* by the side of *Yerros*. In both plays error is punished and virtue rewarded. But the outcome of Calderón's play depends upon the behaviour of each of the characters involved, not upon an accident of nature. In *Yerros* Matilde was, literally, fated to be killed and Polidoro to be restored to the throne. Matilde's death at the hands of Segismundo has nothing to do with her guilt, nor Polidoro's restoration with his innocence. Fate may seem to be at work also in *La vida es sueño*; as the stars predicted, Poland has a civil war and Basilio is prostrated at the feet of his rebel son. Yet the important consequences of the play are not predicted. Basilio is pardoned, not killed, and at the end there is peace and harmony. Even the extent to which the horoscope is fulfilled is due primarily to the moral error of Basilio; and its complete fulfilment is prevented by the forbearance and endurance of the chastened Segismundo. All the characters of *La vida es sueño* are shown to bring about, and to deserve, the fate that overtakes them. The characters are not the puppets of an alien force, their fate predetermined; they are persons who shape their own destiny.

This close nexus between behaviour and subsequent events is found in all the plays which have been studied here, with the exception perhaps of *Los cabellos de Absalón*. Amón, it is true, brings a violent death upon himself by his incestuous passion and Absalón pays with his life for his unscrupulous ambition. But both were pardoned by David; and it is evidently the theme of pardon which is intended to give unity to the different incidents. Throughout the play mercy is commended and revenge condemned. Yet David's forgiveness of Amón provides Absalón with the opportunity to murder him, and forgiveness of Absalón leads directly to rebellion and war. Precisely because the connexion between conduct and later events is here less close, *Los cabellos de Absalón,* for all its dramatic force, its fine poetry and deep humanity, is untypical of Calderón's best work.

Every action in Calderón's plays is motivated. If in *Polifemo y Circe* the plan to lure Ulises away from Circe is spontaneous, in *El mayor encanto amor* it is suggested by Ulises' reaction to the alleged attack upon Circe, which is wrongly interpreted as a response to the call to arms. The refuge which Coriolano finds with his enemies, which is unexplained in *El privilegio de las mujeres*, in *Las armas de la hermosura* is an act of gratitude by Astrea for her release by Coriolano in Act I. Calderón motivates even the least important incident. In *Los cabellos de Absalón* Jonadab is made to suspect the cause of Amón's indisposition and to listen secretly to the exchanges between him and Tamar; in *La venganza de Tamar* he was simply told of his master's passion. Similarly, in *Los cabellos de Absalón* David revisits Amón because of his concern for his health and his wish to see him privately; in Tirso's play he was sent for. And Calderón does not perpetuate the whimsical and unexpected entrances and exits of characters of the earlier plays. In his *El médico de su honra* Prince Enrique's admission to the house of Mencía, which is not accounted for in the source, is arranged by the slave-girl Jacinta; in Act III the King does not arrive by chance at Gutierre's house but is taken there by Coquín.

Another factor which contributes to the cohesion of Calderón's work is the anticipation of the play's *dénouement*, usually from the very outset. Some of the source dramatists had themselves adopted this procedure, but Calderón both extended and refined it, and resorted to a wide range of devices to give it effect. His first scenes are particularly important in this connexion. In place of the long expository scene in Portugal of *La fortuna adversa*, *El príncipe constante* opens in Fez with the exchanges of Christian prisoners which, in a play concerned with the conduct of a captive, pose the whole problem of captivity. In *El mayor encanto amor* the storm at sea, the desolation and horror of the countryside, the dark, awe-inspiring woods and other details foreshadow the moral dangers that are in store for Ulises. The fall of Enrique in the first scene of *El médico de su honra* augurs the tragedy that will later occur. The opening lines of *Las armas de la hermosura*, on the other hand, in which Coriolano and Veturia declare their love, betoken a happy ending. The first lines of *El alcalde de Zalamea* offer a vivid picture of soldiers in a play which hinges on the conflict between soldiers and the peasants of Zalamea. Often the outcome is explicitly predicted. In *Los cabellos de Absalón* Teuca foretells the fate of Absalón, in *El príncipe constante* an old hag prophesies that Fénix will be exchanged for a corpse. But the predictions are all ambiguous and enigmatic, necessarily so since the person whose fate is predicted has it within his power to overrule the stars. Absalón and Fénix both misinterpret the prophecies concerning them, and Segismundo gives the lie to his horoscope.

Calderón rarely limited himself to any one device. Amón's death is foretold by Teuca, but it is also hinted at when Tamar in self-defence wounds him at the end of Act I. Lesser characters are made to comment upon the imprudence of the conduct of their superiors : Ginés repeatedly cautions Gómez Arias, and Antistes and Iris warn Ulises. Bad omens are often presented : Enrique falls from his horse in *El médico*, Ulises narrowly escapes shipwreck and sees birds of ill-omen in *El mayor encanto*, another Enrique trips on landing in *El príncipe constante*. Most important of all, perhaps, are the hints at subsequent developments by means of a song or an image or a classical allusion, to which I shall refer later. By a combination of devices, Calderón was able to make the foreboding of a play's end cumulative. He begins with a mere suggestion by means of an image or an ambiguous phrase; then, as the play progresses, the suggestions accumulate and at the same time become more explicit. If Leonor's prophetic curse at the end of Act I of *El médico* prepares us for a tragic ending, the exchanges at the end of Act II predict precisely what form the tragedy will take. Only rarely did Calderón find inspiration for these points in the source-plays.

Again, most of the plays studied in these pages are more concentrated than their models both in respect of time and place. Calderón certainly did not restrict himself to any particular period of time, but he would have agreed with González de Salas that many Spanish plays would have been improved had they been more circumscribed :

> Doctrina que de la misma suerte hoi podra mejorar mucho nuestras dramáticas representaciones. [1]

Certainly in his recastings he avoided extremes of the kind ridiculed by El Pinciano and Cervantes, if only by the simple method of leaving indeterminate the time which elapses. The action of most of our plays proceeds without any serious breaks as in *El mayor encanto amor*, *El alcalde de Zalamea* and *La vida es sueño*. A few days

---

[1] *Nueva idea de la tragedia antigua* (Madrid, 1633), p. 22.

elapse between the acts of *La niña de Gómez Arias*. In *El príncipe constante* Calderón is discreetly silent about time, but events which spanned some thirty odd years are compressed in what appears to be a matter of weeks, and the action is continuous. The two plays whose structure Calderón preserved more or less intact have no serious breaks in the action. *Los cabellos de Absalón* is the only one in which I have noted a reference to the passing of years, in the interval between Acts II and III. Spanish preceptists called attention also to the excessive geographical spread of Spanish plays; one recalls the mocking comment of the canon in *Don Quixote*, XLIII. Here again Calderón is seen to have imposed certain limits upon the material of the source-plays. *El médico de su honra* is set in or near Seville, *Las armas de la hermosura* in or near Rome, *El mayor encanto amor* in Sicily, *La niña de Gómez Arias* in the area between Granada and Guadix, *Los cabellos de Absalón* in or near Jerusalem, *El alcalde de Zalamea* in Zalamea and *La vida es sueño* in and near the Polish Court. This is often in marked contrast to the procedure of the source dramatist. The author of *La fortuna adversa*, for example, opened his play in Portugal, moved to Africa for the Tangier landing, and returned to Portugal for the first scene of Act II; most of the latter part of the action necessarily takes place in Africa, but even so he allows himself two further visits to Portugal. In contrast, Calderón's play is set exclusively in Africa, in a single, ungeographical Fez-on-Sea!

Calderón's contribution in this direction has not been recognized. Don Eugenio Frutos, for example, though rightly remarking that Calderón did not observe the unities, contrasts his success in achieving unity of action with his perpetuation of the multiplicity of scenes of the Lopean *comedia:*

> En cambio no se cumplen las otras unidades clásicas: la temporal y la espacial. Las mutaciones escénicas son tan frecuentes, y en muchas comedias tan aparatosas, que recuerdan la actual técnica cinematográfica. [1]

Yet Calderón substantially reduced the number of scenes of many of the source-plays. Where scenes are clearly differentiated, his norm seems to be two scenes in each act, at least in the first two

---

[1] E. Frutos Cortés, *Calderón de la Barca* (Barcelona, 1949), p. 240.

19

acts; the increased pace and the requirements of the *dénouement* result sometimes in more scenes in Act III. But he often bridges the interval between scenes: persons required by one scene remain on stage to introduce those of the second, or musicians are employed specially for this purpose. Don Angel Valbuena has commented on the ironic references in Calderón's plays to the device of making a character who is alone on stage soliloquize. [1] More significant still is Calderón's use of a shifting scene which moves with the action from one place to another without noticeable breaks. In *El alcalde de Zalamea* the scene follows the action like a spotlight; we move from the countryside outside Zalamea in the play's opening lines to Zalamea itself and then through the street to the house of Pedro Crespo without a break. Though for the first act of *Los cabellos de Absalón* Calderón added a new scene which might have interrupted the continuity of Tirso's act, he interlocked the beginning and ending of the scene with the rest of the act in such a way that the action is continuous and the stage is never empty. In Act II of *El mayor encanto amor* we move imperceptibly from Circe's garden to a mountain and later to a sheltered glade without an abrupt scene-change. Calderón evidently was concerned to avoid both the multiplicity of scene and the empty stage which were technical short-comings of the Spanish *comedia,* though Lope himself had called attention to the latter point in his *Arte nuevo:*

> Quede muy pocas vezes el teatro
> sin persona que hable, porque el vulgo
> en aquellas distancias se inquieta
> y gran rato la fábula se alarga;
> que, fuera de ser esto un grande vicio,
> aumenta mayor gracia y artificio.   (240-245)

Many of Calderón's changes are evidence simply of more subtle handling. In recasting a scene or a ·situation he had a sure eye for achieving the maximum dramatic effect. In *El médico de su honra* he dispenses with an informative dialogue between a mistress and her servant, and allows the relationship between Mencía and Enrique to emerge from their conversation; and he extracts far more than his predecessor from the situation in which the husband goes to embrace his wife with dagger in hand. *Los cabellos de Absalón* does not

---

[1]   A. Valbuena Prat, *Calderón* (Barcelona, 1941), p. 153.

perpetuate Tirso's clumsy device of making Amón invent the story of a love-affair with an Ammonite girl so that he could ask Tamar to act her part. Instead, Calderón ingeniously brings the dialogue between Amón and his sister round to a point where Amón addresses her as if she were his beloved. One might set the whole of Act II of *Las armas de la hermosura* against the second act of *El privilegio de las mujeres* by Montalbán, since both dramatists are aiming at much the same effect with the same material. The structural differences between *El príncipe constante* and *La fortuna adversa* were required in the first instance by Calderón's recognition that, in presenting the story of a hero whose greatness lay in endurance rather than in action, he must exploit to the full those instances of active resistance which occurred in the source-play, and devise new ones. But most of the superbly handled scenes of this play, as of *El alcalde de Zalamea* and *La vida es sueño*, are without precedent. Calderón's plays are overwhelmingly superior to the source-plays by their certainty of aim and by the clarity and subtlety with which the dominant issues are presented and developed.

In the conception of his plays Calderón had in mind, I have suggested, a theme which the plot or story was intended to illustrate; and aspects of this theme are represented by the different characters. A study of the characters shows, in the first place, how remarkably consistent Calderón was both in their number and in their distribution. The table below analyses the plays here studied:

PARTS OF STANDING

PLAY	MEN	WOMEN	TOTAL	OTHER NAMED PARTS	TOTAL
El médico de su honra	5	2	7	5	12
Las armas de la hermosura	6	2	8	3	11
Los cabellos de Absalón	7	1	8	5	13
El mayor encanto amor	5	3	8	14	22
La niña de Gómez Arias	6	3	9	5	14
El príncipe constante	7	1	8	6	14
El alcalde de Zalamea	6	2	8	4	12
La vida es sueño	4	2	6	1	7

It will be recalled that these plays derive from earlier plays whose characters range from a mere half-dozen to nearly forty. The total number of speaking parts is around twelve or fourteen. The only exception is *El mayor encanto amor* which is mythological, intended in part as spectacle, with crowd scenes and choruses; so, instead of the norm of two or three servants, Circe has six maids who correspond to the six followers of Ulises. The principal rôles in all the plays are six, and the persons of standing rarely exceed nine. The parts are variously distributed, depending upon the particular plot, but they are mostly for young men, with one and sometimes two for old men. At least two of the main parts are for women, except in *El príncipe constante,* and all the women are young. The *gracioso* has the most important servant part, and he appears in all the plays except *Los cabellos de Absalón* and *El alcalde de Zalamea* where Jonadab and Rebolledo respectively have a similar function. *El médico de su honra* and *Las armas de la hermosura,* the only plays in which the distribution of characters was left unchanged by Calderón, fit almost exactly into the pattern which he imposed upon the other plays.

Calderón rejected all those characters of the source-plays who could contribute nothing to his basic theme; he retained and admitted only those to whom he could assign a specific and distinguishable rôle. Hence both the economy and the consistency of his plays. The test applies even to minor characters. Servants are found in all Calderón's plays and they provide usually the moments of humour. But they serve at the same time as foils to their masters and mistresses. In general their behaviour is shown to be inferior to that of the persons of standing; their cowardice, selfishness and lack of scruple are contrasted with the valour, generosity and integrity of their masters. The servant, of course, lacking the power and influence of his master, lacks also his responsibility. But the contrast is not always in favour of the master. In exposing the harshness and inhumanity of the code of honour, the servants are often made to show pity and affection. Coquín has neither the integrity of Gutierre nor his cruelty. The sympathy of Ginés in *La niña de Gómez Arias* contrasts with the brutality of Gómez. Except for Rebolledo and La Chispa, Calderón's servants are less alive than those of the source-plays and the humour they provide is often stereotyped and dull. The *gracioso,* however, is given a new and greatly extended rôle. Besides being a figure of fun and throwing into relief the conduct of his master, in many of Calderón's plays

he makes a serious and quite distinctive contribution to the dramatic exposition of the play's theme.

Coquín, for example, in *El médico de su honra* is more than
a jester. His contract with the King is a persistent reminder that the
King is incapable of laughter. He has important comments too
upon the behaviour of Gutierre and Mencía. It is Coquín, as we
have seen, who makes the strongest indictment of Gutierre's adherence to principle, even to the extent of sacrificing an innocent
human life for the sake of appearance. And words of Coquín epitomize the kind of society portrayed in the play, where values are
distorted and love is smothered by honour, a society 'al revés' in
which there is room neither for the laughter of happiness nor the
tears of pity. Clarín's antics with the giant Brutamonte in *El mayor
encanto amor* were inspired by the experiences of Chitón with
Poliphemus in *Polifemo y Circe*, but, like Coquín, he has far more
than a comic rôle. His fate symbolizes that of his master. Just as
he pays for his over-confidence by being transformed into a monkey, so Ulises pays for his temerity by being converted into someone
who bears no resemblance to his former self. Later Clarín is restored to human form, when he looks at himself in a mirror. Ulises
also, mirrored as it were in the words of Achilles, overcomes his
passion for Circe and recovers his former stature. In *La vida es
sueño* another Clarín has a major part which is both comic and
serious. Clarín tries to avoid the major issues of life, and in the
battle between the forces of Basilio and Segismundo he is the only
casualty. Like Segismundo, Basilio and Astolfo, he is undeceived;
he pays for his over-confidence with his life.

Most of Calderón's plays give greater prominence to the protagonist than did their sources. This is partly the effect of removing
or reducing the sub-plots and of discarding dispensable characters;
the characters that survive have larger parts. It was the rôle of
the protagonist which was most extended. The principal addition
in *La niña de Gómez Arias* is Gómez's abandonment of Dorotea,
in *El príncipe constante* Fernando's refusal to accept freedom at
the expense of Ceuta, both expanding primarily the part of the
leading character. The new incidents of *Las armas de la hermosura*
increase the importance of Coriolano and Veturia. At the same
time Calderón used other means of accentuating the protagonist.
In *El médico de su honra* and *La vida es sueño* monologues direct

attention to Gutierre and to Segismundo, as well as to the problems with which they are confronted. In other plays there are extended duologues, between Ulises and Circe in *El mayor encanto amor,* between Gómez Arias and Dorotea in *La niña de Gómez Arias,* between Fernando and the King in *El príncipe constante,* between Crespo and Don Lope in *El alcalde de Zalamea,* between Segismundo and Rosaura in *La vida es sueño.* All are without parallel in the source-plays. Yet another method was to allow other characters to discuss the protagonist so that, even when not on the stage in person, he is kept before the audience. A new scene in Calderón's *El médico de su honra* between Don Arias and Leonor throws more light on their own characters and allows a discussion of Gutierre, thereby clinching points which have emerged from the play's action; at the play's end a speech by the *gracioso* Coquín serves much the same purpose. The other plays provide countless examples of the same device: Antistes's comments on Ulises in *El mayor encanto amor,* those of the *gracioso* Ginés on Gómez Arias in *La niña de Gómez Arias,* the hearsay which the sergeant passes on to the captain about Crespo in *El alcalde de Zalamea,* Basilio's account of the horoscope of Segismundo in *La vida es sueño,* the testimony of Muley and Fénix to the conduct of Fernando in *El príncipe constante.*

Calderón's plays also show a clearer subordination of characters to the protagonist. Their parts are conceived in terms of his, their qualities and behaviour throw his into relief. The foil technique was of course used by Calderón's predecessors, and it has been taken even to be a distinctive feature of the plays of Mira de Amescua. That Calderón extended its use is clear from these studies. A series of parallels and contrasts has been seen to exist between the protagonist and the remaining characters. In *El médico de su honra* we have an instance of almost perfect symmetry in its seven parts for persons of standing. In *Las armas de la hermosura* the three characters of Aurelio, Lelio and Enio are closely associated; so are Veturia and Queen Astrea. In *Los cabellos de Absalón* Amón and many of the minor characters are grouped with Absalón, all bringing death upon themselves, and all contrasted with David. In *El mayor encanto amor* Ársidas and the *gracioso* Clarín are linked with Ulises. In *La niña de Gómez Arias* El Cañerí is set beside Gómez Arias, and Beatriz beside Dorotea. Alfonso mirrors

Fernando in *El príncipe constante,* as do Isabel and Juan Pedro Crespo in *El alcalde de Zalamea.* On the other hand, Fernando's courage and cheerfulness are contrasted with the fear of Enrique and Fénix's melancholy in the face of adversity, and Crespo's honour with the mere label of honour of Don Mendo and the dishonour of the captain; a different kind of contrast is established between Crespo and Don Lope. Segismundo in *La vida es sueño* is offset on the one hand by Basilio, Astolfo and Clarín and on the other by Clotaldo and Rosaura. Calderón's protagonist usually towers above the other characters who are conceived to throw him into relief.

The stories of the plays which Calderón chose to recast were extraordinarily diverse: a husband murders an innocent wife, a general is persuaded to spare the town he has threatened to destroy, a brother rapes his half-sister and a son conspires against his father, a veteran warrior all but abandons his calling on account of a siren, a villain seduces a girl on a promise of marriage and sells her to the *moriscos,* a prince suffers death in captivity to save a Christian town, a peasant mayor has two army captains garrotted, the rightful heir to a throne is the victim of his sister's ambition until restored by a stroke of fortune. Each of these stories is accommodated to Calderón's philosophy; a single coherent view of life informs them all. Only two of these plays have leading characters whose conduct is illicit by the values of the natural order, whose deeds are both morally wrong and punishable by the state. Absalón is a murderer and a conspirator, Gómez Arias is a ruthless villain. Both survive in the source-plays, both meet violent deaths in Calderón's. Two other characters, Amón and the captain in *El alcalde,* also offend against the moral law and the law of the state, and both die. A third protagonist, Segismundo, inclined by birth and upbringing to behave like a brute, overcomes his baser nature. The remaining characters are well-intentioned and, by the standards of the society in which they live, good. Yet they are guilty of moral error because of their distorted values or because their reason is clouded. Sometimes they bring tragedy upon themselves, their friends and their family; sometimes they are spared by the wisdom of others. Moral error, committed in pursuit of either good or evil, is shown to lead, in society to conspiracy and war, in the family to suspicion, hatred and dishonour.

Calderón's search for a significant theme and his insistence that each character should fit into a thematic pattern necessitated often the distortion of history or legend. Coriolano is impeached not for attempting to deny the tribunes their rights but for championing the cause of women, and the siege is not of Corioli by the Volscians but of Rome by the Sabines in revenge for the rape of the Sabine women. Such changes were not, as Menéndez y Pelayo claimed, arbitrary and capricious. By this means the theme of the play could be the superiority of mercy to revenge, and the championship of woman's rightful place in society. Calderón changed the historical setting of *La niña de Gómez Arias* so that the behaviour of Gómez Arias could be related to that of the *moriscos* and of their leader El Cañerí. Even the facts of near-contemporary historical incidents were changed, sometimes reversed. Henry the Navigator, whose very recklessness was one of the causes of the Tangier disaster, is changed by Calderón into one who was cautious and fearful. As the play's protagonist, Fernando has to take precedence over Enrique. But Calderón not only makes the prayerful, retiring Fernando of history lead the expedition, he invests him with the qualities of a Christian crusader who scorns superior numbers and ill-omens. Enrique, in contrast, is diffident and defeatist. The failure of critics to approach Calderón's plays through their themes has blinded them to his intentions and made them censure him for the liberties which he took with history. In his plays dramatic necessity takes precedence over historical truth.

In general it may be said that Calderón's characters were of interest to him primarily for the dominant qualities which they embodied. It is for this reason that he was able to fit them into the complex pattern of his plays. But this does not mean that he did not create characters of flesh and blood, or portray profoundly moving human situations. On the contrary, close and intelligent reading of his plays reveals that the characters are far more complex, varied and rich than earlier scholars have allowed. His themes are presented in terms of human experience, not expounded by arid argument; and we have noted a number of instances in which he surpasses the source dramatist in humanity. *El alcalde de Zalamea* is a striking example, with some of the most poignant human situations of Spanish drama. But it has no monopoly of such situations. It is matched by *La niña de Gómez Arias* with its scene of Dorotea's desertion by

Gómez Arias in Act II and her sale in Act III. Gutierre's interview with the King in Act III of *El médico de su honra* and David's conversation with Amón in Act I of *Los cabellos de Absalón* both exceed in warmth and pathos the corresponding scenes in the source-plays.

One final point: in so far as Calderón's plays have a new unity and are more concentrated in time and place, they may be said to be more classical than the source-plays. This classicizing process may also be noted in Calderón's choice and conception of characters. The ancient doctrine of the different levels of literary represent-ation was not of course accepted by Golden Age dramatists. The Spanish drama was an outgrowth of the popular drama of the sixteenth century and it required no strict separation of styles. In this matter Calderón identified himself with Lope, and it would be easy to quote examples from his plays of the alternation of tragic and comic scenes, of comic characters mixed with tragic in the same scene, and of single characters shifting from tragedy to comedy. Even so, one can detect a tendency towards the classical separation in Calderón. With the notable exception of Pedro Crespo, the protagonists of his plays are almost all of high social rank. Even in taking over Crespo Calderón omitted a number of details which were in his view unbecoming to a tragic figure; for example, he is no longer illiterate. Similarly, in *Los cabellos de Absalón* Tamar was removed from the kitchen. The alternation of elevated and low scenes is much rarer in Calderón's plays than in their sources and such comic passages as do appear are virtually restricted to servants; we recall the antics of Clarín in *El mayor encanto amor* and the brief appearances of Brito in *El príncipe constante*. Again, of the serious plays of Calderón only to my know-ledge *El alcalde de Zalamea* offers anything to compare with the vivacious gossip of the peasant girls in *Peribáñez* or with the mayor's speech to the Queen in *La prudencia en la mujer*. And it is perhaps significant that, in appropriating an act of *La venganza de Tamar* for his *Los cabellos de Absalón*, one of the very few changes which Calderón appears to have made was to remove the comic relief which Tirso, so characteristically, provided in the form of shepherds' dialect and song. The most striking change of mood in the plays studied here is produced by *capa y espada* situations, like those of *El mayor encanto amor* and *La niña de Gómez Arias*. Certainly,

Calderón's plays have nothing of the secluded sublimity which isolates Racine's characters from everything ordinary, nor do they exclude what Auerbach has called the "creatural" —man's subjection to suffering and transitoriness. [1] Calderón had a strong sense of literary decorum. He was careful to omit anything which might detract from the dignity of his characters; the creatural takes an exalted form.

The language of these *refundiciones* is as authentic and truly original as that of any of Calderón's plays. It is in fact remarkable that in those instances in which he keeps close to the source-play he is so rarely tempted to take over lines and phrases. The appropriation of a whole act of *La venganza de Tamar* is unique and certainly requires some special explanation. For the first part of Act III of *Las armas de la hermosura* he adopts the same scheme of versification as Coello, and both here and in some passages of Act I he borrows a number of lines. Sometimes, as for Veturia's speech in Act I, Calderón systematically expands a passage of the source-play, extending for example pairs of lines to four. He uses a similar procedure for Circe's long speech in Act I of *El mayor encanto amor*. All the plays have some lines that were directly inspired by the source. We recall in particular the exchanges between Pedro Crespo and Don Lope in *El alcalde de Zalamea*, the sale of 'la niña' in *La niña de Gómez Arias* and the dilemma of Ulises in *El mayor encanto amor*, not to mention almost the whole of *El médico de su honra* and *Las armas de la hermosura*. Yet such was Calderón's desire to be independent that he deliberately avoided words or expressions used by the source dramatist. Rewriting two short passages of *La fortuna adversa* for *El príncipe constante*, he uses *monte* for *cerro, una tropa de jinetes* for *gran multitud de lanzas, cadenas* for *hierros*, and *sarga humilde y pobre* for *un capote viejo*.

For many of our plays Calderón's new conception of the source material required so radical a reconstruction that he could preserve few of the earlier scenes or situations. Even so, all the plays except

---

[1] *Mimesis. The Representation of Reality in Western Literature* (Princeton, 1953).

La vida es sueño have at least some scene in which Calderón was writing within the same general limits as the source dramatist and with a similar aim in view. The correlation of such scenes in the foregoing pages, brief though it has been, will have thrown into relief the principal features of Calderón's style, or at least those features which distinguish it from that of the source dramatists. Perhaps the most striking difference is quite simply the extraordinary care with which Calderón wrote and, as a result, the importance of every detail. Calderón, of whom G. H. Lewes had the effrontery to write:

> [We] shall scarcely expect to find his dramas unfolding new beauties at each perusal and remaining endless monuments of study and admiration. [1]

was, we now know, one of the most painstaking and subtle dramatists of all time. In his best work every phrase —an image perhaps or a classical reference, a parallelism or a contrast— is significant and has its place in the scheme of the play. This is not true of even the best work of Lope. The point is well made by M. Aubrun and Sr. Montesinos in their edition of *Peribáñez*:

> Il s'agit, ici comme d'ailleurs, d'une improvisation. Lope n'était capable que de produire torrentiellement, à flots, et ses comedias les plus soignées se ressentent parfois de sa précipitation. Notre poète eut toujours du goût —un goût bien espagnol et romantique— pour le *naturel*, pour ce qui jaillit spontanément et sans effort, et, aussi bien, il n'éprouve qu'indifférence —une indifférence à la fois espagnole et romantique— pour les enfantements laborieux de l'esprit. [2]

In a comparison of the two *El médico* plays it is Calderón's imagery which is conspicuous. The language of the source is by no means colourless and Calderón has taken from it some of the associations of his own play, in particular the basic image suggested by the title. What the source-play lacks is the brilliance of many of Calderón's images and, at the same time, the consistent pattern into which most of them are fitted. The association of life with light, for example, is immortalized in the words of St. John:

vita erat lux hominum

and it occurs in the first *El médico*: Doña Mayor is associated with

---

[1] *The Spanish Drama* (London, 1846), 240.
[2] Ed. *Peribáñez* (Hachette, 1943), xlvi.

light, and light with life. Yet only in Calderón's play do we have a chain of images relating the darkness in which so many of the situations occur with moral blindness. Mencía is the sun whose shining honour is obscured by the cloud Enrique; but she is also the light which Gutierre extinguishes. The play's images point unmistakably to its meaning. Gutierre is the physician of his honour; by bleeding his wife, his good name is not compromised. But he is abased by the barbarity of the code he follows. His jealousy consumes his heart like a fire, poisons it like a viper. Like a thief he works in the dark, and in his confusion he is doubly blind.

The association of error with darkness and disorder, of moral *confusión* with physical confusion, is probably the most common of all Calderón's associations. Dorotea elopes with Gómez Arias after the chaos at her father's house at the end of Act I. Like Isabel in *El alcalde de Zalamea* she is assaulted in a wood that is dark and labyrinthine. Amón, obsessed by his incestuous love for Tamar, shuns the light of day and retires to a room with closed shutters. Isabel, after her dishonour, pleads with the sun not to rise. The handsome Absalón is compared with the sun, and his vanity and ambition are related to the idea of ascent. But, as with Phaethon, presumption brings about his downfall and he dies in an *espesura*, his hair entangled in an oak tree. In *La fortuna adversa* Fernando's spirit appears with a lighted torch to encourage Muley, and in *El príncipe constante* to guide the Portuguese army; but what is an isolated incident in the source-play becomes in *El príncipe constante* part of a scene which depends for much of its meaning upon the symbolism of light and darkness. Throughout the play the sun represents both the radiant beauty of Fénix and the shining faith of Fernando. In *Yerros* the darkness of the prison-tower is linked by a series of metaphors with death, but these associations have been multiplied and enriched in *La vida es sueño*.

The distorted sense of values of Gutierre in *El médico* relates him to the Roman patricians in *Las armas de la hermosura*. Their moral confusion is linked with the confusion and chaos of the battle scenes. In *El mayor encanto amor* the dominant association is that of man's degradation with animals. But in the scene in which Ulises chooses to remain with Circe and later when Achilles comes to upbraid him, his effeminacy and degeneracy are compared with blindness, deafness, dumbness, madness, sleep, lethargy, oblivion, slavery, poison, imprisonment and death, as well as with darkness, all familiar associations of Calderón. Ultimately, like Theseus he will escape from the labyrinth, and like Oedipus solve the riddle. These are a few of the principal images commented on in earlier chapters. Few of them are original, and a good many occur in the source-plays. But in Calderón's plays they take their place in a complex but consistent pattern of imagery in which honour and dishonour, reason and passion, prudence and imprudence, are associated in turn with light and darkness, day and night, sun and shade, ascent and descent, head and feet, right and left, white and black, sanity and madness, waking and sleeping, sight and blindness.

Calderón's rewriting of a scene of *La venganza de Tamar* for the opening scene of *Los cabellos de Absalón* is remarkable for its balance and symmetry. In Tirso's play a long speech of David's, in which he describes the assault on Rabbah and greets those who have come to welcome him, is followed by lively exchanges with all the apparent spontaneity and triviality of ordinary conversation. Calderón's scene in contrast is highly mannered. Each of David's four children has four lines of *silva*, with parallel phrases and images; and David replies, first with a formal greeting, then with a word for each of his children, and finally with a brief account of his victory. This formality of Calderón's writing, with the attention paid to pattern and symmetry, is reflected in the numerous examples of correlation and parallelism in his plays which Don Dámaso Alonso has studied. [1] We have seen how, elaborating upon some lines of *El privilegio de las mujeres,* Calderón added to the number of parallel phrases, how the rewriting of the climax of Vélez's *La niña de Gómez Arias* led to a finer example of enumeration and recapitulation, and how Circe's memorable speech in the first act of *El mayor encanto amor* is constructed throughout on the basis of correlations and parallelisms. Many scenes and acts end with balanced lines or phrases which epitomize a basic conflict of the play. There is the clash, for example, between *amor* and *honor* in *El médico de su honra:*

> D.ª MENCÍA.   tuve amor, y tengo honor;
> esto es cuanto sé de mí.   (189a)

---

[1] *Seis calas en la expresión literaria española* (Madrid, 1951), 115-86.

and between *amor* and *deseo* in *La niña de Gómez Arias:*

DOROTEA. Amor, ¿qué no haré por ti?
GÓMEZ. ¿Qué no haré por ti, deseo? (368b)

not to mention the exchanges between Crespo and Don Lope in *El alcalde de Zalamea.* We recall Lope's remarks in the *Arte nuevo*:

Remátense las escenas con sentencia,
con donayre, con versos elegantes,
de suerte que, al entrarse, el que recita,
no dexe con disgusto al auditorio. (294-97)

Casuistry is another feature which distinguishes these plays from their sources. The characters are made to enunciate rules of behaviour and then apply them to the case in point. Calderón, rewriting the scene in which David visits Amón, replaces the simple exchanges of Tirso, with its tender pleadings of a loving father and the blunt replies of an embittered son, with logic and gentle philosophizing: "If the cause of Amón's melancholy is known, then David will remove it; if unknown, the result simply of his character and temperament, he has the power to overcome it." Time and again Calderón's characters are confronted with conflicting obligations and they are made to weigh them against each other in monologues or asides. The dilemma of Enio, for example, in *Las armas de la hermosura* is threefold: he is faced with obligations to the *plebs,* to his friend and to a lady. In *El médico de su honra* Gutierre, in his long soliloquy in Act I, presents aloud to himself the whole case of his honour and the conflicting evidence with the logic and the clarity of a trained lawyer; he is even made to congratulate himself on the fine distinctions that he has drawn:

¡Oh!, ¡cuánto me estimo haber
hallado esta sutileza! (200b)

Calderón's characters are adept at dialectic, and few exchanges between them are free from quibbling and sophistry of one kind or another. Mencía's comment on Gutierre, after listening to his strained argument to justify his departure for Seville:

Muy metafísico estáis. (189a)

is one which could be applied to many of the personages of Cal-

derón's plays. Take, for example, the syllogistic reply of Gómez
Arias to his servant Ginés in *La niña de Gómez Arias:*

GINÉS.	...¿Cuál es la razón?
GÓMEZ.	Esta.
	Para ser perfecto amor,
	perfecto ha de ser por fuerza
	el objeto que se ame.
GINÉS.	La mayor concedo.
GÓMEZ.	Espera.
	No hay tan perfecta mujer
	que algún defecto no tenga.
GINÉS.	Concedo la menor.
GÓMEZ.	Luego
	preciso es que me concedas
	que no hay tan perfecto objeto
	que todo un amor merezca.
	Luego querer yo el aliño
	de una, de otra la belleza,
	de otra el ingenio y de otra
	la calidad y las prendas,
	es tener perfecto amor,
	pues quiero en cada una dellas
	la perfección que hay en todas.
GINÉS.	Concedo la consecuencia. (359a)

Later in the same play we have the cold argument with which
Gómez counters the rather improbable reasoning of Dorotea in
Act III. A large part of the second act of *El mayor encanto amor*
is taken up with the ingenious argument between Ulises and
Ársidas as to whether it is easier to affect a love you do not feel
or dissemble a love which is true, and later with their attempt to
justify their reactions to the false alarm.

Long monologues are far more common in Calderón's plays than
in the sources. Many are narrative speeches; they occur in the
first act and provide the audience with the background for the
events which follow, or they make known incidents which have
happened off stage. Enio reviews the events which have led to
the Sabine attack and Pasquín describes the Senate's edict in *Las
armas,* Muley describes the Portuguese threat to Tangier in *El
príncipe constante,* Basilio tells of the birth and imprisonment of
Segismundo in *La vida es sueño,* Ulises recounts his experiences to
Circe and Circe replies in *El mayor encanto amor.* Such narrative

speeches take the place of action, sometimes action which the source dramatists included: Muley's single speech in *El príncipe constante*, for example, replaces the long opening scene of *La fortuna adversa*. Other speeches are soliloquies which reveal the thoughts and the mental conflict of the person speaking: Gutierre meditating upon his honour, Enio and Aurelio balancing their different obligations, Amón vainly trying to resist his passion. But the most characteristic orations of Calderón's plays are those in which the protagonist or a principal character releases his pent-up feelings after an emotional crisis or grave decision: Veturia inveighing against the iniquitous edict of the Senate and castigating Coriolano for refusing peace-terms, Dorotea's bitter denunciation of Gómez Arias, Fernando's indictment of Mohammedanism and his death-bed refusal to agree to Ceuta's return, Isabel's confession of her abduction by the captain, Segismundo's triumph over himself. Such speeches occur usually at the climax of the action towards the end of the third act. They represent the culmination of the dramatic movement which has been developing with mounting tension throughout the play; and they are often a final restatement of the basic theme. Veturia maintains the superiority of mercy over revenge, Dorotea condemns lust and villainy, Fernando defends Christian fortitude, Segismundo proclaims man's self-mastery.

All these speeches have a legitimate dramatic purpose. They contain also much of Calderón's finest poetry. Muley's account of the Portuguese attack in *El príncipe constante* is, significantly, lyrical rather than narrative. But it was the violent, frenzied speech which evidently commended itself most to Calderón's audience, declaimed at them in high-sounding, rhetorical language. Spaniards of the seventeenth century, like the Elizabethans, delighted in words for their own sake; they were beguiled by their music and stirred by the sheer virtuosity of the playwright and, doubtless, the actor. Such speeches in Calderón's plays run to a great length, often to two or three hundred lines. They are constructed with all the skill of an accomplished architect; they follow a consistent plan, they are admirably varied in pace. And they incorporate all the familiar devices, in particular parallelism, correlation, repetition and recapitulation. Proof of the appeal and popularity of monologues of this type is provided by the fact that so many of them were reprinted, as Wilson points out, in eighteenth- and early nineteenth-century chap books. [1] The plays of Calderón, in short, are more stylized than their sources. The language of *Los cabellos de Absalón* is far more studied and formal than that of *La venganza de Tamar*. Tirso's dialogue gives the appearance of spontaneity. Calderón's, on the other hand, is formal, less direct. Tirso's ingenuity finds an outlet in word-play, Calderón's in skilful dialectic. This is characteristic of Calderón's plays in general. Their carefully-conceived plan of images, their balance and symmetry, their long speeches, their rhetorical devices, combine to give them the studied artificiality which is in marked contrast to the style of most of the source-plays.

Calderón's favourite stanza-forms are *romance* and to a less extent *redondilla*, in contrast with the combination of *quintilla* and *redondilla* preferred in the earlier plays of Lope; and *silva*, *décimas* and the sonnet tend to replace the earlier *endecasílabos sueltos*, *tercetos* and *octavas*. Calderón's break from the language of the source-plays was, at the same time, a break from their versification. As with the language, the influence was sometimes negative. Where he has retained a scene from the source, his procedure was normally to refrain from using the same stanza-form. Though he follows, for example, the scene pattern of Act I of the first *El médico*, *romance-redondilla-romance-redondilla-romance-redondilla* give way to *redondilla-romance-décima-silva-octava-romance*, the two strophes in common, *redondilla* and *romance*, being used in different places. In *Las armas de la hermosura* he shuns the verse-forms of the source for most of the first two acts, but he adopts those of Coello in Act III. In the first act of *Los cabellos de Absalón* the *décima*, which is the only metre used by Tirso in his corresponding act, is not used in the same scene. The same is true for the rest of the plays. It is very doubtful whether the source-plays exerted any positive influence on Calderón's versification. The large proportion of *décimas* and *silva* in *El médico de su honra* cannot, for example, be accounted for by the source, nor can the high percentage of *quintillas* and the low percentage of both *décimas* and *silva* in *La niña de Gómez Arias*.

Reference has already been made to Calderón's reduction of

---

[1] E. M. Wilson, 'Some Calderonian *pliegos sueltos*', *Hom. Van Praag* (Amsterdam, 1956), 140-44.

the number of scenes of the source-plays and his resourcefulness in avoiding an empty stage. For other differences between the staging of these pairs of plays one has to rely often upon the stage-directions of the texts that have happened to survive, which can be misleading; I have noted only the most striking. In those plays in which Calderón borrowed the structure of his source, he seems to have kept most of the details of staging. In the two *El médico* plays a screen is used, in Act I to hide the second lady and in Act III to hide the husband. Calderón varied the settings of his play by shifting two scenes from the husband's house to the garden and he appears to have dispensed with one of the three 'discoveries'. But the most significant change is the setting of the inner stage at the play's end when the wife is revealed lying dead upon her bed; and here we can be certain of Calderón's intentions since he incorporates a detailed description of the scene in the dialogue. The gruesome spectacle of the dishevelled Mayor of the source-play has been replaced by one of calm and peace. Mencía's face is covered, two candles are lit on either side of the bed and above it hangs a crucifix. She has made her peace with God whose divine forgiveness contrasts with the vengeance of Gutierre. Sometimes Calderón's reconstruction of the source-play involved the omission of *tramoyas,* like the miraculous appearance of a font for Iataf's conversion and of the Virgin Mary, St. Anthony and St. Michael to attend Fernando on his death-bed in *La fortuna adversa.* But he gave *El príncipe constante* a more spectacular ending; Fernando makes two appearances with a flaming torch and, in full view of the audience, his coffin is lowered from the walls of Fez. Fernando's final appearance alive on stage is unusually realistic: he is described by Muley as a corpse on a dunghill. In contrast, if one can judge by the stage-directions of the Vera Tassis text, the more gory details of the 'discovery' of the murdered Amón in *La venganza de Tamar* were omitted from productions of *Los cabellos de Absalón.*

Only two of our eight plays, *El mayor encanto amor* and *Las armas de la hermosura,* require elaborate staging. Calderón added considerably to the spectacle of *Polifemo y Circe* which has nothing to correspond, say, with the appearance of Galatea in her triumphal car and the transformation of Circe's palace into a volcano belching flames. Similarly, the complicated sets of *Las armas de la hermosura* for the banqueting scene with which the play opens and for the investiture in Act II have no parallel in *El privilegio de las mujeres*. Both *El mayor encanto amor* and *Las armas de la hermosura* make striking use of choruses. Music, we have seen, serves a dramatic purpose in Calderón's plays, sometimes to bring out the harmony of life lived in accordance with the laws of God, sometimes to further the cause of evil. [1] The love of Coriolano and Veturia in *Las armas de la hermosura* is reflected in the songs of the two choruses in the play's first scene. Thereafter, through the confusion of war, the lovers are estranged and separated until they are reunited in the last scene, when music is again heard. Music here symbolizes the peace and harmony of true love. In contrast, in *El mayor encanto amor*, the music provided by Circe is beguiling and false, enticing Ulises from the path of honour. In the same way, the musicians of *Los cabellos de Absalón* assist Amón in his incestuous assault upon Tamar. In *El alcalde de Zalamea* the contrast between the two kinds of music is found in a single scene: the friendship between Pedro Crespo and Don Lope is symbolized by the natural music of the wind and stream. It is this peaceful scene that the Captain and his serenaders disturb, and their appearance is marked by the strumming of guitars and the singing of a *jácara*.

Songs are used by Calderón for a variety of purposes. Sometimes they anticipate later developments in the action, either in the course of the play itself or even after the play has ended. In *El médico de su honra* the King overhears a street ballad telling of the imminent departure from Seville of Prince Enrique and predicting the tragedy of Montiel; following upon the King's delirious vision of his bloody death it points unmistakably to the fate that awaits him. Often the songs are less explicit. In Act III of *El mayor encanto amor* they evoke the mood of love; in the first lines of *El príncipe constante* they underline the conduct required of a captive. The words of La Chispa's song in *El alcalde de Zalamea*, like those of Teodora to her mistress in the second act of *El médico de su honra*, vaguely forebode tragedy and so increase the dramatic tension. In *El mayor encanto amor* Circe's musicians remind the audience of Ulises' renown for courage and discretion at the very moment when he is being effeminate and indiscreet. Like other minor characters,

---

[1] This distinction between what Calderón calls good and bad music has been studied by J. W. Sage, 'C. y la música teatral', *BHi*, LVIII (1956), 275-300.

musicians were occasionally used by Calderón to bridge intervals between scenes. Sometimes he included songs and dances simply, or at least primarily, for entertainment, as for example in the soldier scenes of *El alcalde. de Zalamea.*

Calderón was attracted to the source-plays in question by their potential as drama, a potential which the source dramatists had failed to actualize. They provided a plot or a dramatic situation or characters which, conceived anew, could become the vehicle of a significant theme. The structural differences between Calderón's play and its source depend upon the extent to which he was able to accommodate his new conception to the original pattern of acts and scenes. In some, his conception corresponds so closely to that of his predecessor that he could preserve the general outline of the source. In others he was obliged to reject completely the original structure, retaining only relics of earlier characters and situations. And between these two extremes there are many and various degrees of approximation to the source-play. All eight plays surpass their sources in their dramatic unity, in their complexity and cohesion, in the richness and brilliance of their language and imagery. Yet to suggest that Calderón's plays are superior to the source-plays only in respect of technique is to ignore the testimony of all the preceding chapters. Calderón's recasting of the source-plays in terms of a theme not only provided them with a single unifying idea; it gave them depth and gravity. He penetrated beneath the multifarious and seemingly capricious incidents of the stories of the sources to an underlying idea of universal application. All his serious plays have, at bottom, but one subject and one theme: man, subverting the order of natural values by his moral error and human frailty, or in the labyrinthine confusion of life groping towards the light by the aid of reason and discretion. Calderón emerges from these studies as a meticulous and subtle craftsman, whose stagecraft at its best was impeccable, and as a poetic dramatist of deep human significance.

BIBLIOGRAPHY

CALDERONIAN CRITICISM SINCE 1900[1]

PRINCIPAL EDITIONS

Auto sacramental de las órdenes militares, ed. E. Walberg, in *BHi,* V (1903), 383-408, VI (1904), 44-66, 94-113, 235-58.

La vida es sueño, ed. W. W. Comfort (New York, 1904).

La vida es sueño, ed. G. Gröber (Strasburg, 1905).

El mágico prodigioso, ed. W. v. Wurzbach (Strasburg, 1909).

La selva confusa, ed. G. T. Northup, in *RHi,* XXI (1909), 168-338.

La vida es sueño, ed. M. A. Buchanan (Toronto, 1909).

La española de Florencia, ed. S. L. M. Rosenberg (Philadelphia, 1911).

Teatro: La vida es sueño y El purgatorio de San Patricio, ed. M. de Toro Gisbert (Paris, 1913).

Troya abrasada, ed. G. T. Northup, in *RHi,* XXIX (1913), 193-346.

El alcalde de Zalamea, ed. J. Geddes (New York, 1918).

El alcalde de Zalamea, ed. I. Farnell (Manchester, 1921).

Three plays: Casa con dos puertas, La vida es sueño and La cena del rey Baltasar, ed. G. T. Northup (Boston, 1926).

Autos sacramentales, 2 vols., ed. A. Valbuena Prat (Madrid, 1926-1927).

El mágico prodigioso, ed. T. Heinermann (Münster, 1927).

La mojiganga de la muerte, ed. A. Valbuena Prat (Madrid, 1927).

La vida es sueño, ed. A. Gasparetti (Roma, 1928).

El mágico prodigioso, ed. J. N. Birch (London, 1929).

Comedias religiosas: La devoción de la cruz, El mágico prodigioso, ed. A. Valbuena Prat (Madrid, 1930).

El alcalde de Zalamea, ed. Elena Taliento (Roma, 1930).

Yerros de naturaleza y aciertos de la fortuna, ed. E. Juliá Martínez (Madrid, 1930).

Comedias mitológicas, 2 vols., ed. A. Valbuena Prat (Madrid, 1931).

La vida es sueño, ed. L. Dubois (Paris, 1931).

El mágico prodigioso, ed. A. R. Ferrarin (Milano, 1932).

Obras completas (Dramas), ed. L. Astrana Marín (Madrid, 1933).

El príncipe constante, ed. A. A. Parker (Cambridge, 1938).

El secreto a vozes, ed. J. M. Osma (Kansas, 1938).

---

[1] This bibliography includes all the significant items of criticism known to me, excluding unpublished dissertations, newspaper articles and reviews. I do not claim that it is complete, but I hope it may be useful. It is arranged in chronological order, with the items of each year listed alphabetically.

Autos sacramentales: El gran teatro del mundo, La devoción de la misa, ed. A. Valbuena Prat (Zaragoza, 1940).
La vida es sueño, ed. R. Gastón (Zaragoza, 1940).
No siempre lo peor es cierto, ed. J. M. Hill and M. M. Harlan in *Cuatro comedias* (New York, 1941).
El alcalde de Zalamea, ed. G. Espino (Zaragoza, 1943).
Auto sacramental alegórico del gran teatro del mundo, ed. F. Selva (Barcelona, 1944).
La dama duende, El gran teatro del mundo, El príncipe constante, ed. J. M. Mohedano (Madrid, 1945).
Psalle et Sile, ed. L. Trénor (Valencia, 1945).
La devoción de la cruz, ed. I. Montiel (Zaragoza, 1946).
El mágico prodigioso, ed. I. Montiel (Madrid, 1948).
La cruz en la sepultura, ed. H. C. Heaton (New York, 1948).
El verdadero Dios Pan, ed. J. M. Osma (Kansas, 1949).
No hay más fortuna que Dios, ed. A. A. Parker (Manchester, 1949).
El príncipe constante, ed. P. Pou Fernández (Zaragoza, 1950).
El alcalde de Zalamea, ed. A. Nougué (Toulouse, 1952).
La dama duende, ed. H. Koch (Halle, 1952).
Obras completas, III: Autos sacramentales, ed. A. Valbuena Prat (Madrid, 1952).
Comedias de capa y espada, II: La dama duende y No hay cosa como callar, ed. A. Valbuena Briones (Madrid, 1954).
La vida es sueño, ed. M. de Riquer (Barcelona, 1954).
El mayor monstruo los celos, ed. E. W. Hesse (Madison, 1955).
La vida es sueño, El alcalde de Zalamea, ed. A. Cortina (Madrid, 1955).
Dramas de honor: I. El secreto agravio secreta venganza, II. El médico de su honra, and *El pintor de su deshonra*, ed. A. Valbuena Briones (Madrid, 1956).
Obras completas, II: comedias, ed. A. Valbuena Briones (Madrid, 1956).

CRITICISM

GORRA, E., "Il dramma religioso di C", in *Fra drammi e poemi* (Milano, 1900).

READE, H., "How did C know Shakespeare's plays?", *Westminster Review*, CLX (1903), 84-88.

BALMONT, K. D., "Kalderonovskaya Drama Lichnosti", *Gornye Vershiny* (Moscow, 1904), I, 26-42.

BREYMANN, H., "C auf dem deutschen Theater", *Allgemeine Zeitung*, LXXXV (1904).

HART, H., "Zwei 'Representative men': C und Milton", *Zeitung für Literatur, Kunst und Wissenschaft*, XXV (1904).

LINDNER, E., *Die poetische Personifikation in den Jugendschauspielen C's* (Leipzig, 1904).

BREYMANN, H. W., *C-Studien: die C-Literatur* (München, 1905).

Catalogue des ouvrages de C conservés au département des imprimés de la Bibliotèque Nationale (Paris, 1905).

LUDWIG, A., "Vergleichende Studien zu C's Technik", *Studien zur vergleichenden Lit*, V (1905), 297-322 and VI (1906). 41-76.

PÉREZ PASTOR, C., *Documentos para la biografía de C* (Madrid, 1905).

BALBÍN DE UNQUERA, A., "Dramas históricos de C", *Revista contemporánea*, CXXXII (1906), 641.

FLERES, U., "Un capolavoro del teatro spagnuolo: El alcalde de Zalamea", NA, CCVII (1906), 83-98.

GÜNTHER, E., "C — Literatur", *Literarischer Handweiser*, XLIV (1906), 753-66, 801-10, 893-99, 941-58.

BUCHANAN, M. A., "Notes on C: The Vera Tassis edition; The text of *La vida es sueño*", MLN, XXII (1907), 148-50.

BUCHANAN, M. A., "Notes on the Spanish drama. The Date of C's *La vida es sueño...*", MLN, XXII (1907), 215-18.

FARINELLI, A., "Apuntes sobre C y la música en Alemania", *Cultura española*, V (1907) 119 ff.

FARINELLI, A., "Divagaciones bibliográficas calderonianas" in *Cultura española*, VI (1907). 505 ff.

BUCHANAN, M. A., "Segismundo's Soliloquy on Liberty in *La vida es sueño*", PMLA, XXIII (1908), 240-53.

AMEZÚA, A. de, "Un dato para las fuentes de *El médico de su honra*", RHi, XXI (1909), 395-411.

PITOLLET, C., *La querelle caldéronienne de J. N. Böhl von Faber et J. J. de Mora* (Paris, 1909).

LOSADA Y DIÉGUEZ, *Simbólica e ideas filosóficas contenidas en "La vida es sueño"* (Santiago, 1910).

NORTHUP, G. T., "*Los yerros de naturaleza y aciertos de la fortuna* by D. Antonio Coello and C", RR, I (1910), 411-25.

SCHEVILL, R., "A Note on C's *La vida es sueño*", MLN, XXV (1910), 109-10.

THOMAS, L. P., "La Genèse de la Philosophie et le Symbolisme dans *La vie est un songe* de C", *Hom. Wilmotte*, II (1910), 751-83.

KEIDITSCH, O., *Der Monolog bei C* (München, 1911).

MARGRAFF, N., *Der Mensch und sein Seelenleben in den Autos sacramentales des C* (Bonn, 1912).

MÜNNIG, E., *C und die ältere deutsche Romantik* (Berlin, 1912).

STIEFEL, A. L., "Über den Verfasser der Comedia *La española de Florencia*", ZRP, XXXVI (1912), 437-67.

MONTEVERDI, A., "Le fonti di *La vida es sueño*", SFM, VI (1913), 177-210.

TIEGHEM, P. VAN, "Notes et réflexions sur deux thèses récentes de littérature comparée", *Revue de synthèse historique*, XXI (1913), 213-24.
VALLVÉ, M., *Historias de C* (Barcelona, 1913).

FARINELLI, A., "Mistici, teologi, poeti e sognatori della Spagna all'alba del dramma di C", *RFE*, I (1914), 289-333.
FARINELLI, A., "Preludi al dramma: *La vita è un sogno*", *NA*, CCLVII (1914) 3 ff.

ALONSO CORTÉS, N., "Algunos datos relativos a C", *RFE*, II (1915), 41-51.
FAULHABER, M. V., *C, der Meistersänger del Bibel in der Weltliteratur* (Freiburg, 1915).
RÍOS DE LAMPÉREZ, B. DE LOS, *De C y de su obra* (Madrid, 1915).

BOTKIN, S., "Dramatourg-mystik", *Vyestnik Yevropy* (1916), 153-77.
FARINELLI, A., *La vita è un sogno* (Torino, 1916).
FARINELLI, A., "C", *NA*, CCLXVI (1916) 10 ff.
MONTEVERDI, A., "Tre commedie famose di C", *RI*, XIX (1916), No. 10.

KASPERS, W., "C's metaphysik nach den Autos sacramentales", *PhJ*, XXX (1917), 416-32.
REYES, A., "Un tema de *La vida es sueño*. El hombre y la naturaleza en el monólogo de Segismundo", *RFE*, IV (1917), 1-25, 237-76.

MORALES SAN MARTÍN, B., "El teatro griego y el teatro español. Esquilo y C. Prometeo y Segismundo", *RQ*, VI (1918), 260-75, 342-59.
TORO Y GISBERT, M., "¿Conocemos el texto verdadero de las comedias de C?", *BRAE*, V (1918), 401-21, 531-49; VI (1919), 3-12.

HENDRIX, W. S., "The Theme 'Life is a dream'", *MLN*, XXXIV (1919), 505-06.
JÜNEMANN, G., "Glosas críticas. Los dos *Alcaldes de Zalamea*", *RCC*, XXXVI (1919), 131-35, 194-202.
PEIPER, T., "La traducción polaca de *El príncipe constante* de C", *La Lectura*, III (1919), 4-5.

EGUÍA RUIZ, C., "C. Nuevas minucias biográficas", *RyF*, LVII (1920), 466-78.
MADARIAGA, S. DE, *Shelley and C and other Essays on English and Spanish Poetry* (London, 1920).
PITOLLET, C., "A propos de deux traductions italiennes de *La vida es sueño*", *HisP*, III (1920), 365-68.

LENZ, A., "La source d'une comedia de C *[Para vencer a amor]*", *RHi*, LIII (1921), 603-13.
MEREJKOWSKI, D., "C", *HisP*, IV (1921), 125-41.
PFANDL, L., "Zur Quellenfrage von C's *Argenis y Poliarco*", *ASNSL*, CXLII (1921), 133-35.
PRAAG, J. A., VAN, "Les traductions de *El mayor encanto amor* de C en néerlandais", *N*, VII (1921), 8-19.
SUSSMANN, J. H., "Ein Lustspiel C's und der Dichter selbst in Neuer Auffassung", *Spanien*, III (1921), 25-29.

CASTILLO, C., "Acerca de la fecha y fuentes de *En la vida*", *MPh*, XX (1923), 391-401.

CANTELLA, A., *C in Italia nel secolo XVII* (Roma, 1923).

CORNEJO, S., "Observaciones a la crítica de un libro *[MLN*, XXXIV (1919), 420-428, 482-92, F. O. Reed on *El alcalde*, ed. Geddes]", *RHi*, LX (1924), 532-45.

COTARELO Y MORI, E., *Ensayo sobre la vida y obras de C* (Madrid, 1924).

DÍAZ GALDÓS, T., "Un autógrafo de C", *RBAM*, I (1924), 102-05.

REED, F. O., *The Calderonian Octosyllable* (Wisconsin, 1924).

SANZ, R. M., "El amor en *La vida es sueño*", *RUBA*, VI (1924), 229-45.

THOMAS, L. P., "François Bertaut et les conceptions dramatiques de C", *RLC* (1924), 199-221.

VALBUENA PRAT, A., "Los autos sacramentales de C", *RHi*, LXI (1924), 1-302.

ALONSO CORTÉS, N., "Carta de dote de la madre de C", *RHV*, II (1925), 158-67.

BUCHANAN, M. A., "*Culteranismo* in C's *La vida es sueño*", *Hom. Pidal*, I (1925), 545-55.

DEPTA, M. V., *C* (Leipzig, 1925).

FARINELLI, A., "C y la música en Alemania", in *Ensayos y discursos*, II (1925), 563 ff.

FARINELLI, A., "Variazioni in *quintillas* sui titoli dei drammi calderoniani" *Hom. Pidal*, I (1925), 533-43.

HERRERO GARCÍA, M., "El Madrid de C", *RBAM*, II (1925), 110-40.

KÜCHLER, W., "Esther bis C, Racine und Grillparzer", *Jahrb. für Phil.*, I (1925), 333-54.

MILLÉ Y GIMÉNEZ, J., "Una nota a *La vida es sueño*", *RHi*, LXV (1925), 144-45.

NORTHUP, G. T., "Some Recovered Lines from C", *Hom. Pidal*, II (1925), 495-500.

PARIS, P., "La mythologie de C: *Apolo y Climene, El hijo del Sol, Faetón*", *Hom. Pidal*, I (1925), 557-70.

SCHÜK, M., "Hat C Shakespeare gekannt?", *Shakespeare-Jahrb.* (1925).

SUSSMANN, J., "C in bisheriger Auffassung", *SpPh*, 5 (1925), 1-2.

THOMAS, L. P., "Les jeux de scène et l'architecture des idées dans le théâtre allégorique de C", *Hom. Pidal*, I (1925), 501-30.

VISING, J., "En Comedia om drottning Kristina av Sverige av C", *Obi*, XXXIV (1925) 65-76.

BERENS, P., "C's Schicksaltragödien", *RF*, XXXIX (1926), 1-66.

FIGUEROLA-CANEDA, D., "La edición cubana de C", *CUC*, XL (1926), 233-37.

GÜNTHER, A., "C's *Alcalde de Zalamea* in der deutschen Literatur", *ZFEU*, XXV (1926), 445-57.

MARTIN, H. M., "Corneille's *Andromède* and C's *Las fortunas de Perseo*", *MPh*, XX (1926), 407-15.

RÍOS DE LAMPÉREZ, B. DE LOS, "*La vida es sueño* y los diez Segismundos de C* (Madrid, 1926).

STEINBERGER, H., *Zu C's Gestaltung Komischer Bauernfiguren* (München, 1926).

STEINER, A., "C's *Astrólogo fingido* in France", *MPh*, XXIV (1926), 27-30.

WEISSER, H., *C und das Wesen der katholischen Dramas* (Freiburg, 1926).

CARRERAS ARTAU, T., "La filosofía de la libertad en *La vida es sueño*", *Hom. Bonilla*, I (1927), 151-79.

GÜNTHER, A., "C's *Alcalde de Zalamea* in der deutschen Literatur", *ZFEU*, XXVI (1927), 445-57.

PORENA, M., "Cristina di Svezia in una commedia di C", *Colombo*, V (1927), 201-07.

SCHRAMM, E., "Corneilles *Heraclius* und C's *En esta vida*", *RHi*, LXXI (1927), 225-308.

VALBUENA PRAT, A., "Los autógrafos de los autos de C", *RBAM*, IV (1927), 484-86.

WURZBACH, W. VON, "Eine unbekannte Ausgabe und eine unbekannte Aufführung von C's *El secreto a voces*", *Hom. Bonilla*, I (1927), 181-207.

BIRKHEAD, H., "The Schism of England: C's Play and Shakespeare's", *Modern Languages*, X 1928), 36 ff.

OLMEDO, F. G., *Las fuentes de "La vida es sueño"* (Madrid, 1928).

OSMA, J. M., "Estudios sobre C. Notas a la comedia *Con quien vengo, vengo*", *HisB*, XI (1928), 221-26.

SCHONS, D., "A C Document", *RR*, XIX (1928), 157.

VALBUENA PRAT, A., "Los autos del *año santo* de C", *RBAM* (1928), 60-73.

VALBUENA PRAT, A., "Una representación de *El gran teatro del mundo*: La fuente de este auto", *RBAM*, V (1928), 79-82.

ALTSCHUL, A., "Vorbilder für einige Szenen und Motive in C's *Alcalde de Zalamea*", *ZRP*, XLIX (1929), 309-18.

BAEZA, J., *C. Su vida y sus más famosos autos sacramentales* (Barcelona, 1929).

HEATON, H. C., "On *La selva confusa*, attributed to C", *PMLA*, XLIV (1929).

MICHELS, W., "Barockstil bei Shakespeare und C", *RHi*, LXXV (1929), 370-458.

ALTSCHUL, A., "Lopesche Motive in C's *La vida es sueño*", *ZRP*, L (1930), 222-37.

FEY, E., "C und Shakespeare", *NM*, 1 (1930), 419-72.

GUIGNARD, R., "C dans le *Frauentaschenbuch*", *RLC*, X (1930), 733-46.

HAEMEL, A., "C. Eine Einführung", *Germ. Rom. Monatsschrift*, XIX (1930), 448-61.

HANE, P. R., "Die Einsiedeler Calderonspiele", *ANW*, LXIV (1930), 863-66.

VALBUENA PRAT, A., "La escenografía de una comedia de C", *AEAA*, XVI (1930).

VALBUENA PRAT, A., "Sobre *El año santo en Madrid*", *RBAM*, VII (1930), 75-77.

EOFF, S., "The Sources of C's *A secreto agravio secreta venganza*", *MPh*, XXVIII (1931), 297-311.

HEATON, H. C., "A Passage in C's *Mágico prodigioso*", *MLN*, XLVI (1931), 31-33.

KRAUSS, W., "C ·als religiöser Dichter", *Kunstwart*, 44 (1931), 490.

MARTIN, H. M., "The Perseus Myth in Lope and C", *PMLA*, XL (1931), 450-60.

SPITZER, L., "C", *Neue Jahrbücher*, VII (1931), 516-30.

VOSSLER, K., "C", *Corona*, II (1931), 43-54.

ALTSCHUL, A., "Zur Beurteilung von C's *La vida es sueño*", *ZRP*, LII (1932), 99-113, 223-236.

BUCHANAN, M. A., "The Presidential Address: C's Life is a Dream", *PMLA*, XLVII (1932), 1303-21.

SALLEY, W. C., "A possible influence of the Abencerraje story on C's *El príncipe constante*", *RR*, XXIII (1932), 331-33.

WILLE, JUTTA, *C's Spiel der Erlösung* (München, 1932).

MARTIN, H. M., "The Apollo and Daphne Myth as treated by Lope de Vega and C", *HR*, I (1933), 149-60.

SCHEVILL, R., "*Virtudes vencen señales* and *La vida es sueño*", *HR*, I (1933), 181-95.

Cossío, J. M. DE, "Racionalismo del arte dramático de C", *CyR*, XXI (1934), 39-76.

DALE, G. I., "Agustín de Rojas y *La vida es sueño*", *HR*, II (1934), 319-26.

FARINELLI, A., "Wagner e C", *NA*, CCCLXXI (1934), 193-212.

SOFER, J., *Die Welttheater Hugo v Hofmannthals und ihre Voraussetzungen bei Heraklit und C* (Wien, 1934).

BEODO, F., "Segismundo ¿es el Contraquijote?", in *Lope de Vega* (Madrid, 1935).

Cossío, J. M. DE, "La 'secreta venganza' en Lope, Tirso y C", *Fénix* (1935), 501-15.

G. QUIJANO, P. M., "Una vez más Lope y C", *Fénix*, I (1935), 611-29.

IRIARTE-AG, J., "En el tercer centenario de *La vida es sueño*", *RyF* (1935), No. 107, 58-72, 457-74; No. 108, 350-69; No. 109, 165-82.

MATULKA, B., "The Courtly Cid Theme in C's *Afectos de odio y amor*", *HisB*, XVIII (1935), 63-76.

PÉREZ, Q., "Lope de Vega y C", *RyF* (1935), No. 109, 31-47.

PITOLLET, C., "*El médico de su honra* à Paris", *LMer*, XXX (1935), 19-21.

SCHULHOF, H., "Grillparzer und C", *Jb der Grillparzer-Ges*, XXXIII (1935), 53-65.

VERHESEN, F., "Nuevos autógrafos de C", *RBAM*, XII (1935), 103-05.

CURTIUS, E. R., "C und die Malerei", *RF*, L (1936), 89-136.

GONZÁLEZ, E., "Los autos marianos de C", *RyC*, XXXII (1936), 319-32.

KOMMERELL, M., "Übertragungen aus C", *Die Neue Rundschau*, XLVII (1936), 449-63, XLVIII (1937), 309-28.

LANCASTER, H. C., "C, Boursault and Ravenscroft", *MLN*, LI (1936), 523-28.

SPITZER, L., "Kenning und C's Begriffspielerei", *ZRP*, LVI (1936), 100-02.

TREVIÑO, S. N., "Nuevos datos acerca de la fecha de *Basta callar*", *HR*, IV (1936), 333-41.

VALBUENA PRAT, A., "Sobre el tono menor y el estilo en la escuela de C", *Hom. Rubió i Lluch* (Barcelona, 1936), I, 627-49.

WILSON, E. M., "The Four Elements in the Imagery of C", *MLR*, XXXI (1936), 34-47.

GATES, E. J., "Góngora and C", *HR*, V (1937), 241-58.

GATES, E. J., "Shelley and C", *PhQ*, XVI (1937), 49-58.

HEATON, H. C., "On the *Segunda Parte* of C", *HR*, V (1937), 208-22.

McGARRY, M. FRANCIS DE SALES, *The Allegorical and Metaphorical Language in the Autos Sacramentales of C* (Washington, 1937).

OSMA, J. M., "Nota a *Gustos y disgustos*", *HisB*, XX (1937), 47-54.

PFANDL, L., "Ausdrucksformen des archaischen Denkens und des Unbewussten bei C", *Gesammelte Aufsätze zur Kulturgeschichte Spaniens*, VI (1937), 340-89.

RODRÍGUEZ EMBIL, L., "El soñar de Segismundo", *Revista Cubana*, VII (1937), 105-12.

TREVIÑO, S. N., "Versos desconocidos de una comedia de C *[Basta callar]*", *PMLA*, LII (1937), 682-704.

VOSSLER, K., "Magische Einsamkeit in C's Fronleichnamsspiel", *Corona*, VII (1937), 568-83.

HILBORN, H. W., *A Chronology of the Plays of C* (Toronto, 1938).

HILBORN, H. W., "The Versification of *La selva confusa*", *MLN*, LIII (1938), 193-94.

SCHNEIDER, R., "Zu Cs Weltbild", *DL*, XL (1938), 721-24.

SCHULTE, I., *Buch-und Schriftwesen in Cs Weltlichen Theater* (Bonn, 1938).

SILVA, R., "The Religious Dramas of C", *BSS*, XV (1938), 172-94.

SPITZER, L., "Eine Stelle in C's Traktat über die Malerei", *NM*, XXXIX (1938), 361-70.

VOSSLER, K., "La solitudine magica nell' auto sacramental di C", *Civiltà Moderna* (1938), No. 10, 353-64.

IDEN, O., "Der Einfluss Lope de Vegas und C's auf die deutsche Literatur", *ZFEU*, XXXVIII (1939), 159-62.

MALKIEWICZ, M., "Un remaniement français de *La vie est un songe*", *RLC*, XIII (1939), 429-44.

OSMA, J. M., "Réplica: *El secreto a vozes*", *HR*, VII (1939), 250-52.

TURKÉVICH, L. B., "C en Rusia", *RFH*, I (1939), 139-58.

WERCKSHAGEN, C., "C und Shakespeare", *Hess. Landestheater Darmstadt*, 14 1939-40), 137-47.

WILSON, E. M., and ENTWISTLE, W. J., "C's *Príncipe constante*: Two Appreciations", *MLR*, XXXIV (1939), 207-22.

ACCHIARDI, P., "Antecedentes de *La vida es sueño*", *INET* (1940), No. 12, 109-27.

MOGLIA, R., "Una representación de C en Buenos Aires en el siglo XVIII *[Afectos de odio y amor]*", *RFH*, II (1940), 48-50.

WEIR, LUCY E., *The Ideas Embodied in the Religious Drama of C* (Lincoln, 1940).

CIROT, G., "*El gran teatro del mundo*", *BHi*, XLIII (1941), 290-305.
CIROT, G., "*La loa de La vida es sueño*", *BHi*, XLIII (1941), 65-71.
FUCILLA, J. G., "Italian Manuscript Versions of *La vida es sueño* and *El delincuente honrado*", *Ital*, XVII (1941), 109-11.
HESSE, E. W., *The Vera Tassis text of C's plays [Parts I-IV]* (Mexico, 1941).
JOHNSTON, H. L., "The sources of C's *La lepra de Constantino*", *HR*, IX (1941), 482-88.
JULIÁ MARTÍNEZ, "C en Toledo", *RFE*, XXV (1941), 182-204.
KOMMERELL, M., "*C-Übertragungen aus La hija del aire*", *RF*, LV (1941), 105-12.
PRAAG, J. A. VAN, "Una fuente de *La vida es sueño* de C", *N*, XXV (1941), 250-51.
VALBUENA PRAT, A., *C. Su personalidad, su arte dramático, su estilo y sus obras* (Barcelona, 1941).

ALPERN, H. and MARTEL, J., *The Story of C's "La vida es sueño"* (Boston, 1942).
HILBORN, H. W., "*C's agudos* in Italianate Verse", *HR*, X (1942), 157-59.
JULIÁ MARTÍNEZ, E., "Una fundación de C", *RFE*, XXVI (1942), 302-07.
KOMMERELL, M., "*Übertragungen aus C*", *RF*, LVI (1942), 33-48.
MALLARINO, V., "*El alcalde de Zalamea y Fuenteovejuna* frente al derecho penal", *RInd*, XIV (1942), 358-67.
VALBUENA PRAT, A., "El orden del barroco en *La vida es sueño*", *Esc*, VI (1942), 167-92.

CARLISKY, M., "Sócrates y Segismundo", *Nos*, VIII (1943), 256-72.
CROCE, B., "C. I. *La hija del aire*. 2. Sulla critica calderoniana", *Cri*, XLI (1943), 173-88.
GONZÁLEZ PALENCIA, A., "El arte de C", *RNE* (1943), 18-37.
HILBORN, H. W., "*C's silvas*", *PMLA*, LVIII (1943), 122-48.
PARKER, A. A., *The Allegorical Drama of C* (Oxford, 1943).
WARDROPPER, B. W., "The Interplay of Wisdom and Saintliness in *El mágico prodigioso*", *HR*, XI (1943), 116-24.

CASELLA, M., "*La vita è un sogno*", *NA*, CDXXXI (1944), 81-98.

ENTWISTLE, W. J., "Justina's Temptation: An Approach to the Understanding of C", *MLR*, XL (1945), 180-89.
FRUTOS CORTÉS, E., "Origen, naturaleza y destino del hombre en los autos sacramentales de C", *RFi* (1945), No. 15, 525-58.
REYES, A., "El enigma de Segismundo", *RAmer*, II (1945), 353-65.

BERGAMÍN, J., "Por debajo del sueño (C, calderoniano)", *RNC*, VII (1946), 3-18.
CEBALLOS GARCÍA, G., "El sentido del sino en los personajes de C", *UAC*, 75-76 (1946), 393-426.

HESSE, E. W., "The Two Versions of C's *El laurel de Apolo*", *HR*, XIV (1946), 213-34.

SILVA, R., "The religious dramas of C" in *Liverpool Studies in Spanish Literature*, II (1946), 119-205.

WILSON, E. M., *"La vida es sueño"*, *RUBA*, IV (1946), 61-78.

BERGAMÍN, J., "C", *Le Cheval de Troie* (1947), No. 4, 565-84.

GATES, E. J., "Proverbs in the Plays of C", *RR*, XXXVIII (1947), 203-15.

HAYES, F. C., "The Use of Proverbs as Titles and Motives in the *Siglo de Oro* drama: C", *HR*, XV (1947), 453-63.

HESSE, E. W., "Court References in C's *zarzuelas*", *HR*, XV (1947), 365-77.

LANCASTER, H. C., "Still More about C, Boursault and Ravenscroft" *MLN*, LXII (1947), 385-89.

LEAVITT, S. E., "A Rare Edition of Plays Attributed to C", *HR*, XV (1947), 216-18.

RUNDLE, J. U., "More about C, Boursault and Ravenscroft", *MLN*, LXII (1947), 382-84.

ENTWISTLE, W. J., "C's *La devoción de la cruz*", *BHi*, L (1948), 472-82.

ENTWISTLE, W .J., "La controversia en los autos de C", *NRFH*, II (1948) 223-38.

FRUTOS CORTÉS, E., "La voluntad y el libre albedrío de los autos sacramentales de C", *Universidad*, I (1948), 1-2.

HESSE, E. W., "The First and Second Editions of C's *Cuarta parte*, *HR*, XVI (1948), 209-37.

HESSE, E. W., "The Publication of C's Plays in the 17th Century", *PHQ*, XXVII (1948), 37-51.

HILBORN, H. W., "C's *quintillas*", *HR*, XVI (1948), 301-10.

HORT, G. M., "The Shakespeare of Spain", *Cont. Rev.*, CLXXIII (1948), 341-46.

OPPENHEIMER, M., "Addenda on the *Segunda parte* of C", *HR*, XVI (1948), 335-40.

OPPENHEIMER, M., "Supplementary data on the French and English Adaptations of C's *El astrólogo fingido*", *RLC*, XXII (1948), 547-60.

OPPENHEIMER, M., *"The burla* in C's *El astrólogo fingido"*, *PhQ*, XXVII (1948), 241-63.

PALACIOS, L. E., *"La vida es sueño"*, *Finisterre*, II (1948), 5-52.

PARKER, A. A., "Henry VIII in Shakespeare and C. An Appreciation of *La cisma de Inglaterra*", *MLR*, XLIII (1948), 327-52.

RUNDLE, J. U., "Footnote on C, Boursault and Ravenscroft", *MLN*, LXIII (1948), 217-19.

ALVAR, M., "D. Francisco de la Torre, amigo de C", *RFE*, XXXI (1949), 151-61.

AVILA, P., *"La cisma de Inglaterra y Ana Bolena"*, *Rev. Iber.*, XIV (1949), 91-96.

FRUTOS CORTÉS, E., *C* (Barcelona, 1949).

GATES, E. J., "A Tentative List of the Proverbs and Proverb Allusions in the Plays of C", *PMLA*, LXIV (1949), 1027-48.

HORST, K. A., "C's geistige Welt", *Deutsche Beiträge*, III (1949), 44-58.

KRASZA, H., "*El alcalde de Zalamea:* estudio psicológico-penal", *AUG*, I (1949), 280-92.

LEBOIS, A., "La révolte des personnages: de Cervantes et C à Raymond Schwab", *RCL*, XXIII (1949), 482-506.

LORA RISCO, A., "El Segismundo histórico de *La vida es sueño*", *RUBA*, 12 (1949), 379-464.

RUBIÓ, D., "La fuente de *La vida es sueño* de C", *BICC*, V (1949), 301-07.

RUNDLE, J. U., "Wycherley and C: A Source for *Love in a Wood*", *PMLA*, LXIV (1949), 701-07.

CROCE, B., "C: *La hija del aire;* Sulla critica calderoniana", *Letture di poeti*, XXXIX (Bari, 1950), 21-42.

CURTIUS, E. R., "George, Hofmannsthal und C", in *Kritische Essays zur europäischen Literatur* (Bern, 1950), 172-201.

ENTWISTLE, W. J., "C et le théâtre symbolique", *BHi*, LII (1950), 41-54.

GONZÁLEZ, E., "Notas para una introducción al estudio de los autos sacramentales de C", *Studia*, 251 (1950), 65-70.

HESSE, E. W., "Courtly Allusions in the Plays of C", *PMLA*, LXV (1950), 531-49.

IRVING, T. B., "Hamlet y Segismundo ante la vida", *Univ. de San Carlos*, XIX (1950), 7-18.

KRAUSS, W. "C-Dichter des spanischen Volkes", *Sinn und Form*, II (1950), No. 2, 34-52.

LEAVITT, S. E., "Did C have a sense of humor?", in *Hom. Dey* (Chapel Hill 1950), 119-21.

OPPENHEIMER, M., "The Baroque Impasse in the Calderonian Drama", *PMLA*, LXV (1950), 1146-65.

SCIACCA, M. F., "Verdad y sueño en *La vida es sueño* de C", *Cla*, I (1950), No. 2, 1-9.

SLOMAN, A. E., *The Sources of C's "El príncipe constante"* (Oxford, 1950).

VALBUENA PRAT, A., "C y el Año Santo de 1650", *Cla*, I (1950), No. 1, 27-36.

VILANOVA, A., "El tema del *Gran teatro del mundo*", *BRABLB*, XXIII (1950).

VOSSLER, K., "C", in *Südliche Romania* (Leipzig, 1950), 204-14.

WARDROPPER, B. W., "The Unconscious Mind in C's *El pintor de su deshonra*" *HR*, XVIII (1950), 285-301.

ALONSO CORTÉS, N., "Genealogía de C", *BRAE*, XXXI (1951), 299-309.

ALONSO, D., "La correlación en estructura del teatro calderoniano", in *Seis calas en la expresión literaria española* (Madrid, 1951). 115-86.

ARÁUZ, A., *Notas sobre Lope de Vega y C* (Mexico, 1951).

COE, ADA M., "Unas colecciones de comedias sueltas de C comparadas con *Literatur...* de Breymann", *Est*, VII (1951), 111-69.

CONSTANDSE, A. L., *Le baroque espagnol et C* (Amsterdam, 1951).

Eguía Ruiz, C., *Cervantes, C, Lope, Gracián. Nuevos temas crítico-biográficos* (Madrid, 1951).

Frutos Cortés, E., "La filosofía del barroco y el pensamiento de C", *RUBA,* IX (1951), 173-230.

Heaton, H. C., "C and *El mágico prodigioso", HR*, XIX (1951), 11-36, 93-103.

Hesse, E. W., "C y Velázquez", *Cla,* II (1951), No. 10, 1-10; and *HisB,* XXXV (1952), 74-82.

Hilborn, H. W., "The Calderonian *gracioso* and marriage", *BC*, III (1951), No. 2, 2-3.

Martín, H. M., "Notes on the Cephalus-Procris myth as dramatised by Lope de Vega and C", *MLN*, LXVI (1951), 238-41.

Oppenheimer, M., "A Spurious Edition of the *Segunda Parte* of the Vera Tassis Edition of C's *Comedias", HR*, XIX (1951), 346-52.

Osma, J. M., "Apostilla al tema de la creación en el auto *El divino Orfeo* de C", *HisB,* XXXIV (1951), 165-71.

Palacios, L. E., "*La vie est un songe", Laval théologique et philosophique,* VII (1951), 123-49.

Sciacca, M. F., "Verità e sogno", *HumB,* VI (1951), 472-85.

Sloman, A. E., "Scene Division in C's *Alcalde de Zalamea", HR*, XIX (1951), 66-71.

Wilson, E. M., "La discreción de Don Lope de Almeida [*A secreto agravio]*", *Cla,* II (1951), No. 19, 1-10.

Anón., "La tradición eucarística en los autos sacramentales", *Est,* VIII (1952), 227-33.

Frutos Cortés, E., *La filosofía de C en sus autos sacramentales* (Zaragoza, 1952).

Giusso, L., "C e la poesia dell'allegoria" in *Spagna e Antispagna* (Mazzara, 1952).

Hesse, E. W., "Obsesiones en *El mayor monstruo del mundo* de C", *Est,* VIII (1952); 395-409.

Oppenheimer, M., "Two Stones and One Bird: A Bird Lore Allusion in C", *MLN,* LXVII (1952), 253-54.

Ritter, F. de, "*El gran teatro del mundo", RNC,* XIV (1952), 133-53, and in *Panorama,* II (1953), 81-98.

Sloman, A. E., "*El mágico prodigioso:* C Defended against the Charge of Theft", *HR*, XX (1952), 212-22.

Sloman, A. E., "*La selva confusa* Restored to C", *HR*, XX (1952), 134-48.

Valbuena Prat, A., "Los autos calderonianos en el ambiente teológico español", *Cla,* III (1952), No. 15, 33-35.

Wilson, E. M., "Gerald Brenan's C", *BC*, IV (1952), No. 1, 6-8.

Atkins, S., "Goethe, C and Faust: Der Tragödie zweiter Teil", *Germanic Review,* XXVIII (1953), 83-98.

Dunn, P. N., "The Horoscope Motif in *La vida es sueño", Atl,* I (1953), 187-201.

GÓMEZ DE LA SERNA, R., "La vida como sueño en C y Unamuno", *CUC*, 40 (1953), 5-20.

HESSE, E. W., "La concepción calderoniana del príncipe perfecto en *La vida es sueño*", *Cla*, IV (1953), No. 20, 4-12.

HESSE, E. W., "La dialéctica y el casuismo en C", *Est*, IX (1953), 517-31.

ROSSI, G. C., "C nella polemica settecentesca sugli *autos sacramentales*", *Studi mediolatini e volgari*, I (1953).

SALAZAR LARRAÍN, A., "Segismundo y 'el hombre natural' ", *Mar del Sur*, IX (1953), 72-74.

SLOMAN, A. E., "C and Falconry: A Note on Dramatic Language", *RPh*, VI (1953), 299-304.

SLOMAN, A. E., "One of C's minor characters: Lelio in *Las armas de la hermosura*", *Atl*, I (1953), 130-35.

SLOMAN, A. E., "The Structure of C's *La vida es sueño*", *MLR*, XLVIII (1953), 293-300.

ZUDAIRE, E., "Un escrito anónimo de C", *HisM*, XIII (1953), 268-93.

CHAPMAN, W. G., "Las comedias mitológicas de C", *RLit*, V (1954), 34-67.

CIORANESCU, A., "C y el teatro clásico francés", *Estudios de literatura española y comparada* (La Laguna, 1954), 137-95.

CROCKER, L. G., "*Hamlet, Don Quixote* and *La vida es sueño*. The Quest for Values", *PMLA*, LXIX (1954), 278-313.

DILTHEY, W., "Das Volksschauspiel und C", *Die grosse Phantasiedichtung* (Göttingen, 1954), 114-22.

FREDÉN, G., *La cena del amor. Estudios sobre C* (Madrid, 1954).

HESELHAUS, C., "C und Hofmannsthal", *ASNSL*, CXCI (1954), 3-30.

JARRETT-KERR, M., "C and the Imperialism of Belief" in *Studies in Literature and Belief* (London, 1954).

KÜCHLER, W., "C's Comedia *El alcalde de Zalamea* als Drama des Persönlichkeit", *ASNSL*, CXC (1954), 306-13.

ORTIGOZA VIEYRA, C., *Los móviles de la comedia en Lope, Alarcón, Tirso, Moreto, Rojas, C* (México, 1954).

SCHOLBERG, K. R., "Las obras cortas de C", *Cla*, V (1954), No. 25, 13-19.

C in Italia, ed. G. Mancini (Pisa, 1955).

FRADEJAS LEBRERO, J., "Un cuento de Don Juan Manuel y dos comedias del Siglo de Oro [Lope, *La pobreza estimada* and C, *El conde Lucanor]*", *RLit*, VIII (1955), 67-80.

FRIEDRICH, H., *Der Fremde C* (Freiburg, 1955).

GROULT, P., "La *Loa* de *El verdadero Dios Pan* de C", *LR*, IX (1955), 39-54.

HESSE, E. W., "C's popularity in the Spanish Indies", *HR*, XXIII (1955), 12-27.

JONES, C. A., "Honor in *El alcalde de Zalamea*", *MLR*, L (1955), 444-49.

PIETSCHMANN, K. R., "Recepción e influencia de C en el teatro alemán del siglo XIX", *Cla*, VI (1955), No. 35, 15-25.

ROSSI, G. C., "C nella critica spagnola del settecento", *FiR*, II (1955), 20-66.

SHERGOLD, N. D., "C and Vera Tassis", *HR*, XXIII (1955), 212-18.

FUCILLA, J. G., "Una imitazione dell' *Aminta* nel *Mágico prodigioso* di C", *Studi Tassiani*, 6 (1956), 29-33.

HESSE, E. W., "El arte calderoniano en *El mayor monstruo los celos*", *Cla*, VII (1956), No. 38, 18-30.

KOSSOFF, A. D., "*El médico de su honra* and *La amiga de Bernal Francés*" *HR*, XXIV (1956), 66-70.

PAGÉS LARRAYA, A., "El nuevo mundo en una obra *[La aurora en Copacabana]* de C", *At*, CXXV (1956), 108-29.

SAGE, J. W., "C y la música teatral", *BHi*, LVIII (1956), 275-300.

VALBUENA BRIONES, A., "Consideraciones en torno de la fuente de *Amor, honor y poder*", *BC*, VIII (1956), No. 2, 1-4.

WHITBY, W. M., "C's *El príncipe constante:* Fénix's rôle in the Ransom of Fernando's body", *BC*, VIII (1956), No. 1, 1-4.

WILHELM, J., "La crítica calderoniana en los siglos XIX y XX en Alemania", *CHA*, 73 (1956), 47-56.

WILSON, E. M., "Some Calderonian *pliegos sueltos*", *Hom. Van Praag* (Amsterdam, 1956), 140-44.

ABBREVIATIONS

AEAA	Archivo Español de Arte y Arqueología. Madrid.
ANW	Alte und Neue Welt. Einsiedeln.
Arb	Arbor. Madrid.
ASNSL	Archiv für das Studium der Neueren Sprachen und Literaturen. Braunschweig, Berlin.
At	Atenea. Concepción, Chile.
Atl	Atlante. London.
AUG	Anales de la Universidad de Guayaquil.
BBMP	Boletín de la Biblioteca Menéndez y Pelayo. Santander.
BC	Bulletin of the 'Comediantes'. Wisconsin.
BHi	Bulletin Hispanique. Bordeaux.
BHS	Bulletin of Hispanic Studies. Liverpool.
BICC	Boletín del Instituto Caro y Cuervo. Bogotá.
BRABLB	Boletín de la Real Academia de Buenas Letras de Barcelona.
BRAE	Boletín de la Real Academia Española. Madrid.
BRSV	Boletín de la Real Sociedad Vascongada. San Sebastián.
BSS	Bulletin of Spanish Studies. Liverpool.
CHA	Cuadernos Hispano-americanos. Madrid.
CL	Comparative Literature. Eugene, Oregon.
Cla	Clavileño. Madrid.
Cri	La Critica. Napoli.
CUC	Cultura Universitaria. Caracas.
CyR	Cruz y Raya. Madrid.
DL	Die Literatur. Berlin.
Esc	Escorial. Madrid.
Est	Estudios. Madrid.
FiR	Filologia Romanza. Torino.
HisB	Hispania. Baltimore.
HisM	Hispania. Madrid.
HisP	Hispania. Paris.
HR	Hispanic Review. Philadelphia.
HumB	Humanitas. Brescia.
INET	Instituto Nacional de Estudios de Teatro. Buenos Aires.
Ital	Italica. Chicago.
LM	La Merced. Madrid.
LMer	Les Langues Méridionales. Paris.
LR	Les Lettres Romanes. Louvain.
MLN	Modern Language Notes. Baltimore.
MLR	Modern Language Review. Cambridge.
MPh	Modern Philology. Chicago.
N	Neophilologus. Amsterdam.

NA	Nuova Antologia. Firenze.
NFRH	Nueva Revista de Filología Hispánica. Mexico.
NM	Neuphilologische Mitteilungen. Helsingfors.
Nos	Nosotros. Buenos Aires.
OBi	Ord och Bild. Stockholm.
PhJ	Philosophisches Jahrbuch. Fulda.
PhQ	Philological Quarterly. Iowa.
PMLA	Publications of the Modern Language Association of America. Baltimore.
QIA	Quaderni Ibero-Americani. Torino.
R	Romania. Paris.
RABM	Revista de Archivos, Bibliotecas y Museos. Madrid.
RAmer	Revista de América. Bogotá.
RBAM	Revista de la Biblioteca, Archivo y Museo del Ayuntamiento de Madrid.
RCC	Revista Católica de Santiago de Chile.
RF	Romanische Forschungen. Erlangen.
RFE	Revista de Filología Española. Madrid.
RFH	Revista de Filosofía Hispánica. Buenos Aires.
RFi	Revista de Filosofía. Madrid.
RHi	Revue Hispanique. Paris-New York.
RHV	Revista Histórica. Valladolid.
RI	Rivista d'Italia. Roma.
RInd	Revista de las Indias. Bogotá.
RLC	Revue de Littérature Comparée. Paris.
RLit	Revista de Literatura. Madrid.
RNC	Revista Nacional de Cultura. Caracas.
RNE	Revista Nacional de Educación. Madrid.
RPh	Romance Philology. Berkeley.
RQ	Revista Quincenal. Madrid.
RR	Romanic Review. New York.
RUBA	Revista de la Universidad de Buenos Aires.
RyC	Religión y Cultura. Madrid.
RyF	Razón y Fe. Madrid.
S	Symposium. Syracuse, New York.
SFM	Studi di Filologia Moderna. Catania.
SPh	Studies in Philology. Chapel Hill, North Carolina.
SpPh	Spanische Philologie. Hamburg.
Thes	Thesaurus. Bogotá.
UAC	Universidad de Antioquía. Colombia.
ZFEU	Zeitschrift für Französischen und Englischen Unterricht. Berlin.
ZNU	Zeitschrift für Neusprachlichen Unterricht. Berlin.
ZRP	Zeitschrift für Romanische Philologie. Tübingen.

INDEX OF NAMES

Geddes, J., 217.
Gerusalemme liberata, 133, 147.
Godínez, F., 111.
Gómez de Baquero, E., 129.
Góngora, L. de 131, 193.
González de Salas, J. E., 12, 288.
Gracián, B., 129.
Guardati, Masuccio, 218.
Gyraldi, 128.

Hall, H. B., 6.
Hartzenbusch, J. E., 14, 18, 59, 61, 94, 128, 142, 159, 160, 188, 217, 238, 250.
Heaton, H. C., 15.
Henry of Trastamara, Prince, 18, 41, 281, 282.
Henry the Navigator, Prince, 188, 191, 203, 296.
Hesse, E. W., 123.
Hilborn, H. W., 100, 160, 252.
Homer, 129, 131.

Jardín de Falerina, El, 13.
Johnson, Samuel, 130.
Jonson, Ben, 283.
Juliá Martínez, E., 251, 262.

Kannegeiser, K. L., 189.
Keil, J. J., 18, 59, 94, 128, 159, 188, 217, 250.
Kelly, J. Fitzmaurice, 14.
Kennedy, Ruth L., 10, 61.
Krenkel, M., 14, 189, 217, 218, 220, 240, 250.

Lazaraque, *vide* Al-Azrak.
Lewes, G. H., 299.
Lista, A., 59.
Lo fingido verdadero, 11.
López de Ayala, A., 221.
López Pinciano, A., 12, 288.
Lotti, C., 131, 155, 156.

Maccoll, N., 189, 250.
Mágico prodigioso, El, 15, 144.
Martínez de los Ríos, J., 20.
Mawlay Sayh (Muley Xeque), 205.
Mayor encanto amor, El, 13, 16, 128-58, 279, 286, 287, 288, 289, 290, 291, 292, 293, 294, 297, 298, 300, 301, 303, 306, 307.

Mayor monstruo los celos, El, 212, 274.
McClelland, Ivy L., 107, 111.
Médico de su honra, El (Anón.), 13, 18-58.
Médico de su honra, El (Calderón), 5, 13, 14, 16, 18-58, 63, 79, 84, 85, 94, 125, 245, 281, 282, 285, 287, 288, 289, 290, 291, 292, 293, 294, 297, 298, 299, 300, 301, 302, 305, 307.
Mejor amigo el muerto, El, 275.
Menéndez y Pelayo, M., 14, 18, 23, 25, 60, 96, 130, 156, 159, 169, 220, 221, 250, 296.
Mesonero Romanos, R. de, 159, 160.
Metamorphoses, 131.
Metford, J. C. J., 96, 100.
Mier, E. de, 14.
Mira de Amescua, A., 13, 14, 100, 131, 132, 133, 134, 149, 157, 294.
Montesinos, J. F., 299.
Moreto, A., 10, 11, 12.
Morley, S. Griswold, 20, 218.
Mudanzas de la fortuna y sucesos de Don Beltrán de Aragón, Las, 14.

Niña de Gómez Arias, La (Calderón), 13, 14, 16, 159-87, 230, 279, 280, 281, 289, 291, 292, 294, 296, 297, 298, 302, 303, 305.
Niña de Gómez Arias, La (Vélez), 13, 14, 159-87, 301.
Northup, G. T., 251, 259.
Nueva idea de la tragedia antigua, 12.

Odyssey, 129, 131, 134.
Olmedo, F. G., 250, 251.
Ovid, 131.

Palacios, L. E., 252.
Parker, A. A., 6, 46, 184, 188, 192, 211.
Parker, J. H., 61.
Pasajero, El, 11.
Pellicer, C., 131, 156.
Pérez de Montalbán, J., 5, 13, 61, 63, 68, 69, 70, 71, 84, 88, 131, 291.
Pérez de Moya, J., 128.
Peribáñez, 297, 299.
Peter the Cruel, 18, 41, 281.
Philip II, 234, 281.